A White Scholar and the Black Community, 1945-1965

Essays and Reflections

August Meier

<small>AFTERWORD BY</small> *John H. Bracey, Jr.*

The University of Massachusetts Press
Amherst

LC 92–3205
ISBN 0–87023–809–4 (cloth); 810–8 (pbk)

Designed by Susan Bishop
Set in Linotron Palatino by Keystone Typesetting, Inc.
Printed and bound by Thomson-Shore, Inc.

Library of Congress Cataloging-in-Publication Data
Meier, August, 1923–
A White scholar and the Black community, 1945–1965 : essays and
reflections / August Meier ; afterword by John H. Bracey, Jr.
p. cm.
Includes index.
ISBN 0–87023–809–4 (alk. paper). — ISBN 0–87023–810–8 (pbk. :
alk. paper)
1. Meier, August, 1923– . 2. Afro-Americans—Civil rights.
3. Civil rights movements—United States—History—20th
century. 4. Civil rights workers—United States—Biography.
I. Title.
E185.98.M55A3 1992
323.1′73′09045—dc20 92–3205

British Library Cataloguing in Publication data are available.

For
Richard P. Thornell
and
David L. Lewis
and
Preston T. King

Contents

PART II

The Civil Rights Movement: Analyses by a Participant   149

Preface

SOME YEARS ago my friend Louis R. Harlan, of the University of Maryland, suggested that it would be worthwhile to publish a collection of the essays I had written early in my career about my experiences teaching at black colleges and participating in the civil movement during the two decades following the Second World War. Nothing came of this proposal at the time. But over the past two or three years another friend, John H. Bracey of the University of Massachusetts-Amherst, came up with a similar idea. He did not share my doubts about the viability of such a venture, and from time to time, encouraged by Bruce Wilcox, director of the University of Massachusetts Press, continued to press me on the matter. I really did not take the matter very seriously until, upon a visit to Amherst, he informed me that we had an appointment for lunch with Wilcox. So it was clear that a decision had to be made. For the next day and a half he and I discussed what the table of contents of such a book might look like, and on the third draft came up with a list and an organization that seemed suitable. I will even have to confess that the very appropriate titles for the book and its various parts were based on his suggestions.

The papers presented here are exactly like the originals (except for minor changes in the footnotes for consistency in style). No attempt has been made to eliminate the occasional redundancies that result. Nor has any attempt been made to update the essays in the light of changing conditions and new perspectives. Rather this collection is offered as representing my point of view in those earlier years. In fact I hope that presented in their original form, they may be helpful for historians by offering some illumination on developments in that period, which of course provided a context quite different from today's pattern of race relations.

Most of the articles in this volume have not been reprinted before and one is published here for the first time. The few that have been reprinted elsewhere are included as they are probably among the most significant of the articles based upon my personal observations and experiences as a participant in the black protest movement.

A White Scholar and the Black
Community, 1945–1965

"A Liberal and Proud of It"

SOMETIMES IT seems like only yesterday that I first arrived at Tougaloo College. Seven miles into the countryside north of Jackson we turned off the highway, past a tiny, pathetic railroad flag stop, carefully labeled "colored" on one side and "white" on the other. There followed a drive of perhaps a mile on a semipaved road, then through the arch at the entrance to the campus, under a grove of oaks festooned with Spanish moss, and on to the unpretentious antebellum plantation big house that now housed the small (student body of four hundred) college's administrative offices.

Thus began two decades of teaching at black colleges and of civil rights activism, a period when in most years I lived in the black community in a way that would seem virtually inconceivable today. Coming to Tougaloo was in one sense the beginning of what was probably the most important period of my life. Yet in another sense my arrival there was the end of the beginning. For in retrospect I had had a background and series of experiences that now make the score of years that followed seem almost inevitable.

The Making of a Liberal, 1923–1945

The first part of my life, growing up in Newark, New Jersey, witnessed what I think can best be described as the making of a liberal. In this process my parents were extremely important. My German father and my East European Jewish mother both came from working-class backgrounds and had met shortly after World War I in the Socialist party. My mother, in addition, came from a large family of radical intellectuals whose political affiliations ranged from anarchism to communism and Trotskyism and rightward to democratic socialism. Actually by the middle-1930s my parents were liberal in their thinking—left-wing New Dealers really—though still proud of their working-class origins, and socialists now only in a sentimental sense. But they made me sharply aware of the plight of the poor and the oppressed. The question of ethnic identity was of course a constant presence. Anti-Semitism was talked about (especially after the rise of Hitler in Germany) and minimally experienced, but my parents resolutely taught my brother and me that we were neither German nor Jewish but simply American—an assimilationist (and anti-Zionist) ethic that would prove enormously important in shaping my later life.

For my mother (who was a teacher and school principal) and my father (who was a chemist) intellectual interests were high on the agenda, and from the reading of serious books to the cultivation of appreciation for classical music, they passed this quality on to us. (Curiously in spite of their concern about the welfare of the common people, they were entirely negative toward popular music and jazz—and most movies as well—so that in certain ways I judge that I might be called "culturally deprived.") All of these things—ideology, ethnicity, and my intellectual orientation—served to alienate me from my peer group in the white Protestant upper-middle-class neighborhood in which I grew up. In short, I buried myself in my books. Part of this was related I am sure to my personality and I have tended toward a certain kind of social marginality, which quite likely had a significant influence in shaping my social interests and intellectual career.

There was one environment however in which my particular combination of interests flowered, and that was the Pioneer Youth Camp, near Kingston New York, where, beginning when I was eleven, I spent a half-dozen summers during the years 1934–1939. Pioneer Youth of America had been founded in 1924 by a heterogeneous group of reformers—anarchists, Communists, socialists, pacifists, union leaders in the garment trades, liberals and, very important, Progressive educators. (Thus, for example, I can recall that during the 1930s, the Communists' "angel" Frederick Vanderbilt Field made substantial financial contributions, and that people like Eleanor Roosevelt, John Dewey, and A. Philip Randolph were on the national advisory committee.) The progressive education orientation led the camp to emphasize individual freedom, and to adopt a practice of having the campers themselves decide democratically on what their activities would be. Thus, as much as possible, decisions about what was done were in the hands of the children rather than their counselors.

The organization also had an outreach to the labor movement, working with children of trade unionists not only in New York City, but among both West Virginia coal miners and North Carolina textile workers during certain major strikes. (The effort to establish an interracial summer camp in North Carolina not surprisingly did not last more than one or two seasons.) Pioneer Youth camp had both black campers and counselors—evidently the first summer camp, and one of the few in the 1930s, to practice such a policy.

(Walter Wallace, the Princeton University sociologist and I were on friendly terms during the summers he was there.) Intellectual interests were definitely encouraged. The freedom to do what I liked (often spending an afternoon reading in my tent), the recognition of the importance of intellectual pursuits, the obvious interracial policy, and the intense exposures to radicals of all sorts proved enormously stimulating and influential on my development. As one who called myself a liberal, I was in a minority in this environment.

Those were the years when the Spanish Civil War and the Italo-Ethiopian war were intensely important matters for discussion in left-wing circles (my eighth grade English teacher was most perplexed when I returned to school and wrote compositions on these topics). These were also the years of the debate about the Moscow treason trials, and of controversy between socialists and Communists about isolationism and collective security as means to preserve peace in the face of the growing Fascist threat. These were, in addition, the years of the Popular Front, and efforts of the Communist party to win control of liberal organizations, with the intention of having them endorse the Party line on foreign policy. (The Communists were very committed and very optimistic about what they could do. I recall one Communist counselor, who was black, having a long conversation with my mother and afterwards telling me that if he had been able to speak with her another fifteen minutes he was sure she would have signed the "red card.")

I observed the attempt at Communist domination occur first at Pioneer Youth where the struggle over the Communists' role came early, in 1938. The liberals and socialists won that fight, though the Communists' ouster took away something of the liveliness of the camp, I will admit. Later on I witnessed, from the sidelines, the way in which the Communist attempt to dominate liberal organizations destroyed the American Youth Congress in 1940. (I heard the Communists boo President Roosevelt when the chief executive addressed the throng of delegates gathered on the White House lawn. Directly after the president's speech I was fortunate enough to accompany the delegation from Pioneer Youth's organization in North Carolina on a visit to the White House. It would seem that through contacts possessed by one of the few remaining Communist-leaning individuals still in the organization we had secured an invitation from Eleanor Roosevelt. At the time she had heroic proportions in my eyes, because of her resignation the preceding year from the Daughters of the American Revolution when that organization refused to rent Constitution Hall for a recital by Marian Anderson. We had lunch in the state dining room with the leaders of the organizations represented at the Congress, and afterwards a tour of the White House, personally conducted by Eleanor Roosevelt.) In any event the many battles with the Stalinists in Communist-influenced organizations provided an exceedingly important learning experience for me; in my mind organizations like Americans for Democratic Action and the NAACP, who bitterly fought the Communists after World War II, were following their own agenda from the experiences of the 1930s, rather than being the victims of a cold war mentality.

Thus, all in all, it would be difficult I think, to overestimate the influence that those half-dozen years with Pioneer Youth had on my interest in social issues, my growing commitment to racial equality, and my persistent anti-Stalinism—as well, as will be indicated below, shaping the style of my activity in the black student protest movement of the 1960s.

IT WAS FORTUNATE, though rather accidental, that I attended Oberlin College. Oberlin had both high standards and a reputation for being "liberal," an image that stemmed largely from its nineteenth-century identification with the abolitionist cause but that was, I learned, in considerable part myth. I found it to be, however, not only a highly intellectual place, but also one that was tolerant of unconventional people. My first two years were spent in hard study, and I was introduced to intellectual history by Frederick B. Artz. His course in European history (my taking this course with him rather than with one of the other uninspired professors teaching it was also purely accidental) opened my mind to all kinds of new ideas, especially in philosophy. This came at a very important point in my intellectual development, for the clash between what my parents had taught me and the values and ideas expressed in school and by my peers had led me toward a skepticism of all values and ideologies, and of all knowledge for that matter.

But I was fascinated with the Enlightenment and the values of freedom, egalitarianism, and government by the people, as expressed by the thinkers associated with it. More important, in my sophomore year Artz had us read William James's *Pragmatism*. Here was a philosophy that enabled me to return with renewed commitment to many of the ideals with which my father and mother had imbued me, and that provided for a relativist like me a justification for activism in a morally uncertain world.

During the academic year 1942–1943 I worked in Newark in a War Department agency that employed nearly ten thousand people, one-third of them black. This experience provided me with my first significant contact outside of the Pioneer Youth Camp with college-educated blacks, and with two of them I formed close and enduring friendships. During this time my consciousness was raised by events such as the riots in Harlem and Detroit; the special issue of *Survey Graphic* entitled "Color: Unfinished Business of Democracy"; and the debate over the Red Cross's practice of segregating plasma in its blood blank, this last controversy especially ironic given the role of Dr. Charles Drew of Howard University in the invention and development of the blood bank. I recall angering the captain in charge of my section by refusing to make a contribution to the Red Cross. Yet this act of protest had what was for me the fortunate result of landing me in another unit which was headed by a black man who was easily the finest supervisor on the floor, a person who had been with the agency since its founding, but who, because of his race, had been denied the promotions to the higher positions for which he was qualified by experience and expertise.

All of these exposures served to crystallize my plans and to give direction to my life. I decided that I wanted to teach at a black college, and inaugurated a program of intensive reading on race relations and the black experience. Much of the best relevant literature at the time was in sociology and anthropology, and through this route I was led to read books on other topics in these fields, especially in anthropology, work that would later provide the basis for the kind of interdisciplinary scholarship in which I became engaged.

My last two years at Oberlin were activist years. Discrimination in the dormitories had led a small group of black male students to move into a house in town, and my brother and I both had rooms there. We were accepted without a question, and I will always recollect fondly those years of study and fellowship together. We were also active in a campus group of secular liberals that protested issues such as the jim crow blood bank and joined in the campaign against the discrimination of the white barbershops. (This project started as a sit-in by students in the graduate school of theology—and I recall being vaguely puzzled at the time by this and by the fact that we were able to hold our meetings at the student Christian center: I thought of religion as basically "pie in the sky," and did not understand the Christian student movement of the era. Only when I learned much later how the Christian student movement had provided the seedbed for the founding and early activities of CORE did I come to understand.) In the end, we took the lead in establishing an interracial barbershop, with a Nisei barber—a project that we found had wide support among our fellow students. (However, when we attempted to secure a contribution from President Ernest Hatch Wilkins, we were met with a brusque reply and were quickly ushered out of his office.)

These were also the years of the appearance of those milestone monographs: Melville J. Herskovits's *Myth of the Negro Past;* Gunnar Myrdal's *American Dilemma;* and St. Clair Drake and Horace Cayton's *Black Metropolis.* (Wilkins, clued into foundation networks, offered to buy a copy of Myrdal's study for any dormitory that requested it!) Myrdal of course spoke to my liberal sensitivities, and all three of these works—especially *Black Metropolis*—were to have an important influence on my own writing. Finally, I must again refer to the influence of Artz, who introduced me to the study of nationalism. It struck me that the modern nationalism of Europe was akin to racism in the United States, and so I embarked on a reading program on the history of nationalism under Artz's direction, with the aim of learning more about the nature of American racism. In the end of course this inquiry helped me not so much to illuminate white American racism but to understand a quite different form of ethnocentrism: black nationalism in America.

Tougaloo, 1945–1949

The black college where I first taught was Tougaloo College in Mississippi, which like Oberlin had had historic ties to the Congregational church and the American Missionary Association. My first knowledge of Tougaloo, however, came not from a knowledge of the history of Oberlin or of the history of education among the freedmen, but from two staff members there who had been with us at Pioneer Youth Camp. In fact, it was quite a surprise to me when President Wilkins informed me at the commencement reception of the historical connection between the two colleges and of Oberlin graduates having served as presidents and teachers at Tougaloo.

Tougaloo was not only small, (most departments, for example, having only one teacher) but when I came there was steeped in a religious and conservative tradition. (I found it helpful to at least join the Unitarian church.) The president was a well-meaning, elderly, paternalistic, and rather authoritarian white Yankee minister, with no administrative talent. The year I arrived was the first one in which dancing was permitted, and the first time that male and female students were not restricted outside of classroom hours each to their own side of the campus. I fell in with a small group of about four young black faculty, two of whom were, like myself, new to Tougaloo. They really took me in, insisting on using their own nickname for me, "Gus" (although I never liked it, preferring the name "Augie" I had received as a freshman at Oberlin, which stays with me to this day). They did their best to teach me to jitterbug and to play bridge, though I am afraid I became adept at neither. We also went to Jackson together, to the black restaurants and theaters on Farish Street, and even to the "Gold Coast," where bars and clubs dispensed illicit liquor, Mississippi having prohibition at the time. (There were of course separate black and white areas there too.) I was, as they said, "passing for colored," and I figured that as long as I was consistent and stayed on one side of the color line there was no danger, since no white folks in Jackson's rather small population were likely to know the difference. (In fact, my first experience in this role had been when my Oberlin friend, G. Allen Price, invited me to his home in Jackson in June 1944. His parents were determined to entertain any friend he had, but his mother—the first black social worker in Mississippi—thought that to avoid the possibility of any unpleasant consequences, it was best to have me "pass," and told her neighbors that I was a Negro.) At Christmas a group of us went North on the train from Jackson together, and to get to the half of the coach that was the jim crow car we had to pass through the back half of the coach that was reserved for white smokers. As we entered the forward compartment a voice called out loudly, "Hey, Boy!" After the second such call I assumed I was probably being addressed. I turned to a fat white man who said to me, "that's the nigger section up there." I replied, "I's sorry sir, but I'm colored myself," and turned away as my interlocutor turned crimson.

Later this particular clique dissolved, but I developed other strong friendships among the faculty at Jackson State and had other highly educational experiences. There were the Senate committee hearings on Theodore Bilbo about charges that violent intimidation had occurred during his most recent election. I recall that I myself had gone down to the courthouse in Jackson some months previously, and had seen hundreds of blacks, almost all of them obviously working class from the clothes they wore, lined up around the inside of the courthouse and beyond trying to register to vote. Tougaloo's campus minister was president of the Jackson and state NAACP, and his life had been threatened. During the hearings, I was privileged to be present for the testimony of one of our students, who had been physically prevented from registering. One Sunday a student drove me to a rural church where I was exposed to the black preaching tradition in a way that later helped me to understand the impact of the cadences of Martin Luther King, Jr. And then there was the revealing experience I had when I was invited to attend one of the monthly luncheons of a black businessmen's club in Jackson. I forget now who took me along, but I recall vividly the address given by the president of Jackson State College, who told us of the ways in which he had to humiliate himself in order to get the funds from the legislature that would enable him to build the institution. He was an "Uncle Tom," if you please, but one who came across as very human and very honest.

As at all of the black colleges at which I taught, my rapport with the students at Tougaloo was better than with most of my colleagues. (One of them, the historian Arvarh Strickland, a good friend, was the first student of mine to earn a Ph.D.) The students were not as yet affected by the cynicism of their elders, and white teachers, like black ones, were accepted or rejected on their individual merits. We had very open discussions in all my classes, especially the one in Negro history (which the students satirically called "Spookology"), and in other classes as well. It was in fact in a discussion in a class on the history of Western civilization (in the days before academe started to teach world civilization courses) that we got to talking about the question of the mixed racial ancestry of American Negroes. Originally my interest in this topic had been piqued by my reading Melville J. Herskovits's early research on the subject. In any event I passed out some papers and requested that each student anonymously outline his genealogy as far as he or she knew it. That was the genesis of what became my first published article, "The Racial Ancestry of the Mississippi College Negro."

The next president of Tougaloo (also a white minister), was if anything more paternalistic than the first one. When a black woman, the pianist Frances Walker who had been at Oberlin with me, came to visit, he assumed we were going together. Since I was about to take a leave to pursue further graduate work, he took the occasion to force me to resign. (Ironically, Walker came to teach at Tougaloo, and she and my successor on the faculty, also white and also from Oberlin, got married at the end of the next school year.)

Columbia and Fisk, 1948–1957

During my last year or so at Tougaloo, I had pursued a master's degree at Columbia University, my thesis being a study of black American nationalism prior to Marcus Garvey. It was a study to which I brought much of the conceptualization about the history of nationalism I had learned under Frederick Artz. In doing the research for the thesis I discovered Ralph J. Bunche's unpublished memoranda on black thought and race advancement organizations drawn up for the use of Gunnar Myrdal, and these proved to be of incalculable value in developing the kind of conceptualization that underlay much of my future work. Beyond that the master's essay proved to be of fundamental importance to my later work, since what I learned about the question of what we would now call black identity especially influenced the treatment of Negro thought in my dissertation and in later books.

After leaving Tougaloo, I began work on the Ph.D., and at first I found it difficult to select a satisfactory dissertation topic. I thought of doing a biography of James Weldon Johnson, whom I greatly admired, but someone else was working on that topic at the time. I had long been curious about Booker T. Washington—What, I wondered, did he really believe?—but I never seriously considered the idea of doing a biography of him since he was not, after all, a man I admired. As an intellectual historian I was really interested in his thought—and in Afro-American thought of the period as it related to the race question. So I began to work on the larger project. While Columbia at the time was hardly a department with much interest in interdisciplinary work (Richard Hofstader and David Donald being exceptions), there were helpful influences. From Jacques Barzun's course on nineteenth-century Western European thought I was made aware of how one could relate the ideas of leading intellectuals to the social conditions of their time. Although I never took the classes of the sociologist Robert K. Merton, I was greatly struck by the way he had addressed himself in *Social Theory and Social Structure* (1949) to the question of the relationship between the development of science and the religious and economic changes in seventeenth-century England.

But these influences did not really come together until my attention was called to a dissertation fellowship program of the Social Science Research Council. I then put forward an ambitious plan of interdisciplinary work, along the lines evident in *Negro Thought in America, 1880–1915*. That agency turned me down, but advised me to submit my proposal to the American Council of Learned Societies, which had a program of giving fellowships in the area of Negro studies. I did not know until decades later that the chair of the ACLS committee was Melville J. Herskovits, who had encouraged me and then had found a publisher for my study of the ancestry of Mississippi blacks. A lot of things crystallized as I drew up the proposal for this fellowship (and my adviser, Henry Steele Commager, though a very traditional intellectual historian who knew virtually nothing about the history of American blacks, obligingly wrote the appropriate references). It is not too much to say that without this award, *Negro Thought in America, 1880–1915*, in its scope and methodology would have been inconceivable.

Meanwhile, during my periods of study and writing at Columbia, I lived with my parents in Newark, where I became active in the Newark branch of the NAACP. In retrospect this branch was not very lively, and I learned later that its leadership had ties to certain machine politicians. Mostly I came to meetings regularly and observed things quietly—although on one occasion when the branch's lone Communist member introduced a resolution opposing the draft not only because the armed forces were segregated but also on foreign policy grounds, I took to the floor in a successful effort to delete the second part of the resolution. It must have been around 1951 that the branch secretary resigned and I was asked to take over the position.

I learned a good deal from this experience since this branch, like most others, had no salaried officer, so that the branch secretary really had the duties of an executive secretary. (I also have vivid recollections of the major lobbying effort with members of Congress, conducted by the NAACP and allied organizations—the Civil Rights Mobilization of early 1950.) My position as a white branch secretary was so unusual—and I guess I made myself relatively diligent—that I came to the attention of the national office, forming a long-term acquaintanceship with people such as Gloster Current, director of branches, and James W. Ivy, editor of the *Crisis*. The *Crisis* in turn proved to be a good medium for me to review books and publish some interesting articles, three of which appear in this book. After accepting the ACLS fellowship I stepped down as secretary, but not without realizing that the status and influence of high office encourage even idealistic people to operate so as to remain in office even if that is not good for the welfare of the organization or movement. I resolved that if I ever was in a similar situation I would not hold office for more than three or four years. Though I served briefly again as branch secretary around 1956, the lesson I learned would be of enormous value to me when I encountered the student movement in the 1960s.

The year on fellowship proved to be an incredibly rewarding experience. It enabled me to move beyond the fine resources at the Schomburg Collection in New York, where Jean Blackwell Hutson and her staff were more than helpful, and spend considerable time at other major depositories, including six months in Washington at the Library of Congress and at Howard University, where Dorothy Porter generously permitted me to work in the stacks. (As was also the case with the Schomburg Collection, there was scarcely anyone else using the Moorland-Spingarn Collection at Howard, a big difference, Dorothy Porter would often say, from the heavy use the collection received during the period between the two world wars—but a situation that, in retrospect, reflects what black intellectuals and students were thinking about in the integrationist optimism of the 1950s.)

During my travels I was fortunate to meet many leading black intellectuals for the first time. I had known Benjamin Quarles ever since he was the dean at Dillard University and I had met him while I was pursuing my study of the ancestry of college Negroes. Now, one of my first stops was at Lincoln University, Missouri, to meet Lorenzo J. Greene, who had published a condensed version of my master's thesis in his *Midwest Journal*. (Rayford Logan, as editor of the *Journal of Negro History* at the time, had turned it down—evidently because it smelled of the Communist "black nation" thesis, and indeed Herbert Aptheker's essay "Consciousness of Negro Nationalism to 1900" had appeared in *Political Affairs* in June 1949). Since I was going to Atlanta University Greene provided me with helpful introductions there: most notably, I recall, to Samuel Z. Westerfield of the economics department, and Clarence Bacote of the history department. In addition, in the men's dormitory where I stayed in Atlanta I got to know young black intellectuals who resided there such as the sociologist Hylan G. Lewis. While in Washington I lived at Carver Hall (built by the government to house black men who came to Washington to work during the war and now owned by Howard, which still accepted many non-students as residents), and I took breakfast and lunch at the university. Here of course I came to know John Hope Franklin, whose house was always open; Sterling Brown; Alain Locke, who filled me with gossipy tidbits about the Harlem Renaissance period; Rayford W. Logan; E. Franklin Frazier; Inabel Burns Lindsay, the head of the school of social work; the anthropologist Mark Hanna Watkins; and Emmett Dorsey, the political scientist who later was the first Howard University faculty member to obtain a microfilm copy and read my dissertation. Not least, there was the ever helpful Dorothy Porter.

HOWARD UNIVERSITY at this time was undoubtedly in its heyday, and, even more than Atlanta, it was an intellectually exciting place to be. But what was striking there and everywhere else I went was the ease with which one met these well-informed black intellectuals, their openness and cordiality. I found myself and my work warmly received wherever I went. It was a period I suppose when black intellectuals had considerable optimism about the long-range future, considerably more than now. Yet there were very few whites seriously working at the time in black studies, and those few found that they experienced the kind of interest that for me, at least, made that year one that I have cherished ever since.

The end of the year, December 1952, found me at Fisk University, where the librarian Arna Bontemps, who was also doing some work on Booker T. Washington, proved most helpful. I still had more research, and virtually all of my writing to do. Dorothy Porter had informed me about the unprocessed American Missionary Association archives at Fisk, and since I needed part-time employment, suggested I explore with Bontemps the possibility of working on these. Bontemps agreed to take up the matter with President Charles S. Johnson, who was fortunately in town, and next day I had a conference with the well-known sociologist and southern black moderate. At the end of an hour of rather exhaustive and careful querying about my research and my thinking about it, he offered me a position that had nothing to do with the AMA papers; I became, in fact, a research assistant to Charles S. Johnson himself.

I spent the next three and a half years at Fisk. Though both Tougaloo and Fisk were old American Missionary Association schools, the difference between the two was substantial. Fisk was far more cosmopolitan than Tougaloo, drawing its roughly seven hundred students from across the country and possessed of a faculty that was both more renowned and more secular. I think chiefly because Charles S. Johnson had good contacts with the philanthropies and seemed willing to try virtually any experimental program if it brought attention and money to the school, Fisk was in what must have been one of its most exciting periods. The problem was that much of the funding was such that it brought temporary glitter, but little in the way of long-range benefits. Easily the most exciting aspect of Fisk at this period was a foundation-funded early entrant program, under which bright young students, fresh from their junior or even sophomore year in high school, were attracted to the university and provided with an enriched program. These students and the revamped general educational curriculum that accompanied the program served Fisk briefly but well—a relatively high proportion of distinguished graduates came from this highly select group. It was to be my pleasure to teach for three years in this program.

But meanwhile there was both my research work and the work for Johnson to do. That first semester, the spring of 1953, gave me the opportunity for the final maturation of my scholarly approach.

Johnson was committed to writing a revised edition of *The Negro in American Civilization* and wanted me to help with it. In the great tradition of black sociologists trained at Chicago, Johnson was interested in providing historical context, and like me he was interested in the interrelationships among the different aspects of a society and its culture. In the working papers I prepared for him, I developed these thoughts, and then put my own ideas together in a paper entitled "Some Social Forces in Negro Thought on the Race Problem in America." Although I came to find much to criticize about Johnson, these first months of working with him provided exactly the opportunity that I needed to finally get my thoughts together and compose an essay whose contents provided the underlying conceptual framework for *Negro Thought in America*. I must concede that Johnson provided me with an unparalleled opportunity at a critical juncture in my intellectual career.

Our collaboration—if I may call it that—lasted just one year. I found that (as an enemy of Johnson had warned me would be the case) Johnson wanted me not simply to be a research assistant but that he wanted me to do his writing also. (Johnson himself believed that, as in his own case, this kind of thing doing other people's research and writing was just the way to embark upon a scholarly career. In fact I recall being puzzled on those occasions when he would pull off the shelf books like *The Negro in Chicago*, and Emmett J. Scott's *Negro Migration during the War*, and point out to me that he was actually the author of both volumes, though the books did not reveal the fact.) In January 1954 I returned from my Christmas vacation, having spent most of the holidays "drafting" his article on American Negroes for the *Encyclopedia Americana*. As he told me more than once, my "first drafts" were like "final versions," and in fact he used this piece verbatim, with only one small change. I felt that if I could write his materials, I would be better off writing my own. I made an appointment and told him that I did not want to be his ghostwriter. Upon hearing this the Fisk president peered at me intently out of the bottom of his bifocals, and thus ended my experience as research assistant to Charles S. Johnson. It was also the end of Johnson's plans to subsidize the publication of my lengthy article, "The Rise of Industrial Education in Negro Schools," in a special issue of the *Journal of Negro Education*. (Ultimately Lorenzo Greene accepted it for publication, in two parts, in the *Midwest Journal*.)

This is not the place for a detailed discussion of Fisk under Johnson, but Fisk did present a seeming paradox: a bright faculty with low morale. Evidently there was a price paid for this in high turnover among younger faculty who were initially attracted by

Fisk's reputation, standing, and cosmopolitan air. Johnson, the proud holder on an honorary doctorate from the University of Edinburgh, was a poor administrator, reluctant to delegate authority. Although he was away half the time on important duties connected with his various boards and committees, he insisted on making virtually all decisions, even on matters of detail.

Moreover, he played a somewhat Machiavellian game with his faculty members. For example, one can cite his dealings with his allegedly Communist faculty members, which produced the somewhat celebrated Lee Lorch case. Lorch, who had received considerable attention for his civil rights activism in New York, was an able mathematics professor who, because of his political reputation, was available at a very modest salary, even though good mathematics professors were hard to find. The year that Lorch became eligible for tenure the board of trustees had suspended all tenure procedures, pending a review of tenure policy, and savvy people on campus said that this was done in order to avoid giving Lorch tenure. When, during my period on the campus, a congressional committee called Lorch to testify and Lorch took the fifth amendment, Johnson decided not to renew Lorch's contract. Lorch sought to mobilize student sentiment against the president, and appealed for support from an acquaintance, the Fisk alumnus, W. E. B. Du Bois. (I once had a phenomenal interview with Du Bois in which he lucidly recalled the ideologies of his contemporaries fifty years before.) Du Bois declined to intervene and Johnson ignored the students. Johnson's cynical strategy became evident when, once the dismissal had been made, he and the board quickly came up with their new regulations on tenure. To Johnson's credit, however, I must say that when Myles Horton of Highlander Folk School was charged with being a Communist, Johnson spoke out in his behalf; and when later W. E. B. Du Bois suffered from similar charges, the aged black leader also had Johnson's support.

Johnson was a great admirer of Booker T. Washington. On reflection the two men were comparable in many ways. In Johnson's view Washington had the ideal strategy for his era, and Johnson himself was a skillful moderate. Although after his death the *New York Times Magazine* published posthumously an article in which he unmistakably set forth Negro goals and aspirations, he had adhered to an old-fashioned view, long held among many southern black leaders, of how to bring about social change. Thus when some of the Fisk faculty members were involved in a lawsuit against the municipal golf courses, Johnson took the occasion of a faculty meeting to

urge them to desist. He carefully explained his strategy: he personally, through his contacts with influential whites, would see that a
change in policy was made—as indeed it was. As his son, the
sociologist Robert Johnson, would tell me some years later, if he had
lived, Charles Johnson would have been totally unprepared for
what happened during the 1960s.

Moreover Johnson, like Washington, had a desire for power, and
probably considered himself the most powerful black man in America (a position Washington had held in his own day). Johnson's
views along these lines became painfully evident when during my
last year he attempted to block the publication of an essay critical of
his administration in a student publication. While Johnson was
unsuccessfully badgering the author of the offending piece in his
office, Johnson's closest friend on the faculty was informing a good
friend of the author that the article should be withdrawn since
Johnson was, after all, "the most powerful Negro in America." This
claim, given Johnson's powers over the careers of black academicians through his influence with foundations, had a certain truth in
it (though certainly things had changed radically from the time
when one could quite accurately describe Booker T. Washington in
these terms).

At any rate, I certainly developed a rather cynical view of Charles
S. Johnson, and out of my direct experiences with him came my
discussion of his role in the review-essay published in *Social Forces*,
"Black Sociologists in White America." Written long after I had left
teaching at black colleges, it is included here because of my reflections on both Johnson and Fisk.

At Fisk most of the faculty, black, white, and Asian, lived on
campus, and administration policy welcomed the kind of interaction between students and faculty that this situation made possible.
I have never witnessed college students so frequently visiting faculty in their homes, and indeed I judge that at few, if any, schools
have students interacted so intensively with faculty. I had certain
good friends on the faculty, most particularly the poet Robert Hayden, and the historian Edward Pessen, but intellectual stimulation
for me came chiefly from the gifted students who came to Fisk
through the early entrant program. Here were youth who not only
performed well, but effectively challenged a professor's assumptions and ideas. Interestingly enough I am still in touch with several
of these students. The one who is best known to historians is the
prolific scholar David L. Lewis, who collaborated with me on my
early article on the history of the black upper class in Atlanta, and at
whose urging many years later Elliott Rudwick and I embarked

upon the book that became *Black History and the Historical Profession.* But there were also people like Preston T. King, who is a leading political scientist in the United Kingdom; Richard P. Thornell, professor of law at Howard University; Isaac Hunt, dean of the law school at the University of Akron; and Niara Sudarkasa, president of Lincoln University, Pennsylvania.

TEACHING AT FISK during the height of the McCarthy Era and the social changes and litigation that culminated in *Brown v. Board of Education* in 1954 and in the Montgomery bus boycott of 1955–56, was an exhilarating, if sometimes frustrating, experience. In the spring of 1956 Charles S. Johnson, peeved at a satirical piece I had written about Fisk for a student magazine, used the occasion of a structural change in faculty arrangements to fail to renew my contract. At Fisk, as at Tougaloo, a brush with an authoritarian college president put me out of a job.

My departure from Fisk came at a time when my dissertation was still unfinished. Fortunately I had very supportive parents, and I spent the academic year 1956–1957 putting the final touches on what turned out to be an opus of nearly a thousand pages. Upon reflection, it is clear that by encouraging me to finish my dissertation and get my degree at Columbia, my dismissal had been the best thing that could have happened to me at that point.

Morgan State and the Student Movement, 1957–1963

Employment in academe was hard to come by as I finished my dissertation and entered the job market in the spring of 1957. Largely— if not entirely—through the support of Benjamin Quarles, head of the history department, I received an appointment as an assistant professor at Morgan State College. Morgan, a former Methodist school taken over by the state of Maryland, had certain distinctive features. With its student body of about three thousand it was the largest school I had thus far taught at. At the time, it probably had more Ph.D.s on its faculty than any other black school except for Howard University, a situation that was the result of three factors: the growing number of blacks earning doctorates; the threat of desegregation which led many southern states to raise salaries at black colleges, including Morgan; and Morgan's location in a border state, where blacks voted and the racial lines were not drawn as rigidly as farther South. Because so many freshly minted Ph.D.s had already been hired as full professors—due to the competition from other southern black state institutions—the top ranks were filled, and I was in a situation often faced by young academicians in recent years of having to make myself comfortable with a low rank.

THE PERIOD I spent at Morgan coincided with the greatest days in Morgan's history. This was largely because it had in President Martin D. Jenkins an extraordinary leader who was determined to raise the school's intellectual standing and was even more determined that Morgan would be a great teaching institution. Although most of our students came from poor neighborhoods and scored low on standardized tests, Jenkins had an abiding faith that with good teaching many of them would be prepared to do well at graduate and professional schools and be in a position to take advantage of the economic opportunities that were slowly opening for college-educated blacks. President Jenkins was on a crusade—and provided an environment in which teaching even the least gifted students became for some of us an exciting and rewarding experience.

Unlike Fisk and Tougaloo where there were approximately equal numbers of black and white faculty, at Morgan the professors were overwhelmingly (90 percent) black. They lived mostly on the other side of the city in the large black community of northwest Baltimore, with a small number in a nearby black enclave, Morgan Park. With the college located in northeast Baltimore in what was still a predominantly white area, it was something of a problem for me to secure housing in a black neighborhood within walking distance of the school. Mostly I succeeded. For about three years I rented a furnished house in Morgan Park, a black upper-class area established in the 1920s; just around the corner from me resided Carl Murphy, publisher of the Baltimore *Afro-American* and chairman of the Morgan board of trustees.

In certain respects my niche in Morgan's black community was unusual. I socialized mostly with a group of single black men, and with the family of a young white professor who was taking his degree from Johns Hopkins. During my last two years I rented a room in the home of a black colleague. In general the black faculty accepted me with some bemusement. Many of them would introduce me to people by saying "Be careful what you tell him; he knows more about us than we do!" In part this was based upon the kind of knowledge I had shown in my review-essay on Franklin Frazier's *Black Bourgeoisie*, which appeared in the *Crisis* at about the time I came to Morgan. But it also seemed to me to be a sign of respect for me in what was in some ways an anomalous situation, a recognition of my interest and knowledge. It was this sort of respect that led Charles H. Thompson, dean of the graduate school at Howard and editor of the *Journal of Negro Education*, to ask me to write a review-essay of Richard Bardolph's *The Negro Vanguard;* as he put it, I was the only person qualified to review the book who was not himself in it.

During my first three years, I devoted myself to my classes and sought in vain to find a publisher for my dissertation (it was too long, and like many young scholars I was very reluctant to reduce its length). Columbia, Princeton, and Johns Hopkins University presses all turned it down. Meanwhile I also pursued research along the lines suggested by the discussion of the relation of ideology to social class and social mobility in my dissertation. It was my aim to write a history of the black upper class, and in fact I did research in several cities—Atlanta, Durham, Charleston, and Nashville—with some work too in Washington and Baltimore. Except for the Atlanta essay, reprinted here, most of this never got published because in the 1960s I developed other concerns. But the information appears in summary in the book that was eventually published from my dissertation, *Negro Thought in America, 1880–1915*. More important for the future, along the way I learned much about Negro leadership and the varying tactics of black advancement organizations that helped to develop my sensitivity to much of the study and writing I was to do later.

It was during my Morgan years, between about 1959 and 1961 that I participated in the campaign to prevail upon the Southern Historical Association to end its practice of holding its conventions at hotels that barred blacks. Of course, given the interests and membership of the SHA this practice was hardly surprising. Still there were hotels in the South that to varying degrees were willing to serve blacks at professional meetings, the result in large part of the changing mores in the upper South that were occurring in the postwar period. I knew in a general way from my years at Fisk that there had been some movement in a positive direction, a trend supported by such scholars as C. Vann Woodward; and I attended the 1954 convention in Memphis at the Peabody Hotel, where one of the speakers at a dinner meeting with addresses on the topic of school desegregation was Morehouse College president Benjamin Mays. But with the rise of massive resistance and the White Citizens' Councils, a reversal set in. The fight was now taken up by a small band of younger white scholars teaching at black schools, such as Howard Zinn at Spelman and myself.

At that time we never thought for a moment of getting in touch with Woodward or any other of that generation of John Hope Franklin's friends—or even with Franklin himself. Rather we viewed

ourselves as young Davids struggling alone against a Goliath represented by reactionaries in control of the SHA. In fact we were quite
unaware of divisions of opinion among our elders, and of the
existence of people, such as a group at the University of Kentucky,
who agreed with our goals. In any event our strategy was different.
Instead of proceeding quietly and behind closed council meeting
doors, as our more senior predecessors had been in a position to do,
our strategy was to make this a public issue, by raising it from the
floor at the annual business sessions. (In retrospect, as young outsiders, we clearly had no alternative).

Zinn was the one who usually spoke from the floor at the business sessions (always well attended since in those days the business
sessions were held in connection with a free luncheon, given by the
local colleges and universities). I recall that at Atlanta, in 1959,
Zinn's attempt to get a motion on the floor was ruled out of order by
the parliamentarian. A year later, at Tulsa, I had to handle things on
my own. I spoke with several top leaders of the SHA, most of whom
wanted to go slowly, and so I was amazed when in speaking with
Secretary Treasurer Ben Wall, at the time a professor at Kentucky, he
leaned over and told me confidentially, in a low voice, that he
thought if I placed a motion on the floor it would pass, since the
meeting was being held so far west. My problem was that I knew
few people whom I could ask to second such a motion, and those I
did know were young professors who, while agreeing with me, felt
that it would damage their careers if they took a public stand. In the
end I raised the issue from the floor, maintaining that it was something the SHA was going to have to face up to. To my utter astonish-
ment, I sat down to an outburst of applause. Afterwards, SHA
president Clement Eaton of Kentucky remarked upon the amount
of applause, but, at the time I just put him down as operating from
purely political motives. Others, especially young scholars, also
stopped to talk with me, usually to express their admiration because they believed that my act would almost certainly hurt my
professional advancement (a point of view I dismissed as utterly
ridiculous, however, given my career of teaching at black colleges
and my plans at the time to continue teaching there indefinitely).

The next year, at Knoxville, I obtained permission to speak to the
executive council on the matter. I found my urgent plea, and threat
of possible picketing if the matter were not settled by the next
convention, received by members with responses that ranged from
frosty to indignant. Wasn't there any compromise possible? I was
asked. Then later at the business meeting Zinn was prepared to
bring up the matter once again, but we were outmaneuvered first

by those who suggested that a Richmond hotel would be glad to serve all our members if permitted to do this "under the table," and then by a motion that in effect tabled the matter. Yet, though no formal decision was ever taken, all future meetings were held at nondiscriminatory hotels.

By this time I was also deeply involved with the Morgan students in their campaign to end exclusion from department store lunchrooms and variety store food counters. Baltimore had been the site of substantial civil rights activism long before I arrived there in 1957. There was the exceedingly active and militant branch of the NAACP, which had been led for more than a score of years by Lillie Jackson and her daughter Juanita Jackson Mitchell. The city boasted one of the most effective Urban Leagues in the country. More recently there had appeared a small interracial CORE group, whose membership overlapped somewhat with the Baltimore chapter of the Americans for Democratic Action which also had a civil rights agenda, although it did not involve direct action; and the Morgan State College students who each spring would mount demonstrations against one of the discriminatory business places in the nearby Northwood Shopping Center.

In addition Baltimore was a city with a quite visible black power structure. At its apex was Carl Murphy, who not only headed the Afro-American newspaper chain and Morgan's trustee board, but also played an active role in the selection of executives and board members for both the local NAACP and Urban League. When feuding among the various race advancement organizations became too serious, it was Murphy who called leaders in and resolved the differences.

In addition to the NAACP and Urban League executives, and the kind of educational leadership represented by Martin Jenkins, there was the influential leader of the Prince Hall Masons, and a group of activist clergymen, mainly Methodist and Presbyterian, who played a significant role in the protest movement. (Baptist ministers, mostly in the anti-King faction of the National Baptist Convention, were not supportive.) Beyond this kind of civic leadership there were the Democratic politicians, from a city council member down, who were aligned with a northwest Baltimore machine whose constituency consisted of blacks and Jews. Finally there was "Little Willie" Adams, a reputed former numbers racketeer, whose money was alleged to be behind two of Baltimore's leading black businesses. He was considered a friend by the likes of Murphy and Jenkins and his wife played an active role in Democratic politics (reputedly she was one of those active in working for Lyndon

Johnson's compromise plan and against the Mississippi Freedom Democratic party at the 1964 convention). It was within this leadership context that the Morgan State College student movement functioned.

As indicated above, the Morgan students had been active in using direct-action tactics from time to time, well before the southwide movement broke out in February 1960. (In fact, shortly before I came to Morgan the Johns Hopkins student who became my closest white friend at Morgan had been arrested while participating in a Morgan student demonstration.) Although I was aware of the demonstrations that occurred each spring it was not until 1960 that I became involved. The way in which I did become involved was essentially serendipitous and, as with so many turning points in my life, appears to me now to have been quite accidental. In fact, I have always had the feeling that if I had been teaching farther south I would never have become involved. Certainly I did not want to get into violent situations, nor did I even want to be arrested. Baltimore, where blacks had a strong political presence and where public and police treatment of the demonstrators lacked the hostility found in states farther south, provided a milieu in which I felt I could function.

In any event what happened that February of 1960 was that after the Morgan students had undertaken their demonstrations protesting exclusion from the restaurant at a branch of one of the downtown department stores in the Northwood shopping center, it was proposed that they hold a demonstration on a Sunday afternoon when Baltimore's leading department store was having a major reception to celebrate the store's renovation. A white Morgan art professor had one or two pictures in an art exhibit for the occasion, and as a result had a few tickets for the celebration. He called this to the attention of the student leaders, and it was agreed that while the students were picketing, a small interracial group of adults would cross the picket line and attend the reception. I agreed to be part of the group, and as we crossed the picket line I noticed some of my students in the demonstration. Afterwards, while we were enjoying the sumptuous refreshments, I felt acutely and with a degree of guilt the irony of arranging for a group of adults, racially mixed though it was, to partake of the delicacies while the students were out on the picket line. Unhappy with myself, I decided the next day to join the picket line at the Northwood shopping center. And having participated once I somehow did not stop. What was intended as a small effort to indicate my support for what the students were doing became a long-term commitment.

Within days as the movement picked up steam and moved to demonstrating at all the downtown department stores during the Easter shopping season, what had been an informally structured movement led by the president of the student government—but calling itself the Civic Interest Group (CIG) in order to dissociate itself from identification with the college—took shape with a more organized and permanent structure. A self-appointed group of the most active participants met, selected officers, and asked the two adults invited to the meeting—a Presbyterian minister who had shown support for the students from the beginning and me—to serve as adult advisers.

Adult adviser? I was always somehow credited with contributing good advice, but the fact was that it was only on the rarest of occasions that I offered any advice. I was faithful about going on demonstrations and being present at meetings and attending court hearings when students got arrested. (I don't think the students fully appreciated the fact that they had the volunteer services of black Baltimore's leading attorney, Robert Watts—a lawyer whose gifts were enhanced by a personality that charmed judges and even hostile policeman and who never, as I recall lost any of our cases.) In any event I can remember only about three occasions when I thought the situation warranted my offering any suggestions or advice. (And in general I felt it wise not to encourage a course of action that I personally was not prepared to participate in.) But I really felt that I knew no more about strategy and tactics than the students did, and influenced by my years at Pioneer Youth I quite consciously acted upon the principle that this was a student movement, and that adults should not play a leadership role. The result was that I kept a low profile. Later, in the spring of 1961, when we secured the assistance of the Howard University Nonviolent Action Group (NAG), Stokeley Carmichael and others saw me as a white person following black leadership—which indeed I was, though I had not conceptualized my role in those terms.

In addition I conceived of myself as playing the role of what sociologists used to call a participant-observer. I do not recall at what point I decided to write about as well as participate in the movement. Although indeed the essay reprinted here about the 1960 department store demonstrations was written very early, I am not conscious of undertaking anything seriously until a good deal later, and my first major essays on the protest movement only began appearing in 1963. Still I was aware that somehow beyond my commitment to the students and the movement I had also a rather different kind of interest as a social scientist. There was of course a tension between these two roles and I felt it important to keep them in balance. From the observer side of the coin, it was probably well that I could never personally respond to charisma. From the participant side of the coin, my effort to be a detached observer was most helpful in enabling me to avoid my usual tendency to get personally involved in arguments and controversies—and this distance in turn was undoubtedly essential if I was to function effectively in the movement altogether. It is true that over time the kind of recognition accorded me for my participation—a recognition that of course I deeply valued—led me to examine my own motives closely, and at times when I felt I was attaching too much importance to my own standing in the movement I would briefly withdraw from activity until I could get things back into an appropriate perspective.

The freedom I had to participate in the movement was facilitated by the attitude of President Jenkins. Given his position as president of a publicly funded institution in a state that had many of the characteristics of those in the Deep South, he had to tread a fine line. Publicly he said nothing about the student movement, but in many ways he was supportive. He informed the movement leaders that they were not to meet in any rooms in college buildings, but then added that of course he was not going around to check on this, and usually we quite freely used college classrooms and the student government office. On one occasion when the governor's office called to complain about my participation in the demonstrations and negotiations held on Maryland's conservative Eastern Shore Jenkins firmly refused to take any action and afterwards indicated his outrage to the faculty. It was about this time that I was promoted to associate professor. The one time I was arrested as the result of a restaurant sit-in, Jenkins called me into his office to confer with him and the dean. Why, he wanted to know, did I have to get arrested? Unspoken, though obvious, was his concern about the response that the newspaper account of this incident might cause in Annapolis, (not to mention the response of the owners of the restaurant, who were reputed to have connections both to organized crime and to leading politicians). Even though I explained that the arrest was unintended, he said he would send me a memorandum to the effect that I would be docked one day's pay for each time I missed a class for a court appearance and that I was to report such absences to the dean. This punitive measure was never carried out, and I speculated that if anyone from Annapolis did get snoopy Jenkins would have his memorandum to show, and final blame would rest on the dean's shoulders. Clearly Jenkins approved of what I was doing but wanted me to maintain my low profile. Even though he would panic in the spring of 1963 when mass arrests occurred, Jenkins, given both his own personality and the importance of the black vote in Maryland, acted far differently than his counterparts in other parts of the South.

In any event CIG, once it had obtained the opening of the department store lunch rooms and restaurants, went on to wage a long but successful campaign to open all of Baltimore's restaurants. It virtually took over a CORE initiated campaign to accomplish the same for the restaurants on the Maryland Route 40 corridor, then the only route for automobile traffic between New York and Washington, and opened a long-range campaign against restaurant discrimination on Maryland's conservative Eastern Shore. For these large demonstrations we were joined by hundreds of students, mainly white, from northeastern colleges and universities. Employment discrimination became the next concern—and this was first initiated at a point where the public accommodations campaigns had temporarily come up against a stone wall of intransigence.

Throughout it often seemed as if CIG was battling on two fronts— one the struggle against discrimination, and the other the fighting with competing organizations engaged in civil rights and race advancement. From the beginning the CIG steadfastly and with unanimity resisted the efforts of adult leaders in the community to tell them what to do. I do not recall their ever going to the NAACP, or Carl Murphy, or the Urban League for advice: on the contrary they fought for their autonomy. First there was the struggle to establish their independence of the NAACP, whose aggressive and militant leadership seemed to want to dominate the civil rights agenda in Baltimore. More than one meeting in Carl Murphy's office was required to set things straight and even yet as late as 1962 NAACP Branch President Lillie Jackson could come to a CIG meeting and rise to say "You still belong to us!" Then there was the off again/on again rivalry with CORE, which was much weaker than CIG but employed the same methods. Typically CIG was able to dominate the situation when it chose. The Urban League was pretty much on the sidelines until CIG suddenly and without warning began to attack job discrimination, an action that drew long-lasting resentment from the local League's executive secretary who thought that the students had invaded his turf. The one group of adults on whom CIG could depend was a group of ministers, headed by Rev. Marion Bascom, who acted as a support organization. Yet the competition among the organizations, while painful, also had its beneficial side; what I have to say in certain of the essays reprinted here about the functions of disunity was originally developed on the basis of my experience and observations in Baltimore.

From the broader national perspective it should be said that CIG was an affiliate of SNCC. Except for our extensive campaigns in Cambridge, on the Eastern Shore—a situation in which the intervention of SNCC's national office was actually resented—CIG's activity was peripheral to SNCC's operations. I would say that politically CIG stood in the right wing of SNCC. The response of the white community to our activities was, as I have indicated, milder than in other places where SNCC operated; arrests were few (except for one late campaign in 1963), and the CIG participants did not undergo the radicalization that SNCC millennarians experienced in the crucible of the Deep South. Thus as early as 1961, when the politically more radical people in NAG began to work with us, CIG leaders were astonished at what they heard from Stokeley Carmichael and others: "Why, they're black nationalists," I was told in amazed tones.

One of the most instructive experiences I had during my years working with the Morgan students resulted from a complicated series of events that involved us with NAG leaders, people in the local and national CORE, and the Baltimore representative of King's SCLC, and that led to my introduction to Bayard Rustin. SCLC actually had almost no presence in Baltimore, and its affiliate seems to have consisted of one Baptist minister who happened to have a fairly popular radio program. What happened essentially was that local CORE had initiated a series of demonstrations in which CIG, with support from NAG, also participated. At one point when the activism was bogging down, the local CORE chairman arranged with King's man to make announcements about the demonstrations. Thereupon the good reverend took the opportunity to skillfully maneuver himself into the center of things, and threatened to take over the whole direct-action movement. At one demonstration NAG and CIG activists had decided to court arrest and spend the night in jail, and King's friend decided to join them. As Marion Bascom and I agreed, the response that his act would engender would radically alter the balance of forces in an important part of Baltimore's black leadership structure, and would do this almost literally over night. Bascom and the other ministers were not anxious to trump the SCLC member by going to jail themselves. The only approach that would undercut his obvious attempt to establish himself in the public's mind as the movement's leader, was to also, of necessity, undermine the NAG-CIG strategy by bailing everyone out of jail—a decision for which I, as an adult speaking with other adult leaders, was responsible for initiating.

With serious trouble in the community and its leadership structure in turmoil, national CORE sent some of its high staff as trou-
bleshooters: first two white officers, field director Gordon Carey
and community relations director Marvin Rich (after Farmer the
most influential man on CORE's staff); and after they proved help-
less program director Norman Hill and his close friend Bayard
Rustin. Though I had never met Rustin I had heard about him ever
since my days at Fisk. It was a Saturday afternoon, and I was
startled to receive a telephone call from this person with an artificial
sounding English accent, telling me that he was Bayard Rustin and
that I simply must come right over to the meeting being held at the
local CORE chairman's home. When I arrived I found a small group
that included not only those speaking for CORE, but a handful of
CIG and NAG people including Clarence Logan, our chair (and one
of the two leaders in CIG who were closest to me), and Stokeley
Carmichael. It seems that they had cooked up a strategy to form an
umbrella coordinating body of several leaders who would act to
contain the Baptist preacher. I was asked to serve as co-chair of this
body. Carmichael and Logan were very firm in their view that this
would be a good idea. I knew Carmichael fairly well by then. When
he first came to Baltimore he had expressed decidedly nationalist
sentiments, expressed amazement at a white like myself following
black leadership, and could not seem to understand how a white
liberal could be involved in the way I was (black bourgeoisie and
white liberals were despised by NAG and many other SNCC militants). We used to have long discussions about the question of
white and black leadership in the movement and on the alleged
deficiency in King's militancy. In the end the NAG people decided to
classify me as a new genre which they thought did not exist elsewhere, a "liberal activist." (Interestingly enough when the NAG
people had criticized the black adult supporters for bailing them out
of jail, I pointed out that I was the one who had made the recommendation—but Carmichael and associates simply dismissed the
matter.) In any event, when I was asked to serve as co-chair of the
leaders' group I flatly declined the invitation. I pointed out that my
role as adult "adviser" was a symbolic one and that I wielded no
power at all. Logan and Carmichael and the local CORE chairman as
well were not prepared to accept my refusal, but Rustin seemed to
understand and after some discussion the matter was dropped. It
was my own view, which events proved correct, that the only way
to regain control of the movement was to carry on activity as usual,
and simply ignore the interloping preacher who would already

have been a force in the movement if he had possessed an activist base of his own.

Rustin was a legend to people active in the movement, even though he did not become a public figure until the 1963 March on Washington. Of course his personal courage was unquestionable, and I was impressed at once with his sagaciousness in dealing with ticklish and complicated situations. I soon began to call him for advice when we were facing difficult problems, and his advice was always sound. At one point, when I disagreed with a line of action many in CIG were advocating but I was reluctant to openly oppose, Rustin advised me to ignore personal considerations of possible criticism and to act on the basis of what I thought was right for the movement. The advice proved absolutely sound. A couple of years later Rustin decided to lend his help to the second New York City school boycott even though he thought it was a bad idea. I was at one of the discussions on this matter and was somewhat disappointed to note that the crux of the discussion centered not on what would be best for the movement, but on how the stand he took would hurt or enhance his own role in the movement. For myself, throughout the remaining years of participation in the movement, I never regretted following the sagacious advice he had given me earlier. At the time I had enormous admiration for Rustin and to this day it has remained difficult for me to accept the cynical views many knowledgeable people in civil rights came to hold about him because of his actions and opinions during the last years of his life.

Meanwhile there had been other important exposures. I learned much from attending some of the SNCC conferences between 1960 and 1962, where I developed at least nodding acquaintanceships with individuals like Charles ("Chuck") McDew, Marion Barry, and Julian Bond. Particularly important was the SNCC executive meeting in Baltimore in the summer of 1961. It was then that I met Ella Baker (who shared with me her reservations about King), and was impressed by the way she played her role as adult adviser—asking questions that led the young people to clarify their thinking, rather than offering advice as such. This was the period when important developments were occurring in SNCC. For one thing there was the debate over using voter registration rather than direct action in a state like Mississippi, with the well-known consequences for civil rights activism in that state. For another a serious breach was developing between King and SNCC, although King himself was present and did his best in a futile attempt to retain a close cooperative relationship. This occasion was also the first time I heard King address a mass meeting, and while I understood the impact of his rhetoric, the charisma he had for so many people, black and white, left me untouched. It was, however, an instructive if somewhat heady experience to be witnessing important developments in the movement that would not appear in the press until several months later.

At about the same time, at the 1961 NAACP convention in Phila-delphia, I ran into an acquaintance, the Durham attorney Floyd McKissick, whom I had come to know back in 1958 in the course of my research on the black upper class. McKissick was now an NAACP lawyer in North Carolina, but over the next couple of years he transferred his allegiance to CORE, where I would know him as both national chairman and after that national director. It was Mc-Kissick who at the 1961 NAACP convention introduced me to the white NAACP labor secretary Herbert Hill.

Hill was a widely read man and seemed to model himself on the two NAACP officials who were race leaders, writers, and sponsors of young creative people during the Harlem Renaissance—James Weldon Johnson and Walter F. White. He knew of my work, evi-dently not only the *Crisis* publications but also some of the articles from my dissertation that had appeared in *Phylon* and the *Journal of Negro Education*. He at once expressed interest in my dissertation, read it himself, and then found a publisher through his contacts at University of Michigan Press. Michigan's readers liked what they read but wanted a shorter study. I still found it hard to reduce the length until one day late in the summer of 1962 at the Schomberg Collection I bumped into another acquaintance, Elliott Rudwick (whom I had come to know because our dissertation topics were in the same area), and he assured me on the basis of his experience that it could certainly be done. I promptly returned to Baltimore, and in three weeks reduced the manuscript by 50 percent. I am thankful to this day that no publisher at the time would publish the original long version; by sacrificing detail and reducing its length I made the book easily accessible to generations of professors and graduate students.

Hill also encouraged my research on the black protest movement, providing me with helpful introductions to NAACP leaders in sev-eral key centers of NAACP work in the South. Soon afterwards, in the late spring of 1963, he prevailed upon me to write my first major essay on the black protest, "New Currents in the Civil Rights Move-ment," for the left-wing Socialist journal *New Politics* (and at one point, when I panicked and found I could not do the article, it was his warm encouragement that enabled me to go ahead and compose the essay that laid the foundation for much of my later work). I have often marveled that my route to academic recognition came so largely by a serendipitous unconventional path through activist, nonacademic sources. I did publish a research note on Booker T. Washington in the *Journal of Southern History* while I was teaching at Fisk, but for the most part I judged that the mainstream journals were simply not interested in publishing essays in black history. This may not have been true. Upon reflection I realize that pieces from my dissertation might well have been accepted for publication in major journals. Subsequently there came a period when the relations between Hill and me became strained for some time, but even though as a scholar I do not personally like his polemical style, I recognize his effectiveness and must credit his encouragement and assistance, at another one of those critical junctures in my life, for doing so much to help my career.

Meanwhile, the first months of the preceding year, 1962, had also provided other important experiences. One was the invitation extended by Laurence Glasco, now a professor at the University of Pittsburgh but then a student at the University of Buffalo, to address the Negro history club there during Negro History Week on the history of the black protest movement. This forced me to pull together all sorts of information I had learned over the years about the twentieth-century black experience, and feeling that I might be treading on thin ice in some places, I put together the outlines of what proved to be the basic overall framework that would inform my scholarship on the movement through the years. Then, later in the spring there was my encounter with Malcolm X.

I had attended the debate between Bayard Rustin and Malcolm X at Howard University and thought it would be instructive to sponsor the same event at Morgan State. One of my friends, adviser to the campus Omega Psi Phi fraternity, proposed the idea to his chapter, and the students came up with the proposal that I, rather than Rustin, be asked to debate the well-known Black Muslim. I accepted the challenge, but aware of Malcolm X's formidable reputation and his strong showing in debating Rustin, I quickly began to rue my decision. So I worked hard at presenting an analysis and critique of the Black Muslims. I did receive help from other sources—not from adults, however, but from students. I will never forget the Saturday evening when some of us were at a NAG party in Washington and Carmichael, Courtland Cox, and others gave me a good deal of coaching in what to say and what not to say. Especially, they told me to avoid anything that could be interpreted as disagreement with Malcolm X's searing indictment of the evils in

American society. I don't suppose I would have done that in any case, but surely their coaching led me to be very explicit about this in my presentation. Then there was the assistance rendered by the Morgan student who was closest to me in the Baltimore movement, Clifton W. Henry, far and away the best debater on the campus. I asked him to accompany me to the small dinner the Omegas had for Malcolm X and me just before the debate, and with Malcolm X appearing a bit grim and rather hostile Henry bombarded him with leading questions that elicited answers that I might find useful in the debate. I must admit that I was so tense that I did not absorb much of this, although in the end I had composed myself and was simply prepared for what I was certain would be an unpleasant evening.

What happened that evening was rather different from what I— and I am sure Malcolm X—had anticipated. To my surprise student sentiment seemed very much in my corner. Partly I suppose this was due to my careful preparation, and to the way in which I couched my argument, especially my insistence that the national- ists and integrationists were both fighting to attain the same goal— recognition of the black people's human dignity—but that integra- tion was the best way to achieve it. But the students' support was also obviously related to my unostentatious participation in the movement. In that era at the height of integrationist hope, it was almost as if the times, rather than my personality, had created in me a somewhat charismatic figure. At the end of his rebuttal Malcolm X lashed out at "blue-eyed white devils" and concluded, "And here is one standing before you!" Afterwards as students crushed around him to ask questions, I went over to say goodbye. To my utter amazement Malcolm X turned, took my hand, and said "Professor Meier, I hope you don't mean goodbye." Afterwards I asked Rustin if Malcolm X meant it, and Rustin assured me that he did. To this day I regret not having taken the opportunity to see Malcolm X in New York. In the debate with Malcolm X I spoke from outline and the event was not recorded. However the debate was reported in a front-page article in the 31 March 1962 issue of the Baltimore *Afro- American* as well as in the 29 March issue of the daily *Baltimore Sun*. My remarks were the basis of the article I prepared at Rustin's request for publication in the pacifist monthly *Liberation*, which is reprinted in this volume.

In the fall of 1962 Morgan students seemed unusually apathetic on the surface, and support for the small core of people who formed CIG seemed to have vanished. Many students were disdainful about having more demonstrations, and took refuge behind President

Jenkins's advice to study hard and prepare for future careers. Then came the momentous explosion of mass demonstrations across the South, whose high point was the events in Birmingham. Just before this explosion CIG was able to overcome the students' apathy to sponsor the only truly mass demonstration in its history—the battle to force the Northwood Theater to open its doors to blacks. This series of demonstrations is the subject of the *Crisis* article "Case Study in Nonviolent Direct Action," reprinted here. On this occasion I came closer to going to jail than at any other demonstration. But I leave further details about my own personal role and experiences in the campaign for an endnote appended to that essay.

Although I did not realize it at the time, that spring of 1963 brought an end both to my participation in the student movement and to my teaching at Morgan State. I went off on a sabbatical leave without the slightest inkling that my career was at another turning point, and that new circumstances would remove me from the school to which I had grown so attached.

Transition: Newark and Chicago, 1963–1965

During the academic year 1963–1964 I returned to my family home in Newark. I attended the March on Washington and, although my recollections are hazy, I am sure I must have been engaged in some form of research on the protest movement. It was perhaps in this period that I had the wonderful interview with Whitney Young, whose personal magnetism caused me to leave his office at the end of the hour with a feeling that I had met one of the finest leaders in the whole movement.

In the fall I traveled through the South from Danville, Virginia, to Selma, Alabama, and to Jackson and Clarksdale, Mississippi. At Danville, where I stayed with Isaac Hunt's parents, I received graphic accounts of the police brutality during the demonstrations the preceding spring, the complex relations between the NAACP branch and the local SCLC group, and the failure of attempts to prevail upon Martin Luther King to return to the city and revive the moribund movement. At Selma I observed the SNCC voter-registration drive, and in Mississippi I observed the experimental "Freedom Vote" that paved the way for the Mississippi Freedom Democratic party. It was also in Mississippi that I got to know the remarkable trio who had created the alliance known as the Council of Federated Organizations (COFO)—Robert Moses of SNCC, David Dennis of CORE, and Aaron Henry of the NAACP. It was on the drive with Moses to Clarksdale to see Henry that I first experienced the fear with which activists in the Deep South lived constantly. And it certainly was comforting, as we sat in Aaron Henry's living room, to know that armed guards were posted outside twenty-four hours a day. This was an important exposure that was reinforced eight months later when I visited Mississippi during the famous "Freedom Summer" of 1964.

Most important, there was the new experience that awaited me in my exposure to Newark, New Jersey CORE, and its chairman, Robert Curvin, whom I also came to admire as one of the finest leaders in the black protest movement. I had at first tried to renew my activity with the NAACP branch but found it tied to machine politics and absolutely dead as a protest organization. On the other hand this proved to be a year in which I renewed my connections with national NAACP officers, most memorably getting to know Roy Wilkins's right-hand man, the unassuming individual admired by nearly everyone in the protest movement, John Morsell. I recall particularly the time that I was informed by James Ivy that Juanita Jackson Mitchell had complained to Gloster Current about some remarks I had made in public that were critical of the Baltimore branch. At her request, Current had asked Ivy not to publish anything further by me in the *Crisis*. I at once went to talk to Current, who taught me a very important organizational lesson, which was that he had to support the troops on the battlefront no matter what the abstract merits of the case might be. After some discussion the importance of what he was saying sank in. Still I was indignant at what seemed to me to be a form of censorship, and I took the matter up with Morsell. He took a broader view of matters and had the decision reversed.

I found Curvin to be one of the most extraordinary people I had ever met, and we are close friends to this day. Although he was essentially a local leader who attained only a modicum of broader recognition as a member of CORE's National Action Council, I regard him as as gifted as any of the movement's well-known national leaders. He was not only a convincing speaker and an engaging personality who clearly knew a thing or two about leadership, but he was also possessed of an acute sense of strategy and tactics and a most refreshing candor. And he was not overwhelmed by any sense of mission or power. He certainly could have remained as chair of Newark CORE for as long as he wished, and I was most impressed when, after four years of service in this office, he gracefully stepped aside for new leadership.

Curvin and I often laughed about it afterwards, but ironically we met quite by accident at a dinner of the rather less-than-militant local Urban League. Its president was a friend of mine who insisted that I come. Assigned to a table where I was bored because I knew no one else, I espied some vacant places at the table where the wife of the president was sitting, and decided to join her. Somewhat later we were joined by a striking couple, who turned out to be Curvin and his wife, Patricia. We quickly became involved in an exciting discussion comparing our experiences, and on Tuesday morning I joined the picket line at Western Electric.

Newark CORE was involved in intensive and successful demonstrations on the job front, and was focusing its attack on major corporations—Sears-Roebuck, New Jersey Bell Telephone, and Engelhardt Industries among them—as well as less successful demonstrations against craft worker discimination on public construction projects. For me there were the usual picket lines, and in addition a challenging round of negotiations as a member of the committee negotiating with New Jersey Bell. The chapter also took up the issue of police brutality, and I will never forget our sit-in at City Hall; I recall telling a CORE colleague who drove me down to the demonstration that I would be damned if I was going to get arrested as the others planned, but when Curvin asked if I would go to jail too it was impossible to say no. But this second arrest was no more eventful than my first; we were released after our arraignment and the charges were later dropped. To the end, amid the scores of demonstrations in which I participated, I personally avoided any stay in jail.

Earlier, in the fall, I had spoken at regional CORE conferences arranged by program director Norman Hill, with my now pretty standard talk on the history of the twentieth-century movement. Rustin appeared on these programs too, and sometimes James Farmer, whom I met for the first time. At one such conference in Syracuse I came to know another most impressive local leader, George Wiley, who like Curvin served on CORE's National Action Council and who would become the highly effective associate national director of CORE during the last year of Farmer's tenure, and afterwards the architect of the National Welfare Rights Organization. I learned a lot about CORE, naturally, and ultimately it was this quite intensive experience with CORE at various levels that I believe led Rudwick and me to inaugurate what we optimistically thought would be a general history of the civil rights movement in the twentieth century, with a monograph on the history of CORE.

Negro Thought in America, 1880–1915, appeared in December 1963 and new career opportunities soon manifested themselves. Flattering contracts from publishers were still in the future, but the most obvious immediate effect was the offer to teach at Roosevelt University, a move I would not have made if Jenkins had arranged a promotion to full professor once the book had appeared. (But then Jenkins for some reason often played a cynical game with promotions, compelling qualified individuals to work an extra year or two beyond the date of their promised promotions.) Roosevelt, of course, had had an unusual tradition of racial egalitarianism since its founding as a secession from the YMCA College over a conflict between the YMCA board and the college's racially equalitarian president. Roosevelt was, in fact, one of the few predominantly white institutions of higher education to have black faculty members at that time. Moreover, Chicago had its attractions. Still my years at Morgan had been so meaningful that I really did not want to leave.

There are at least two different accounts of how I came to be invited to teach at Roosevelt, though they are not really mutually exclusive. One account stresses a personal network, the other the appearance of a good book at the appropriate time. It so happened that the head of the Roosevelt University mathematics department was a close friend of both Jack Roth, history department chairman, and my brother, a mathematical statistician who taught at the University of Chicago. There had been an earlier effort from these people to bring me to the history department's attention, but without a book at least accepted for publication Roth had no interest. Then, in the spring of 1964, this connection was activated again, and as far as the mathematicians ever knew this led directly to the invitation.

John Bracey, involved in my recruitment as both a history major and a black activist at the school, remembers a very different chain of events. Black students—and black faculty like St. Clair Drake— were pushing for the introduction of a course in black history. When *Negro Thought in America* came out they were impressed, perhaps with its attention to nationalism as much as with anything else—and St. Clair Drake reviewed the book favorably in the *American Sociological Review*. There was some discussion as to whether I was black or white—at the time, at least, one could not tell from the content or style of the book itself, and indeed the book was consciously written with the kind of detachment that characterized the best black scholarship of the period, including the work of figures like Charles S. Johnson, Drake, and John Hope Franklin, as well as other historians like Lorenzo J. Greene, Benjamin Quarles, and Luther Porter Jackson. Moreover, my career trajectory—from Oberlin to Morgan State—could well have been that of a black person. I understand that in the discussion at the time they decided that, whatever my race, it was a good book, and they proceeded successfully to press their case with the history department.

WITHOUT MY INTENDING IT to turn out that way, the move to Roosevelt served to mark an end to my activism. The Chicago freedom movement was so large and populated by so many able people that it did not seem possible to make a significant contribution. I did join the group of historians who were part of the March on Montgomery in the spring of 1965, and directly after that once again pulled a lot of diverse thoughts together and wrote what has proven to be my most widely reprinted article, "On the Role of Martin Luther King." It was the fruit not only of my observations of King (I never met him—the time that Rustin took me by his hotel room one night when King was in Chicago, he was already in bed), but also of discussions I had had with Bracey and others in the graduate course on twentieth-century Negro history in which the students expressed doubt about King's militancy. (Bracey and I were—and still are—poles apart ideologically, but from the start we had an enormous respect for each other's knowledge.) As I recognized only a good deal later, in searching for a formula that would reconcile my understanding of King's role with the views of the students, and also take into account King's complexity, I borrowed and adapted a conceptualization employed in a book I was reading with another class—John Blum's *The Republican Roosevelt* (1954) which categorizes Theodore Roosevelt as a conservative kind of Progressive. I recall that once the essay was composed I called Curvin and read it to him over the phone, asking him if he thought the essay was a sound analysis. Assured that things looked pretty much the same from his perspective, I felt confident about what I had written.

All in all, though my black students were still exercising a potent influence on me and my thinking, my two years at Roosevelt proved to be the end of an era. As opportunities for publication multiplied with the growing salience and increasing militancy of black protest, and as white participation in the movement became less and less welcome (a phenomenon I had first observed in old NAG friends when I visited the COFO headquarters in Mississippi during the summer of 1964), the move from a period in my life when activism had taken first place (at Morgan and during the year with CORE) to one in which scholarly activities became dominant seemed quite natural. (Encouraging this shift was the fact that at the very time I began teaching at Roosevelt, Elliott Rudwick and I embarked on what would prove to be a long-term scholarly collaboration.) While teaching at Miles College in Birmingham during the summer of 1966, I traveled with a few white colleagues to Jackson for the end of the Meredith March, which launched the phrase "Black Power" on its remarkable career. I personally elected to stay on the sidelines and did not participate in this final direct-action demonstration. As the march began that last day from Tougaloo College—the place where in a sense for me "it all began"—and Carmichael and Young walked by and cordially shook my hand, I naturally had a feeling of alienation and loss, wondering, as Vincent Harding put it in the title of that illuminating article of his, "Where Have All the Lovers Gone?"

The era of integration had passed and that of "Black Power" had begun. Yet, whatever my personal feelings, in terms of my career I would have to say that the surge of black nationalism was beneficial. The new spirit of the late 1960s, vividly caught by the slogan "Black Power," made the black experience more important than it had ever been viewed by white Americans before, so that ironically one of the unintended consequences of the new developments was to stimulate an enormous interest in scholarship on the subject. Indeed I used to say, with a bit of hyperbole, that it was "Black Power" that "helped make me famous."

And so I am the heir of a rich but bitter-sweet experience. I am esteemed as a scholar and regarded as a success in a way that earlier I would have thought inconceivable. Yet the state of American race relations today is not really part of the world I was hoping to help build. Instead my assessment both of the American scene and of multiracial and multiethnic societies in much of the contemporary world has eroded the liberal optimism with which I started out at Tougaloo nearly a half century ago.

Kent, Ohio
March 1991

PART I

Teaching and Learning behind the Color Line

ONE

The Racial Ancestry of the Mississippi College Negro

As INDICATED in the introduction, this essay, my first published article, grew out of (1) my interest in Melville J. Herskovits's early work on the Afro-American population as an example of "racial crossing," and (2) a discussion of the subject that arose in one of my classes at Tougaloo College. This essay is reprinted here partly because it illustrates the kind of rapport I had with the students, and because it indicates something of the scope of my interests.

Introduction

ABOUT TWENTY years ago Melville J. Herskovits published the results of his pioneering work on the racial ancestry of the American Negro. On the basis of a genealogical survey Herskovits concluded that about 22% of the American Negro population was of unmixed African ancestry, while the rest had varying amounts of Indian and Caucasian admixture (see table 1).

A study of these figures gave rise to a genealogical survey of a similar nature undertaken in the spring of 1947 on the campus of Tougaloo College (Tougaloo, Mississippi) by a small group of students as a class project in a course in Negro history. We too found that the great majority of the Tougaloo faculty and student body was of mixed ancestry, but our data showed certain outstanding deviations from those found by Herskovits, as indicated in table 2. (For purposes of comparison with a college group the Howard University sample of Herskovits is also included.)

As can be seen at a glance there are two points at which the differences between the Herskovits and Tougaloo samples are striking: the lesser incidence of unmixed Negroes, and the greater incidence of Indian ancestry in the Tougaloo sample. The latter is reflected not only in the total incidence of Indian ancestry and in the number showing a simple Indian and Negro mixture, but also in the greater incidence of individuals with an ancestry composed of all three racial groups.

Inasmuch as the majority of individuals in the Herskovits sample

From *American Journal of Physical Anthropology*, n.s. 7 (June 1949): 227–40.

Table 1. Racial ancestry of the American Negro: Herskovits's sample

Class	No. of individuals	Percent of total
Unmixed Negro	342	22.0
Negro, mixed with Indian	97	6.3
More Negro than white	384	24.8
More Negro than white with Indian	106	6.9
About the same amount of Negro and white	260	16.7
The same class with Indian mixture	133	8.5
More white than Negro	154	9.3
More white than Negro with Indian	75	5.5
Total	1551	100.0

resided in the eastern part of the United States a geographical differential was suspected. Acting upon the suggestion of Dr. Herskovits I obtained a larger sampling by extending the survey to four other schools in Mississippi, and, for purposes of comparison, to one school in each of the neighboring states of Tennessee and Louisiana. The following schools participated:

Mississippi: Alcorn A. & M. College, Alcorn
　　　　　　　Campbell College, Jackson
　　　　　　　Jackson State Teachers College, Jackson
　　　　　　　Southern Christian Institute, Edwards
　　　　　　　Tougaloo College, Tougaloo
Louisiana:　Dillard University, New Orleans
Tennessee:　LeMoyne College, Memphis

In addition to college students the sample includes a sprinkling of faculty members (all schools), some senior high school students (Campbell College and Southern Christian Institute), and a number of veterans taking vocational courses, but not working for a degree (Alcorn and Campbell Colleges).

Procedure

Introducing the survey. The first step at each school, once the approval of the administration had been obtained, was to present the survey to the students—ordinarily at a general assembly. In a brief talk I would tell them the basic facts relating to the formation of diverse physical types in the human species, with emphasis upon the role of race mixture in this process; explain why anthropologists are interested in studying the racial composition of the American Negro; indicate the results obtained from the Herskovits study; and explain how it was that I happened to be conducting the survey in

Table 2. Comparison of the Herskovits and Tougaloo College samples

Class	Herskovits's total sample % of 1551[1]	Herskovits's Howard University sample % of 538[2]	Tougaloo sample % of 200
Unmixed Negro	22.0	20.3	8.0
Negro, mixed with Indian	6.3	6.7	27.0
Negro, mixed with white	50.0	47.1	21.0
Negro, mixed with Indian and white	20.9	25.0	45.0
Total of all classes with Indian ancestry	27.2	32.6	72.0
Total of all classes with white ancestry	70.9	73.0	66.0

[1]See table 1.   [2]Herskovits, 1930, p. 179.

that particular school. I also emphasized the voluntary nature of participation in the survey, and stressed the fact that the information (except at Tougaloo) would be given anonymously.

The interviews. The second step consisted of the interviews. Those conducted at Tougaloo College in the spring of 1947 were done on an individual basis by me and a select group of students working under my direction. The Tougaloo freshman class of September 1947 and the participants at all the other schools were interviewed on a group basis by means of a questionnaire. The groups so interviewed ordinarily ranged from thirty to sixty people in size. The form of the questionnaire used is shown in figure 1.

Completing the genealogical diagram in the questionnaire involved placing in the appropriate blanks the racial composition of each ancestor about whom information was known. Four symbols were used: "N" for Negro, "I" for Indian, "W" for White, and "C" for Creole. (The word Creole has various meanings—e.g. an individual of French descent; an individual of French and Negro descent—and in perhaps a majority of the cases the participants did not know just what Creole meant in their ancestry. Consequently it was given a separate classification.) Other groups such as Chinese, Japanese, or Mexican, were to be written out in full where they appeared. Where necessary the chart could be extended by a participant as far back as he knew his ancestry.

Before filling out the questionnaires the participants were given the opportunity of asking any questions they might have regarding the survey or any relevant anthropological material. They were told again that their participation was purely voluntary, and that they would fill out the questionnaires anonymously. The scientific nature of the survey and the necessity for strict accuracy were empha-

TOUGALOO COLLEGE HISTORY CLUB
Survey on Ethnic Composition of Mississippi
College Students and Faculty
Fall Semester, 1947

Name of college ⎯⎯⎯⎯⎯⎯⎯⎯⎯⎯⎯⎯⎯⎯⎯⎯⎯⎯

Your age ⎯⎯⎯⎯⎯⎯⎯⎯⎯⎯⎯⎯⎯⎯⎯⎯⎯⎯⎯⎯⎯

Check one: Faculty ⎯⎯⎯⎯⎯⎯⎯⎯   Student ⎯⎯⎯⎯⎯⎯

Check one: Male ⎯⎯⎯⎯⎯⎯⎯⎯⎯   Female ⎯⎯⎯⎯⎯⎯

County and state of birth ⎯⎯⎯⎯⎯⎯⎯⎯⎯⎯⎯⎯⎯⎯

Present residence ⎯⎯⎯⎯⎯⎯⎯⎯⎯⎯⎯⎯⎯⎯⎯⎯⎯

Genealogical data:

Mother				Father			
Grandmother		Grandfather		Grandmother		Grandfather	
Mo	Fa	Mo	Fa	Mo	Fa	Mo	Fa

Fig. 1. Sample questionnaire

sized. The participants were clearly directed to indicate only what they were sure of—where they were not sure of a person's ancestry they were to leave the space blank. I then demonstrated how the diagram was to be completed by filling out a blackboard model step by step. Questions on the part of the participants were encouraged until all seemed satisfied that they understood the procedure. The students were also encouraged to ask for assistance from either me or their instructor, and a number of them did.

Question can, of course, be raised as to the reliability of the information obtained from a genealogical survey of this nature. In any information passed down by word of mouth from generation to generation inaccuracies are bound to occur because of various psychological factors. It is sometimes said, for example, that Indian ancestry carries a prestige value. This is quite possible, though I did not find any indication of it in my conversations with people while conducting the survey. It is of course impossible to measure the extent of this and any other inaccuracies that may occur in genealogical data obtained by interviews. However, Herskovits has already pointed out that this is obviously the only way to get anything like complete information on the data desired, and like Herskovits I made every effort to eliminate the possibilities of the participants giving false data. In the first place participation was voluntary. In the second place the interviews (except for the first group at Tougaloo where the interviewers were personally known to the participants) were purposely made anonymous. In the third place the necessity for accuracy was stressed. Fourth, I was introduced—usually by the dean of the school—as a teacher at another Negro college, and the administration at each school clearly indicated its support of, and interest in the survey, to the student body. And finally in my talks introducing the survey I was careful to emphasize the widespread occurrence of the phenomenon of race mixture, and to present the subject in a stimulating fashion. Very few declined to participate. In short the rapport was excellent.

Making the calculations. In making the calculations from the data thus secured the following steps were taken:

1. All questionnaires showing inconsistencies in the genealogical data, or indicating no knowledge whatsoever of ancestry were discarded.

2. The questionnaires were then grouped according to the birthplaces of the participants. Two major groups were decided upon: the Mississippi born (1,089) and, for purposes of comparison, those born in the nearby states of Tennessee, Louisiana, Arkansas, Texas, Oklahoma, Alabama, Missouri, and Kentucky (390)—referred to as the "nearby states" in tables 3 and 4. The sample of those born outside of this South-Central area was discarded because it was so very small.

3. In classifying the individuals of these two series I followed the same general method as Herskovits. "This," he writes, "I did as conservatively as I was able to do it. A given individual was classified only on the basis of the actual information given by him. If he stated that, to the best of his knowledge, three grand-parents were unmixed Negro, and if he had no information at all about the 4th grand-parent, then he was classified as unmixed Negro. If he knew of one White grand-parent and of another who was mixed Negro-White, and knew nothing of the other two, he was classified as more White than Negro. In this way 8 classes were formed. . . . Four of these represent differing degrees of Negro blood, and there are 4 corresponding classes for the subjects who were aware of some Indian admixture." Herskovits, however, did not indicate the "amount of Negro blood, . . . since mixture with Indians is not a thing of the recent past" (Herskovits, 1928, pp. 8–9).

I found, however, that for the present sample mixture with Indians appeared to be quite as recent as mixture with whites, and in any case the great incidence of Indian ancestry necessitated the adoption of a larger classification (as will be noted in the following table), though the same procedure of flexible classification was followed.

The Data

In table 3 are shown the various classes, the number in each class, and the proportion of the total contained in each class for the two series of the present survey: those born in Mississippi, and those born in nearby states. It will be noted that the classifications of Creole and Creole with Indian are given without any proportions of Negro, white, and Indian ancestry. This was necessary as relatively few individuals claiming Creole ancestry knew just what it stood for in their particular families, and it would have been hopeless to attempt a percentage classification in such a case. In any event the percentage of Creole ancestry in the Mississippi sample, at least, is negligible.

Discussion

As indicated earlier the two most striking differences between the Tougaloo sample and the Herskovits sample were the greater incidence of Indian ancestry and the lesser incidence of unmixed ancestry in the former. We shall concentrate our attention upon these two items. Before continuing, however, it must be noted that inasmuch as the majority of those interviewed for this survey were college students the sample is probably not representative of all socio-economic groups in any correct proportions. Consequently if there are any significant differences in racial ancestry among the various socio-economic levels they probably are not properly reflected in the conclusions of this survey. (Herskovits's figures, which were obtained not only at Howard University, but also in a West Virginia community, and from the parents of New York high-school children, are quite likely more representative in this respect.)

Table 4 shows comparative figures of the Herskovits sample and the two series of this survey for certain combined classes. (Creole for this purpose is naturally enough considered as containing white ancestry.)

Turning first to the question of the amount of Indian ancestry it will be noted that both series of this survey support the general trend indicated in the first Tougaloo group, with over two and one-half times the incidence of Indian ancestry in my sample as compared with the Herskovits sample. At the same time the incidence of white ancestry appears to be somewhat lower.

In view of the fact that the Herskovits sample came primarily from the Middle Atlantic and Southeastern States, there apparently exists a pronounced regional difference, especially in the amount of

Table 3. Racial ancestry of participants born in Mississippi and in nearby States

Class	Mississippi-born		Born in nearby states	
	Number	% of total	Number	% of total
Unmixed Negro	181	16.6 16.6	50	12.8 12.8
Mostly Negro with Indian	296	27.2	74	19.0
Mostly Negro with Indian and white	209	19.2	76	19.5
Mostly Negro with white	123	11.3	26	6.7
Total, mostly Negro		57.7		45.2
About one-half Negro with Indian	38	3.5	7	1.8
About one-half Negro with Indian and white	85	7.8	33	8.5
About one-half Negro with white	23	2.1	2	.5
Total, about one-half Negro		13.4		10.8
Less than one-half Negro with Indian	6	.6	1	.25
Less than one-half Negro with Indian and white	92	8.4	37	9.5
Less than one-half Negro with white	3	.3	2	.5
Total, less than one-half Negro		9.3		10.25
Negro with Creole	8	.7	22	5.6
Negro with Creole and Indian	19	1.7	53	13.6
Total, Negro with Creole		2.4		19.2
Negro with Oriental (Chinese and Japanese)	2	.2	1	.25
Negro with Oriental and Indian	2	.2	1	.25
Negro with Oriental and white	1	.1	1	.25
Negro, with Oriental, Indian and white	1	.1	1	.25
Negro with Polynesian and white			1	.25
Negro with Indian and Mexican			1	.25
Negro with Indian, Mexican and white			1	.25
Total, with Oriental, Mexican and Polynesian		.6		1.75
Grand total	1089	100.0	390	100.0

Table 4. Comparison of Herskovits's sample with samples of present survey for certain combined classes

Class	Herskovits's sample % of total	Present Survey Miss.-born % of total	Present Survey Nearby states % of total
Unmixed Negro	22.0	16.6	12.8
Negro, mixed with Indian	6.3	30.3	21.0
Negro, mixed with white	50.0	14.4	13.3
Negro, mixed with Indian and white	20.9	37.2	51.1
Total of all classes with Indian ancestry	27.2	68.6	73.1
Total of all classes with white ancestry	70.0	51.8	64.9

Indian ancestry. In the light of historical fact this is not so very surprising. It must be remembered that by the time African slaves were imported in large numbers into the eastern seaboard states most of the Indians had probably been either killed or forced to move further to the west. In addition most of the intermixture that did occur with Indians of that area occurred so long ago that most memories of it have probably been erased. Such is not the case with the Lower Mississippi Valley where Negro slavery was introduced at a more recent date, and right along with white settlement, before the Indians had been either largely evicted or exterminated. This situation undoubtedly made possible a much higher degree of Indian admixture.

It is interesting to note that Herskovits also found a regional differential in the amount of Indian ancestry (Herskovits, 1930, p. 17). Arranging the individuals of his Howard University series in regional groups, he found that forty-four individuals or 45% of those from the South Central Division (the same area covered by the present survey, except that Herskovits does not include the state of Missouri) had Indian ancestry, as against 33% for the whole Howard University series (and about 27% for his whole sample). This was second to New England which had 53% claiming Indian ancestry, and was closely followed by the North Central Division which showed 42% claiming Indian ancestry (which is natural, as the lines of migration were pretty generally directly north).

There still remains a discrepancy between the Herskovits figures for the South Central area and those of this survey. It occurred to me that this discrepancy might be a reflection of a time differential. The Herskovits survey at Howard University was taken about twenty-five years ago—almost a generation. In view of the fact that many individuals of the last generation who had Indian ancestry undoubtedly married individuals without Indian ancestry the total incidence of Indian ancestry had, in all probability, greatly increased. A check on this hypothesis in the case of the Mississippi-born series revealed that of 2,142 parents of those interviewed (not quite twice the 1,089 who participated as in some cases information was available for only one parent) 939 or 43.1% had Indian ancestry, and that of 757 parents of the series born in nearby states 377 or 49.8% had Indian ancestry, as compared with 45% of the Howard University individuals born in the South Central division. Naturally the parents of these two series are not precisely comparable with the Howard University series, but the comparison is very suggestive. Consequently the incidence of Indian ancestry for the Negro population as a whole ought to be a good deal higher today than it was at the time of Herskovits's survey; and the regional differential, while present, is not as great as the uncorrected figures seem to indicate.

Turning now to the group with unmixed Negro ancestry it must be noted that the figures given—16.6% for the Mississippi-born series, and 12.8% for the other series are in all probability too high. Not only were some of the participants undoubtedly unaware of the intermixture that had occurred, but the 159 questionnaires which were discarded because of inconsistencies all claimed a mixed ancestry—so that the proportion having unmixed ancestry should be a few points lower, while the other major classifications should be a few points higher.

The differences between the present sample and the Herskovits sample in regard to the incidence of unmixed Negro ancestry, while not as great as indicated by the first Tougaloo group, appear sizeable enough. The Herskovits sample of 1,551 contained 22% unmixed Negroes, while my Mississippi-born series contained 16.6% and the other group 12.8% unmixed Negroes. Here also I thought it might be valuable to compare the Herskovits sample with the parents of the two series in the present survey, and upon doing so calculated that 738 (out of 2,142) or 30.3% of the Mississippi-born series, and 215 (out of 757) or 28.4% of the series born in nearby states were of unmixed ancestry. Again these figures are merely suggestive—the parents of the present sample and the individuals of the Herskovits sample not being exactly comparable. In any event one may expect that there will be almost no unmixed American Negroes within a few generations.

It may be noted also that the Mississippi-born sample showed a sizeably smaller total incidence of white ancestry than the Herskovits sample. This seems less true of the series from nearby states, as is also indicated in the larger incidence of individuals claiming an ancestry composed of all three races, and in the smaller number of individuals with a simple Negro and Indian admixture in this series. It is likely that this differential in incidence of white ancestry between the two series of the present sample is largely due to the presence of the large number of individuals of Creole ancestry, principally from the Louisiana-born group. That the differential between the total Herskovits series and the two series of the present survey as to incidence of white ancestry is a significant one is shown by a comparison of the parents of the present sample with the individuals of the Herskovits sample. Of the 2,142 parents of the Mississippi-born sample for whom information was given, 727 or 33.5% had white ancestry, and of the 757 parents of those born in nearby states 337 or 44.5% showed white ancestry, as compared with 70% for the total Herskovits sample.

That the increased incidence of Indian and white ancestry during the past twenty-five years is due almost entirely to intermarriage between Negroes and not to any fresh admixture or addition of non-Negro ancestry was shown by a study of the questionnaires. Of the 2,142 parents of the Mississippi-born series only 5 were of the unmixed white ancestry, and only 4 were of unmixed Indian ancestry; while of the 757 parents of the nearby states series there were none of unmixed white ancestry, and only one of unmixed Indian ancestry. Carrying this investigation to the grandparents of those interviewed in the present survey it was found that of 3,912 individuals for whom data were given in the Mississippi-born series only 85 had unmixed white ancestry, and only 112 had unmixed Indian ancestry; while of the 1,410 grandparents for whom information was available in the series born in nearby states only 38 had unmixed white ancestry, and only 26 had unmixed Indian ancestry. In other words substantially less than 20% of those interviewed in the present survey had one or more grandparents of unmixed white or unmixed Indian ancestry. It appears therefore that most of the original white and Indian admixture took place no more recently than three or four generations ago. This of course supports the conclusion of various other studies which indicate that intermixture has been on the decline since the Civil War period, and is now practically at an end.

In conclusion then one may say:

1. That there seems to be a significant geographical or regional differential in the incidence of Indian ancestry, with the Lower

Mississippi Valley showing a greater incidence than the Middle Atlantic or Southeastern States.

2. That there also seems to be a significant geographical or regional differential in the incidence of white ancestry, with the Lower Mississippi Valley showing a lesser incidence than the Middle Atlantic or Southeastern States.

3. That this survey bears out Herskovits's conclusion that the great majority of American Negroes are of mixed ancestry; and that due to the intermarriage of mixed and unmixed Negroes during the past generation the incidence of mixture is undoubtedly significantly greater than it was at the time Herskovits made his survey.

Literature Cited

Herskovits, Melville J. 1928 *The American Negro; a study in racial crossing.* New York: Alfred A. Knopf

————. 1930 "The anthropometry of the American Negro." Columbia Univ. Contr. to Anthrop., *11*

TWO

Tougaloo College Revisited

THIS ARTICLE was written as a response to a fellow Unitarian, a white man who had joined Tougaloo's faculty after I had left. After reading his distorted discussion about the college in the *Unitarian Christian Register*, I and my successor as Tougaloo's history teacher, Chester Slocum, decided to submit a rebuttal.

In reflecting on this piece as it was being considered for publication in this volume, I thought it could be said that Tougaloo was a missionary (Congregationalist) institution, and that both its strengths and weaknesses stemmed from the fact. On the one hand Slocum and I judged that Tougaloo had from its beginnings during Reconstruction a mission of teaching that it still stood for—a fact exemplified by the dedication of nearly all the professors. On the other hand there was an unfortunate expression of this old missionary impulse in the paternalism to be found among some of the white faculty and administrators.

By the 1960s Tougaloo had shed its old parochialism and would be found in the mainstream of black education and Afro-American protest. In fact, its faculty and students would play a major role in the struggle for racial equality in Mississippi.

M R. GILBERT GREDLER'S ARTICLE, "Frank Look at Tougaloo," in the June issue of the *Register*, must have been read with interest by those seriously concerned with minority problems in the United States. It is therefore unfortunate that Mr. Gredler's account of Tougaloo contains not only much that is common knowledge, but also, we believe, serious distortions, unwarranted generalizations, and important omissions. It is our purpose, as former faculty members of Tougaloo College, to correct the false impression created by Mr. Gredler's article, and to give a fuller evaluation of the work of Tougaloo.

Mr. Gredler's observations suffer from the limited experience and perspective of their author. In this connection, it is indeed surprising that any well-informed person, particularly one interested in psychology, education and minority problems, should have found it an "eye opener" that (due to environmental limitations) Negroes do not, on the average, perform as well as whites on intelligence tests. Furthermore, though the title of the article is "Frank Look at

From *Unitarian Christian Register* 130 (November 1951): 27–30 (with Chester Slocum).

Tougaloo," Mr. Gredler states that his objective is "to give . . . an intensive look at the Negro college and the Southern Negro student." The critical reader will at once observe that what Mr. Gredler is actually doing is generalizing about all southern Negro colleges and students upon the basis of a very limited experience—one year at but one Negro college. He altogether neglects to consider such excellent Negro schools as Howard, Fisk, Talladega, Dillard and the Atlanta University system, which have higher standards, greater financial resources, and better equipped students than Tougaloo. His failure to give consideration to these schools is related to his false assumption that the best Negro students in Mississippi go to Tougaloo. Actually the best students, provided they are financially able, tend to leave the state for their college education, because of the better training available elsewhere. Much that Mr. Gredler considers typical of Negro colleges is unique to Tougaloo. Much that he thinks unique to Tougaloo and other Negro colleges is characteristic of American higher educational generally, especially in the South.

We agree with Mr. Gredler as to the deplorable state of educational facilities for Negroes in Mississippi, and the consequent lack of control over the tool subjects which is characteristic of many students at Tougaloo. However, Mr. Gredler ignores the inadequacy of the basic training of many white students attending colleges both North and South, and thereby creates the false impression that Tougaloo, and by implication Negro colleges generally, are unique in this respect. Recent surveys by the *New York Times*, for example, have shown an amazing ignorance, among American college students, of the basic facts of American history and world geography. Similarly Mr. Gredler's criticism of the lack of ability of many students to take lecture notes is valid, but again this is not unique to Tougaloo or to Negro colleges. We also question Mr. Gredler's statements on the circulation of periodicals in the college library. It is true, as he says, that picture magazines such as *Life* and *Ebony* are the most popular; but *Life* undoubtedly heads the circulation list in almost any college library. One may easily question the accuracy of Mr. Gredler's figures on the circulation of newspapers and magazines in the college library, for outside of a few of the most popular magazines which were kept at the reserve desk, no circulation records of periodicals were kept. Again, while Mr. Gredler claims that the *New York Times* and the *Christian Science Monitor* "were never looked at," it is a fact that assignments were given in these newspapers.

Furthermore Mr. Gredler's statement that "the majority of students were from homes of low socio-economic environment" is misleading. While one does encounter some cases of financial need at Tougaloo, nevertheless many of the students are from families of professional and business people who are comfortably well off by any standards. At any rate, those students who cannot afford to attend a private school like Tougaloo tend to gravitate to state colleges.

While Tougaloo is not, as Mr. Gredler implies, the only Negro college in Mississippi that offers a liberal arts program, it is generally agreed that it offers the best education, with the highest standards, available to Negroes in Mississippi. Unfortunately Mr. Gredler fails to discuss the quality of the faculty and curriculum of Tougaloo College. While only one full-time and one or two part-time faculty members had Ph.D. degrees, the faculty is hard-working and effective in its teaching. The curriculum compares favorably with that offered by small liberal arts colleges (Tougaloo has less than four hundred students) in the United States. It must be pointed out, however, that while there is a good student-teacher ratio (about one to fourteen) the wide selection of courses offered by Tougaloo frequently gives faculty members a burdensome course load (often fifteen or more class hours a week). This situation arises from the limited resources and small size of the college. Financial renumeration is low, averaging perhaps something over $2,100 for the school year, though unmarried faculty members live very well, as they can obtain full maintenance from the college for $320 for the school year.

We do not mean to imply that Tougaloo College is the scholastic equal of the average accredited northern college or of the better southern white and Negro schools. But the academic problems and weaknesses evident at Tougaloo College, though more extreme than those of many other institutions, are basically similar to those affecting American higher education today. Tougaloo is not as good as the majority of accredited American colleges; but it is better than some. True there are graduates of Tougaloo, as of other institutions, who cannot write good English. But there are a significant number of Tougaloo alumni, who, as Mr. Gredler himself points out, are now doing creditable work in outstanding northern graduate schools. By not qualifying his remarks, Mr. Gredler has overstated his case and gives a false impression. He has not told us about the eager students literally thirsting for knowledge and working diligently to acquire it; nor has he told us about the able, clear-thinking students who would do superior work in any school. He has not given us the impression, which we gathered from our years at Tougaloo, that considering the inadequacies of the educational system for Negroes in Mississippi, and in view of the slender resources of the college, Tougaloo and its faculty have been doing a remarkable job in the academic preparation of their students.

Mr. Gredler's remarks about the social aspects of Tougaloo College are similarly out of focus. For one thing Mr. Gredler makes a great deal of the lack of student motivation due to limited job and graduate school opportunities available to Negroes, which he says "shifts the focus . . . from the academic field to the field of social activities." While it is well known, as Mr. Gredler points out, that employment opportunities for Negroes are greatly inferior to those for whites, nevertheless a college degree does create for most of Tougaloo's students economic opportunities that otherwise would not be available. To describe the Tougaloo student as "knowing that he will not gain a better job through a college degree" is making a misstatement of fact. As an example, with the raising of teacher qualifications in the Mississippi school system, even in-service teachers are being compelled to complete their college education. We also feel that while it is true that some northern universities maintain restrictive racial quotas, Mr. Gredler exaggerates the difficulties attendant upon getting into graduate school. The National Scholarship Service and Fund for Negroes has a list of between two hundred and two hundred and fifty institutions which, as far as is known, do not discriminate against Negroes. There is no reason why qualified Negro students cannot get into a good graduate school, and indeed Mr. Gredler himself tells us that a high proportion of Tougaloo alumni are pursuing graduate study, a significant number at the best universities in the country. In regard to certain professional, especially medical, schools the picture is of course less satisfactory. But certainly Mr. Gredler should have pointed out that the situation with regard to the professional and graduate school opportunities for Negroes is constantly improving at the present time.

Therefore, while we are aware of the restricted vocational, graduate and professional educational opportunities for Negroes, and while we are aware of the sociological and psychological studies indicating the frequently adverse effects of caste upon the motivation of Negro students, and while we agree that some of the students at Tougaloo therefore reflect a certain amount of hopelessness and lack of interest in their work, nevertheless we feel that Mr. Gredler has largely exaggerated the effects of these factors upon the motivation of Tougaloo College students. Furthermore we are reminded of the lack of motivation characteristic of students in almost all American colleges. Mr. Gredler may complain that few Tougaloo students do extended outside reading—but how many students at any school do more than is required, or indeed do all that is required? Here, again we are dealing with a characteristic phenomenon of American college life; at worst the situation at Tougaloo, due largely (as Mr. Gredler himself points out) to discouragement caused by the unusually poor training that many students have had in basic academic skills, is rather more extreme than in most other accredited schools.

Mr. Gredler then goes on to say that this lack of academic motivation is an important cause of what he feels is an extreme emphasis at Tougaloo upon athletic and social life, and upon the social prestige to be gained by acquiring a college degree. Actually social prestige accrues to almost anyone, regardless of race, with a college education, and is a major factor in bringing large numbers of white students to college. It is true, however, that a formal education is an important symbol of status in the Negro community. Because the class structure of the Negro community is skewed, as compared with the class structure of the white community, with a much larger proportion of poor and ill-educated people, and a much smaller proportion of well-to-do, highly educated individuals, the college professor or other professional person enjoys a higher status in the Negro community than he does in the white community.

Eminent sociologists such as Gunnar Myrdal and E. Franklin Frazier have pointed out that the caste pressures of American society have led to compensatory activities in the Negro community, such as great emphasis upon conspicuous consumption and highly formalized social life among the upper classes. So it is hardly surprising that at Tougaloo, with its basically middle- and upper-class orientation, social activities should be an important element of student life. However, Mr. Gredler does not take into account the fact that in most colleges there are large groups of students to whom athletic and social events are the primary interest. Nor does he take into account the special circumstances involved in the case of Tougaloo. The small size of the college community and its physical isolation in a rural area serve to highlight the importance of all social functions. For students residing on campus, movies and other social events assume an importance that would hardly be the case in a college located in an urban center. Three formal dances during the school year 1949–1950 can hardly be called excessive.

Mr. Gredler also focuses critical attention upon what he considers to be the exaggerated social role played by the choir and dramatic club. It is true that membership in both is actively sought, and a source of considerable prestige, perhaps more than in the usual white college. Yet one must point out that ever since the Fisk Jubilee

Singers started their money-raising tours in the 1870s the Negro college choir has been recognized as an important asset to the institution, and characteristically makes the extended tours, bemoaned by Mr. Gredler, even during periods when school is in session. What Mr. Gredler fails to recognize is that the importance attached to the college choir at many Negro institutions is due to vital historical tradition, not the desire for social prestige. He also fails to recognize that in church schools like Tougaloo, the choir assumes extra importance because of its role in the Sunday service. Furthermore, contrary to the implication of Mr. Gredler's article, the dramatic club at Tougaloo is a unique institution, its preeminence as a social and cultural factor in college life being due almost solely to the personality of the present dramatic director.

It is indeed strange that Mr. Gredler should regard all these matters as due exclusively to the character of Negro life and culture, and altogether neglect the leading role played by the white president of Tougaloo in creating the emphasis upon athletic and social events. The president not only actively encouraged the introduction of fraternities and sororities, but used funds which could have been applied to urgent academic needs for the construction of an unnecessary new football field. Mr. Gredler complains that basketball games on weekdays caused the closing of the college library on certain evenings; but he does not tell us that it is the white president who was responsible, in spite of the opposition of the Negro dean, for instituting these midweek athletic activities. So it is hardly correct to say that Tougaloo's emphasis on social and athletic life arises solely, or even principally, from the supposedly unique cultural characteristics of the Negro college community.

Mr. Gredler speaks enthusiastically of the social contacts between Negroes and whites made possible by the interracial faculty of Tougaloo College. While, contrary to the impression created by Mr. Gredler, Tougaloo is not the only college in Mississippi with an interracial faculty, we agree with him as to the excellent possibilities for improving intergroup relations that are inherent in the situation. Yet we feel that the situation at Tougaloo is far from ideal. Apparently Mr. Gredler does not see what we consider to be one of the great weaknesses of Tougaloo College—the fact that, in spite of its ideological patterns of racial equality and human brotherhood, some of the white faculty members, motivated by an "old-fashioned missionary spirit," are essentially paternalistic and are condescendingly sentimental toward Negroes, rather than realistic and genuinely equalitarian.

By "missionary spirit" we mean the old fashioned "do-gooder," "convert-the-heathen" attitude, characterized by the idea of doing things *for* an inferior or degraded people, rather than working *with* individuals on a socially democratic level. One white faculty member admitted to "serving" at Tougaloo, because of a "guilt complex" concerning her attitude toward Negroes. Distinctly associated with this "missionary spirit" is what we may call the "martyr complex," well reflected in the general attitude held by many Negroes and whites connected with Tougaloo, that the white faculty members are to be praised and thanked for the "great sacrifices" they are making for the "cause," rather than to be evaluated and accepted as individual personalities like everyone else.

This "missionary spirit," strongly evident in much of Tougaloo's publicity literature, is historically related to the fact that Tougaloo is a church school. Through the American Missionary Association it is connected with the Congregational church. The typical Tougaloo College president has been a white Congregational minister. All this is not in itself unfortunate. Religious idealism generally, and the Congregational church and the American Missionary Association particularly, have made notable contributions to Negro advancement and Negro education. Nor has Tougaloo been narrowly sectarian: members of all religious faiths have been represented in its faculty and student body. The man now president is a former Presbyterian minister. Yet we feel that the time has passed when old-fashioned missionary techniques, when patronizing, paternalistic and sentimental attitudes are satisfactory at Tougaloo. We do not mean to generalize; at its best the religious tradition has produced some remarkable individuals. Perhaps the most forward-looking, socially aware, and educationally progressive person on the administrative staff during our years at Tougaloo was a specialist in religious education, deeply imbued with religious idealism; and the most universally admired, loved and respected faculty member at Tougaloo today represents the finest flower of this religious and missionary spirit. But we feel these individuals to be exceptional.

Specific examples of what we mean by this white missionary attitude in its more unfavorable aspects are numerous. There is the white woman faculty member who told a student who did not rise when she entered the room in which he was working that "a polite white boy" would have stood up when she came in. Another white person indicated to a Negro faculty member that she felt he was such an interesting and able person that it was too bad he was colored. Then there was the individual who at times expressed disgust and pity over the treatment of Negroes in Mississippi, yet strongly opposed the establishment of a campus chapter of the National Association for the Advancement of Colored People. This same person was annoyed when he felt that Negro faculty members tended to avoid sitting with white faculty members in the college dining hall, yet was terribly upset and irate when a Negro woman from another state happened to visit a while male faculty member for a few days. Some of the white faculty were in fact mildly and unconsciously prejudiced toward Negroes, tended to feel socially distinct from Negroes and to refer condescendingly to Negroes as "your people," or "his people," or "their people." Some white members of the college staff became obsessed with the idea that the Negroes as a group would not associate socially with them, were prejudiced against whites, and desired their removal from the faculty.

Naturally, attitudes such as these can scarcely undo the hostilities and resentments engendered in Negroes by the American caste system. And so there is another side to the coin. Students were agreed that a few of their teachers were prejudiced. We have been informed by certain Negro faculty members that some of the Negro faculty did not care for the white faculty, would rather they were not at Tougaloo, and did not care to associate with them. And there was the student who frankly told one of us that she didn't like white people, and would rather not associate with them at all. Revealing indeed was the incident reported to one of us by a Negro member of the college staff, who said that when a new president was being appointed in 1947 some of the colored faculty members expressed the point of view that Tougaloo College was not yet ready for a Negro president. Such an attitude of course reflects an unsound social relationship between Negroes and whites at Tougaloo College, and the persistence of traditions of missionary paternalism.

So while race relations at Tougaloo are much better than in the general segregated pattern of southern life, conditions are not really ideal. Many Negroes and whites on the faculty were of course unprejudiced, and enjoyed splendid social relationships with each other and with their students. Nor are we generalizing about other Negro colleges with an interracial faculty, on the basis of our experience at Tougaloo. Friends who have been at such schools tell us that relationships between whites and Negroes there are fully satisfactory, and unmarked by the tensions and stresses felt at Tougaloo. Undoubtedly the whole situation is related to the general question of intrafaculty tensions at Tougaloo. The fact that there was a turnover of almost one-third of the faculty in 1949, and almost one-half in 1950, suggests a rather fundamental maladjustment.

Another aspect of social life at Tougaloo is the characteristic paternalism pervading all phases of college life. It is related in part to the missionary spirit we have discussed above, but it is far more inclusive. As is to be expected, no one is more aware of this than the students. All student activities, including the college newspapers, the fraternities and sororities and other clubs, and class activities and functions are closely supervised by faculty members. College women going to town, and all coeducational social functions are carefully and ostentatiously chaperoned. Students are permitted to do very little of consequence entirely on their own. Registration procedures are a case in point. Instead of supplying each student with a copy of the college catalogue so that he can at his leisure and using his own initiative draw up a program of studies to be approved by his faculty advisor, the college merely makes available a few catalogues at registration time, and allows almost the entire responsibility of arranging the students' schedules to fall upon the teachers. A number of students simply allow teachers to make their decisions for them. In this situation, as in others, student initiative and self-reliance are discouraged.

We are glad to say however that there was no administrative interference with classroom activities. In general, however, we feel that behind the facade of republican institutions such as the College Council and the monthly faculty meeting, there is a genuine conflict between two of Tougaloo's fundamental ideologies—between the democratic ideal of training for self-government and participation in American society, and the more authoritarian ideal of the "Tougaloo Family"—and, that in this conflict, it is the paternalistic ideal of the "Tougaloo Family" which emerges as the core of the "Tougaloo Way of Life." Similar conditions of course are all too common in many of our institutions of higher education; we do not mean to imply that they are unique to Tougaloo.

In conclusion then we feel that Mr. Gredler was mistaken in much of what he said, and left much of significance unsaid. If accepted, Mr. Gredler's generalizations would create a new stereotype of American Negro life. While there is much to be criticized at Tougaloo we feel that the school has great possibilities. But difficulties lie ahead. Tougaloo can succeed only if it fulfills vital functions not supplied by most other institutions. We feel—and here we agree with Mr. Gredler—that the college has two functions to fulfill: to serve as a center of liberal arts education for Mississippi Negroes, and as an oasis of interracial understanding and good will. To do the first it cannot rest on its laurels or divert money to athletics in the false and smug assurance that as the best Negro College in the state

all the best students attend it. Indeed, on the contrary, fresh appro-
priations are rapidly strengthening the state colleges for Negroes in
Mississippi, and these may soon threaten the preeminence Tougaloo has enjoyed. To maintain its status Tougaloo must strengthen its
faculty and course offerings, constantly raise its academic standards, and make a real effort to insure effective and satisfactory race
relations on its own campus, which shall serve as a model for good
human relations throughout the state. Tougaloo is still at the cross-
roads. If it does these things, its future will be even more fruitful
than its past.

THREE

Race Relations at Negro Colleges

THIS ESSAY is based upon experiences and observations growing out of my teaching and research at black colleges. My optimistic assessment at the time was that, as the author and Fisk University librarian Arna Bontemps put it, the social cleavages along racial lines that tended to be the norm among faculty at black colleges were due to the fact that these institutions attracted different kinds of people from the two racial groups.

The schools discussed, while not named, are in the order of their appearance in the article as follows: Tougaloo College, Hampton Institute, Fisk University, Atlanta University, and Morgan State College. The college described in the *Social Forces* article is undoubtedly Talladega College.

A FEW YEARS ago a colleague of mine spoke wistfully of how, just before she began her work at a leading Negro university in the upper South her sophisticated New York friends had waxed enthusiastic over the model of interracial relations she was undoubtedly about to witness. For though some would deny that the situation at this university is less than ideal, it had taken her but a few months to grasp that, to a striking extent, social groupings there followed racial lines.

There has been little serious discussion of race relations at Negro colleges with mixed faculties. Until recently only certain church related schools employed white teachers, and it was assumed that Christian brotherhood was the rule at such institutions. Even when secular liberals began teaching at Negro colleges in significant numbers, comparable ideological considerations discouraged detached analysis of social relationships on mixed faculties.

Two studies, however, deserve mention. Recently a graduate student at Stetson University, on the basis of a survey conducted by mailing questionnaires, concluded that "all but five percent of the white teachers in the study claimed 'good rapport' with their Negro colleagues."[1] It should be noted, however, that only about a third of the people who received questionnaires responded,[2] and it is likely that a number of those who did respond glossed over certain matters and rather gilded the lily.

From *The Crisis* 65 (November 1958): 535–43.

Actually, for this sort of investigation, careful case-studies are necessary. A significant step in this direction was an article by "a former faculty wife" that appeared in *Social Forces* about ten years ago. Describing the situation among the married couples on the campus of a small liberal arts college during the war, she concluded that significant cultural differences between Negroes and whites caused the personal "friction," that is present at any college, to roughly "follow racial lines" at that particular school. The white couples, she reported, tended to be the "Quaker-work-camp variety of liberal," opposed to fraternities, "pacifists, co-operators, folk-dancing enthusiasts, committed to internationalism and interracialism . . . advocates of the simple life, and . . . generally 'religious.'" The Negro couples on the other hand were usually deeply involved in fraternity life, tended more to conspicuous consumption, were Christians but relatively indifferent to religious matters, were not pacifists, were not particularly interested in social issues other than the race problem, and preferred a formal social life. Thus she concluded that in all matters, except racial attitudes, the Negro teachers had more in common with typical middle-class whites against whose values the white teachers were actually in "rebellion." Since there was a lack of shared values, "the result is that when people really want to enjoy themselves, they do it in a segregated social life, in this haven of interracial concord."[3]

The following pages are in the nature of a prolegomenon to the scientific analysis of race relations at Negro colleges. They are based upon a total of eight years teaching experience at three Negro colleges, visits to several more, and such relevant information as colleagues and other informants were generous enough to share with me. Only colleges about which I feel I have enough material to draw a valid picture are discussed. However, the reader should bear in mind that the conclusions reached in the following pages are tentative in nature, since the discussion is based chiefly upon personal experiences at certain colleges at certain times. Individuals of a different temperament, or of a different cultural background than the author's, might very possibly have received different impressions; and there is good reason to believe that the situation at some schools has altered radically within the space of a few years.

Social Isolation

At a leading small liberal arts college in the lower Mississippi Valley where I taught from 1945 to 1949, I was, according to one of my Negro colleagues, perhaps the best "integrated" white member

of the faculty. This was so especially my first year, when, despite the
social fragmentation characteristic of faculty life on the campus, and
the social isolation experienced by many faculty members of both
races, I found myself the only white member of a clique of four
younger teachers who exercised such social leadership as existed
there. The "cabal," as the dean jocularly labeled us, despite its
interracial character, patronized restaurants and theaters in the
nearest city (four miles from the rural campus). On campus the
"cabal" gave dances and parties that were the envy of the unin-
vited, and with its "satellites" played bridge at least once—and
often twice—daily (so that I eventually became an indifferent bridge
player).

This clique soon fell apart, and the realities of faculty life at this
school emerged in clear focus. It appeared that in spite of its ideological patterns of racial equality and human brotherhood some of
the white faculty, motivated by a "missionary spirit," were essentially paternalistic and condescendingly sentimental toward Negroes, rather than genuinely equalitarian. By "missionary spirit" I
mean the old-fashioned "do-gooder" attitude, characterized by the
idea of doing things *for* a degraded people rather than working with
individuals on a democratic level. One white teacher admitted to
"serving" at the college because of a "guilt complex" concerning her
attitude toward Negroes. Distinctly associated with this "missionary spirit" was a sort of "martyr complex," well reflected in the
attitude widely held by many Negroes and whites connected with
the school, that the white faculty were to be praised and thanked for
the "great sacrifices" they were making for the "cause," rather than
to be evaluated and accepted as individual personalities.

This "missionary spirit," strongly evident in much of the school's
publicity literature, was historically rerelated to its Congregational
church connection. This is not in itself unfortunate. Religious idealism generally has made notable contributions in the field of Negro
education. And at its best the religious tradition has produced some
remarkable individuals. The most universally admired, loved and
respected faculty member during my years at this institution was a
man who represented the finest flower of this religious and missionary spirit (though even he was not "social"). But such individuals are exceptional.

More characteristic were the paternalistic white presidents and
the condescending white faculty. The wife of one of them told a
Negro faculty member that he was such a fine person that it was too
bad he was colored. The wife of another white administrator informed a new white faculty member that they were on "pins and

needles" because the head of the English department was a Negro who, that year, had only white women working under him. One of the presidents at times expressed pity over the treatment of Negroes in Mississippi, yet strongly opposed the establishment of a campus chapter of the NAACP. This same person was annoyed when he felt that discrimination on the part of Negro faculty members was what led to largely segregated eating patterns among the faculty in the college dining hall, yet was upset when a Negro woman from another state visited a white male faculty member for a few days. Then there was the white woman who told a student who did not rise when she entered the room in which he was working that "a polite white boy" would have stood up when she came in. Some of the faculty were in fact mildly and unconsciously prejudiced toward Negroes, tended to feel socially distinct from them, and always referred condescendingly to Negroes as "your people" or "their people." Others became obsessed with the idea that the Negroes generally would not associate with them, were in fact prejudiced against whites and desired their removal from the faculty.

Cultural Differences

Naturally such attitudes could scarcely undo the hostilities and resentments engendered in Negroes by the American race system. And so there was another side to the picture. Certain Negro colleagues have informed me that some of the Negro faculty actually did not care for the white teachers, and would have preferred their not being at the college. On one occasion all the children of the Negro faculty were invited to a party, but the only two white children on campus were not, even though they were neighbors who played together daily. Moreover, many of the Negro teachers were distinctly ambivalent in their attitude toward whites.

Revealing indeed was the incident reported to me by a Negro member of the college staff who said that when a new president was being selected in 1947, some of the colored teachers expressed the view that the college was not yet ready for a Negro president. Such an attitude of course reflected an unsound relationship between Negroes and whites at this particular school and persistence of the traditions of missionary paternalism.

Other differences in cultural background and personality types also undoubtedly played their role in setting the tone of interracial relationships at the institution we have been describing. Quite unique for this school was the case of the liberal white pacifist who was looked down on by the Negro faculty because he lacked their

middle-class tastes, paid scant attention to dress and drove a battered small imported car (before such cars were as fashionable as
they are now). The majority of the faculty and administrators professed a deep concern with the Christian way of living, but many of
the Negro faculty had a hedonistic orientation toward life quite out
of keeping with the attitude of the more straitlaced "missionaries."
Moreover, Negroes had a fraternal life not shared by any of the
whites. That many faculty members of both races were not completely emancipated on the matter of interracial relations became
evident in the objections widely voiced when a colored faculty
member became engaged to one of the white teachers.

It should of course be emphasized that some Negroes and whites
on the faculty did enjoy wholesome social relationships with each
other. Nevertheless, to the extent that there were social cliques,
they tended, to a remarkable extent, to follow racial lines.

Interracial Hostility

Another school where missionary traditions seem to have fos-
tered interracial hostility on the faculty is a noted industrial school
founded by a Union general shortly after the Civil War in the upper
South. Visiting the school for a week of research in 1952, I found it
evident, just from observing the seating arrangements in the faculty
dining room, that race and social clique were highly correlated.
According to the Chinese teachers—who by virtue of their acceptance by both of the other races, were unusually good informants—
the social relations between whites and Negroes were "rotten."
Many of the whites associated with white townspeople, and on
crucial occasions adopted the latter's point of view. The one young,
liberal white teacher I met seemed to be snubbed by some of his
Negro colleagues.

As a matter of fact an examination of the school's history and the
attitudes of its founder and early presidents would lead one to suspect that unfortunate traditions of missionary paternalism would
linger long there. As late as the 1930s, as a person who taught there
at that time has told me, most of the Negro teachers were in the
trade school: two-thirds of the college department was staffed by
whites, who were paid more than the Negro teachers. There were
no Negroes in policy making positions; those who held administrative posts were generally regarded as acquiescing in white decisions. The school even hired local white high school graduates as
secretaries instead of employing its own graduates. White admin-

istrators in policy making positions, and retired white teachers who still lived on the campus, set the dominant tone in race relations. They felt constrained to prohibit anything that might be offensive to the local white community, and frequently in their personal attitudes were condescending rather than equalitarian. Negroes in fact regarded some of them—including a leading administrator—as prejudiced. In earlier years there had even been incidents of white faculty members refusing to sit next to Negroes in the faculty dining hall. Many of the older white faculty associated socially with local whites, and Negroes felt that they were influenced by the views of their southern friends. This group of administrators and older white faculty members avoided discussion of the race problem; a favorite phrase was "We have no problem." And they opposed agitation against disfranchisement and segregation, they said, because Negroes were not ready for integration. As the school's founder had held, when Negroes were ready, they would get their rights without difficulty. Newer white faculty members tended to be more liberal; a few socialized with Negroes. But most of the "newer whites" found it wise to either conform to the pattern set by the dominant white element, or to resign after a year or so.[4]

Far more cosmopolitan than either of the schools thus far discussed was the distinguished university of the upper South where I worked from 1953 to 1956. Here the missionary spirit had practically disappeared, and the motivations prompting the white faculty to teach there were highly varied. There were, of course, a few of the old fashioned missionary group, like the mediocrity who was acutely conscious of the value of her "contribution" to Negro education. Many years before she had begun teaching at a Negro college as preparation for missionary work in Asia. After a year at the Negro college, however, she decided that there was plenty of missionary work to be done right here, and consequently she had remained at Negro colleges ever since. There were also a few of the latter-day missionary type, like the young faculty wife who told me that because whites had made Negroes suffer for so long, white faculty members should willingly accept unfair actions from their colleagues as long as they are Negroes. A small group of what appeared to be Communists or fellow travelers were active in protest movements against discrimination; but, despite considerable student support, they were not liked by most of their colleagues, white or Negro. There were also a handful of secular liberals; a number of older mediocrities, who—like their Negro counterparts—had no place else they could go; and a sizeable group who were there simply because the school was a highly-rated institution. Most of the Negroes were typically middle class, interested in fraternities, clubs, and card games. Several were persons of considerable distinction nationally.

Racial Lines

Like the two schools described above, though for different reasons, social clique lines at this university tended to follow racial lines, and that tendency has increased in the past few years as more white faculty members have bought homes in town rather than living on campus. It was common for Negro faculty members to accept dinner invitations to the homes of the white faculty, without returning the invitation. The faculty club was split between those who wanted card games, formal dinners and dances, and those who wanted more informal entertainment or some sort of cultural activity; and this division was in considerable part correlated with racial lines. Official functions, of course, were interracial—though one colleague informed me that during the preceding administration it had always been the white women who poured tea. At one faculty party, before I came to the university, it was reported that after the whites had departed, around 10:00 P.M., the party really began. Recently, at another party held at the home of a white faculty member, the Negroes left early and a couple of whites regaled the remaining guests with shocking remarks to the effect that Negro youth were unable to understand great literature, or sing the musical classics. Personally I shall never forget one night when I visited one of my closest friends on the campus, a cultured and intellectual Negro faculty member. He informed me that a faculty wife had called and invited him to a gathering at her home in honor of some distinguished visitors. When told that I would be visiting him, she naturally invited me also. It was distinctly a gathering of campus elite, and many of the more distinguished faculty celebrities were present. Needless to say it was readily apparent that I was the only white person present. So widely practiced was this segregated social life that one white professor talked proudly of how he and his wife were the first white persons to be invited to a certain Negro colleague's home, and of how they were the first white people asked to join a Negro social-musical club. Illustrative of the parochial attitudes engendered in Negroes by the American race system were the remarks of one sophisticated administrator, a widely traveled, eminent and puissant scholar, who once explained to me that the continued existence of the Negro college was justified because

Negroes who attended white colleges failed to develop a realistic view of the world and consequently—he alleged—displayed a remarkable tendency toward suicide.

There seemed to have been a variety of reasons for the considerable correlation of social and racial lines at this university—though as elsewhere there were some striking exceptions to this generalization. Perhaps to some extent the situation was a survival from earlier missionary traditions; the preceding president, for example, who had done much to restore the school's tarnished intellectual reputation, was widely regarded as rather anti-Negro (though it was also said that townspeople thought him too radical). More significant perhaps is that a substantial group among the Negro faculty were upper-class Negroes with the values and attitudes of an upper-class toward the middle class whereas the white faculty was definitely middle-class whites. As a group of distinguished Negro professors told a *Time* reporter at a luncheon I was privileged to attend at the president's house, they regarded themselves as socially on a level with upper-class whites. To some extent the situation was due, undoubtedly, to the fact that the local Negro community had its own club and fraternal structure in which college people played a leading role but in which whites had no part. Finally, there was undoubtedly a cleavage of interest between most of the Negroes and the group of intellectual and liberal whites. As E. Franklin Frazier has pointed out, the interests and values of middle-class Negro professors are actually closer to those of middle-class prejudiced whites than to those of the liberal intellectuals on the campus.[5] A number of white faculty members were disillusioned by the lack of true intellectual interest at the university, noted though it was for its scholarly and artistic tradition. That this dissimilarity of interests rather than race feeling was at the bottom of much of the social distinctions between the races at this school was forcibly brought home to me on a visit to nearby state university. At the conclusion of the panel discussion in which I had participated, a faculty wife discreetly inquired of me if I played bridge. My negative reply naturally led her to pursue the subject no further, for I was simply not available for card-playing society.

Variety of Factors

Illustrative of the large variety of factors that can enter into social relationships at Negro colleges with mixed faculties is a noted university and college center in the southeast, which I have visited several times in the past half dozen years. While most of the white professors there tend to be very peripheral socially, a few of them have moved freely in Negro upper-class circles. In part this may be due to the rather congenial manner of certain of the white teachers; in part it may well be due to the emancipated attitude of many among the city's Negro upper class—widely enough travelled both in the United States and abroad to have absorbed cosmopolitan attitudes, and secure enough in their wealth and social position to accept whites as individuals more readily than upper-class Negroes in other southern cities. Other factors involved may include the fact that the city enjoys unusually good race relations for the Deep South, and the social patterns set by certain leading Negro administrators in the colleges themselves.

Personally I found at this university and its affiliated colleges the most complete acceptance as an individual that I have enjoyed at any Negro school. In addition to the factors discussed above, this seemed to have been due to the excellent introductions I came with, to the congeniality of intellectual interest I had with several of the people I met, to the sophisticated character of many of the faculty (educated at the best northern and western universities), and perhaps most of all to the fact that I stayed at the graduate dormitory where many other single young faculty lived and took their meals. This situation encouraged a sort of social relationship that was not possible at other schools where the faculty lived in more scattered fashion and where there were few single young men and women teachers.[6]

State Schools

A relatively new phenomenon are Negro state schools with white faculty members. In contrast to most of the private schools I have observed, not only is a long tradition of mixed teachers lacking, but the white professors are in a tiny minority.

Because the state college where I have taught since the fall of 1957 is a much larger institution than any of the others discussed, and because unlike the other schools at which I have taught the faculty do not live on the campus, it is difficult to generalize about race relations there. The school is located in a border state, and the administrative policy is one of integration—the college has both white faculty and students. The handful of white faculty all appear to have come to the institution simply for a job. The Negro faculty range from persons who have white spouses and those who seek participation in interracial civic organizations to those who are reputed to feel that the college should not employ white teachers.

An article on integration a few years ago by one professor indicated his essential ambivalence toward integration by citing certain advantages to be derived from segregated schools, though he concluded that the advantages of integration certainly outweigh those of a segregated system. Certain department chairmen feel that they have to be careful about employing too great a proportion of white teachers, lest they incur criticism from some of their Negro colleagues.

As far as I can ascertain social relationships off the campus between white and Negro colleagues are generally quite limited, though it should be pointed out that outside of several cliques the college is not characterized by an active social life among faculty members. During my first year there I was invited to the homes of three Negro professors for purely social purposes; though as at the noted university in the upper South described above I was on excellent terms professionally with members of the Negro faculty who did not invite me to their homes socially. A white professor at the state college who entertains considerably receives significantly less invitations from Negroes than he extends. One white professor was elected to an important committee; however, it has been said (though I am not able to say how widely this view is shared) that his election was due to his equable temperament and to the fact that he was not involved in the personal frictions and politics existing among the Negroes themselves. On the other hand there is at least one white teacher who is on very friendly terms with a couple of the colored teachers.

That the white teachers at this state college function to a considerable extent as a minority group is evident from the view of some Negro colleagues who warned me that if a white teacher missed a faculty meeting he was conspicuous by his absence (even though certain of the Negro teachers, who are as fair as the white teachers in complexion, would not be noticed if absent). As to the factors responsible for what would appear to be the significant correlation between social clique and race at this state college, I judge that cultural and personality factors comparable to those described in connection with the upper South university are responsible.

Thus it would appear that at most of the schools with which I have had extended contact there is a significant correlation between race and social grouping, though the number of interracial friendships should not be minimized. Nor do I mean to suggest that because the situation is not ideal that mixed faculties have been a failure. On the contrary, given the sort of society in which we live, it would be surprising to have perfection; and the interracial faculties at Negro colleges have certainly made an important contribution in furthering intergroup understanding. At some it may be chiefly the Quaker type of social idealism that sets off the white from the Negro faculty; at others it may be primarily a gap in intellectual interests. Significantly, in all the colleges where I have taught, to the extent that there are people who accept individuals without regard to race and who share mutual values and interests, the correlation between race and social clique disappears.

Notes

*Thanks are due to the *Unitarian Register* for permission to use in revised form August Meier and Chester Slocum's "Tougaloo College Revisited," 130 (November 1951): 29–30.
1. Paul Decker, "A Study of 'White' Teachers in Selected 'Negro' Colleges," *Journal of Negro Education* 24 (1955): 503.
2. Ibid., 501.
3. A Former Faculty Wife, "A Note on Intergroup Conditioning and Conflict Among an Interracial Faculty at a Negro College," *Social Forces* 27 (October 1948): 430–33.
4. For description of missionary attitudes at Negro schools during the 1920s see Langston Hughes's *The Big Sea*, (1940) and Worth Tuttle Hadden's fictionalized account of Straight University, New Orleans, Louisiana, *The Other Room* (1947).
5. Frazier, *Black Bourgeoisie* (Chicago, 1957), passim.
6. On the other hand it should be pointed out that comparable living arrangements at this school were not able to overcome the unfortunate attitudes engendered there for other reasons.

FOUR

Black Sociologists in White America

THIS REVIEW-ESSAY, though not written until 1977, reflects both my long acquaintance, beginning in my undergraduate days, with the sociological literature on American blacks and my personal observations of and experiences I had while working with Charles S. Johnson at Fisk University in the mid-1950s.

Black Sociologists: Historical and Contemporary Perspectives. Edited by James E. Blackwell and Morris Janowitz. Chicago: University of Chicago Press, 1974.

Morris Janowitz in his introduction to this volume quite correctly divides "the history of black sociologists" into three periods, although he fails to grasp their full import. The first, from the end of the nineteenth century through the 1930s, was "a period of founding," dominated by three giants, W. E. B. Du Bois, Charles S. Johnson, and E. Franklin Frazier. Then came a period of about two decades when, building on an institutional base in southern black colleges, the numbers of Negro sociologists grew "despite meager resources and complete segregation as far as employment opportunities were concerned." Finally, the years since 1965 have been a period when black sociologists became highly visible as they sought "to alter the institutional setting in which they work and teach." It was in this third period, amidst the polarization and conflict in the American Sociological Association occasioned by the rise of the Caucus of Black Sociologists, that Janowitz arranged for the University of Chicago to sponsor a conference on the contributions, status, and problems of black sociologists. The fruits of this conference, held in May 1972, have been published in this provocative although disappointing volume.

Black Sociologists is a diverse and loosely structured book, but underlying nearly all of the essays is a unifying theme: the tensions involved in being a black sociologist in white America. As coeditor James Blackwell observes, black sociologists have been characterized by a dualism rooted in their identity as both "sociologist-scholars" and "members of a racial or ethnic category" that "engenders status ambiguities, role conflicts, isolation, and contention." Three interrelated subthemes emerge from the discussion. First,

From *Social Forces* 56 (September 1977): 259–70.

there is the inherent tension felt by those who simultaneously perceive their work as both scholarship and an instrument of racial protest or social reform. As Richard Robbins expresses it in his essay on Charles S. Johnson: "Given the depth and pervasiveness of racism in the United States, if a man or woman is an historian and black, a sociologist and black, then he or she is compelled to work out a distinctive role-balance between scholarship and advocacy, between creativity and commitment." Second, there is a curious trajectory in the history of black sociologists: Why did the output decline so markedly after 1945, following the golden age which produced a number of distinguished and seminal monographs? Finally, within the academic discipline historically most hospitable toward black scholars, there has been nevertheless a vexing problem of overcoming discrimination by—and securing adequate recognition in—the graduate schools and professional societies.

At the outset we must note two striking paradoxes that are neither recognized by the editors nor referred to by the several contributors. First of all, there is the striking fact that, beginning in the milieu of a highly racist social science in the 1890s, sociology over the next half century produced the most distinguished group of black scholars in any academic discipline at the time. Second, around the middle of the century, the sociological profession was electing blacks to high office in both the national and regional associations— including the presidencies of the American Sociological Association, and the eastern and southern societies—in a way that had no parallel in any of the other learned societies; yet throughout, as this volume so eloquently attests, there have been ambiguities and contradictions that in the end relegated race relations and black sociologists to a minor place in the discipline, and inhibited the maintenance of a major school of sociological research. In my judgment, the volume is seriously marred just because it does not deal systematically and in a spirit of scientific inquiry with these paradoxes. Instead it tends (although with certain significant exceptions) to stress advocacy above scholarship, and to celebrate rather than analyze the work of the major Negro sociologists. There is no recognition, for example, of the fact that the greatness of the major monographs produced by Du Bois, Frazier, and St. Clair Drake was in large part actually rooted in the creative tension between their scholarship and their social commitment. (It is unfortunate that the volume nowhere includes a good discussion of Drake, apparently because he holds his degree in anthropology.) And the book is also seriously marred because—despite all the attention it lavishes on Charles S. Johnson, the most political and the most powerful of the black sociologists, and despite some magnificently candid data on his role supplied by Butler Jones—it simply does not come to grips with the crucial role Johnson played.

The earliest black sociologists did their work at a time of intense racism in the social and biological sciences. Yet serious scholarly study of the black community and the early important research of the Negro sociologists were rooted in another strand of the relatively undifferentiated sociology of the time—the reformist impulse, with its strong ties to the Progressive movement and to social work, that perceived sociological inquiry as the basis for solving society's ills. It was widely believed that careful empirical research, done in an objective spirit, would both educate the literate public and decision makers, and suggest appropriate courses of social action. In his sociological scholarship, Du Bois was, as Elliott Rudwick points out, passionately devoted to this point of view. So also were his early twentieth-century successors: George Edmund Haynes, Richard R. Wright, and Kelly Miller. And after them came Bertram W. Doyle, Charles S. Johnson, and E. Franklin Frazier, who imbibed this point of view from their mentor, Robert E. Park (who was, of course, a major influence in stimulating and shaping the direction of research on race relations and the black community in the three decades after he came to Chicago in 1914). As Charles U. Smith and Lewis Killian express it in their essay: "The dictum advanced by Du Bois and Park, that good social science research constituted a form of protest, protected [the early black sociologists] from the intrinsic tension between these two worlds."

There were important, even profound, differences in the ways in which various scholars balanced the tension between the claims of scholar and reformer. Du Bois ultimately became disillusioned and by 1910 left the world of scholarship for the world of protest. His *The Philadelphia Negro* (commissioned by social work reformers and modeled on Booth's *Life and Labour of the People in London*); the work of George Edmund Haynes, a founder of the National Urban League; and Johnson's *The Negro in Chicago* (1922), commissioned as part of an attempt to solve the problems brought to public attention by the Chicago race riot of 1919, were all explicitly tied to the social reform tradition of American sociology. Not only was Haynes an Urban League executive, but Johnson served for several years as the organization's research director, and his successor, Ira DeA. Reid, did much of his major work while holding this post. Frazier, on the other hand, had a more radical bent—he had been a Socialist during his undergraduate days at Howard University—and was always more outspoken. He became known not only for his fine empirical work, but also for his acerbic and polemical critiques of both white Americans and the black bourgeoisie.[1] But even Johnson, who was a great admirer of Booker T. Washington and essentially a racial moderate operating for many years in a southern context, could on occasion be quite outspoken in his denunciation of American racism. Yet different as these men were, they were similar in being attracted to sociological scholarship as a tool of social reform. In a sense, it can be said that this first school of black sociological scholarship came to a climax in Gunnar Myrdal's *An American Dilemma* (1944), a synthesis blending dispassionate scientific inquiry with explicit moral judgments, a work in which the line between empirical analysis and policy orientation was never clearly drawn. Even a superficial reading of Myrdal's justly celebrated book reveals the debt it owes to the work of black scholars like Du Bois, Johnson, Frazier, and Reid, and the research memoranda that several of them contributed directly to the project.

In the increased output by black sociologists during the past decade, the tension between scholarship and advocacy has usually been resolved quite differently. The tilt has been more toward advocacy and protest than toward dispassionate scholarship and analysis. (Among the important exceptions is William J. Wilson's *Power, Racism and Privilege*, 1973.) Moreover, much of the recent writing has tended toward a nationalist or separatist perspective, in contrast to the assimilationist assumptions that guided the labors of earlier scholars. (One should of course be careful not to oversimplify here; separatist themes were to be seen in some of the early work also, most notably in that of Du Bois.) Charles U. Smith and Killian in their illuminating essay describe the shift and its roots in the changing nature of black protest during the 1960s. Despite a degree of confusion on certain points (as in a tendency to equate militance with nationalism in the history of black ideologies, and in the curious assertion that the civil rights movement did not begin until the mid-1950s), this is an important and suggestive piece. The social changes which they describe had important consequences for the work of black sociologists who, like the radical white sociologists, have tended to become more ideological and political, and less analytical and empirical. The impact of this development can be seen, for example, in G. Franklin Edwards's overly defensive analysis of Frazier's work in this book. Frazier's contributions need no defense, even though they have been viewed with disdain by many of the latest generations of black sociologists.

Yet the fact is that when the transition explicated by Smith and Killian took place, in the late 1960s, sociology had for some time lacked a strong tradition of scholarship in the area of the black experience, written by either whites or blacks. The impressive series of community studies, inaugurated by Du Bois, and including works like *Shadow of the Plantation, Negro Youth at the Crossways,* and *Deep South,* virtually ended with the publication of Drake and Cayton's magnificent opus, *Black Metropolis,* in 1945. Frazier continued to be active, pulling together and expanding on earlier research and ideas in such titles as *The Negro in the United States* and *Black Bourgeoisie;* Hylan Lewis in *Blackways of Kent* and G. Franklin Edwards in *The Negro Professional Class* produced significant volumes that, like the studies of the 1930s and early 1940s, cried out for replication in other communities; and in 1948 appeared Oliver Cromwell Cox's theoretical analysis and radical critique, *Caste, Class, and Race.*[2] Yet, in the aftermath of Myrdal's synthesis and Park's retirement from Chicago, there was a curious hiatus in the scholarly productivity of black sociologists. This development is of central importance to any systematic treatment of the history of Negro sociologists, but the book under review fails to mention it, much less account for it. Given the earlier giants, descriptions of the discrimination faced by black scholars do not by themselves fully explain what happened. The following is an attempt to explore this subject, although my explanation (drawn largely from personal observations—particularly as a research assistant to Charles S. Johnson) must be regarded as tentative.

One can suggest various explanations for the decline in productivity of black sociologists during the years following World War II. Older figures like Johnson and Reid moved into administrative positions, and always there was the lure of consulting and applied research. More important is a phenomenon mentioned in passing in several places in *Black Sociologists*—the change in the nature of sociology as a discipline in the 1930s and 1940s. The movement away from social reformism to ethical neutrality and quantification, the decline of the influence of Park and the University of Chicago, and the emergence of Harvard, Columbia, and Berkeley as dominant centers—all meant that interest focused on matters other than race relations and the black experience. Except for the white-only University of North Carolina, where the concern with race relations on the part of Howard Odum and his associates still survived, race and the black experience became a sociological backwater as far as the white graduate schools were concerned. Indeed few scholars, black or white, were doing distinguished work in the field. Race relations did not lend itself readily to quantification, and the holistic community studies, invaluable though they were, were not con-

tinued. The major departments and the famous teachers who produced most of the distinguished students had other interests. In
short, although the contributors to *Black Sociologists* fail to take note
of the fact, the passing of Park and W. Lloyd Warner and the kind of
training and encouragement they supplied must be accounted a
major factor in the decline of both the study of blacks as a field and
the productivity of black sociologists.[3]

In addition, as this volume so well documents, blacks seeking
careers in sociology suffered from white racism and discrimination.
Despite the relative liberalism of the profession, white universities
would not employ even the finest black sociological scholars. (Ira
Reid's going to Haverford was an exception, and that of course was
an undergraduate institution.) While some white professors were
genuinely sympathetic to the aspirations of their black graduate
students, and while the majority of course subscribed to a racially
egalitarian psychology, the mainstream of white sociologists was
indifferent to racial issues. Among those who displayed an interest,
blacks often detected a degree of paternalistic condescension. Black
sociologists were relegated to black institutions, a milieu that usually did not encourage scholarly publication. Small southern institutions, struggling for funds, dedicated to teaching, offered little
opportunity for research. Even where white universities with good
libraries were close by, they were usually closed to blacks. (This was
the case at Vanderbilt University, for example, as late as the early
1950s.) In addition, as Butler Jones so effectively points out in his
essay on "The Tradition of Sociology Teaching in Black Colleges,"
paternalistic white presidents of black colleges, who were missionaries rather than scholars, were not interested in scholarship. Black
presidents, as Jones indicates, prized the prestige Negro Ph.D.s
brought to their institutions (and the contribution this made to ac-
creditation with the Southern Association of Colleges and Secondary Schools), but were often jealous of the professional standing of
those with doctorates, and resentful of the independent spirit they
often exhibited. Yet some great teachers emerged, like Charles G.
Gomillion at Tuskegee and Walter R. Chivers at Morehouse. (Morehouse has been widely known as the mother of black college presidents; it would even more appropriately be described as the mother
of black sociologists.) Two other factors accentuated the non-re-
search orientation of black colleges. As Jones points out, the scarcity
of job opportunities for blacks and the high prestige accorded to
professors meant that economic and social pressures, more than
intellectual interests, tended to be the motivation behind obtaining
a doctoral degree. And as Frazier so bitterly pointed out in his *Black*

Bourgeoisie, the social and fraternity-sorority orientation of black colleges had a debilitating effect on intellectual endeavor. Edwards notes that even at Howard University, which under the New Deal and the presidency of Mordecai Johnson became the leading institution of Negro higher education during the 1930s, Frazier found his hopes for a substantial program of research in the social sciences frustrated.

Part of the reason for Frazier's disappointment at Howard was that the philanthropic foundations interested in supporting social science research at black institutions concentrated their efforts at Fisk. What happened, as Butler Jones brilliantly demonstrates, was that Charles S. Johnson, when he moved from the National Urban League, created in Nashville a "Fisk Machine," that enabled him to function as the " 'prime mover,' 'overseer,' or 'establishment nigger' in sociology, . . . the new Booker T. Washington, . . . 'the black' for other blacks to see in matters relating to financial support for, or, in some instances, academic recognition of social science research." Fisk's president, Thomas Elsa Jones, recruited Johnson as part of his effort to build the university into a major center of learning. In turn, Johnson brought not only his own prominence, but connections with leading sociologists across the country and with all the philanthropies significantly involved in black higher education. As a result, except for the race relations interests at Chapel Hill and the Carnegie Corporation's funding of the Myrdal project, what research money there was for the study of black sociology and for black sociologists tended to go to Fisk. Johnson's "Fisk Machine," in Butler Jones's view, had both functional and dysfunctional aspects. It helped secure funding for the training of black sociologists and the study of the black community. But it also stimulated such "jealousies and feuding" among the leading black sociologists that Johnson was unable to assemble "a faculty of the strength and diversity needed to create a first-rate center for graduate training in sociology," made it hard for other black graduate institutions to obtain much-needed funds, and "tended to force all research by black sociologists in a direction favored or at least not opposed by [Johnson]."

Johnson is, in fact, central to any discussion of what was happening to black sociologists and the study of the black community during the 1930s and 1940s. While he gets more attention than any other figure in *Black Sociologists,* his true role nevertheless remains obscured. Unfortunately both Robbins's essay on Johnson, and Stanley H. Smith's lackluster discussion of "Sociological Research and Fisk University" are uncritical in their assessment of this man and his accomplishments. None of the contributors observes how little of Johnson's later work was actually his own, and Jones alone recognizes that the Fisk sociologist's role had dysfunctional aspects; it seems to me however that Johnson's negative impact was even greater than Jones suggests.

Johnson was an extraordinarily complex person. He was probably the best informed of the black sociologists of his generation, possessing an impressive grasp of historical and sociological data, and a keen analytical mind. Nevertheless his published work is actually less impressive than that of contemporaries like Frazier and Cox, both of whom, as Jones indicates, considered Johnson their intellectual inferior. The fact was that Johnson seldom published his most thoughtful and original ideas.[4] Instead he tended to limit himself to empirical description, to keep abreast of the most recent research in the field, but—acting cautiously—not to move beyond it. Just because he was so abreast of current research, contemporaries, confusing the up-to-date quality of his writing with originality, were impressed. But nowhere in Johnson's publications does one find the challenging, if debatable, theses of a Cox or a Frazier, or the sensitivity of a St. Clair Drake. The unoriginality of Johnson's published work is all the more curious because of a fact unfortunately passed over by Jones and missed by Robbins in his celebration of the team research that became the hallmark of the Fisk social science department: much of Johnson's later work was undoubtedly not his own, but that of a succession of "research assistants."

Jones correctly observes that the "Fisk Machine" developed bit by bit, rather than as part of a grand design or organized conspiracy among white sociologists and philanthropists. Yet Johnson's own role in creating the "Fisk Machine" remains obscure—and, given Johnson's habit of not leaving records behind, will probably always remain so. Actually he undoubtedly worked hard to build this machine, shrewdly cultivating relations with scholars like Park and the people at Chapel Hill, southern civic leaders and New Deal administrators like Will Alexander, and philanthropists like Edwin R. Embree of the Rosenwald Fund, the officials of the General Education Board, and John Hay Whitney. In the end, he established a unique power not only over black sociologists but over the entire black intellectual community. Jones writes of Johnson's "control over, or relatively exclusive access to, research and other support funds available to blacks," as not only funneling donations to Fisk, but even making it "difficult for black sociologists with different interests to get unbiased evaluation of their research support proposals." Actually, with Johnson sitting on practically every board that seriously entertained applications from blacks for fellowships or grants, there was scarcely a young black intellectual in any field who could get an award if he disapproved. Johnson undoubtedly liked to think of himself in the way that one of his closest associates at Fisk described him—"the most powerful Negro in America"— like the earlier Booker T. Washington whom he so much admired.[5]

With his hands at key financial levers, Johnson was able to attract an able group of young scholars to the social science department at Fisk—mostly black, but whites and Orientals as well. Once at Fisk, however, these people became immersed not in their own work, but Johnson's. Not only did the "Fisk Machine" discourage research that diverged from the general direction of Johnson's, but it seems to have inhibited promising young people from doing much of their own scholarly work altogether, so that Johnson never even developed a school of scholars who followed in his footsteps. Most of those who served as his research assistants have only praise for Johnson and do not admit that much of his later work was ghostwritten by them. But it is interesting to note that the people who emerged from the "Fisk Machine" as publishing scholars in their own right were individuals who had either established a significant reputation before coming to Fisk or left in disillusionment after the nature of their research for Johnson became clear to them.[6] Evidently the acknowledgment in one of Johnson's later books to the person who really wrote most of it may be taken literally rather than figuratively.

Thus I would emphasize, even more than Jones, the dysfunctional aspects of the "Fisk Machine." It seems to me that the philanthropic foundations that sought to encourage serious study of the black community by building the Fisk sociology department unwittingly helped to discourage the continued development of the promising school of black sociologists that had emerged earlier in the century. Too many bright young minds became caught up in doing Johnson's work rather than their own, and their potential for becoming important sociologists in their own right was never fulfilled. Of course, Johnson's control would not have been possible if race and the black experience had remained an important concern of mainstream sociology, and if the racism of the academic world had not permitted the creation of a little jim crow fiefdom at Fisk, with power over black intellectuals. Thus the racism that the contributors to this volume so properly stress had, I believe, a far more subtle and profound effect than even they have recognized.

With scholarly study of race relations and the black experience a peripheral concern for the major departments of sociology; with perhaps two decades of black sociological scholarship dominated by Charles S. Johnson at Fisk; with a lesser graduate department like Ohio State University producing a disproportionate number of the black Ph.D.s after midcentury; with the graduate departments at predominantly white universities hiring only white professors, perhaps it is no wonder that black sociologists functioned primarily as teachers in the Negro colleges rather than as published researchers. Not until the 1960s, when the sociological profession suddenly became aware of the importance of the black experience as a field of inquiry and when, responding to the pressures of the time, mainstream graduate departments turned systematically to recruiting black students and hiring black faculty, did a substantial amount of new published research by black scholars appear again. And when it did appear, its approach and style represented something quite new in the history of black sociologists.

Given the changing research priorities within the discipline, and given the mixture of racism and benevolence, discrimination and paternalism, that made the Fisk machine possible, blacks developed strong feelings of ambivalence toward the professional associations and the sociological establishment. To be sure, around midcentury Negroes received recognition in the form of high office unparalleled in other scholarly disciplines, and the American Sociological Association (responding to an embarrassing incident of discrimination against Charles S. Johnson in the early 1930s) became the first professional organization to adopt a policy of not meeting in segregated facilities.[7] Still, blacks were acutely aware that their status in the profession remained marginal. Of course, professional standing and advancement depend only in part on the quality of one's work. Factors such as the topicality of one's research, personality characteristics, and the nexus of personal contacts are also important. So if Negroes were underrepresented in the major professional journals and in the offices of the professional organizations, it was hard to know if this was a reflection of the significance of their published scholarship, a result of outright prejudice, or a sign that faculty at little-known black colleges (disproportionately Ph.D.s from less prestigious graduate departments) lacked helpful personal contacts. Accordingly, like other marginal academics, blacks were uncomfortable in the professional associations. Blackwell, in one of the most useful essays in the book, cogently describes the alienation of the black sociologists, and the way in which they therefore tended to band together and ignore whites at professional meetings.

Such matters need more systematic study, with careful attention to variation over time. Yet it must be emphasized that the criticisms voiced by Blackwell and other contributors are not placed in the comparative context of racism in the broader academic world outside sociology. The fact is that in no other profession have blacks enjoyed as much recognition or as high a share of prestigious offices. To suggest that blacks were consistently ignored by the sociological profession distorts history. For example, in turning to the 1947 volume of the *American Sociological Review,* in order to peruse once again Frazier's "Sociological Theory and Race Relations," I found that Frazier and Earl Moses contributed two of the sixty articles the journal published during the year; that Frazier was listed as first vice-president, Charles S. Johnson as an at-large member of the executive committee, and Ira DeA. Reid (along with Robert K. Merton, Kingsley Davis, and Howard Becker) as one of the *Review*'s six assistant editors. Of course, this likely represents an apogee: with the changes described above, the recognition accorded blacks fell sharply in the following decades. Nevertheless, this whole question requires careful and intensive study. As Janowitz so forcefully argues in defending the University of Chicago's department and the editors of the *American Journal of Sociology* from Rudwick's charge that they ignored Du Bois, a careful content analysis needs to be made before any definite conclusion can be reached. Indeed one wonders why Janowitz justifiably disputes the complaints about racism at his own institution seventy years ago, while ignoring the unmitigated condemnation of the whole profession over the years. Blackwell could have made a profound contribution if he had studied the changing practices of the profession in order to understand how things happened rather than simply condemning the injustices that existed. As it stands, there is simply no explanation offered for the fact that—as measured by scholarly eminence and achievement, receipt of research funds, and election to professional offices—prior to the 1960s blacks achieved far more in sociology than in any other field.

In any event, black sociologists felt themselves in no position to do much about discrimination and lack of professional recognition until the late 1960s. By then, the lessons of the civil rights revolution had made blacks more militant and white sociologists more sensitive, and as Killian and Charles Smith point out, the successes of the radical white sociologists softened up the sociological power structure and paved the way for concessions to black demands. In one of the most useful sections of this volume Blackwell charts the rise and history of the Black Caucus, and analyzes the way in which it pressed successfully in 1969–72 for a greater share of offices and committee assignments. Blackwell also describes the conflict between the younger, nationalist group in the caucus, and the generally older group which had an assimilationist emphasis—not " 'bellicose radicals' given to meaningless rhetoric, but . . . people who understood the nature of formal organizations, the conditions that engender subsystems, parallel structures, and processes which serve either to heighten or reduce alienation." It was the latter group which developed a temporarily productive strategy of pressing the Association to accord blacks greater recognition. Under Blackwell's leadership the caucus achieved significant successes, including a share of offices more than commensurate with the number of blacks in the organization, a minorities fellowship program, and a biennial award honoring the memory of Du Bois, Frazier, and Johnson.

Actually the distinction between assimilation and separatism is not as simple as Blackwell suggests, and similar complexities and confusions affected other aspects of the blacks' struggle for recognition in the profession as well. For example, is the Du Bois-Johnson-Frazier prize, administered by an interracial committee, but deliberately awarded exclusively to blacks, an example of integration or separatism? And, in limiting the prize to blacks, was the committee encouraging the highest standards of scholarship and thus assimilating blacks into the mainstream of the profession, or providing a place where works by Negroes, even if of lesser quality than by white specialists in black studies, would be granted a jim crow award? Nathan Hare, in his essay, reports ambivalences and ambiguities in the attitudes of black sociologists toward the struggle for separate black studies departments, waged at the same time as the struggle for recognition within the ASA. Wilson Record and William J. Wilson describe different aspects of another dimension of this drive—the claim that only blacks can do valid research and teaching in the black experience. Thus Wilson, in his discussion of the " 'Insiders and Outsiders' Controversy," observes that for some this demand for a "black monopoly in the field of race relations" is a genuine intellectual position, while for others it is "motivated by a desire to enhance their own professional status by removing white competition." It would have been helpful if one of the volume's contributors, or perhaps the editors, had systematically analyzed the complexities and psychological ambivalences involved in this struggle for recognition and status.

In any event, the progress within the ASA in the end was not as great as Blackwell had hoped. It proved impossible to sustain the relatively high number of blacks in important committee posts and other offices, and, indeed, in 1976 only one black was chosen for elective office. To many of the black sociologists it appeared that the racial stance which had prevailed in the Association before 1968 remained essentially intact. Accordingly, dissatisfied elements in the Black Caucus have now formed a separate organization, the Association of Black Sociologists. In this they were acting as their counterparts in political science and psychology had previously. It is still too early to say what impact this will have on the participation of blacks in the ASA. If the withdrawal is as great as it has been in psychology and political science, it may mean that the power structure within the profession can largely ignore the demands of the protesters, and black influence within it may actually diminish further. Or if the black sociologists adopt a strategy akin to that of the black psychiatrists, remaining active within the predominantly white association while simultaneously functioning in their own independent organization, the tactic of maintaining pressure on the white sociological establishment will continue.[8]

In the end *Black Sociologists* raises more questions than it answers. As the editors indicate, the volume was not intended to be a systematic or definitive treatment. The quality of the papers, as in any symposium, is highly uneven. Moreover, certain obvious topics crying for discussion are omitted, such as a systematic evaluation of Park's influence; a coherent treatment of Johnson's role; a rigorous analysis of the decline in black officeholding in the professional organizations after midcentury and the reasons for this; an evaluation of the quality and significance of the upsurge in published scholarship by black sociologists that has appeared in the past decade. Also unfortunate is the tendency to discuss the sins of the profession without placing its behavior in the broader context of what was going on in other disciplines—a tendency that produces the failure to explain why it was that such a distinguished group as Johnson, Du Bois, Frazier, and Reid ever appeared at all. Except for Wilson, the contributors fail to grapple with—or even seriously consider— the anti-intellectualism posed by the demand that whites withdraw from studying and teaching about black life and culture. And nowhere does anyone develop the very telling point made by Janowitz in his introduction that there is no viable distinction between black sociology and white sociology as such, that despite the distinctiveness of the subject matter and the uniqueness of the black experience in America, "The sociological study of black society [is] a part of the larger enterprise of understanding society."

Yet *Black Sociologists* has raised important questions in the areas of race relations and the sociology of knowledge—about how changes in the social milieu, in the attitudes of sociologists black and white, and in the structure of the profession affect ongoing research in this crucial subject. Accordingly the volume, with all its limitations, is a most welcome contribution.

Notes

1. How Janowitz can describe the essentially polemical *Black Bourgeoisie* as being done with objectivity is something of a mystery to me.
2. This volume, with its Marxist cast, though conceived before 1945, lay outside of the then-dominant school of black sociologists oriented toward empirical description and reformist social change. Butler Jones, quite aptly classing Cox as "an aberrant among black sociologists," observes that "unlike his black brethren whose descriptive and analytic essays on particular features of Negro-white relations were aimed at documenting the failures of the American system . . . , Cox used the race experience in the United States to document not merely the shortcomings of the country's system but the more fundamental position that the system was incapable of organizing itself to correct the situation."
3. In this discussion I have been considerably influenced by Edward Shils's "Tradition, Ecology, and Institution in the History of Sociology," in *Daedalus* (Fall 1970). His comments on the decline of interest in blacks (pp. 806–809) are suggestive; I would agree with him that it was significantly related to the patterns of institutional dominance in the field, although I would disagree with his view that changes in methodologies and research techniques were not relevant to this development.
4. One has only to compare his *Patterns of Negro Segregation* with the unpublished draft of it to be found in his papers, to grasp this.
5. During my last year at Fisk a revealing incident arose when Johnson, hearing of an article highly critical of his administration that was about to appear in the student newspaper, sought to have it withdrawn prior to publication. Johnson himself pressed the student who had written the piece, while his close associate, a well-known black administrator at the university, advised the student's best friend that since Johnson was "the most powerful Negro in America," the item should be withdrawn if the student wished to receive a fellowship for graduate work. The young man stood firm, and whether or not Johnson in the mid-fifties could have stood in his way, the fact is that he pursued his advanced training abroad.
6. Frazier, who had already become known for significant work before he went to Fisk, and left that institution swearing that he would never write another word for Johnson, is the best authenticated instance. My own experiences were probably similar to his. Working for Johnson while I was completing my doctoral dissertation, I at first found the job stimulating and challenging with Johnson exceedingly open to fresh ideas. Only gradually did the true nature of my "research assistantship" emerge, as I was asked to help Johnson out of emergencies by "drafting" overdue reviews and articles. His essay on the American Negro in the *Encyclopedia Americana* was drawn from my draft virtually verbatim. When, upon the completion of this task I indicated to Johnson that I was unwilling to continue ghostwriting for him, I was relieved of further research assignments.
7. Blackwell errs in saying that the action in this meant that it was adopting a practice characteristic of learned societies in general.
8. A comparison of the rise and fate of the various black caucuses, such as Wilson Record is doing for political science, psychology, and sociology, will be most

useful. It would also be useful to investigate at the same time why it is that a black caucus has never appeared among historians. Possible factors one should consider include the fact that there existed already the Association for the Study of Afro-American Life and History, which has held annual scholarly conventions for sixty years; the fact that the historical profession in the 1960s and 1970s placed blacks in important positions on councils and committees and in the presidency of both the Southern Historical Association and the Organization of American Historians without organized pressure from blacks; the possibility that history may attract a different kind of person, both among whites and blacks, less prone to radical activism; the newly won recognition of black history as a legitimate historical specialty; and the nature of the eminence achieved in the profession by John Hope Franklin, who has served as president of both the Southern Historical Association and the Organization of American Historians.

In addition the fact that a black caucus did not develop among historians may be related to the history of research in Afro-American history by black and white scholars, contrasting markedly as this did with what happened in sociology. Between the two world wars, contemporaneous with the work of Park's black disciples, there flourished a school of black history inspired by the Harvard Ph.D. and founder of the Association for the Study of Negro Life and History, Carter G. Woodson. But unlike the case in sociology, none of this was stimulated by white reformers or white scholars. By the 1940s, however, there was a rising interest in black historical studies among a small but growing group of radical and liberal white scholars, although these men, like the earlier black group around Woodson, were essentially on the periphery of the profession. At the end of the 1940s two additional major black historians emerged—Benjamin Quarles and John Hope Franklin. But during the 1950s a curious irony appeared; for reasons that are not yet understood, no additional black scholars of note appeared, while simultaneously leading white historians like Kenneth Stampp and C. Vann Woodward became interested. By 1960, at a time when race relations and the black experience had become a backwater in sociology, major works in black history were appearing and others were in the works. This legitimization of research into the black experience on the part of the mainstream of the historical profession undoubtedly had a good deal to do with the way black historians acted amidst the ideological changes of the late 1960s and the early 1970s, though one can only speculate as to the precise nature of the connection.

I am indebted to Wilson Record of Portland State University, who is making a study of black and women's caucuses in selected professional organizations, to the psychiatrist James Comer of Yale University, to Cora Marrett of the department of Sociology at the University of Wisconsin, to James Blackwell, and to John Blassingame of the history department at Yale, for sharing with me helpful information and suggestions on the whole question of the development of black caucuses. Needless to say the statements in my discussion of the matter do not necessarily reflect the views of these individuals.

FIVE

Some Observations on the Negro Middle Class

OVER THE YEARS I had of course come to know many people who belonged to what E. Franklin Frazier referred to as the "Black Bourgeoisie." There was considerable excitement among the Fisk students when the original French edition, *Bourgeoisie Noire*, appeared and I did a brief review of it for the student newspaper. When the English edition appeared in 1957 I called James Ivy to see if I might do a review-essay for the *Crisis*, and I recall his asking what I thought of it. When I responded that I intended to explore both its strengths and weaknesses—both its telling points and its distortion and hyperbole—Ivy agreed to my doing the review.

This essay, while based primarily on personal observation, also owed much, in its historical criticisms, to the research and writing I had done for my dissertation and first book.

IN HIS IMPORTANT and provocative essay, *Black Bourgeoisie* [Glencoe, Ill.: The Free Press, 1957], E. Franklin Frazier has etched in acid his portrait of the American Negro middle class. According to Frazier, the Negro business, professional, and white collar groups—the bourgeoisie or middle class—though the highest status group among American Negroes, occupy an anomalous and insecure position in American society.[1] Largely dependent for their income upon the patronage of lower-class Negroes (though in recent years a significant number have been employed in white collar positions by "white" business firms), this tiny bourgeoisie lacks a firm foothold in the larger American economy, and is unable to match the large fortunes of wealthy white Americans. Yet the members of the black bourgeoisie look down upon the masses of the race and scorn their culture. Illustrative of their attempt to disassociate themselves from the majority of Negroes is their condescension toward the spirituals and toward the culture of Africa.

But they are rejected by the white middle class, and so they are, says Frazier, culturally rootless, and beset by feelings of inferiority, insecurity, and even hatred of the race and of themselves. While masking their real sentiments under talk of race pride, they actually

From *The Crisis* 64 (October 1957): 461–69, 517.

disparage the physical and cultural characteristics of the majority of American Negroes. They complain of white discrimination and wish to be accepted by whites, yet ambivalently fear to enter into direct competition with them—even where fully qualified to do so—but prefer to enjoy their little monopolies and social life established behind the walls of segregation.

Instead of being realistic about its situation, the frustrated Negro bourgeoisie retreats into a "world of make-believe." It engages in extreme exaggeration about the success of Negro business, creating a myth about the extent of its enterprises, and the possibilities of business based on the Negro market. Moreover, it indulges in an elaborate social life, characterized by extreme manifestations of conspicuous consumption which hardly any of its members can afford. This "world of masks" is a compensation for inferiority feeling resulting from rejection by whites. At the same time the bourgeoisie fails, even disdains, to meet the intellectual standards and professional competence of members of the white middle class. Even the Negro colleges exhibit a woeful lack of intellectual interest. Faculty members are primarily interested in the position and income that make it possible for them to participate in the extravagant middle-class social life, while the students are chiefly interested in the fraternities and view college education chiefly as a means of achieving middle-class status. Members of the bourgeoisie, in fact, consider their fraternal and social life (especially poker) as more important than their work. Money, not real culture, or even respectability, is the key to success in this world of make-believe.

The NAACP and the Urban League reflect the outlook and aspirations of the middle class, which is actually not interested in the welfare of the masses of the race. The Negro press also, while it pretends to represent the aspirations of the race, actually exhibits the outlook of the bourgeoisie. It reflects the feelings of insecurity and inferiority among the black middle class by exaggerating Negro achievements, the importance of Negro "society" and incidents indicating white recognition of individual Negroes. Despite all this pretense, concludes Frazier, "in reality the black bourgeoisie . . . seems to be in the process of becoming *Nobody*," since "when Negroes attain middle class status, their lives generally lose both content and significance."

It is true that *Black Bourgeoisie* suffers from certain faults. For a judicious and scholarly approach that would carefully explore the wide range and variety of middle-class activities and attitudes, Frazier has substituted highly critical and often sweeping, and therefore misleading, generalizations. Much of the historical discussion is of questionable validity. And most unfortunately Frazier has dealt with his subject as an isolated social phenomenon, even though he does recognize that the "behavior" of the black bourgeoisie "is a reflection of American modes of behavior and American values," and that its distortions of American patterns of behavior and thought are due to the fact that "the Negro lives on the margin of American society." If Frazier had discussed his subject from this frame of reference, he would have placed it in far better perspective and drawn a more meaningful and better-balanced picture. Yet these criticisms should not lead one to underestimate the value and significance of Frazier's contribution. Above all he has had the courage to discuss important matters that very much deserve discussion.

Since Frazier has a deeper realization of the relevance of history to his field than have most sociologists, it is unfortunate that historians have failed to investigate materials pertinent to this study.[2] It is undoubtedly the lack of adequate historical foundation that has led Frazier to describe the black bourgeoisie as "a group which began to play an important role among American Negroes during the past two decades," and to minimize "the spirit of business enterprise" among the "Negro elite" prior to the Civil War. Actually the professional and entrepreneurial groups have played a leading role among Negroes throughout American history, and "the spirit of business enterprise," absorbed as it was from the surrounding American culture in which the "gospel of wealth" played such an important role, owed nothing to the Freedmen's Bank to which Frazier attributes its emergence.

Frazier advances the thesis that occupational differentiation associated with the urbanization that followed the First World War resulted in the rise of a "new middle class" that replaced in importance and status an "old middle class." High social status in the pre-World War I period, according to Frazier, was based upon family background (including white ancestry), education, and conventional behavior, in contrast to the postwar and present emphasis on income and occupation. However, our research indicates that occupation and income were as important as the other criteria mentioned by Frazier for membership in the elite before the First World War.[3]

In the 1890s for example, the upper stratum of Negro society in the larger towns and cities consisted of some civil servants and politicians, a handful of professional people, and an *entrepreneurial* group that included independent artisans, barbers, blacksmiths, grocers, restaurateurs, caterers, draymen, hackmen, undertakers, and in some cases hotel owners, coal and brickyard owners, real estate dealers and contractors, as well as a scattering in other occupations. (The high social status earlier associated with some of the families engaged in domestic and personal service had pretty much disappeared by the twentieth century.) This group was imbued with the "spirit of business enterprise," as its occupational distribution indicates.[4]

Nor does Frazier discuss one very significant development in the history of the Negro bourgeoisie. This was the shift, under way by 1900 and completed during the 1920s, of the economic base of Negro business from primary dependence upon white customers to primary dependence upon Negro customers. This process was related to several developments: (1) the growing prejudice of whites, which made it less fashionable for them to deal with Negro businessmen; (2) the decline of certain types of small business in which Negroes played an important role (such as hacking, draying, catering, blacksmithing), due to changes in technology and business organization; (3) a growing spirit of racial self-help and racial solidarity in the face of increasing white hostility, a spirit that called for Negro support of Negro business in order to advance the race; and (4) the urbanization of Negroes, which by the end of the century had become significant enough to afford a profitable market that could be exploited by Negro entrepreneurs and professional men. Some business men (such as newspaper publishers, undertakers, many grocers) had always depended on Negroes for their support; but banks, insurance companies and numerous small enterprises serving the Negro community rapidly increased in number beginning about 1890, and especially after 1900. A few of the older elite, men like barbers John Merrick of Durham and A. F. Herndon of Atlanta, successfully moved into the newer businesses, in their case insurance; descendants of some of the older economic and social elite served Negroes as professional men; certain members of the older elite families managed to retain their status by judicious marriages with successful conductors of the newer enterprises; elsewhere the older aristocracy has decayed and been bypassed by the newer business and professional men who now compose the elite group.

It was the newer entrepreneurial group (which gradually came to dominance roughly during the generation after 1900), that was responsible for much of what Frazier has described as the "Myth of Negro Business"—the myth that by patronizing Negro business, Negroes could build up great enterprises. Curiously enough, though Frazier quite correctly ascribes much of the force behind this ideology to the propaganda of the National Negro Business League, founded by Booker T. Washington in 1900, he somehow does not relate the phenomenal development of the League in the first years of the century to the changing class structure.

Frazier, in addition, has errors of fact and interpretation, of which we can give only a sampling. The Garvey Movement is called "the only serious Negro nationalist movement to arise in the United States," although certainly the nationalistic emigrationist movement in the 1850s was exceedingly important.[5] According to Frazier, Atlanta and Fisk Universities, which were founded by the American Missionary Association with the assistance of the Freedmen's Bureau, were founded by the Bureau alone. He calls "Paul Lawrence [sic] Dunbar the first Negro poet to treat with humor and sympathetic understanding the Negro rural folk," though Dunbar wrote in the stereotyped plantation tradition which pictured Negroes as happy under slavery. On page 40 Frazier states that the United Order of True Reformers was founded in 1887; on page 91 he gives the date as 1867. The correct date is 1881. Frazier states that there were only seven Negro banks in existence in 1905. Actually there were about thirty.

Frazier perpetuates Horace Mann Bond's error (stated in the latter's *Negro Education in Alabama*) to the effect that the Slater Fund became interested in industrial education due to the influence of Booker T. Washington, when actually it was the Slater Fund that was the chief agent responsible for creating, during the 1880s, the vogue for industrial education which in turn provided the basis for Washington's fame and ascendance.[6] To state: "As the black bourgeoisie has grown in importance in the Negro community during the past two decades, the Negro press has focused attention upon activities of the Negro in business and his achievements in acquiring wealth" gives a false impression, because there is less emphasis on these matters in the Negro press today than there was thirty or sixty years ago.

Again, the ideology of Negro support of Negro business (or the creation of what Du Bois and others called a "group economy") as a solution for the economic problems facing Negroes was not "formulated . . . during the last decade of the nineteenth century," as Frazier says it was, but enjoyed a considerable vogue during the 1850s when it was espoused by Frederick Douglass and other eminent leaders, and had been becoming increasingly popular during the 1880s. And Frazier's further assertion that this "myth" was "created by a small group of Negro intellectuals and Negro leaders who accepted racial separation as the inevitable solution of the race problem," overlooks the fact that this ideology was regarded by its supporters as a temporary device to build Negroes economically to the point where they would be integrated into the larger American economy.

Frazier is undoubtedly at his best in his sociological analysis. Here, in the writer's estimation, Frazier's discussion, though at times exaggerated, is perceptive and, in places, brilliant. That large segments of the Negro bourgeoisie have as their chief interest a social life characterized by extreme standards of conspicuous consumption, and a highly competitive struggle for status within Negro "society," would appear to be undeniable. Too often, as Frazier points out, Negroes manifest interest in interracial social action organizations only when it becomes a socially satisfying activity. Thus in some cities liberal leaders plead that they can not obtain Negro participation, while in other places, where socially prominent whites are active participants in liberal movements, it is said that the Negro members seem chiefly concerned with the social prestige which they feel accrue to their belonging to these organizations.

Other observers have noted the lack of intellectual interest characteristic of Negro institutions of higher learning, the tremendous interest in the Ph.D. as a prestige symbol rather than as proof of scholarly achievement, and the precedence social life takes over learning. There are, of course, a handful who resist this tendency, and they are significant, but usually those who fail to compromise with the dominant trend feel isolated. As Frazier suggests, the average Negro professor has more in common with prejudiced middle-class whites than with the liberal white professors on the campus. To idealistic white liberals, in fact, whose interest in race relations is closely related to their dislike of empty social striving and unjust social distinctions and discriminations, and who tend to be interested in intellectual matters, Frazier's description appears to be, by and large, sound, and his criticisms justified.

Yet, given the nature of Negro-white relations in the United States it is only natural that the Negro elite would tend to imitate, even as Frazier implies, caricature the behavior of far wealthier upper-class whites in order to build up its own self-esteem. In many ways, in fact, as Gunnar Myrdal has suggested, middle-class Negroes are exaggerated middle-class Americans. Frazier condemns the lack of intellectual atmosphere in the Negro colleges, even those that pride themselves upon their intellectual traditions; but most American colleges lack such an atmosphere, and are primarily engaged, as are the Negro colleges, in preparing their students socially and occupationally for participation in American middle-class life. Frazier, with considerable justice, criticizes the black bourgeoisie for being indifferent and even hostile to the interests of the Negro masses, but he seems to expect too much of human nature, for the white bourgeoisie has the same attitude toward the white masses.

Often, in fact, Frazier's criticisms are as applicable to whites as to Negroes, as in his statement that "The activities of 'society' are not simply a form of social life engaged in for pleasure. . . . They are engaged in primarily in order to maintain status or as a part of the competition for status." It is true, as Frazier says, that the emphasis on status symbols and the competition for social status represents an effort to overcome an inferiority complex. But this sort of thing is as true of whites as it is of Negroes, the only difference being that race discrimination serves to heighten feelings of inferiority and therefore increases the felt need for status symbols that enhance one's self-esteem. Unfortunately Frazier has not attempted a careful comparison of the striving for social status among middle-class whites and middle-class Negroes, a comparison that would place his statements in a much-needed perspective.

His ignoring of the impact of the attitudes and patterns of life of the white middle class on the Negro middle class is particularly evident in his ascribing the rising number of divorces and scandals among the new Negro middle class to the fact that this new middle class "is recruited" from the lower classes, without noting the increase in divorces among whites and the scandals reported in the daily press about Hollywood celebrities and white "society" as a likely factor.

Frazier makes exaggerated statements and cites atypical instances in a way that suggests that they are representative. He criticizes the Negro bourgeoisie for being "insulted if they are identified with Africans," and for refusing "to join organizations that are interested in Africa." While there is undoubtedly some ambivalence in regard to this matter, it would appear that if the bourgeoisie despised Africa its current interest in Ghana, for example, would be puzzling. In criticizing Negro business he underestimates the prejudice exhibited by white banks as a factor in their failure to extend loans to colored entrepreneurs. In attacking the myths widely held in regard to Negro business enterprise, he does not, unfortunately, inform us that there are at least a few (such as the eminent businessman who frankly described the largest Negro businesses to me as "so-called large business") who do have a realistic view of the subject.

In his criticism of the Negro press, the NAACP, and the Urban League, for reflecting the concerns of the middle class rather than advancing the interests of the race as a whole, he undoubtedly underestimates their constructive influences. In fact, he scarcely mentions the protest activities of the Negro press, which he says "provides a romantic escape for Negro city-dwellers." And it certainly would take more than Frazier's mere assertion to prove a relationship between the middle class's alienation from the religion of the masses and an alleged worship of chance and fortune as exhibited in the emphasis on poker in society's "world of masks."

On the other hand, Frazier throws out a number of highly suggestive generalizations that should make provocative subjects for further research. We can point out only a few here. To what extent, for example, has the outlook of Negro intellectuals been dominated by the ideas of wealthy philanthropists, whom Frazier pictures as wielding enormous influence? To what extent has the bourgeoisie's one-tracked interest in "society" led "gifted Negroes" to abandon "altogether their artistic and scientific aspirations?" Naturally, a few individuals have resisted this pressure, and it would be interesting to analyze the sources of their alienation from middle-class culture. In this connection Frazier suggests that the writers of the Harlem Renaissance, with their interest in the Negro folk and in Africa, were in fact alienated from the middle class, a thesis independently advanced and explored in some detail by a recent doctoral dissertation at Yale.[7]

The role of the middle class in the NAACP needs study and elucidation. Frazier, like other writers on the subject, does not discuss the trade union, nor the socialistic leanings of many of the leaders in the early years of the NAACP. It is also generally assumed that it is the Negro intellectuals who have dominated the affairs of the NAACP, though Frazier believes that the NAACP reflects the aspirations of an unintellectual, not to say anti-intellectual, bourgeoisie. These questions take on added pertinence in view of the fact that the middle class leadership of many NAACP branches does not consist of the highest social status individuals in their communities, and even more in view of the fact that in some branches leadership is now passing from the middle to the working classes, a fact related to the increasingly mass base of NAACP membership.

This last statement suggests that the middle class may be losing one bastion of its power in the Negro community, a power which Frazier believes centers in its control of the churches, fraternities, and uplift organizations. In this connection Frazier advances the thesis that some members of the Negro bourgeoisie obtain escape from their frustrations and inferiority complex by "delusions of power" growing out of posts they hold in the white community (even where such posts are merely a "token" integration and carry little weight), and out of "the position of power which they occupy in the Negro world," a position which "often enables them to act autocratically towards other Negroes, especially when they have the support of the white community." Many examples of this sort of thing can be cited, though in accounting for the authoritarianism of Negro leaders in certain types of situations, one should not over-look the fact that the institutional structure of the Negro commu-nity, and its relation to the white community, make the exercise of such power easier than in the larger American society. This, natu-rally, is a situation that ambitious men, no matter what sort of frustrations they may or may not have, would take advantage of.

From the point of view of theoretical orientation, however, per-haps Frazier's most significant contribution lies in his underlying hypothesis that in their behavior the Negro masses and the Negro bourgeoisie each represent a distinct subculture in American so-ciety. The culture of the masses, writes Frazier, is in the tradition of the peasant, modified in recent years by the impact of urbanization; while middle-class Negro culture is today a modified derivative of the culture of the antebellum southern gentleman, which the free Negroes imitated (a thesis that, we feel, certainly is oversimplified). On the one hand Frazier implies that the Negro bourgeoisie has basically not had much of a business tradition, but, like the gentle-man, has been more interested in spending money than in ac-cumulating it. On the other hand, he asserts that the middle class has been alienated from the folk traditions of the Negro masses. It is this alienation, coupled with rejection on the part of upper-class whites with whom the Negro elite wishes to identify, that has, according to Frazier, given to the black bourgeoisie a feeling of self-hatred and an inferiority complex which it attempts to escape by a flight into the illusions of its isolated, competitive, social world. To this writer it would appear to be more fruitful to employ the concept of ambivalence toward both races (as Frazier himself occasionally does) rather than to speak of self-hatred and a wish to be white. Yet there does seem to be considerable heuristic merit in Frazier's anal-ysis, however overstated it may be, and however much it ignores the striving for status to overcome inferiority feelings that character-izes so much of humanity.

Frazier's thesis implicitly involves acceptance of the work of the personality-and-culture school of anthropology, and the thesis that race prejudice and discrimination have a baneful effect on the per-sonality of middle-class Negroes, which in turn is reflected in what Frazier obviously regards as the pathological aspects of their culture. Unfortunately, while this hypothesis seems quite plausible, little work has been done to prove it, and Frazier's uncritical use, in this connection, of Kardiner's *Mark of Oppression*, with its grave methodological shortcomings, is unfortunate. It should be noted, however, that some support is lent to this line of reasoning by the material summarized in the brief on school desegregation submitted to the Supreme Court by the NAACP, in which the NAACP pointed out the harmful effects segregation has on the self-esteem of Negro youth.[8] Nevertheless, here is an underlying theoretical framework that, though undoubtedly oversimplified, would undoubtedly have significant and fruitful results if tested by further extensive research and modified and refined where necessary.

Finally, as we have insisted all along, in spite of our criticisms, *Black Bourgeoisie* must be treated as an important and valuable discussion. Despite its errors and its hyperbole, it says many many things that need saying. And it will have served a useful purpose if it stimulates further research on the questions it raises, and if it creates a spirit of detached analysis about itself on the part of the black bourgeoisie.

Notes

1. Frazier uses the phrase "middle class," as originally employed by European social scientists, to describe the urban professional, business, and white collar people as differentiated from the titled landed aristocracy. This is in accordance with the usage accepted by sociologists like David Riesman and C. Wright Mills. On the other hand, Frazier's middle class includes what are members of both the middle- and upper-status groups among Negro Americans. Frazier apparently lumps them together as an upper-status group or elite, rather than describing the gradations within the group discussed.

2. The following critique of the historical aspects of the *Black Bourgeoisie* is based primarily upon relevant material in August Meier's "Negro Racial Thought in the Age of Booker T. Washington, Circa 1880 to 1915," especially Chap. 11, "The Development of Negro Business and the Rise of a Negro Middle Class." Doctoral dissertation, Columbia University, 1957. Also examine subsequent research in the history of the Negro upper class in Atlanta, Georgia.

3. Frazier in fact is somewhat contradictory on this point, but does indicate that "the members of the [old] upper class depended on a number of skilled occupations for a living, though there was a sprinkling of teachers, doctors, educated ministers and small businessmen among them."

4. In this connection it should be pointed out that Frazier, though somewhat contradictory and not altogether clear on the matter, minimizes the emphasis on economic accumulation in the Negro schools of the late nineteenth and early twentieth centuries, and consequently overdramatizes the transition in Negro education in the 1920s as being "From the Making of Men to the Making of Money-Makers."

5. See Howard H. Bell, "A Survey of the Negro Convention Movement, 1830–1861." Doctoral dissertation, Northwestern University, 1953.
6. See August Meier, "The Rise of Industrial Education in Negro Schools," *Midwest Journal* 7, 1 (Spring 1955): 21–44; and 7, 3 (Fall 1955): 241–66.
7. Robert Bone, "A History of the Negro Novel from the Civil War to World War II." Doctoral dissertation, Yale University, 1954.
8. See also Kenneth Clark, *Prejudice and Your Child* (Boston: Beacon Press, 1955), Ch. 3.

SIX

Comment on E. Franklin Frazier's *Black Bourgeoisie* at Morgan State College Faculty Meeting, January 19, 1960

As INDICATED in the introduction, my review of Frazier's book appeared just after I had arrived at Morgan in the fall of 1957, and I received the distinct impression that it was well regarded by colleagues. In any event, a couple of years later—in January 1960—Martin Jenkins arranged to have Frazier come over from Washington and discuss the book with the faculty. The anthropologist Irene Diggs and I were asked to present brief critiques to which Frazier responded. I print this hitherto unpublished paper here, because its approach differs from my *Crisis* article in formulating some of my observations more sharply.

Afterwards there was a heated discussion from the floor, with Frazier replying to questions in his characteristically caustic and witty way. Why, he wanted to know, for example, did white school teachers travel to Europe while black school teachers spent their money on shoes? In response to a defense of the black church, Frazier irreverently (and irrelevantly) exclaimed that the Christian god was not a god of people originally transplanted from Africa. And so it went. I recall that the faculty was about equally divided between those who grimly sat through the proceedings and those who greeted the Howard sociologist's sallys with hearty laughter.

IT SEEMS TO me that people's reactions to E. Franklin Frazier's *Black Bourgeoisie* make an excellent illustration of the sociology of knowledge—of how people's beliefs and social perceptions are shaped by their social and cultural experiences, by the statuses they occupy and by the roles they play. This was strikingly exemplified by the comments of members of a class in Negro history who read the book last spring. Several, chiefly those who did not appear destined for high social status, tended to agree with Mr. Frazier. The fraternity and sorority members, on the other hand, were critical. One of them testified to the veracity of Mr. Frazier's description, but defended the type of social life which Mr. Frazier denounced, because it was the sort of life he himself was expecting to live. Finally one student, a white woman who was not familiar with the subculture being discussed, admitted to being hopelessly confused by the book; she finally decided that it was probably a satire.

Perhaps this last judgment is not too wide of the mark, after all. For the element of hyperbole that led this student to conclude that *Black Bourgeoisie* must be a satire is exactly the feature of Mr. Frazier's writing that has made his book such a noteworthy polemic. As a work of scholarship, it is true, *Black Bourgeoisie* leaves something to be desired. But as a polemic it has been, to say the least, brilliantly effective, as the storm of indignation it has aroused so eloquently testifies.

Though it should be emphasized that I regard *Black Bourgeoisie* as a book of significance and value, it is true that it suffers from certain faults. For a judicious and scholarly approach that would carefully explore the wide range of middle-class activities and attitudes, Mr. Frazier has substituted highly critical and often sweeping, and therefore misleading, generalizations. Much of the historical discussion is of questionable validity. And unfortunately Mr. Frazier has dealt with his subject as an isolated social phenomenon, even though he does recognize that the behavior of the Negro middle class "is a reflection of American modes of behavior and American values," and that its distortions of American behavior patterns and thought are due to the fact that "the Negro lives on the margin of American society." If Frazier had discussed his subject from this frame of reference, he would have placed it in a far more meaningful perspective.

Admittedly this would be difficult to do. For one thing it is hard to decide which group in white America Mr. Frazier considers most comparable to the Negro middle class. According to Mr. Frazier's definition, the black bourgeoisie consists of those engaged in entrepreneurial, professional, and white collar occupations. Some appear to belong to an elite in the Negro community, while others are not necessarily members of the elite though they aspire to belong to "society." This difficulty is compounded by the fact that Negroes who possess an occupation and income that would go with middling status among whites, are included among the elite groups in the Negro community, and, as Mr. Frazier points out, frequently aspire to emulate the life of the wealthy high-status whites. Would it be most appropriate then to consider the class whom Frazier describes as being most comparable to elite groups like, say, Amory's "Proper Bostonians" and Baltzly's "Philadelphia Gentleman"? Or would a more comparable model be the upper class of the Lynds', Middletown, or some segment of society in Warner's "Yankee City"; or would it be perhaps Whyte's "Organization Man," or Riesman's

"Lonely Crowd," or C. Wright Mill's "White Collar Class," or possibly Vance Packard's "Status Seekers"? Or would it perhaps be some combination of these types?

Historically Mr. Frazier has made a number of factual errors. I disagree with him also on certain matters of interpretation that are too technical to be discussed in the short space of time allotted to me this evening. My chief historical criticism is that it seems to me that Mr. Frazier underestimates the importance of occupation as a criterion for membership in the higher status groupings.

Mr. Frazier is undoubtedly at his best in his sociological analysis. Here, it seems to me, Mr. Frazier's discussion, though at times exaggerated, is perceptive and, in places, brilliant. That large segments of the Negro bourgeoisie have as their chief interest a social life characterized by extreme standards of conspicuous consumption, and a highly competitive struggle for status within Negro society would appear to be undeniable.

A number of observers have noted the lack of intellectual interest characteristic of Negro institutions of higher learning, the tremendous interest in the Ph.D. as a prestige symbol rather than as proof of scholarly achievement, and the precedence social life takes over learning. This is evident, for example, in the tendency to define culture as being concerned with dress, coiffure, and manners, rather than with intellectual and artistic interests. There are, of course, a handful who resist this tendency, and they are significant. But usually those who fail to compromise with the dominant trend feel isolated. As Mr. Frazier suggests, the average Negro professor has more in common with prejudiced middle-class whites than with the liberal white professors on the campus. In fact, to idealistic white liberals whose interest in race relations is closely related to their dislike of empty social striving and who tend to be interested in intellectual matters, Mr. Frazier's description appears to be, by and large, sound, and his criticisms justified.

Yet, given the nature of Negro-white relations in the United States it is only natural that the Negro elite would tend to imitate, even as Frazier implies, to caricature the behavior of far wealthier upper-class whites in order to build up its own self-esteem. In many ways, as Gunnar Myrdal has suggested, middle-class Negroes are exaggerated middle-class Americans. For example, Mr. Frazier justly condemns the lack of intellectual atmosphere in the Negro colleges, even those that pride themselves upon their intellectual traditions. But the majority of American colleges lack such an atmosphere and are primarily engaged, as are the Negro colleges, in preparing their students socially and occupationally for participation in American middle-class life. It is possible, as Frazier suggests, that the emphasis on status symbols represents an effort to overcome an inferiority complex, and that since race discrimination serves to heighten feelings of inferiority it increases the felt need for status symbols that enhance one's self-esteem. Unfortunately, however, Mr. Frazier has not attempted a careful comparison of the striving for social status among middle- and upper-class whites and among middle- and upper-class Negroes, a comparison that would place his statements in a much-needed perspective.

On the other hand Mr. Frazier throws out a number of highly suggestive generalizations that should make provocative subjects for further research. We can point out only a few here. To what extent, for example, has the outlook of Negro intellectuals been dominated by the ideas of wealthy philanthropists? To what extent has the bourgeoisie's one-tracked interest in "society" led "gifted Negroes to abandon altogether their artistic and scientific aspirations"? What are the sources of the alienation from middle-class values of those few individuals who have resisted these pressures? And what about the authoritarianism of Negro leaders in certain types of situations? Has this been due, as Frazier holds, to the effort to escape from frustrations and from an inferiority complex by "delusions of power" obtained by holding positions in which an individual can act autocratically toward other Negroes? Or is this due to certain particular aspects of the institutional structure of the Negro community, and its relation to the white community, which make the exercise of such power easier than in the larger American society? To what extent does the Negro middle class and lower class, as Mr. Frazier holds, possess a distinct subculture within the larger American culture? (I here use culture in the anthropological sense of a way of life characteristic of a group of people.) And if such a subculture is empirically identifiable, to what extent is it an outgrowth of the baneful effects that discrimination has on the Negro personality—effects on the personality which Frazier believes are responsible for what he regards as the pathological aspects of the culture of the Negro bourgeoisie?

Finally, in spite of our criticisms, *Black Bourgeoisie* must be treated as an important and valuable discussion. Despite its errors of fact and interpretation, despite its hyperbole, it says many, many things that need saying. And it will have served a useful purpose if it stimulates further research on the questions it raises, and if it helps to create a spirit of detached analysis about itself on the part of the Negro middle class.

SEVEN

History of the Negro Upper Class in Atlanta, Georgia 1890–1958

THE RESEARCH for this essay grew out of my interest in the history of the Afro-American class structure which had been with me ever since I had read those sociological caste and class studies of the late 1930s and early 1940s, including the attempt to relate the analysis of class structure and social mobility to the ideologies explored in *Negro Thought in America, 1880–1915*.

Needing more information to test the thesis I had developed in my dissertation, I turned to expanding my research on the subject, primarily through interviewing people who could be identified as "upper class," and, to some extent, other knowledgeable individuals. I chose to study Atlanta first in large part because one of my Fisk students, David L. Lewis, was from Atlanta and could provide valuable entree into upper-class circles there. The result is the rather preliminary and experimental essay, which Lewis and I wrote together.

DOWN TO THE close of the nineteenth century the entrepreneurial class in the Negro community depended in considerable part upon the support of white customers. Though the range of occupations varied in different cities, this group was composed primarily of blacksmiths, tailors, barbers, and other skilled artisans, hackmen, and draymen, grocers and, less frequently, hotel owners, caterers, real estate dealers, and contractors. Along with civil servants, teachers, pullman porters of good family background, domestic servants in the most elite white families, the more eminent and better educated ministers, a few doctors, and an occasional lawyer, the more successful among these entrepreneurs formed the upper stratum in the Negro community during the late nineteenth century.[1]

By about 1900, however, significant economic and social changes were under way in the Negro community. A growing antipathy on the part of whites toward trading with Negro businessmen, and changes in technology and business organization, forced many of these small entrepreneurs out of business. At the same time the increasing urbanization of Negroes supplied a base for business

From *Journal of Negro Education* 28 (Spring 1959): 129–39 (with David L. Lewis).

dependent on the Negro market. Such businesses included banks (the first two founded in 1888), cemetery and realty associations, insurance enterprises, and numerous small retail and service establishments. Of course certain businesses—such as newspapers, undertakers, and some barbers and retail merchants—had always depended on the Negro market, and this group now increased in number. At the same time there appeared larger numbers of doctors and lawyers who, like the ministers and the great majority of teachers, served a segregated community. This shift in the economic base of the Negro bourgeoisie proceeded at an uneven pace, earlier and more rapidly in some cities than in others. Moreover the process was relatively gradual extending from the 1890s through the 1920s, by which time the newer enterprises were dominant.[2]

We were interested in ascertaining the extent to which this shift in the economic base of the Negro bourgeoisie had affected the class structure of the Negro community. To what extent had the older upper-class families of around 1900 survived (a) as an economic elite and (b) as a social elite? To what extent had individuals of a more obscure origin come to occupy a dominant place in the economic life of the Negro community, to what extent had they achieved upper-class status, and to what extent had they replaced the older upper-class families in status? It is our hypothesis that it was for the most part a newer rising group of men that formed the backbone of the entrepreneurial group that depended on the Negro market, and that in time they and their families came to constitute not only the economic elite, but the social elite as well.

Very little research has been addressed to this problem. About the only relevant study is that of Drake and Cayton, who report that in Chicago during the 1920s the pre–World War elite, largely economically dependent on the white community, for the most part lost its status to a parvenu group, which catering to the needs of the Negro community became the dominant figures in "Black Metropolis."[3]

The city of Atlanta was selected for this pilot study because of its importance as an industrial city of the New South. In view of the nature of the data most of our information was perforce obtained through interviews with residents who because of their social status, their length of residence in Atlanta, or their professional interests, would be expected to possess information relevant to this study. We interviewed about thirty people—social scientists on the faculties of the five schools comprising the Atlanta University Center (Atlanta and Clark Universities, Morehouse, Morris Brown and Spelman Colleges), prominent businessmen, professional people, descendants of old families, and women of high status. We asked our informants whom they considered upper class at the turn of the century and whom they considered upper class today; we sought information as to the changing criteria for upper-class status; and we attempted to secure as many complete family histories as possible of Atlanta families prominent in the past, the present, or in both periods. The important role of the social clubs in Atlanta society led us to pay special attention to their membership.

In view of its historical nature this study did not lend itself to the use of statistical techniques. Under the circumstances, and in view of the paucity of relevant historical documents, we felt that the data obtained by interviewing a variety of well-informed individuals, supplemented by information from such documentary sources as were available, would supply as close an approximation to the actual state of affairs as one is likely to get.

Among the Negro entrepreneurs in Atlanta in the 1890s the druggist, most of the several grocers, and the one or two undertakers appear to have had primarily a Negro clientele; but the shoemakers (including the city's leading one) and draymen served both races; the chief barber shops for whites were owned by Negroes; a rock contractor and at least one outstanding building contractor (both of whom employed both white and colored workers), and at least two realtors did business almost entirely with whites.[4] Of this group several of the grocers, barbers, and draymen, one undertaker, the contractor, and the realtors enjoyed upper-class status. Three doctors, a couple of politicians, at least one minister, probably one lawyer, in some instances the resident bishop of the African Methodist Episcopal church, several postal employees and college teachers rounded out the membership of this group.[5] In contrast to cities like Augusta and Savannah, with their antebellum free aristocracies, the early elite in Atlanta came from the mostly mulatto house-servant group, who were in a few cases aided by whites with whom they maintained close relationships, but who ordinarily seized the advantages (as compared to the field hands) enjoyed by this group to pull themselves up by their own bootstraps.

Life for the mulatto aristocracy of old Atlanta (circa 1890–1910) centered primarily on the respectable First Congregational Church, select Atlanta University, and perhaps half a dozen exclusive social clubs. Many of the elite had themselves been educated at Congregationalist Atlanta University (or its affiliated grammar and secondary school) and ordinarily sent their children there to be prepared for teaching and other white-collar occupations. However a minority, connected with the A.M.E. church, the Methodist church, North, and its affiliated Clark University, or with Atlanta Baptist (later

Morehouse) College, were accorded recognition in the highest
social circles. The leading women's social club for example was
founded by the daughter of an A.M.E. bishop. With but few exceptions all of these families lived in the then fashionable Auburn
Avenue section of Northeast Atlanta. (Many of the families who
now live on the West Side still refer nostalgically to "family home-
steads" across town). Here they were set apart from the less fortunate groups, who were largely concentrated in western Atlanta.[6]

The shift from a bourgeoisie with its economic roots largely in the
white community, to one with its economic roots almost entirely in
the Negro community, actually began during the period we have
been describing. Prominent among these were the so-called "cooperative" insurance and real estate businesses. Negro leaders as early
as 1890 founded the Georgia Real Estate Loan and Trust Company.[7]
Illustrative of the trend were the activities of Alonzo F. Herndon,
whose career encompasses the transition. Arriving at Atlanta a poor
man, he established himself as the most prominent barber in the
city, and then ventured into the rapidly expanding field of Negro
insurance, founding the Atlanta Life Insurance Company in 1905[8]
(today one of the leading Negro enterprises in the country). To
cite another instance, at about the same time white discrimination
against Negro customers led a graduate of Atlanta University to
open a shoe store which race leaders urged Negroes to support.[9]
Again, one family was wise enough during the time of the First
World War to turn from a declining hack business and invest its
capital in an undertaking establishment.

However, it is generally agreed that the chief stimulus to Negro
business enterprise in Atlanta was the audacious vision of Hemon
Perry, who arrived in the city in 1908. The son of a Texas grocer and
farmer, Perry had received only a sixth or seventh grade education,
but had been a successful cotton sampler and insurance agent in his
native state. On the basis of his experience with such companies as
the Equitable and the Manhattan Life, Perry in 1911 launched the
Standard Life Insurance Company, the largest Negro enterprise of
its time. During the next dozen years there appeared a series of
subsidiary and related companies: a bank, the Citizens' Trust Company (1921), and a half dozen organizations intended to "serve" the
needs of Negro consumers. These included the Service Company (a
laundry and dry-cleaning establishment, 1917), the Service Phar-
macies, the Service Realty Company, the Service Engineering and
Construction Company, and the National Fuel Corporation (which
owned coal mines in Tennessee).[10] In spite of glowing prospects the

insurance company began encountering serious legal and financial difficulty by 1925 and failed a few years later.[11]

But Perry's failure was chiefly a personal one. For on the ruins of his empire a few energetic and better trained men who had worked under him established many of the most important businesses of present-day Atlanta. They include the reorganized Citizens' Trust Company (the only Negro bank belonging to the Federal Reserve System), the Yates and Milton Drug Stores, and the Mutual Federal Savings and Loan Association. Moreover, the opening up of the new fashionable West Side of Atlanta as a well-to-do residential area, grew out of the Perry Service Companies. Three of the most important businessmen in Atlanta today first entered Atlanta businesses through the Perry enterprises. Other businesses that have appeared in the last thirty-five to forty years have included a radio station, a cosmetic factory, a daily newspaper, another pharmacy, and—especially since the Second World War—a number of realty and contracting companies. All of these concerns depend upon the Negro market.[12]

It is noteworthy that the chief enterprises, save for the Atlanta Life Insurance Company and the smaller of the two drug concerns, were created by men who were not members of the turn-of-the-century Atlanta elite. Even the majority of the directors of the Atlanta Life, though Congregationalists and graduates of Atlanta University, are from families who were not upper class in Atlanta fifty years ago. The question then arises, to what extent has the economic dominance of this new elite affected the old social structure?

Considerable insight into the composition of the contemporary social elite is given by an examination of the social clubs. For purposes of analysis we have selected what Atlantans consider to be the two leading women's clubs and the two most prominent men's clubs. The former are "The Twelve," a social club, and the "Chautauqua Circle," a literary society composed of fifteen members. Both date back to about 1900. The two leading men's clubs, both established in the 1920s, are the local "Boulé" of the Sigma Pi Phi, a national business and professional fraternity, and the somewhat more recent "Twenty-Seven Club."

Approximately half of the original thirteen members of the Boulé belonged to old elite families. Today, however, practically all of its nearly doubled membership are individuals whose families were not upper class in Atlanta before the First World War.[13] The Twenty-Seven Club[14] is similarly composed for the most part of the newer business and professional men. The few members of these clubs who are descended from old elite Atlanta families are themselves prominent in the business life of present-day Atlanta. On the other hand economic and professional status is not the only criterion for membership in these clubs, for certain prominent and wealthy individuals either do not care to join or are excluded on the basis of personality characteristics.

Judging by the composition of these men's clubs (whose membership overlaps considerably), and judging also by other data supplied by our informants, the men who form the core of the upper class in Atlanta today are the presidents of the six institutions of higher education, the leading businessmen (all of whom are connected with businesses based on the Negro market), some of the more distinguished physicians, a few professors who play strategic roles in the affairs of the Negro community, and a handful of other professional men. Of this group many are from respectable families, though only a few are from really prominent families at the apex of the social pyramid in Atlanta or elsewhere. On the other hand it would appear that only a few of them rose from lower-class backgrounds. On the fringes of this core group, and associated with its members to a considerable extent, are a number of college professors and professional and business men who do not rank with the highest elite socially, though comparable to its members in wealth or professional attainment or both. (Some parvenus are not really socially acceptable at all.) One can also find an occasional example of an individual who is a small businessman, but is rather well accepted socially because of his family background. Significantly civil servants, who once comprised a considerable part of the elite, now tend to occupy a middle-status position. It is noteworthy, too, that grocers and undertakers no longer play the role that some entrepreneurs in those occupations once did, while the group of artisan-entrepreneurs who served the white community has quite disappeared.[15] It is thus apparent that the increasing economic differentiation of the Negro community has been reflected in the criteria for membership in the upper class, though now as earlier college education is an important criterion of upper-class status, many of the most eminent businessmen in the city retaining close connections with the Atlanta schools either as alumni or professors in the business school. It should also be pointed out that due in large part to the fact that Atlanta University discontinued its undergraduate program over twenty-five years ago, the correlation between Atlanta University training and Congregational church membership on the one hand, and social prominence on the other, has diminished.[16] Thus it is clear that only a handful of men who belong to the old elite families have a significant economic and social role in present-day Atlanta.

On the other hand, in contrast to the men's clubs, about half the members of the two leading ladies' clubs, the Chautauqua Circle and The Twelve, are members of the city's old elite families. With them must be classed a lady who came from a neighboring state about fifty years ago, but who became thoroughly identified with the old aristocracy and an important social arbiter. The other members of these two clubs owe their social prominence to the fact that they are married to men who have themselves achieved upper-class status in Atlanta during the last forty years. A few of this latter group come from distinctly elite families outside of Atlanta; the others have gained acceptance by virtue of the social power created by a combination of their husbands' standing and their own personalities. (There are cases of women whose husbands stand at or close to the top of Atlanta's social hierarchy, but are themselves unacceptable to the social arbiters among the women.) Membership in both of these clubs, with their old-family leadership, is still a coveted honor; in part this is undoubtedly for the very reason that the club leaders have astutely admitted a judicious selection from the wives of Atlanta's new male elite. Moreover the influence of the old aristocratic families is not limited to these older clubs. For example, two other leading clubs, the Junior Matrons founded perhaps thirty years ago, and the recently established chapter of the new, nationwide Links, exhibit the same pattern of membership, with descendants of old families forming about half the membership.[17] That family background is still a significant criterion in upper-class status is indicated by the fact that many older members of these clubs, who are financially unable to move to the now fashionable West Side, are still regarded as among the social elite.

What has happened to the older elite families that no longer enjoy the highest status in Atlanta society? In the evidence made available to us, cases of marked downward social mobility are rare. It is, however, not uncommon to find people whose parents were at the top of the social hierarchy and who are themselves respectable and respected professional and business people, but who, unlike their parents, are on the fringe of the upper class, are peripheral socially, rather than belonging to the most elite social groupings. Even more significant has been the large number—especially among the men—who have left Atlanta for other cities. The descendants of one socially very prominent grocer at the turn of the century have all left Atlanta, and several of them have become very prominent elsewhere. One exceedingly distinguished New York surgeon was also from an elite Atlanta family; in another case the descendant of a leading Atlanta physician is married to the president of a noted medical school. These two, of course, have enjoyed upper-class status in the cities of both their birth and their adoption.

In general then the data indicate that there has been a considerable elite circulation in Atlanta, though the continuing role of the older families, especially among the women, should not be minimized. There is, moreover, still something of a correlation between color and upper-class status,[18] though this is not nearly so striking as it was half a century ago. On the other hand the fact that there appear to be so few extreme cases of downward mobility, and the fact that the disappearance of old families from Atlanta's upper class is due largely to migration to other cities, suggests that to a considerable extent the situation might be described as a broadening of the base of the upper class, rather than an actual substitution of new families for old families constituting that class. Moreover, as the upper class has increased in size and as Atlanta Negroes have moved upward economically, greater social differentiation has taken place, so that many of those who today are what might be called "lower upper class," though their parents were at the pinnacle of the social hierarchy, would have retained the highest status if the economic status of Negroes had remained unchanged, or if the upper-class population had remained smaller.

To what can one attribute the continued importance that Atlantans attach to the old families as evidenced by the continued importance of the older social clubs and the leadership that certain descendants of the old aristocracy exercise in social affairs in modern Atlanta? In part this is undoubtedly due to a natural lag between the shift in economic leadership and that in social leadership. However it is our belief that the most important factor was undoubtedly the fortunate marriages made between certain daughters of the old families and some of the newer business and professional men— marriages that have tended, to a remarkable degree, to unite the descendants of the older aristocracy with the newer economic-social elite.

This tendency is revealed by several of the following family histories, which are illustrative of the developments described above:

One of the most distinguished families among Atlanta's old mulatto aristocracy was that of a man who came from a northwestern Georgia town to Atlanta University and established his realty business about 1890. From then until his death about twenty years ago, his clientele was almost entirely white. His wife, whose forbears

had been the house slaves of a distinguished Georgia planter family, became a member of the Chautauqua Circle. All of the children
attended Atlanta University. Two of them became professional people and later left Atlanta; a third married a physician of some
prominence in the new Atlanta, who came originally from central
Georgia where his father had been the town's only iceman. This
couple's children have entered professional work and left town.
Meanwhile the wife carries on the family tradition of Chautauqua
membership. And although she now resides on the fashionable
West Side, she nostalgically recalls her pleasant childhood days in
the old section of the city when, as she expressed it, "family and
character were more important than they are today" as criteria of
social acceptability.

Among the small circle of people with whom this lady associated
as a youngster were the children of one of Georgia's two or three
most distinguished federal officeholders during the administrations
of Presidents McKinley and Roosevelt. This man, who owned a
Decatur Street barbershop frequented by white politicians and who
headed up the Georgia Real Estate Loan and Trust Company mentioned above, married the daughter of a Reconstruction congress-
man, and sent all of his children to Atlanta University. One of his
daughters married the outstanding colored contractor in Atlanta in
recent years, a new settler, but a man who has been consistently
influential in the development of the West Side. Though preferring
the solitude of their sprawling estate to the glitter of Atlanta's social
life, this couple must be regarded as belonging to the city's upper
crust.

Of the three leading men formerly connected with the Hemon
Perry enterprises, none of whom were natives of Atlanta, two have
married into old elite families. One of them was descended from
residents of a midwestern northern city since before the Civil War,
where one grandfather was in the dray business and the other one a
barber. Coming to Atlanta University from a neighboring state
where his father was a retail businessman with both Negro and
white customers, he became connected with Perry and married a
descendant of one of the most prominent white families of antebellum Atlanta. Both his wife and her parents were also graduates
of Atlanta University, and her father was a Congregationalist minister from Savannah. Her mother founded a noted charity which the
daughter now directs, and was a charter member of the Chautauqua and The Twelve. The daughter, active in both groups, is widely
regarded as the chief social arbiter among Atlanta ladies. When she

and her husband built a West Side home in the middle twenties, it heralded the exodus of Atlanta's elite from the Auburn Avenue section.[19]

Another of Atlanta's leading businessmen, son of a border city high school teacher and graduate of a famous northern university, was certainly far from wealthy when he married the Atlanta University–educated granddaughter of two of Atlanta's old elite businessmen—one an undertaker, and the other a grocer with white customers. The undertaker, born a slave, like many others of the late nineteenth-century mulatto elite had migrated to Atlanta from a smaller Georgia town. With only the most informal of educational backgrounds, he worked as a railroad porter, acquired some land, and entered the undertaking business around 1880. Quite unusual for a family that belonged to the elite, his family belonged to the A.M.E. church, though the children went to Atlanta University. While the family as a group must still be counted among Atlanta's upper stratum, the granddaughter who married the successful businessman from the border states was the one selected by the Chautauqua to carry on the family membership, and her marriage in time certainly enhanced her own and her family's position. Her husband's grandparents were on one side trusted house slaves, and on the other side of free ancestry. After the Civil War one grandparent was a chef at a prominent hotel, the other a doorman for an important government official—both coveted jobs at the time. His father's professional training and occupation as teacher illustrate the rising educational attainments of the late nineteenth-century Negro bourgeoisie; the distinguished Atlanta businessman himself illustrates the continuing mobility of his family.

Not generally regarded as in the very highest circles, but still representative of the mulatto elite was the family of a lady who ran a hack stand during the late nineteenth and early twentieth centuries, while her husband was a shoemaker and grocer. Both of their businesses and their home were near Atlanta University on the western side of town rather than in the Auburn Avenue Section. After her husband's death, and before the hacking business had petered out—as it was doing by the time of the First World War—she and her sons shrewdly established an undertaking business that is still run by one of her daughters-in-law. Several of her children left the city, but one of them married a man who for about ten years around 1900 ran the only restaurant for whites in a noted antebellum town. Of the six children of this union, all but one daughter (who was graduated from Clark) finished at Atlanta University. The son became an elementary school principal. Four daughters left the city, two of them, as many Atlantans say, "marrying up" into the family of a very eminent grocer, all of whose descendants, however, have also left the city and are leading distinguished lives elsewhere. The fifth daughter married a postal employee and obtained a home in northeast Atlanta shortly before the move to the West Side began; this lady carries on her mother's club membership in the Inquirers, an old and distinguished literary club, although somewhat below the Chautauqua in the social hierarchy.

Rather rare are the descendants of the old elite who have maintained or increased their wealth without marrying into newer families. Yet even today few families could rank in status with the descendants of a postal employee and important official in the Congregational church half a century ago, who was an alumnus of Atlanta University. His wife belonged to both the Chautauqua Circle and The Twelve. Their children went to Atlanta University and entered the professions, the youngest becoming a noted race leader nationally. Of the two daughters who remained in Atlanta, one married the Atlanta University trained son of a respectable postal employee and Congregationalist, who unlike others did not leave the city to seek his fortune, but became a leading figure in the business community. He was thus one of the few sons of old families who acquired a prominent place in the business life of present-day Atlanta, thus perpetuating and perhaps improving his family's position among the economic and social elite. His wife of course carries on her mother's affiliation with the Chautauqua and The Twelve.

The findings of this study then indicate that economic leadership in the Atlanta Negro community has very largely passed into the hands of a group of professional and businessmen who have come to Atlanta or risen to prominence there in the past thirty-five years, and that connected with the shift in economic power there has been a related change in the composition of the upper class, with the very highest social status being accorded to certain men prominent in business and professional life today, even though most of them are not of distinguished old Atlanta families. The few male descendants of the old social and economic elite who are recognized as important social leaders today are those who have successfully made their place in the new economic world whose chief enterprises are the Atlanta Life Insurance Company, the Citizens' Trust Company, and the Mutual Federal Savings and Loan Association. Among women on the other hand, a high proportion of descendants of the old families still retain the highest social status. This is especially true of those who have married the founders of the newer fortunes, and their social connections with other old families (especially through the women's clubs) have served to bolster the prestige of the older aristocracy. Though considerably diminished, the social role of descendants of the old aristocracy is still significant. It is possible that the displacement of the older upper class has been less complete in southern cities than in northern cities, if the findings of Drake and Cayton in regard to Chicago are representative. Future studies should be conducted therefore to ascertain to what extent this pattern has been followed in other cities North and South.

Notes

*Part of the research for this article was done under a research grant from Morgan State College.

1. On the role of Negro business and businessmen in the late nineteenth century see W. E. B. Du Bois, *The Philadelphia Negro* (Philadelphia, 1898), 115–31; Jeffrey R. Brackett, *The Colored People of Maryland Since the War* (Baltimore, 1890), 28–29, 37–39; Du Bois, ed., *The Negro in Business* (Atlanta University Publications No. 4, 1899) passim: St. Clair Drake and Horace Cayton, *Black Metropolis* (New York, 1945), 433–34; *Christian Educator* 5 (July 1894): 167–68; *Proceedings of the National Negro Business League, 1900* (no imprint, 1900) passim; Robert A. Warner, *New Haven Negroes: A Social History* (New Haven, 1940), 233; Du Bois, "The Negroes of Farmville, Virginia: A Social Study," *Bulletin* of the Department of Labor No. 14 (1898): 17–19, 20; Du Bois, "The Negro in the Black Belt: Some Social Sketches," *Bulletin* of the Department of Labor, No. 22 (1899): 403, 407, 408, 412, 413, 415; Abram L. Harris, *The Negro as Capitalist* (Philadelphia, 1936), chaps. 3–8.

2. Harris, Ibid.; Joseph Pierce, *Negro Business and Business Education* (New York, 1947), chap. 1; Drake and Cayton, *Black Metropolis*, 434–37; Du Bois, ed. *Some Efforts of Negroes for Their Own Social Betterment* (Atlanta University Publications No. 3, 1898): 18–27; Du Bois, *Economic Co-Operation Among Negro Americans* (Atlanta University Publications No. 12, 1907), passim; Mary White Ovington, *Half a Man* (New York, 1911), chap. 5; George Edmund Haynes, *The Negro at Work in New York City* (New York, 1912), Part 2; R. R. Wright, Jr., "The Negro in Philadelphia," A.M.E. Church *Review*, 24 (July 1907): 137–39; R. Wright, *The Negro in Pennsylvania* (Philadelphia, [1909]), 30–33; Booker T. Washington, "Durham, North Carolina: A City of Negro Enterprise," *Independent*, 70 (1911): 542–50; E. Franklin Frazier, "Durham: Capital of the Black Middle Class," in Alain Locke, ed., *The New Negro* (New York, 1925), 333–40; Ray Stannard Baker, *Following the Color Line* (New York, 1908), 39–44; Warner, *New Haven Negroes*, 233–36; Du Bois, "The Economic Revolution in the South," in Washington and Du Bois, *The Negro in the South* (New York, 1907), 95–101; Annual *Reports* of the National Negro Business League (imprint varies), 1900 et seq.; Ira De A. Reid, *The Negro in the American Economic System* (memorandum for the Carnegie-Myrdal Study of the Negro in America, 1940), 3 vols.; E. Franklin Frazier, *Negro Youth at the Crossways* (Washington, 1940) passim; Du Bois, *Philadelphia Negro*, 115–31; John Daniels, *In Freedom's Birthplace* (Boston, 1914), 362–73.

3. Drake and Cayton, *Black Metropolis*, 543–44. Unfortunately E. Franklin Frazier's provocative *Black Bourgeoisie* (Glencoe, Ill., 1957), does not deal with how the historical development of the class structure was related to the economic process

we have described. John Daniels in his study of Boston Negroes just prior to World War I described an upper class economically and socially allied with the white community, and a rising middle class many of whose members were entrepreneurs serving the Negro community. (*In Freedom's Birthplace*, 174–85.)

4. For partial accounts of Negro business in Atlanta in the 1890s see Clarence A. Bacote, "The Negro in Georgia Politics, 1880–1908" (Doctoral dissertation, University of Chicago, 1955), 5–7 (Bacote also mentions a Negro dentist who had white customers at least as late as 1890); E. R. Carter, *The Black Side*, (Atlanta, 1896) passim; Robert J. Alexander, "Negro Business in Atlanta," *Southern Economic Journal* 17 (1951): 452–54. For a partial account of Atlanta business about 1907 see Baker, *Following the Color Line*, 38–44.

5. Interestingly enough men of the cloth, though important in the affairs of the Negro community, do not usually appear to have attained the highest social status. This situation was related to the fact that the bulk of the clergy belonged to denominations such as the Baptist, A.M.E. and A.M.E. Zion, rather than the elite churches.

6. At that time only three of the schools, Atlanta University, Atlanta Baptist College, and Spelman Seminary (now College) were located on the West Side. For descriptions of slums near these schools see Ridgely Torrence, *Story of John Hope* (New York, 1948), 139.

7. Bacote, "Negro in Georgia Politics," 6.

8. For a brief discussion of Herndon see Baker, *Following the Color Line*, 43.

9. Ibid., 39–40.

10. These concerns constituted a small interlocking empire. Funds of the insurance company formed the chief deposits of the bank; the bank in turn could finance the operations of the service companies; the construction company built the houses on the lands sold by the realty company, whose sales were made possible by mortgage loans made by Standard Life, whose chief investments were in unimproved lands on the West Side of Atlanta.

11. A useful compendium of materials on Perry is available in C. L. Henton, ed., "Hemon E. Perry: Documentary Materials for the Life History of a Business man," (Master's Thesis, Atlanta University, 1948). Perry left the city and died soon after.

12. For some material on the recent economic developments in Atlanta see Emmet John Hughes, "The Negro's New Economic Life," *Fortune*, 54 (Sept. 1956): 248, 250. For material on conditions in the late 1940s see Alexander, "Negro Business in Atlanta," 455–61.

13. For roster of original and 1952 members of Atlanta Boulé see Charles H. Wesley, *History of the Sigma Pi Phi* (Washington, 1954), 361–62.

14. In addition to its social functions, the Twenty-Seven Club functions in the political power structure of the city. Negroes in Atlanta in fact exercise unusual political power for a southern city, and their votes are generally credited with the recent reelections of Mayor Hartsfield. (See Douglass Cater, "Atlanta: Smart Politics and Good Race Relations," *The Reporter*, July 11, 1957, esp. p. 19.) One informant, however, insisted that the belief that Negroes hold as to their role in the political power structure of the city is mostly myth.

15. The pattern of exclusion of ministers from elite circles noted above continues. Perhaps half a dozen clergymen may be said to occupy positions in the core of the upper class; of these, four are college presidents, and it is to be presumed that their social positions are attributable to this fact. That power and social status may be quite distinct is illustrated by the fact that the minister who

probably has the most power in the Negro community, by virtue of his influence with the masses, is not considered upper class; the same is true of a leading and respected fraternal figure. Nor is the NAACP presidency held by a member of the upper class.

16. To some extent Morehouse College has taken over Atlanta University's role as a road to economic and social status for young men.

17. This discussion of social clubs is based on interview material and lists of club members. In a perceptive study of a sampling of voluntary associations in Atlanta, Lois E. Johnson, utilizing a modified form of Warner's Index of Status Characteristics, places both the Chautauqua Circle and the Twenty-Seven Club at the pinnacle of Atlanta society, with a membership upper and upper-middle class in terms of its economic and educational attainments. (Miss Johnson did not include The Twelve and the Boulé in her study.) See Lois E. Johnson, "Voluntary Associations: A Study in Status Behavior," Master's Thesis, Atlanta University, 1952, esp. p. 24.

18. Though it is widely held that skin color is no longer a criterion of social status among Negroes, the statements of those informants who discussed the matter—with one exception—and such observations as we ourselves made support the view that there still exists *some correlation* between social class and skin color in Atlanta, especially among the women.

19. Census tract data and Block Statistics derived from the 1950 census support the information derived from informants as to the residential distribution of the upper class. For example the homes with the highest assessment are located in certain blocks of tract 29 in the older northeast area, and in certain West Side tracts, especially tracts 24 and 40. See U. S. Bureau of the Census, *U.S. Census of Population*, 1950, Vol. 3, *Census Tract Statistics*, chap. 2 (Washington, 1952); and Ibid., Vol. 5. *Block Statistics*, part 9 (Washington, 1952). Since 1950 the movement to the West Side has continued, and the residential area for middle- and upper-class Negroes has expanded considerably.

EIGHT

The Successful Sit-Ins in a Border City: A Study in Social Causation

THIS ESSAY, on the department store restaurant sit-ins by Morgan State College students in the early spring of 1960, was an effort to explain why the Baltimore demonstrations took the course and achieved the results they did. In addition to writing on the basis of my own participation in the movement, I interviewed a number of department store executives and leaders in black advancement organizations. It is also interesting to note that excellent material on the Hochschild-Kohn department store's interest in desegregating its lunchroom as early as the 1930s has turned up in the NAACP Papers at the Library of Congress.

AMONG THE EARLIEST successes of the student sit-in movement during the spring of 1960 was the opening up of the Baltimore department store restaurants to Negro customers.[1] In this city, moreover, it was notable that the demonstrations were unmarked by the violence that attended demonstrations in cities farther south, and the students attracted an unusual amount of support among white citizens.

In this article I shall explore the reasons for the character and success of the student sit-in movement in Baltimore during the spring of 1960, by placing the movement and its achievements in the context of social change that has been going on in Baltimore over the past decade, and tracing in some detail the sequence of events initiated by the student demonstrations that began in the middle of March 1960. The analysis will involve an examination of the activities of the students, of store managements, and of intergroup relations agencies.[2]

The Setting

Baltimore is a border-state city of almost a million people, of whom over one-third were Negroes in 1960. In race relations its practices had been largely southern until well after the Second

From *Journal of Intergroup Relations* 2 (Summer 1961): 230–37.

World War. Segregation was complete in education (with the exception of the University of Maryland Law School) and in publicly owned recreational facilities. Negroes were barred from theaters, restaurants and other places of public accommodation, and they faced extreme discrimination in employment.

From the point of view of subsequent change, however, Baltimore was fortunate in several respects. Negroes were not disfranchised and there was no segregation on trains and buses. Moreover, the city possessed unusually vigorous units of both the NAACP and Urban League, a crusading Negro newspaper whose publisher played an important role in civic affairs, several active interracial civic groups such as the United Church Women, Americans for Democratic Action and the Congress of Racial Equality, and beginning late in 1951 an effective Governor's Commission on Interracial Problems and Relations. All of these agencies, acting sometimes in concert, more often autonomously, and at times at cross-purposes, helped to make significant dents in the system of segregation and discrimination during the postwar years.

Progress in the immediate postwar period seemed minimal, but 1951–1952 proved to be a turning point. In those two years there was a significant breakthrough in employment when taxi and bus companies began hiring Negro drivers, the University of Maryland began admitting Negroes to all its graduate and professional schools, and the city's only legitimate theater abolished segregated seating.

From then on the pace of social change quickened. In 1954 the Board of Education voluntarily decided to desegregate its schools promptly after the Supreme Court's decision of May 17. Also in the wake of this decision the Housing Authority of Baltimore decided the time was ripe to desegregate its public housing operations. The predominantly Negro residential sections of the city had been growing rapidly in extent following the Supreme Court decision against restrictive covenants in 1947, and except for one incident (which was promptly quashed by the police) neighborhood transitions had been peaceful. Moreover since 1956 there has been some progress in efforts to promote integrated neighborhoods. In 1956 also a legal battle of several years finally resulted in the complete integration of the city's recreational facilities.

In the economic area the Urban League reported modest successes in widening employment opportunities; in 1957 the city council created an Equal Employment Opportunities Commission (without enforcement powers, however); and the local physicians' and lawyers' association began admitting Negroes.

Meanwhile there had also been significant political development. In 1954 three Baltimore Negroes were elected to the state legislature, marking the first time any Negroes had served in that body; and the following year the first Negro councilman since the city had been redistricted in the early 1930s was elected. In the middle fifties, also, Governor McKeldin appointed several Baltimore Negroes to judicial and other positions in the city and state.

Some Earlier Gains

In the area most pertinent to this paper—that of public accommodations—there was also some improvement. In 1954 and 1955, chiefly as a result of CORE sit-ins, downtown variety store lunch counters opened to Negroes, and in the latter year a sit-in demonstration by Morgan State College students at the Northwood shopping center opened the Read drugstore chain lunch counters. Between 1956 and 1958 the downtown movie houses opened their doors to Negroes; in 1958 and 1959 several of the major downtown hotels ended their discriminatory policies; and as the fifties drew to a close a tiny handful of restaurants also changed their policies.[3]

Curiously department stores had been more discriminatory in Baltimore than probably anywhere else in the country. Beginning in the 1920s they effectively discouraged Negro trade by refusing Negroes charge accounts and refusing to permit them to try on or return articles. Certain firms, it appears, in effect rejected Negro patronage entirely. It was only during and after the Second World War that, under the pressure of various interested groups and agencies, the department stores gradually—and in piece-meal fashion—modified their discriminatory policies.

By 1960 beauty shops, eating facilities, and the more intimate women's garment departments were the chief pockets of discrimination left in the department stores. Meanwhile, on their own, the stores had been gradually moving toward elimination of segregated rest-room and dining facilities for their employees, had ventured modestly into the area of hiring Negroes for white-collar jobs, and in at least two instances had begun the employment of Negro salesclerks.

The Northwood Demonstrations

In this movement toward opening up places of public accommodation, Morgan State College students had played a significant role by their sit-in demonstrations at the Northwood shopping center, located less than a mile from the college. These, beginning in 1955, had as their chief targets lunch counters, which they successfully desegregated, and the movie theater, whose owner stubbornly refused to alter his policy.

Typically the demonstrations were organized under the leadership of the student council, began sometime during the spring of each school year, and usually ended with at least one success, but with the theater owner and some other proprietors proving obdurate.

In order to disassociate themselves from the college, and to emphasize their status as citizens asking for the rights of citizens, the students carried on their work as the Civic Interest Group. In 1958 and 1959 the students had unsuccessfully attempted to open the Rooftop Dining Room at the Hecht-May Company's Northwood branch department store.

It was in this atmosphere of social change in Baltimore, and in the context of past successes (and failures) at Northwood that during the school year 1959–1960 the student leadership at Morgan was, as usual, thinking of again starting the annual demonstrations. Eventually, about six weeks after the southern student sit-in demonstrations had begun on February 1 at Greensboro, North Carolina, the Morgan students renewed their efforts at Northwood—this time aiming at the movie theater and more particularly at the department store restaurant.

For several days their mass sit-ins thoroughly disrupted service at the restaurant; subsequently the management barred their entrance, and the students then confined their activity to picketing at the two outside entrances to the restaurant. Five students were arrested during the ten days or so of demonstrations at the Northwood department store restaurant—one charged with assault in a pushing incident, and the other four charged with trespass when they temporarily seemed to be blocking an entrance walkway. These were the only arrests made during the entire period of department store demonstrations, and the charges were later dropped in all cases (though there have since been a number of arrests in connection with demonstrations against other restaurants during the summer and fall of 1960). And in contrast to the early years of the student demonstrations at Northwood, the police acted fairly, and in fact almost seemed to be apologizing for arresting the "trespassing" students at the request of the restaurant manager.[4]

Shortly after the demonstrations began the executive secretary of the local Urban League, a skilled tactician highly regarded by many of the city's businessmen, came out to the campus to speak with the student leaders. He felt that the students would be unable to attain their objectives without putting pressure on the Hecht-May Company's competitors, and he therefore urged that the students demonstrate downtown at all of the four major department stores. (In the course of my research it later developed that this was precisely the course of action desired by the Hecht-May Company itself, and that in fact the Urban League secretary and the firm's executives had discussed the idea together before it was broached to the students.)

To the surprise of this experienced and outstanding community leader, the students' response to his suggestion was negative. As the student council president expressed it, it was manifestly impossible for the students at Morgan, in an outlying section of the city, to arrange effective demonstrations downtown, several miles from the college.

The students picketed at Northwood as much as twelve hours daily, though participation declined from two or three hundred students to a few dozen by the end of a week. In contrast to the strong hostility exhibited toward the student demonstrators in the middle fifties, few passersby made nasty remarks. Some bottles tossed off the roof of the store one evening were the sum total of violence from teenage roughs, who were usually shooed away by the police before they could cause any trouble.

At the behest of the Governor's Commission negotiations between the students and the department store were instituted, but ended in failure. A request by the company for temporary suspension of the demonstrations while negotiating continued was rejected by the students, because of negative results when they had agreed to a similar proposal the year before.

Finally, in desperation, about ten days after the demonstrations had started, the department store obtained relief in the courts, in the form of a temporary injunction limiting the students to two pickets at each entrance to the restaurant. In their complaint the store management charged that the demonstrations had cost them 49 percent of their restaurant business, and 35 percent of their retail store trade, as compared with the same period a year before.[5]

Broadening the Attack

Ironically the granting of this injunction was probably the best thing that could have happened to the Civic Interest Group at that time. This was so for two reasons. First, it served to perk up flagging student interest (in fact it had become difficult to obtain pickets during the daytime). Second, it led the students to take up the suggestions of the Urban League Secretary which they had earlier rejected, and to adopt the tactic which—unknown to the students— the department store management wished they would take. In short the students did what had previously appeared to them to be impossible: they went downtown—to the "seat of the trouble" as they said.

What made possible this belated fulfillment of the Urban League secretary's suggestion was a few hundred dollars put up by the NAACP for chartered bus transportation. And so it was that on a tense Saturday morning, late in March, a couple hundred students and a handful of their instructors staged sit-in demonstrations at Baltimore's four major department stores.

The Hecht-May Company was prepared, for guards stationed at the restaurant entrance turned the students away. A second store simply closed its dining room. At Hutzler's, considered Baltimore's leading department store, the students were permitted to sit in the restaurant and at the basement lunch counter until closing time, but the facilities themselves ceased serving for the day. The fourth store, apparently out of a mixture of what it deemed to be the ethical thing and what it judged to be sound business practice at this juncture in the city's history (though admittedly it was taking a definite risk), had earlier decided to serve the students if they should appear. Consequently, to the surprise of the demonstrators, they were courteously received as customers. So unprepared were the students for this unexpected turn of events that they had scarcely enough money to buy anything.

Sitting-in and picketing downtown gave the students something they had lacked before—adequate coverage in the city's media of mass communication. And Hochschild-Kohn's courageous decision to change its policy was crucial to the success of the movement, for it facilitated the mobilization of public opinion against the other stores. Indeed, practically at once there was a dramatic rallying of public opinion to the support of the students.

Quite spontaneously and without any prompting from the students a number of Negro and interracial—even predominantly white and relatively conservative—organizations got busy. Some, like the YWCA, passed resolutions commending the store that had opened and urging that the others do so. Money seemed to be flowing in as others, especially the churches and voluntary associations in the Negro community, as well as numerous individuals of both races, sent in contributions, though the students had not made a general appeal for funds. Many organizations urged their members to write letters and cancel charge accounts, and many individuals did this spontaneously.

Public Support

Unlike in other cities this was not a centralized, coordinated movement, but came about partly as the result of the spontaneous actions of many individuals, and partly as the result of the unsolicited efforts of leaders in a number of organizations. Especially striking was the fact that economic action was taken not only by Negroes but by many whites as well.[6] The fact that the demonstrators were students seemed to be particularly effective in eliciting the support of many white people. Indicative of the response of the white community were the communications received by the store that had changed its policy. Overwhelmingly they favored the change, and many of the letters came from the finest residential sections of the city.[7]

The heaviest pressure was exerted against the city's leading department store, for the other stores had indicated that they would change their policy if Hutzler's did—that, as one executive said, they were hitching their wagon to Hutzler's star. Furthermore, it was alleged by other department store executives and by leading figures active in intergroup relations that Hutzler's had all along been the most intransigent on the matter, for its management had never so much as agreed to sit down and discuss the situation. Though Hutzler's has denied these charges, it was clear that this store's policy was the key to the solution of the situation.

Prodded by one of the chief figures among the city's intergroup relations leaders, some of the most prominent white people in the city individually visited the officials of the various stores, and informed Hutzler's that inasmuch as the other two were willing to alter their policy, and they personally favored the change, they really thought that Hutzler's ought to do so.

Meanwhile the demonstrations continued two or three days a week (on Saturdays and on evenings when the stores were open late). The demonstrations were always orderly, the policemen and others commending the students on their excellent behavior. The crowds out for Easter shopping did not jostle with the students, there was no violence, and there were no arrests. In an effort to avoid any incidents, Hutzler's president, upon leaving town for a few weeks shortly after the demonstrations began, had left word that the dining rooms were to close down whenever the students appeared. In fact, on one occasion, shortly before the stores gave in, eight demonstrators closed all four dining places at Hutzler's. All in all there was something downright genteel about this phase of the Civic Interest Group's operations in Baltimore.

Further efforts at negotiation with the department stores had borne no fruit. The students refused to go along with a two-week cooling off period because they reasoned that their demonstrations would be less effective once the pre-Easter buying season was over. Nevertheless student interest was again flagging, and it was well that Hutzler's president returned from his cruise and arranged a conference.

Victory

This meeting was attended by four student leaders, two Urban League officials, and the NAACP lawyer who was the students' legal counsel. Though the students were thus armed with adult aid adequate for difficult negotiations, the presence of the latter proved unnecessary, for the firm's president announced his change of policy at once and complimented the students upon their behavior during the demonstrations. Though this decision was a surprise to the other two stores they both followed suit immediately.

Thus within three weeks from the time the students had started demonstrating downtown, victory was won. Victory had been achieved relatively easily because of the support of both the Negro community and the white community. Baltimore was perhaps unique in the degree to which the economic pressure was not only a Negro "withdrawal" but an interracial one. Victory was also achieved because of the support the students received from community organizations professionally interested in race relations, as well as from churches and other voluntary associations whose chief concern was not race relations as such.[8] To a considerable degree this support came to the students unsolicited. Much of the work— especially of the Urban League and the United Church Women— was unknown to the students.

The spontaneity of this support accorded the students not only among adult Negroes—which was typical throughout the South— but also among sympathetic whites, was notable indeed. Just as Hochschild-Kohn's unexpected reversal of policy on the occasion of the students' first downtown demonstration seems to have been essential for the students' ultimate victory, so also it is hard to see how the students—whose efforts were waning when victory came—could have succeeded without this dramatic demonstration of public support.

It is true that then, as later in the history of the Civic Interest Group, the students have tended to act autonomously of the established leadership in the community, even when, as in this instance, its assistance was so important in their victory. This has tended to exasperate adult leaders, especially in the Baltimore NAACP and Urban League, who felt that the students have lacked appreciation for their help and guidance.

Yet fundamentally it was, after all, the students' victory. This was so in their eyes, and it was so in the eyes of the public. They were the heroes, for they were the ones who had picketed for hours, they were the ones who had run the risk of being arrested, and they were the ones who had pointed the way to the community. Hutzler's in a statement to the public gave credit to the students for calling attention to the situation and for accomplishing what the stores themselves had not been able to do. As the students' lawyer said, "They were way ahead of me. If they had followed me, we would still be in court arguing the case on a demurrer."

In short, by dramatizing the issue, the student demonstrations had harnessed both the Negro community's desire for change and the white public's readiness for it. Certainly in Baltimore, as elsewhere, the students' action speeded up spectacularly the whole process of change in the pattern of race relations.

Notes

1. Probably the only earlier instance that spring of a change in store policies due to student sit-in activity was at Galveston on April 5. There were of course earlier instances of successful sit-ins by school youth, as in the case of the activities of the Oklahoma City NAACP youth councils in 1959.
2. The following account is baed chiefly on information obtained as a result of being a participant-observer in the student sit-in movement in Baltimore, and from interviews with store officials and leaders in intergroup relations agencies.
3. Many of the business firms involved were reluctant to change their policies, and economic interest was often an important factor in their shift of policy. Thus the downtown movie houses and one of the restaurants were compelled to alter their practices by the changing character of the neighborhoods in which they did their business, while the major hotels were influenced by the growing number of groups who would hold conventions only at integrated hotels.

    For an excellent summary of most of the changes discussed in the preceding paragraphs see *Toward Equality: Baltimore's Progress Report* (Baltimore: The Sidney Hollander Foundation, 1960). Also helpful were the annual reports of the Governor's Commission and a number of interviews.
4. In general the higher police officials have acted fairly throughout the year and a half during which the demonstrations have been going on, though there have been instances of discriminatory actions by individual policemen. For the most part also the city magistrates proved impartial, and in some cases were in obvious

sympathy with the student demonstrators. During the summer of 1960 one magistrate actually expressed disappointment that he did not get the opportunity to dismiss charges against one student, because, before he could even hear the case, the student's lawyer had requested that the case be transferred to a state court.

5. While much of the drop in trade in the store was due to the loss of Negro customers, the drop in restaurant business was probably due to whites staying away in order to avoid what seemed to them to be possible unpleasant incidents.

6. It would be hard to say how much business the discriminating stores actually lost, especially as the period covered by the downtown demonstrations was relatively short. The Baltimore *Afro-American* on April 16 (the day before the department stores all gave in), citing Federal Reserve figures, stated that there was an 8 percent decline in department store business as compared with the same period in 1959. The downtown department stores all denied that there had been any significant change in their trade, however.

7. This store, however, did suffer a temporary drop in its restaurant patronage.

8. The Baltimore *Afro-American* on two or three occasions stressed—in very general terms—the contribution of white ministers, though I did not happen to find out about this in the course of my own research.

NINE

The Black Muslims

IN THE INTRODUCTION there is a discussion of how I came to debate Malcolm X at Morgan State College in late March 1962.

Although the debate was not recorded, my presentation was the basis of an essay entitled "The Black Muslims" which, at the suggestion of Bayard Rustin, was published in the pacifist journal *Liberation*. This version of my interpretation of the Black Muslims is presented below.

For a journalist's description of the debate, see Baltimore *Afro-American*, March 31, 1962.

PERHAPS THE MOST impressive development in the years since the Second World War has been the movement toward independence and freedom on the part of colored peoples throughout the world. In Africa and in Asia, darker-skinned peoples have successfully thrown off the rule of white men, obtained recognition of their dignity as human beings, and achieved influence in the councils of the world. Part of this larger movement for freedom and dignity has been the stirrings among American Negroes. Most notable have been the nonviolent direct-action demonstrations, such as sit-ins and Freedom Rides on the one hand, and the various nationalistic movements, of which the Black Muslims are the most important, on the other.

There are, in fact, notable similarities between the Black Muslims and the nonviolent direct-action movement. Essentially, the aim of both movements was summed up by the student demonstrators in Baltimore, during the early months of 1960, who, as they picketed, would chant, "We walk for human dignity." Both movements are manifestations of a rejection of white doctrines of Negro inferiority, and of white policies of discrimination. Both reflect the new self-image of American Negroes, arising out of the emergence of the independent states of Africa. Both exhibit dissatisfaction with the traditional Christianity of the Negro masses. The Black Muslims claim that they reject Christianity entirely (though actually their brand of Islam is significantly influenced by Christian organization and doctrine), while the nonviolent demonstrators reject the old-fashioned, "pie-in-the-sky" kind of Christianity which accepted the racial status quo and promised rewards for the meek in heaven.

From *Liberation* 8 (April 1963): 9–13.

Both thus insist upon changes in the pattern of American race relations, and insist that they be made at once; both preach what appears to most white people to be a revolutionary resistance to the old order of race relations; both indicate that Negroes will no longer tolerate a subordinate position in the American social order, that gradualism in race relations must go.

Though most American Negroes would not agree with the program of Elijah Muhammad, the leader of the Black Muslims, it is important to point out that most of them would agree with his indictment of the American race system:

My people, the so-called American Negroes, have long been the victims of attacks by their slavemasters. . . . America tells the Negro he is an equal citizen, but America denies him justice. The so-called Negro has been declared an equal citizen. Where is this equal citizenship? It is only in words! It has not been in deeds! . . . The United States Constitution declares equal justice for all. This equal justice is never practiced on the so-called Negro.

Thus the difference between the Black Muslims and other Negroes lies not in the Muslim criticism of the prejudice and discrimination practiced by American whites and of American hypocrisy in regard to the treatment of Negroes. Rather, the difference lies in their proposed solutions to the problem. Most Negroes hope that integration and constitutional rights can be achieved, that Negroes will be accepted as fellow citizens without discrimination. The Black Muslims do not believe that this is possible. In a nutshell, most Negroes still have faith in the American white man; the Black Muslims do not.

And the Black Muslims can cite impressive evidence to back up their belief on this score. Pointing to cases of discrimination, violence, and police brutality, they claim that the white American will never live up to his democratic ideology in regard to the Negro. Those whites who appear to favor integration are worse than open segregationists, for the white liberals are hypocrites; they are like foxes who are trying to deceive the Negro by holding out the promise of integration. Says Elijah Muhammad:

There is no security for even one black life in America. What chance have we against well-armed devils who are free to use their arms on the poor unarmed black people? This country's police force, using the tactics of brute savages, have behind them the government to kill us.

And again:

The evil slavemasters know that they can never sincerely accept their slaves as their equals. In fact this is against the very nature of the white race; they were not created to accept the black man as their equal. . . . There are none who are actually seeking justice for the so-called Negroes but Allah and myself, His Servant. It makes me ashamed to read and hear over the radio, and to see my people on the TV in Washington praying and begging the same murderer for justice. . . . If they would only accept their own god and religion [Islam] and follow me, they would enjoy Freedom, Justice and Equality at once. . . . Though the government of America claims you are free, she is still the greatest hindrance to your exercising the freedom that she claims you have.

So profound is this distrust of the white man that observers have concluded that the Black Muslims actually preach hatred of the whites, though the movement's leaders deny this. One authority (C. Eric Lincoln, *The Black Muslim in America* [Beacon Press, 1961]) has written of their "consuming and potentially violent racial and religious hatred. . . . They find no mandate except that of temporary expediency, for peace and submission between whites and blacks." In their literature the white race is described as "the human beast—the serpent, the dragon, the devil, and Satan." A play written by one of the Black Muslim ministers charges the white man with being the greatest liar on earth, the greatest drunkard on earth, the greatest gambler on earth, the greatest robber on earth, the greatest deceiver on earth, the greatest troublemaker on earth. And since it was white men who robbed Negroes of their freedom and made them slaves, since it was white men who spawned a numerous mixed blood progeny out of adultery with Negro slaves, since white people have talked of democracy and equal rights while denying these things to 10 percent of our population, and since whites to this day keep Negroes in second-class citizenship, these charges contain a core of truth that gives the Black Muslims a potent appeal.

As we have noted, according to the Black Muslims even white liberals cannot be trusted. As they say, "The Caucasians are great deceivers. Their nature is against friendship with black people, although they often fool the black people . . . claiming they are sincere friends." Northern whites, say the Black Muslims, are concerned about race relations in the South only because maltreatment of Negroes is bad for international relations. After all, says Malcolm X, one of the movement's chief spokesmen, American society is like a ship on which whites kept Negroes on the lowest decks until their ship was sinking; now why should Negroes want to integrate with whites when whites are going to drown anyway?

Fundamentally, the Black Muslims claim that the two races can never get along together, and they insist therefore upon the separation of the races as the only solution to the problem. Associated with this idea of separation is the belief that black men need race unity and race cooperation more than anything else, and that along with this they need a vigorous racial pride. In instilling this racial pride, and in giving the American Negroes a sense of identity and self-respect, they glorify the African background of American Negroes, and identify this African background with a rather unorthodox type of Islam. The founder of the Black Muslims, W. D. Fard, is regarded as the incarnation of Allah, sent to lead the persecuted American Negroes out of their bondage, and the present leader, Elijah Muhammad, has the title of "The Messenger of Allah." Actually Islam did not penetrate to the areas from which most of the New World Negroes came. But the achievements of the racially mixed ancient Egyptians, and the great Negro Muslim kingdoms of West Africa in the Middle Ages—most notably Ghana, Mali and Songhai—form the basis for a historical tradition, which is supplemented by the belief that all the colored peoples of the world can be classed as black men.

WHAT ARE the precise goals of the Black Muslims? For purposes of analysis we may divide their ideology into two parts—the extreme views and utopian ideals on the one hand, and their more immediate program on the other. Now the most extreme views of the Muslims are not always stated, and are at times denied. It can be said, however, that they assert the physical and moral inferiority of the white men, and the divinity and superiority of the black men. The Black Muslims hold that the six thousand years of white domination of the world is about to come to an end, and that Allah is about to usher in a struggle between the forces of good and evil which will eventuate in the destruction of the white race and the ascendancy of the black race. This Armageddon will result in a this-worldly utopia for black men—for the Black Muslims do not believe in a future life but assert that heaven and hell are right here on earth. As a song by Minister Louis X of Boston puts it, "A white man's heaven is a black man's hell." Allah, it is anticipated, will soon reverse this situation.

The Black Muslims' more immediate program stresses four chief elements: a plea for greater race unity and race pride; an advocacy of Islam as opposed to Christianity; an economic and moral program composed of a puritanical sexual code, thrift, industry and economic accumulation designed to build up Negro businesses, so that Negroes can obtain employment and services in their own establishments rather than seek these things from whites; and political separatism, or the creation of an independent all-Negro state out of land obtained from the United States government. Says Elijah Muhammad:

We must have some of this earth that we can call our own. We have lost 400 years making our slavemasters rich, powerful and independent. . . . Would you not like to live in peace and be recognized and treated as brother-citizens by your own people, in your own country, rather than to be unrecognized and treated like a "dog" by others than your own kind and country? Allah wants to give you, the so-called Negroes, the best and most permanent home the earth has to offer. . . . We must have some of this earth that we can call our own for a permanent home.

Exactly where this territory is to be the Black Muslims fail to state, and needless to say, it is unlikely that they will obtain it.

Thus though the eschatological prediction of the doom of the white race, and the Utopian vision of a separate territory of their own form an important part of the emotional appeal made by the Black Muslims, their actual practical program is centered upon the economic and moral uplift of their members. This they do by giving their members a sense of identity and self-respect through an appeal to the race's glorious past and a prediction of an equally glorious future, by stressing a high degree of morality, and by supplying some sort of half-way practical answer to the economic problems of the Negro masses. (I say it is a half-way practical answer because the major credit and industrial facilities are in the hands of white corporations, so the quickest and only realistic way of advancing the Negro masses economically is through breaking down the walls of discrimination in employment.) In fact, the movement is known for the number of former criminals who have joined it, have been reformed, and now lead respectable lives.

THOUGH IT IS FEARED that the Black Muslims preach racial violence and revolution, there is no direct evidence to support this. Those who have studied the movement most closely are not in entire agreement on this matter. It is agreed that the Muslims direct their members not to start fights, but that they are urged to resist when attacked. One observer reports that when leaving religious services they are told, "Never be the aggressor; but if the wolf should bite you on the jaw, do not turn the other jaw. Show the wolf that you also have teeth and that you can do battle." One careful student of the movement (E. U. Essien-Udom, *Black Nationalism: The Search for an Identity in America* [University of Chicago Press, 1962]) in fact concludes that the eschatological aspects of the Black Muslim ideology, with its assertion that Allah will miraculously destroy the

white race, actually mitigate the movement's violent and revolutionary potential; that the Black Muslims actually accommodate to
the realities of the white-Negro power relations in the United States
by preaching that Allah will bring about the solution to the Negro's
problems in his own way. However, I feel that implicit in the movement's ideology is a strain of violence and hatred that, given the
right conditions, could easily flower into a significant revolutionary
force, though at present this eventuality seems quite unlikely.

Now why is it that this movement has risen to prominence at this
time? It is of course not the first important nationalistic movement
to have arisen among American Negroes. The Garvey Movement of
the 1920s is simply the most famous of these Negro nationalistic
movements, which go back as far as the eighteenth century. In fact
most of the ideas of the Black Muslims have in one form or another
been held by substantial numbers of American Negroes in the past,
though the particular synthesis they have made is quite unique. But
still the thoughtful observer might well ask why it is that, in a
period when so much progress has been made toward improving
race relations as in the last fifteen years, when conditions for Negroes appear to be better than ever before, such a movement should
thrive. As a matter of fact, the movement, which was founded in
1930, remained small until well after the Second World War; indeed
its chief growth has been from the period since 1954—since, in fact,
the very year of the famous Supreme Court decision on desegregation in the public schools.

For one thing, the advances that have been made in race relations
since the Second World War have caused a revolution in aspirations
among American Negroes. They no longer feel that they have to accept the humiliations of second-class citizenship, and consequently
these humiliations—somewhat fewer though they now are—appear to be more intolerable than ever. And in spite of Supreme
Court decisions, Fair Employment Practices Laws and all the rest,
the pace of change has been disappointingly slow. Thus there is
considerable disillusionment among American Negroes. The sit-in
movement and the Freedom Rides have been an expression of this
impatience among the great rank and file of Negroes. Second, as
mentioned earlier, the rise of colored nations—especially African
nations—to independence has had a profound effect upon the self-
image of American Negroes. If Africans can obtain their freedom,
why should not Afro-Americans have theirs?

Third, an important clue to the phenomenal rise of the Black
Muslims is to be found in the fact that their appeal has been almost
entirely to the very poorest Negroes, in the lowest paid occupa-

tions, many of whom are in fact unemployed, to Negroes living in the over-crowded urban slums and unable to escape to better neighborhoods as the middle-class Negroes do. For these peoples the conditions of life have been growing not better, but worse, in the last eight or ten years. At the very time that the Negroes' aspirations have risen, their situation has deteriorated.

Let us cite some concrete figures to illustrate this. In 1952 the average Negro family's income was 57 percent of the average white family's income; ten years later, despite improvements in race relations, and despite the highly publicized occupational breakthroughs of a minority of Negroes, the average income of Negro families has fallen to 54 percent of the average income of white families. Meanwhile the unemployment rate has increased; and in fact the first real spurt in the membership rolls of the Black Muslims seems to have dated from the first postwar recession, that of 1954. Negro unemployment has been growing constantly since 1958, for unlike whites, Negroes do not recover any of the losses made during recessions. Negro unemployment is now two and a half times that of whites. In some major cities the figures are even more striking. In Chicago, with a total unemployment rate of 5.7 percent, 17.3 percent of the Negroes are jobless; and one-quarter of that city's Negroes are on relief. In Detroit 60 percent of the unemployed workers are Negroes, though only 20 percent of the city's inhabitants are Negroes. In Philadelphia the general unemployment rate is 7 percent, while Negro unemployment is 28 percent; in Gary, Indiana, the community as a whole has an unemployment rate of 6.3 percent, while the city's Negroes have one of 44 percent. According to official A.F.L.-C.I.O. statistics, the over-all rate of unemployment of Negroes is 20 percent, which is higher than the rate of general unemployment during the depression.

Negroes, last to be hired and first to be fired, and for the most part confined to semiskilled and unskilled jobs, are bearing the brunt of the technological unemployment caused by automation. Elijah Muhammad indicated his awareness of this fact when he said:

It is beyond a shadow of doubt that America has no future for the so-called Negroes other than being subjected people. Though she has no labor for the so-called Negroes today that she cannot do for herself with modern machinery, she refuses to allow them to go for self.

THE GREAT MASS of lower-class Negroes thus find the American dream further from reality than ever. Rejected by the dominant whites, and pretty much ignored by middle- and upper-class Negro leadership (and the Black Muslim leaders express nothing but scorn for Negro leaders like those in the National Association for the Advancement of Colored People, whom they regard as toadying to white people), the frustrated Negro masses are ripe for the message of the Black Muslims. For those who are willing to submit to the severe discipline of the Black Muslim movement, this organization serves as a way out. It does this because it gives an identity and a sense of purpose and destiny, a self-respect and a feeling of hope, for its members. In short, then, Black Muslims appeal to those whom integration and the advances of recent years have passed by. To them the Black Muslims have a program that makes sense, for it offers them four things: an explanation of their plight (white devils); a sense of pride and self-esteem (black superiority); a vision of a glorious future (black ascendancy); and a practical immediate program of uplift (working hard and joining together to create Negro enterprise and prosperity).

It is important to note, however, that the ideology and program of the Black Muslims are shot through with paradoxes. In the first place, they exhibit the same sort of prejudices for which they so justly criticize whites. They assume that all whites are bad; and the stereotyped image which the prejudiced have of Negroes is the very image of whites which the Muslims are projecting—that whites are inferior beings, lazy, sexually immoral, dirty and criminal. Second, in their emphasis on thrift, hard work, economic accumulation, and Puritan morality, they seem to be trying to make Negroes over into the old-fashioned middle-class American image. In this, of course, they are imitating not only white middle-class virtues, but also the Negro middle class which they attack so much. They are indeed attacking the lower-class way of life of the very group to which they appeal—and their appeal lies in the very fact that they offer a route of upward mobility, a road to respectability, for people who would otherwise have no hope of improving themselves. Thus, as Essien-Udom suggests, the Black Muslims are as much anti-Negro-lower-class values, and anti-Negro-middle-class complacency and opportunism as they are anti-white injustice. In the third place, the faith of the Black Muslims is racially exclusive, though orthodox Islam preaches brotherhood and equality of all races. There are a number of similarities between the Black Muslim doctrines and Christianity. Like the Black Muslims, the early Christians appealed to the poor and the downtrodden, and they did this by giving them a sense of dignity and self-respect. Both the Christian and Black Muslim eschatologies paint a future of bliss for their righteous followers, and punishment for the wicked who are their oppressors. Both stress righteousness and justice, and both protest against oppression.

Both believe that God was incarnate in a man, the founder of the faith—and in this and other ways W. D. Fard is comparable to Jesus. Both the Christians and the Black Muslims appear to be intolerant of other faiths. And both white Christians and Black Muslims have perverted their religious doctrines to justify racial hatred.

There are paradoxes involved also in the Muslims' espousal of race pride. First, by stressing the Arabic language and Islam, the Black Muslims unintentionally seem to agree with whites who have incorrectly held that the culture of the Negro societies of Ashanti, Dahomey, Yoruba and related peoples—who were the chief sources of New World Negroes—were negligible and inferior. Second, the Black Muslims have attacked Martin Luther King, CORE and the student demonstrators as lacking in self-respect because they want integration—because, as the Black Muslims put it, they are begging to eat and sit in the white man's places rather than building their own. Psychologists have found that people who hate others—as do the white supremacists and the Black Muslims—are the ones who, subconsciously, really feel inferior and actually hate themselves, and therefore need a scapegoat on which to vent their frustrations. Only people with pride and confidence in themselves could display the courage of the nonviolent demonstrators, who have risked jail and even death, instead of being like the Black Muslims, who retreat into their own separate world.

In view of the situation in which lower-class Negroes find themselves, the wonder is not that the Black Muslim movement has grown so much, but that it has not grown far more. The severe discipline and ascetic code of the movement undoubtedly discourage many sympathizers from becoming members. But more important is the fact that fundamentally what most American Negroes want are their full rights as American citizens; that is, though they are forced to think of themselves as a disadvantaged minority group, in part the failure of the Black Muslims to attract larger numbers of people is due to the quest of the masses of Negroes for identification with the larger American society. Even among the Negro lower classes, the dream of full participation in the promise of American life remains a pervasive influence.

I DO NOT MEAN to suggest that the Black Muslim movement does not have a great potential for further growth. Current estimates of its membership range from fifty thousand to a half million; probably the lower figure is more nearly correct, though the true numbers are a closely guarded secret. But the actual influence—and potential influence—of the Black Muslims is several times greater than this, both because the Muslims have many sympathizers in the Negro community, and because they are extremely well organized. While the movement's leaders thus far have discouraged their members from voting, it is not at all unlikely that they could wield an important—and in some cases a decisive—political influence in the major urban areas in the near future. In large part the future influence of the movement depends upon the actions of white Americans. If the slow pace of change in race relations continues and more Negroes become disillusioned, and particularly if something drastic is not done—and soon—to reverse the unemployment rate and improve the economic opportunities for Negroes, it is quite possible that it could become a mass movement that could create serious problems for American whites. Moreover, it is not too difficult to conceive of a combination of international circumstances that could give the movement a very real revolutionary potential. The crux of the situation, it seems to me, lies in the challenge Elijah Muhammad and Malcolm X have hurled at the white people of America, when they charge them with being hypocrites mouthing the language of freedom and equal rights, while according Negroes an inferior place in the American social order. The relatively slow pace of change in race relations, the continued economic deprivation and oppression of the great masses of Negroes, the slowdown on school desegregation, the resistance to Negro voter registration in the South, the frequency of police brutality, the reluctance to employ Negroes in skilled labor, white-collar and managerial positions (even on the part of some individuals well known for their interest in integrating Negroes into American society), the flight of whites from neighborhoods when a Negro family moves in, all support the contention of the Black Muslims that basically Americans do not want to accord equal rights to Negroes, that white Americans do not want to recognize the Negro's essential manhood and citizenship, but are being forced into making grudging changes only because of the pressure of international public opinion and the exigencies of United States foreign policy. And unfortunately it cannot be denied that much of the improvement in race relations over the past fifteen years has been for just this reason. The only way to meet the challenge posed by the Black Muslims and the possible danger they may pose to American society in the future is to show that white Americans really mean what they say when they talk about freedom and the democratic way of life by taking prompt and effective action to end segregation and discrimination at once. Even more than the student demonstrators and the Freedom Riders the Black Muslims have a message for white America—and that message is that not only discrimination but also gradualism in race relations must vanish.

TEN

Case Study in Nonviolent Direct Action

THE NORTHWOOD THEATER demonstrations of the early spring of 1962 brought the student nonviolent direct-action movement in Baltimore to its climax. The theater was the last bastion of exclusion at the shopping center virtually across the street from the college. Its owner's determined resistance led to the largest and most militant demonstrations in the history of Morgan State's Civic Interest Group.

The following account was written with Thomas Plaut, a young white journalist close to the events, and Curtis Smothers, vice chair of Morgan's student government and an active leader in the demonstrations.

For me, this campaign was perhaps the most important and certainly the most intense experience I had during my years of activism in the nonviolent direct-action era of black protest. This article, of course, is written from a more detached perspective than one composed as a personal reminiscence would be. Accordingly I have appended after the essay an extended note on my own personal experience.

IN LATE FEBRUARY 1963, a mass student demonstration forced a suburban movie theater in northeastern Baltimore, Maryland, to open its door to Negro customers.

The demonstration's significance lies not only on the lowering of a racial barrier, but also in indications that the process of integration could be expedited by disrupting civil authority and the normal operations of the city's police, court, and penal facilities.

The demonstration provided Baltimore with the following score card. In six days some 1,500 people picketed the theater and 413 were arrested. A municipal court was daily flooded well beyond capacity. The imposition of high bails on arrested demonstrators failed to discourage others from seeking arrest with the result that police and detention centers had difficulty handling the load. The women's section of the City Jail was overcrowded beyond effective operation. When public concern won jailed students their textbooks, extra milk, and other privileges, the regular inmates organized a sit-down strike in protest. City officials, above all Mayor

From *The Crisis* 71 (November 1964): 573–78 (with Thomas Plaut and Curtis Smothers).

Philip H. Goodman, who was facing a primary election in which his candidacy was strongly contested, felt sufficient pressure to become involved. When integration leaders refused to compromise with the owners, the mayor announced the theater's capitulation. The events which led him to take a strong hand in an emotional issue whose outcome was contrary to many of his constituents' beliefs seems well worth consideration.

For eight years before the final demonstrations that brought integration, the Northwood Theater had been sporadically picketed, primarily by students from Morgan State College, a predominantly Negro institution a few blocks away. During that time, the Morgan students formed the "Civic Interest Group" which organized demonstrations that forced the integration of all facilities except a tavern and the theater at the Northwood shopping center as well as other public accommodations throughout Baltimore city. However, the only movie theater within walking distance of the campus remained segregated.

Plans Formed

On February 4, student government and CIG leaders met in Morgan's student government office. In the course of an hour, they decided that mass picketing alone would be ineffectual without accompanying mass arrests, a technique which had been effective in desegregation campaigns in the Deep South.

It was decided that the basis for arrests would be the Maryland trespass law, originally enacted in 1878 for farmers to keep hunters off their lands. In recent years, the law has provided the legal method for keeping places of public accommodation segregated. Basically, it states the owner's right to admit only those persons he wants. Consequently, only those white and Negro students who were to attempt to gain entrance to the theater were to be arrested, while others would be free to draw public interest by picketing.

The biggest problem facing the demonstration's organizers was creating sufficient interest within the student body to form a mass movement. Several hundred picketeers were needed as well as fifty to one hundred volunteers for arrest.

The answer, they decided, was to enlist the most popular elements of the student body for the first arrests—from the president of the student council to Miss Morgan of 1963. This struggle for equal rights was probably the first in history organized along the lines of a pep rally before a football game.

On Friday, February 15, while some fifty students marched with picket signs in front of the theater, Miss Morgan and twenty-five other students were escorted from the theater lobby to a paddy wagon and a precinct station for the night. At the hearing the following morning, they requested jury trials and were released on their own recognizance by Municipal Court Judge Joseph P. Finnerty, who advised the students that it was best for them to stick to their studies.

The pep rally tactics began to pay off. The demonstration rapidly grew and more arrests followed. By Monday, Judge Finnerty had faced sixty-seven student defendants in his courtroom.

That afternoon a mass meeting at Morgan gathered an audience of more than five hundred students. A week before a similar meeting was attended by only thirty members of a student body of 2,600. The second mass meeting crystalized the demonstration into an effective movement. The chairman of the CIG Adult Assistance Committee, Reverend Marion C. Bascom, urged his audience to fill the jails, "to follow Gandhi's example and go down to the sea and make salt."

Monday night 151 persons were arrested. Such a large number of arrests had not been possible on previous days, CIG leaders explained, because the assistance committee, which was responsible for raising bail money, had not endorsed the policy of mass arrests.

Officials Alarmed

On that same evening, city officials became sufficiently alarmed to start planning their own strategy. A curious meeting of prosecuting police officers and municipal judges was held in the northeastern precinct station. The judges, including Finnerty, declined to tell inquiring newspaper reporters what they were doing there while ranking police officers issued the following statement: "On the advice of the State Attorney-General, due to the large scale of the demonstrations, both charges of disorderly conduct and trespassing will be placed against the arrested students, and it is not necessary to obtain warrants." The next day a defense attorney for CIG was told by Baltimore's chief prosecuting officer that a charge of conspiracy might be placed against a Morgan College professor who had acted as an adviser to the student group.

When the 151 arrested demonstrators requested jury trials on Tuesday morning, they found the charge of disorderly conduct carried a bail of $500, in addition to $100 for trespassing. Total bail that morning was $90,200. "The time has come when I must do something to conserve the peace," Judge Finnerty said.

But the demonstration only continued to grow. Tuesday night Morgan students were joined by white and Negro demonstrators from other colleges, notably Johns Hopkins University and Goucher College. There were 120 arrests bringing the demonstration's total to nearly 350.

As the demonstrations continued to grow, so did the apprehensiveness of city and judicial officials. On Tuesday, Mayor Goodman, with primary election day just two weeks away, offered to mediate the dispute. And the next morning a Negro member of the legislature reported Judge Finnerty had asked her to speak to the governor "and get me off the hot seat."

Wednesday afternoon representatives of the theater, CIG, city, and state met in the mayor's office. Theater representatives said they would agree to discuss integrating their business establishment in five weeks time if the demonstrations were called off immediately. The offer was turned down, and that evening seventy-four more students were arrested while a picket line of 500 students and several professors marched under the glare of television camera lights in front of the theater. The picket line was large enough to draw crowds of shoppers containing many Negroes who cheered the demonstration. Newsmen walking through the crowd heard observers say "We've got to stand up for our rights," or "If you want something, you've got to fight for it." Some brought coffee to the marchers. A few put their parcels down in the middle of the oval of picketeers and joined the line. A type of demonstration usually avoided by Baltimore's public had become contagious.

However the growing strength of the movement was unknown to several hundred students locked in jail. A lack of communication between the ins and the outs, and the unforeseen shock of jail living, especially on the women crowded six and seven to a cell, caused a breakdown in morale, which nearly resulted in the collapse of the demonstration.

Mass Arrests

The announced plans for the mass arrests included the assumption that all those arrested would be bailed out, having served the purpose of calling public attention to the demonstration. The idea of placing additional pressure on the city administration by packing the city jail had not occurred to CIG leaders. They realized it only when the $90,200 bail for those arrested Monday night could not be immediately raised; thus, the jail-packing plan became operational quite by accident.

Consequently, the arrested students who were sent to the city jail on Tuesday following their arraignment in the northeastern court felt lost. With no rhyme or reason to give them purpose, they began to falter when faced with the realities of life in a large jail, an experience for which they were not prepared.

The prisoners received no word from CIG leaders their first afternoon in jail, when the men were herded nude through admission processes and the women were forced to wash their hair with lye soap. They were visited only by a defense attorney who, somewhat stunned by the high bail and his large number of clients in jail, was apprehensive and asked if the demonstrators had not bitten off more than they could swallow.

There were no CIG leaders in jail. They had been arrested in the first two days of the demonstration and had been released. They were "outside." Those inside felt very much alone. Members of this group later reported that by Wednesday morning a "feeling of being used by CIG leaders" became predominant. Many, especially among the women, wanted out.

By late Wednesday night, when the demonstration attained its peak, 74 women students in the city jail had signed a bail-out list for Thursday. CIG leaders informed them of their jail-packing value on that morning, barely preventing a bail-out that might well have snapped the spine of the Goliath they had created.

The CIG leadership by Tuesday began to be torn by strategy disagreements which prevented it from realizing the amount of pressure it had placed on the city jail.

Sunday, the college's president had informed CIG's adult adviser that he would be dismissed if the governor asked the president to fire him.

Monday, the Morgan administration had suggested that students involved in the demonstration might be subject to disciplinary action on campus.

On Tuesday, with the $90,200 bail yet to be raised, a city administration offer to release all those arrested without bail was approved by the CIG's executive council by a five-to-four vote. The offer was rejected only after the council's chairman disqualified four of the five votes favoring the compromise.

But late Tuesday night Reverend Bascom announced the bail had been raised, and the following morning the CIG was encouraged to hear public denunciation of "the high and punitive" bails set on the students.

Encouragement Bolstered

Their encouragement was bolstered that afternoon at the conciliation meeting in Mayor Goodman's office when Morgan College president Martin D. Jenkins said the only solution to the matter would be the integration of the theater and withdrawal of charges against his students. He went on to say that if the theater was not integrated promptly, "there will be 2,400 students in jail by Monday morning."

Mayor Goodman is reported to have told those present at the meeting that the demonstration was not only embarrassing the city, but reactivating his ulcers as well.

The meeting served to show the CIG its own strength. In rejecting a new compromise calling for the release of the students and a five-week cooling-off period before negotiations with theater representatives, the importance of the overcrowding in the city jail became apparent.

Following the meeting, CIG leaders were briefed on the critical morale situation in the jail and decided that some of them should be rearrested that night so that they could organize and keep the jailed students in jail.

They did not, however, realize that they had already won the integration battle by rejecting the second offer. In offering to negotiate, the theater had compromised as far as possible without capitulating.

Mayor Goodman was faced with an increasing number of reasons for stopping the demonstration as soon as possible. Baltimore was receiving unfavorable news coverage on a wide scale. He must have been informed by jail authorities of the growing unrest in the city jail of the regular inmates who resented the "coddling" of the students. On Tuesday, these prisoners had threatened a sit-down strike.

On Thursday, both the male and female regular inmates announced a time for their strike—6:00 P.M.

Jail officials, still smarting from embarrassment caused to their institution by a recent mass escape which had resulted in the warden's suspension for thirty days, felt they were now faced with a situation which could explode into violence. "This place is a powder keg," one prison official confided to a reporter.

The mayor now found himself faced with an ugly time limit. The CIG was stronger than ever and seemingly unwilling to compromise. The theater management was under fire from surrounding businesses who, being integrated themselves, saw bigotry turning their regular customers to other shopping areas.

At 1:30 P.M., the mayor appeared on the steps of city hall to announce that the theater would open its doors to Negroes the following day if the demonstration was called off immediately.

But the city's prosecuting attorney and Municipal Court judges, having cut the bail from $600 to $200, now balked at the CIG's insistence that the mayor had promised the jailed students would be released on their own recognizance.

By 3:00 P.M. the president of the jail's board of directors began to aid CIG efforts to eliminate the bail. The group worked its way up the judicial ladder and finally, at 4:30 P.M., a member of the Baltimore Supreme Bench agreed to drop the bail.

The arrested demonstrators began to emerge from the jail shortly after 6:00 P.M.

Theater management later appeared on television to say it was happy to join the ranks of progressive businessmen in northeastern Baltimore.

Two weeks later a grand jury dismissed all charges against the demonstrators. And Mayor Goodman won his primary.

Endnote

By 1963 the Northwood Theater was, after perhaps eight years of demonstrations, the last item on the agenda for desegregating the Northwood shopping center. The fall and winter of 1962–1963 had been a period when there was an ebb in direct action generally across the country, and the small nucleus of students who formed the active core of the Civic Interest Group were discouraged by the apathy of most of Morgan's student body. There were complaints that other students had even poked fun at CIG activity. (My response to this was that it was probably not such a bad thing—that the students poking fun, rather than revealing apathy, actually felt uncomfortable about their failure to join our demonstrations and could perhaps be mobilized to action.)

The whole situation was thrashed out at a small meeting early in the year before the Birmingham demonstrations, as we discussed various options for attacking the theater situation. In the course of our discussion occurred the one time I recommended a strategy in which I myself would not participate. I called attention to how in Louisville (one of the cities where Herbert Hill helped me to secure entree in 1963), Frank Stanley, Jr., son of the publisher of the Louisville *Defender,* had in 1962 led the black youth of the city in massive demonstrations at numerous restaurants, in which the participants refused to move at police orders. They were arrested in droves for disorderly conduct, and so dramatized the problem that the restaurants in that border city had capitulated. I suggested that a similar strategy might work for us. When the question was raised as to how we could possibly mobilize the student body for such a large-scale demonstration, I suggested use of the tactics described in the article.

Having agreed on a course of action, we approached the leadership of the student government, asking the president to act as chair of CIG, while our regular chair, Clarence Logan, was detailed to exploit contacts he had built over the years with the media. He was very knowledgeable about such matters as, for example, the importance of having arrests occur before 8:00 or 9:00 P.M. if they were to receive attention in the late news broadcasts or in the daily newspaper next morning.

What happened was something beyond my original expectations. Ultimately, it seemed as if every group on the campus found that it had to get involved, and the kinds of students who had tended not to be involved before—most notably fraternity and sorority members and athletes—joined in the demonstrations, prepared to go to jail. I got to understand something of the dynamics involved when observing some of my own students being hauled off in paddy wagons, I felt a strong tug within me urging me to join them. I recall, one night, as hundreds were picketing and singing songs on the sidewalk, I sat with a black faculty friend of mine in a nearby ice cream parlor, and let him talk me out of joining them.

The first nights the arrests were few, and we bailed people out. But after a couple of days we found ourselves without bail money, and Rev. Marion Bascom and his colleagues were hard put to obtain the money. At least one approach was even made to "Little Willie" Adams through a close associate of his, but the response was negative. Trying another possible source of assistance I called the head of the Baltimore Urban League, but instead of providing behind the scenes help as he had done in 1960, he started to argue with me about the CIG moving in on his territory when they attacked job discrimination! (For pretty obvious reasons I guess, no effort was made to obtain help from the treasury of the Baltimore branch of the NAACP. In other cities NAACP branches had provided indispensable help for arrested students, Louisville being a good example.) Meanwhile President Jenkins had been his usual quiet self.

But as the arrests continued to mount Jenkins grew alarmed,

especially I suppose because the school's budget for the next biennium was about to come before the legislature. At any rate it was Sunday morning, when he called me at 7:30 A.M., and asked if I was "the one advising the students," and when I conceded that I was he directed me to be at his home at 9:00 A.M. When I arrived, Jenkins was in his lounging robe, and his brown face was bright red. Although I admitted that I had suggested the strategy, when he asked that the whole campaign be called off, I said the matter was now in the students' hands, and there was nothing I could do. Threatened with possible dismissal, I recall feeling less angry than sad—I guessed he may have been fearful that a political backlash would damage his own position as president, if not destroy what he had built. In any event, as I was leaving, I told him I thought I would go to Washington and consult with the staff of the American Association of University Professors and he agreed that would be a good idea. Monday, the student leaders, deeply concerned about what might happen to me, insisted that I resign as adult adviser.

I do not suppose that Jenkins ever actually learned of this decision on the part of the students. In any event I found myself summoned along with the student leaders to a meeting at President Jenkins's office that afternoon. Attending also were a few of the college's chief administrators. As usual at CIG meetings I was prepared with pen and paper to take minutes, but Jenkins peremptorily forbade me from doing this (as he later said he did not want to find himself quoted in some learned article). He expressed his disapproval of our strategy and indicated that if the demonstrations continued he might have to expel the leaders. The dean of the college seemed, by virtue of his silence, to support the president, but Thelma Bando, dean of women, to our surprise forcefully backed the demonstrations. For their part the student leaders were very forthright in their response to Jenkins and made it clear that a halt to the demonstrations was inconceivable. As usual at CIG meetings I said nothing, and with the students having things very well in hand, I excused myself in order to meet with a class that had been waiting for me.

On Tuesday morning I was in Washington to talk with officials of the AAUP. They felt the fact that I had told Jenkins I would see them indicated an unusual degree of rapport between the two of us. In effect the AAUP executive secretary agreed with the students, and advised that it would probably be advisable for me to drop out. But by the time I returned to campus late that afternoon it was quite clear to me that the only course of action I could take would be to continue working with the students.

By then we had ceased meeting at the student government offices and moved to the Christian student center. Throughout we had the firm support of the college pastor (and in fact it was at a mass meeting of students held there on Monday that Bascom had urged the assembled students to go to jail—to be like Gandhi and go to the sea to make salt). In some ways the situation was looking desperate. Morale among those in jail, especially the women, was very bad. There seemed to be scant hope of finding the bail money. On Wednesday President Jenkins took the occasion of an assembly to criticize the demonstrations and tell the students that they were "following bad advice." Logan was doing a superlative job with the media, and a call was even made to Washington in a quixotic effort to obtain some kind of intervention from Attorney General Robert Kennedy. I decided to skip my classes—Logan said he knew things were serious when I did that, and when I informed Benjamin Quarles, my department chair, he said he would "look in" on them. Things were so tense that I could hardly get to sleep, and I recall wishing that Clifton Henry, who had graduated, was still with us offering his usual sound advice. I recall also that the outlook was such that I seriously suggested to Bascom that we should escalate our tactics by going to jail ourselves, but he flatly vetoed the idea. The one thing that was encouraging was the supportive attitude of Morgan faculty members in this time of crisis. I recall colleagues who usually had only perfunctory relationships with me now greeting me warmly in the hallways.

Though we did not realize it, Thursday, a day of intense negotiations, would bring us victory. In the morning we were joined for the first time by several of the seniors in the ROTC program, and I was detailed to inform their officers that, regardless of the rules, they would be absent that day. By then, as the arrests and concerned adults put the mayor under increasing pressure, Martin Jenkins shifted gears and vigorously supported our activities. Then in the afternoon came the news that the theater had capitulated, and we went to city hall to hear the mayor's statement. (I was rather alarmed when it became clear that the agreement worked out by our lawyer, Robert Watts, and the city administration did not include dropping all charges, and I recall pushing Watts so vigorously to get this accomplished that he finally expostulated that I was behaving like Juanita Mitchell!)

Those arrested were to be released without bail, and I accompanied the CIG leaders to the Baltimore city jail, where we were permitted inside and even allowed to visit the students on the ranges and assure them that they would soon be out. Somehow

Logan's efforts to get us national television coverage had paid off, and as we entered the jail we were greeted by the sight of Walter Cronkite's television crew setting up its equipment.

Although we no longer needed the bail money, by the time the students were being released from jail the cash had been obtained—though I did not learn about this until much later. It seems that the head of the local Masons and, perhaps, City Councilman Henry Park were reported to have convinced "Little Willie" Adams to assist us, and that the needed cash (I understand it amounted to $100,000) had been secured and flown in from New York.

Upon reflection, it afterwards was pretty clear that we had been exceedingly fortunate, and that we were closer to failure than we had realized. It was our good luck that the preceding mayor, whose base was in a white working-class neighborhood, had been elevated to a judicial post, for, as Watts informed me later, he would certainly have simply let the matter be handled by the courts and that would have involved us in depressing long-term litigation without any certainty of winning. Thus City Council president Goodman, with his base in predominantly black and Jewish sections, was acting as mayor quite accidentally. Here was a final lesson learned—that for a major direction effort, one needed to know and understand the political context in which a campaign was carried out in order to evaluate the likelihood of a successful outcome.

PART II

The Civil Rights Movement: Analyses by a Participant

The Revolution against the NAACP: A Critical Appraisal of Louis E. Lomax's *The Negro Revolt*

LOUIS E. LOMAX's *The Negro Revolt* (New York: Harper and Brothers, 1962), its limitations notwithstanding, was a landmark in writing about the black protest movement of the early 1960s. The knowledgeable journalist brought to the attention of the general public important developments in the movement, especially the youths' criticism of the methods and strategy of the NAACP. Its appearance came at the time that I was starting to crystallize my own reflections on the dynamics of the movement, and composing this review-essay laid the foundations for much of my later writing on the subject.

"THE CURRENT Negro revolt," writes Louis Lomax, "is more than a revolt against the white world. It is also a revolt of the Negro masses against their own leadership and goals." Mr. Lomax ranges widely in this vivid, provoking and somewhat poorly organized volume, devoting chapters to assorted subjects from white liberals to Black Muslims. But the main point of the book is that since the mid-fifties the slow pace of social change has made the tactics of the older Negro leadership organizations obsolete, and that the Negro masses, increasingly impatient, have adopted new techniques of action which in turn have propelled to prominence a group of men who have challenged the position and power of the previously established leaders. This "revolt of the masses" (if I may use the phrase coined by Ortega y Gasset) is evident in phenomena as diverse as the student sit-ins, the Black Muslims, and the vitality Whitney Young has infused into the Urban League. No longer can Negro leadership devote itself chiefly to the interests of the elite; to be successful it must relate itself to the new militancy of the masses.

Inevitably ideological questions concerning techniques become focused about organizations and personalities, and tactical disagreements become the basis for power rivalries. In an earlier article in *Harper's* and in this book Lomax discloses to public gaze something of this struggle. And he does not hesitate to enter the fray and

From *Journal of Negro Education* 32 (Spring 1963): 146–52.

take sides, dispensing praise and blame with Olympian sweep and considerable oversimplification. Whitney Young, Paul Zuber and James Farmer are his heroes; Roy Wilkins emerges from the pages of this book as a rather pathetic villain; Martin Luther King is portrayed as a charismatic wonder with feet of clay; and A. Philip Randolph, it is implied, is something of a has-been. Thus Lomax's book has a zestful quality which gives the reader the feeling that the author is revealing the very insides of things.

The volume does, in fact, have some notable sections. The historical materials can be dismissed as generally superficial, often inaccurate, and largely unrelated to what follows. But the chapter on the Negro in the fifties sets forth lucidly the conditions that formed the seedbed of the "Negro Revolt"—the frustration with legalism engendered in the aftermath of the 1954 decision; the deteriorating economic condition of the Negro masses; and the changing self-image of American Negroes as the African states gained their independence. Though one might wish for more details, Lomax has done a real service by telling how the Kennedy administration, working indirectly through liberal wealthy whites who financed the Taconic Foundation, subtly motivated the establishment of the current voter-registration drive in the South. Especially penetrating is the author's analysis of Martin Luther King, who in spite of weaknesses (the most notable of which are a lack of administrative ability, and an eclectic and superficial philosophy), is a superb symbolic leader for the race, and a most effective interpreter of Negro aspirations to white America.

On the other hand, the book gives the impression of careless research and hasty writing, and this is true even of the area in which Lomax is best informed—the contemporary scene. Thus, for example, the reader is informed, on page 123, that "NAACP youth groups had been the first to use the sit-in method," and in general the organization of the book is such that the reader is not made properly aware of CORE's significance in the development of the historical background to the Negro Revolt, in the period before 1960. Again, contrary to Lomax's statement (p. 127), the organization of the Student Non-Violent Coordinating Committee (SNCC) was not entirely a student idea, and it was certainly not a blow to King and the Southern Christian Leadership Conference (SCLC), since it was originally organized under their auspices. The author states (p. 129) that Edward King, Jr., left the post of executive director of SNCC in order to "return to law school at Wilberforce University." Outside of the fact that this does not take into account the internal politics in SNCC that led to King's resignation, the statement as it stands is

demonstrably erroneous because King had previously been studying at Kentucky State College and because Wilberforce has no law
school. Lomax says (p. 133) that the first CORE freedom ride, conducted in the upper South in 1947, was intended to test discrimination on trains, when actually the tests were conducted on buses.
And then there are the careless inaccuracies, such as identifying the
Bruce Boynton case as the Bruce Boyington case, and referring to
the Albany movement's leader W. G. Anderson as G. T. Anderson.

Undoubtedly the author's most serious distortions are to be found
in his criticisms of the NAACP. He recognizes that "it was the work of
the NAACP that set the stage for the Negro Revolt," but he feels that
its program is now hopelessly out of date. The gist of his criticism is
that the NAACP is undemocratic, that it is not responsive to the
needs of the masses and fails to enlist their direct participation in the
civil rights struggle, that it is still too legalistic, and that it has erred
in making school desegregation the cornerstone of its recent program. In a couple of passages Lomax does indicate that part of the
failure to engage in mass action is due to local branch leadership, but
he leaves the impression that the chief fault lies with Roy Wilkins
and the national office. "I have," he writes, "been unable to unearth
a single directive in which the NAACP national office has called for
such action as the sit-ins and freedom rides. And the feeling that the
NAACP national office does not condone such action remains."

Though one must agree that there is much to criticize in the
NAACP, Lomax distorts by the extreme nature of his statements and
by his differential treatment of the various civil rights organizations.
Qualities that he regards as faults in the NAACP do not appear to
him to be faults when they occur in CORE or in SNCC or in SCLC. This
is particularly evident in his charge that the NAACP is undemocratic
and unresponsive to the voice of the rank and file. Because of its age
and size one would naturally expect the NAACP to possess a somewhat unimaginative and conservative bureaucratic structure. As in
mature organizations generally leadership in the NAACP has tended
to shift from the charismatic to the administrative type. And one
will have to concede that the NAACP is not an example of direct
mass participation in the decision-making process. But neither is
SCLC, or CORE, or even SNCC. Any observer of social movements is
aware of the inherent oligarchic tendencies present even in those
possessed of the most democratic of ideologies. Skill, dedication,
experience, and ability are unevenly distributed among the members of a movement; continuity of leadership and tightness of control seem necessary for a high degree of effectiveness; it is easy for
the active few to make the decisions; and on top of this there is the

all but universal desire for prestige and power. One of the big issues at CORE's 1961 convention, for example, was charges of oligarchic rule by a small clique at CORE's national office. The majority of local student movements which I have observed tend to be oligarchic, and were so from a relatively early date. Nor is SNCC itself directed by the rank and file of student groups throughout the South; rather an active clique in Atlanta initiates projects on its own initiative, and enlists the aid of people in the communities in which it decides to work. Because of its size and age the NAACP may be less responsive to the desires of the rank and file than these newer, more flexible organizations; its internal threads of power may be more complicated; but everywhere the story is basically the same. Ideologically we would wish for all of these organizations to be more democratic; practically we will have to struggle continuously to strike a reasonable balance between the advantages that come with the concentration of authority and the ideal of keeping the organization responsive to the desires of the majority of its members.

In other respects also Lomax criticizes the NAACP for not doing what other organizations are not doing either. He excoriates the national office for failing to call in local leaders and outlining a plan of attack to be followed in concert. But neither SNCC nor SCLC appears to have such a procedure. SNCC headquarters has attempted at times to set a national policy, but not with any great degree of success. And one of the big troubles with SCLC is that it really has no program, no long range strategy. If one follows King's career, one observes that, unlike SNCC, he does not initiate situations. Rather he appears on the scene after a crisis has developed, and then functions effectively in his role as charismatic and symbolic leader by rallying people and focusing national and international attention upon the local situation. CORE's most celebrated activities are originated and directed by the national office, but there is evidence that this is not always accomplished with particularly good articulation with local CORE groups—certainly not if the Route 40 demonstrations in Maryland in November and December 1961 are typical.

It is noteworthy that in spite of its bureaucratic nature, and despite its tendency to bask in a glorious tradition of legal successes, the NAACP has moved into direct action—and far more than Lomax is willing to admit. The crux of the situation lies largely with the branches, many of which have been characterized by stodgy leadership. But some branches did engage in sit-in activity during the 1950s. The most noted example was the successful demonstrations of the Oklahoma City youth council in 1958–1959. Adult branches had also conducted sit-ins, as in the case of the Louisville branch in 1959. Lomax himself offers evidence of NAACP activity in the 1960 sit-ins. He refers to the magnificent work done in Savannah, and also records that the NAACP youth secretary, Herbert Wright, was sent south to organize demonstrations after the student sit-ins began in Greensboro. But somehow he manages to give the erroneous impression that Wright's activity was not favored by the national office. As a matter of fact, in spite of Lomax's iterations to the contrary, the national office did get behind the student sit-in movement after it started in February 1960. It deliberately speeded up the formation of youth councils and college chapters with the specific purpose of engaging in demonstrations. And as one official of the NAACP put it to me, he and others from the national office went to the regional NAACP conferences that spring and knocked heads together in a strong effort to obtain local NAACP participation in and support for this sort of mass action. The trouble, in fact, seemed to be more with the local branches than with the national office. Many of the demonstrations in the spring of 1960 were carried on by NAACP youth councils and college chapters, though the actual extent of the activity under NAACP auspices is difficult to measure because the NAACP obscures matters by claiming credit for the activities of all those who happened to be NAACP members even when the NAACP had not organized the demonstrations, and because people in SNCC tend to discount the work of the NAACP. The importance of the work of NAACP youth during the dramatic months of 1960 and 1961 was made very evident at the NAACP 1961 convention, when the NAACP was faced with a serious revolt of its own youth councils and college chapters, which regarded themselves as setting the pace for the adults, and which demanded and received greater autonomy and increased representation on convention committees and on the national board.

Thus to get the real story of the relationship of the NAACP to the nonviolent movement one must make detailed studies of the complexities that obtained in various local situations. The patterns of what actually happened seem infinitely varied. In some cases the adult leadership worked well with the youth, as in Durham. In other cases the adults and youth had some friction, as in St. Louis where adults organized a youth council, then thought the youth were moving too fast and finally, when dramatic youth action brought results, they wished to take credit for the achievement. In some places, as in Memphis, militant NAACP adult leadership maneuvered originally autonomous youth groups into the NAACP, and misunderstanding and some bitterness followed when youth and adults did not agree on tactics. The wonder is not that the

NAACP has done so little in terms of mass action and sit-ins, but rather that, in view of its history, it has done as much as it has. One may attribute this in part to the NAACP's desire to maintain its prominence in the civil rights field; but the fact is that to a considerable extent it did meet the challenge posed by the youthful revolt of 1960–61.

Lomax's method is further revealed by the way in which he subjects claims made by the NAACP to the most careful scrutiny, but accepts without question statements made by SNCC and SCLC. I simply cite two instances. Thus Lomax accepts the information, which he says was supplied by James Foreman, executive director of SNCC, that the sit-in demonstrations held at Cambridge, Maryland, were the most effective sit-in demonstrations organized by SNCC in 1961. In actual fact these demonstrations were held in 1962, they were organized not by SNCC but by the Baltimore-based Civil Interest Group, and they were not effective in desegregating any restaurants.* Again, Lomax accepts the statements of Wyatt T. Walker, executive director of SCLC, as to how SCLC has spent the hundreds of thousands of dollars raised by King. Among other things it is suggested that SCLC gave substantial financial assistance to the Freedom Riders. Actually during the summer of 1961 there was a good deal of dissatisfaction voiced just because SCLC was giving so little financial backing to the Freedom Riders.

The NAACP, Lomax states, is not interested in the Negro masses; and thus he simply ignores, for one thing, the magnificent work done by the NAACP labor secretary, Herbert Hill, in opening up job opportunities in the mass employment industries. As a matter of fact, Lomax's conceptualization of the Negro masses is weak. The masses we are told are the ones who are the supporters of sit-ins, freedom-rides, selective-buying campaigns, and the Black Muslims. Two obvious points that should be made in this connection are that the real activists are a minority in all classes, and that the boycotts have been supported by Negroes of all social levels. If Lomax had probed more deeply he would have distinguished be-

---

*In justification of Foreman's position it should be stated that the CIG is loosely affiliated with SNCC. When, after CIG had initiated the Cambridge demonstrations, SNCC headquarters sent field representatives there without consulting CIG, the tendency among CIG members was to regard SNCC as an interloper trying to take undeserved credit for the project at a time when CIG's demonstrations on the Eastern Shore of Maryland were the chief focus of sit-in activity in the country. It is also true that four restaurants in the vicinity of Cambridge were desegregated—but this came about as a result of the work of the Cambridge Equal Opportunities Commission before the CIG started its demonstrations there, though undoubtedly the fear of possible CIG activity was the main prod that led the commission to act.

tween the different social strata from which the student sit-inners and the Black Muslims are derived. The former are chiefly from upper-lower- or lower-middle-class backgrounds, ordinarily belong to the first generation in their families to attend college, and tend to describe themselves as belonging to the "striving lower class." On the other hand, the Black Muslims draw from a more oppressed, lower-lower-class stratum. To lump both of these groups together as "the masses" leads to a superficial understanding of the dynamics of the two movements. Finally, it is exceedingly important to remember that much of the leadership of the Negro revolt, particularly among the adults, comes from people of middle- and even upper-class background. The case of the leadership of the Albany movement is simply one graphic illustration of this fact.

Now the conflict for prestige and power, which in the past two and a half years has become a four-way struggle between NAACP, SCLC, SNCC and CORE—with the Urban League in the wings—has been in large part a struggle for influence over, and the support of, the great mass of lower-middle- and upper-lower-class Negroes. Many of the youth view themselves as spokesmen for the masses against the middle- and upper-class-dominated NAACP and Urban League and accept without qualification Frazier's description of the "Black Bourgeoisie." And as Lomax himself suggests SNCC bears watching because it could perhaps become "*the* organization to be reckoned with in the Deep South."

When the student movement that swept the South began at Greensboro in 1960, the NAACP still dominated the civil rights field. The Urban League was largely discredited for its policy of moderation. And despite King's glamour, for a variety of reasons SCLC had not effectively challenged NAACP preeminence. But the student sit-ins and the freedom rides changed the situation. From the first the NAACP recognized in the student movement a threat to its position, and as we have stated, encouraged sit-in activity itself, and tried, in some areas, to take over spontaneously organized student groups. (In all fairness it should be noted that the students looked to the NAACP and other adult leaders for financial and legal aid; and quite naturally adults who came to their assistance expected to be consulted by the students.) SCLC realized the potential in the student movement, and helped call the Raleigh Conference at which James Lawson denounced the NAACP and at which SNCC was born. At first SNCC and SCLC were closely allied, and the NAACP withdrew its youth and college groups from participation in SNCC because it did not want to lose credit for what these units were doing. The result was to fortify the impression among SNCC people that they, themselves, were carrying on most of the significant activity. However, SNCC leaders did not want to be dominated by King and SCLC, and gradually drifted away from the close connection with them, though there is still a great deal of cooperation between the two organizations. This drifting apart was very evident by the summer of 1961, by which time student leaders were complaining of various aspects of King's leadership. Though it was not until August that NAACP leaders appear to have become aware of the fact that SNCC was really projecting its own program, by July the NAACP had found itself faced not only with serious unrest against adult leadership on the part of its own young people, but also the revival of CORE and its emergence into the forefront of the civil rights movement as a result of the Freedom Rides. Under the circumstances, as we have seen, the NAACP made significant concessions to its youth groups.

Now Lomax does make clear the threat which the "Negro Revolt" posed to NAACP leadership; and he is also highly critical of the activities of Wyatt T. Walker, who is much disliked for his attempts to project the power of SCLC in local communities where mass-action leaders desire the presence of King as a symbolic figure, but do not wish their own power taken away from them by an outside person (though one might wonder if King himself should not bear some of the responsibility for this situation, since he continues to rely heavily upon Walker). But Lomax has ignored an important part of the dynamics of the whole movement by failing to give a well-rounded account of the intricate rivalry and competition—and cooperation—among the various civil rights groups.

It is as inevitable as it is unfortunate that even the most idealistic social movements should develop power rivalries; and that the more successful the movement the higher the stakes and therefore the fiercer the struggle. It has been my observation that the desire for power and prestige quickly asserted itself in the student nonviolent movement, both in the local groups and in SNCC itself. At SNCC's founding conference both the Nashville and Montgomery delegations hoped to take over the leadership, though neither succeeded in doing so. I have observed youth, originally without a trace of a desire for leadership or prestige, being projected into positions of prominence against their will, and then becoming so enamored of their fame and influence that they wished to perpetuate themselves in office at all costs and to appropriate to their organization the lion's share of credit for advancements in civil rights. The result has been that there is a Kremlin-like quality about leadership in the nonviolent movement (and Lomax himself suggests that King may be swallowed by the revolution he helped to create). Those who endure as individuals of influence in the movement often tend to be those who are least concerned with their own positions in it. They are not always the best known figures, and on the national level this type is best represented by Bayard Rustin, whose name is practically unknown to the general public. (It is a measure of the superficiality of Lomax's book that Rustin isn't mentioned in it at all.)

Thus the idealistic and egoistic motivations among leaders in civil rights organizations become so inextricably intertwined that one often cannot tell where one ends and the other begins. High officials in both CORE and NAACP gave me an honest and convincing picture as to why it was that each had to try to obtain full credit for whatever it did: each needed a good image if it was to attract the members and funds necessary for it to carry on and expand its important and worthwhile work. This goes far to account for the frequency of domineering tactics on the part of the NAACP, whose officials are fond of saying, for example, that because their branch leadership in Atlanta and Nashville was so closely identified with local SCLC affiliates, the NAACP has not received due credit for its role in the civil rights struggle in those cities.

The rivalries between organizations, and the feuding cliques within organizations, can—and at times do—lead to nastiness, bitterness, and even paralysis. Yet they have also proven to be an essential ingredient of the dynamic of the civil rights movement over the past two and a half years. For in their attempt to outdo each other, each organization or clique puts forth stronger efforts than it otherwise would, and is constantly searching for new avenues along which to develop a program. I believe that the past two and a half years have seen new life infused into the activities of the NAACP, which, setting legal victories aside, has made accomplishments unmatched in its previous history. Lomax's strictures notwithstanding, the NAACP appears to me to be more vigorous than ever. CORE in 1960 appeared to be a dying organization, its method appropriated by more lusty successors. In 1961 it emerged, as Lomax says, as the most imaginative of the civil rights organizations, and again seized the lead in the nonviolent technique in which it had pioneered. As a local example one might cite the three-way rivalry between NAACP, CORE and the student-based Civic Interest Group in Baltimore. One could not wish for a more militant organization than the Baltimore Branch of the NAACP, which had, in fact, been engaged in direct action demonstrations before CIG began its career. The bitter quarrel between the two groups developed originally because the NAACP wanted to direct the students; since then it has become a fight for prestige in the civil rights field, with each one trying to outdo the other. Since the tactics of CORE and CIG are identical, only the prestige motive can explain the mild rivalries that have existed between the two in Baltimore, though cooperation between them has been much closer than between CIG and NAACP because of the nonauthoritarian nature of CORE leadership in Baltimore. And despite all rivalries, there is a significant amount of cooperation among all three of these groups. In my judgment the net effect of this competition has been good rather than bad for Baltimore—and more has probably been accomplished for civil rights than if one organization dominated the field, or if there had been no friction among the various groups.

Thus though Lomax's discussion of "The Negro Revolt Against the Negro Leaders" is characterized by distortion and omission, he has raised important questions and offered suggestive insights. Because of the valuable information which the book contains, and because of the illuminating perspective it sheds on the civil rights movement, it is unfortunate that it was not written with care and impartiality.

TWELVE

New Currents in the Civil Rights Movement

I CONSIDER "New Currents in the Civil Rights Movement" to be my first real synthesis concerning the black protest movement in the twentieth century. It and other essays appearing in 1964 and 1965 in turn laid the foundations for *Negro Protest Thought in the Twentieth Century* (edited with Francis Broderick), and the discussion in *From Plantation to Ghetto: An Interpretive History of American Negroes* (written with Elliott Rudwick), which did not appear until 1965–66.

In this 1963 essay I not only analyzed past and current developments, but undertook to make certain predictions that time showed to be in error. Ultimately I learned through experience that one could make no safe long-range predictions about the future course of the movement. I thought it important to reprint this essay, with its errors, both because of its pivotal place in the development of my scholarship and because it expressed the hopes and faith of a white liberal in the movement at that moment in history—the beginning of the summer of 1963. Those who will want to see a somewhat different version of the essay, composed late in the same summer, and eschewing predictions, are referred to my article, "Negro Protest Movements and Organizations," in the Fall 1963 *Yearbook* of the *Journal of Negro Education*.

E VENTS THIS SPRING have made it abundantly clear that gradualism and tokenism in civil rights will no longer pass for progress. The Negro protest movement has become suffused with a new militancy, a new sense of urgency. This is evident in the widespread use of deliberate mass jail-ins, open sneering and jeering at white policemen, a disposition to meet violence with violence, a tendency to package several demands together—to demand "total integration" rather than to work for one reform at a time—and the involvement of greater and greater numbers of people from all strata of the Negro community. "Freedom now!" has become the new slogan.

What happened in Birmingham epitomizes this new militancy, and was itself a major stimulus for the events that have transpired since. But the basic forces operating in Birmingham were operative elsewhere. Birmingham basically functioned as the spark that ignited some highly inflammable material.

From *New Politics* 2 (Summer 1963): 7–32.

Indicative of the new mood was the Northwood Theater demonstration in Baltimore, which occurred in February, over two months before Birmingham. Enjoying unusual support in the white community, a rather fair police force, and often favorable judges, and moving over the years from one victory to another, the Civic Interest Group—as the student nonviolent movement in Baltimore is called—had been characterized by a relatively mild spirit. Seldom had demonstrators stayed in jail even overnight and the notion of deliberate large-scale arrests was dismissed as unworkable, for no one would ever be able to get that many students from Morgan State College to go to jail. But it was a continuing insult to the dignity of the Morgan student that the neighborhood theater, less than a block from the school, should have resisted negotiations and picketing for over eight years, and this in the face of the desegregation of practically every other business establishment in the same shopping center, and of all the other theaters in that part of the city.

When Civic Interest Group leaders and student government officials met once more to discuss the matter early last February, it was obvious that the students were in a mood to employ some new and dramatic techniques. The upshot was that over four hundred Morgan students (and several white students from Goucher College and Johns Hopkins University) were arrested, filling the city jail to overflowing. Punitively high bail set by the judge only encouraged further arrests. Finally, after three days of distressing turmoil, embarrassed by the nationwide publicity and facing a primary election in two weeks, the city's mayor compelled the theater to capitulate.

The Negro community in Baltimore was stirred as it had not been in all the previous years of demonstrations. Students who had been skeptical of direct action found themselves trespassing and going to jail, and for the first time large numbers of fraternity members, honors students, and outstanding athletes participated along with the more anonymous students who had heretofore formed the backbone of Civic Interest Group activity. Adults who wondered about all the fuss over one single theater were told that it was the principle that counted. Parents whose mixed feelings of anger and fear soon turned to pride, even urged that their children be kept in jail until the theater opened its doors. Certain powerful figures in the community, themselves previously sympathetic to the student activists, at first frankly questioned the wisdom of this particular action, but eventually came to give the students their militant support. And at the other end of the social scale, it was reported that for the first time the nonviolent demonstrations were a topic of excited conversation in the lower-class bars of east Baltimore.

The whole experience was clearly a new departure for Baltimore. Few if any towns had witnessed so many arrests at a single place of business. And though the jails were filled at Albany, Georgia, and on the Freedom Ride to Jackson, this was one of the first successful attempts to deliberately disrupt the city's political and judicial machinery by mass arrests and filling the jail. The experienced veterans of the Student Nonviolent Coordinating Committee (SNCC) regarded the Northwood Theater demonstration as a highly significant development. And SNCC, itself, shortly thereafter launched its Greenwood, Mississippi, registration drive, in the heart of the White Citizens Councils' territory—the most difficult and dangerous task any of the civil rights organizations had yet undertaken in their voter registration work. Then came the William Moore memorial trek, Birmingham, and the outbreak of new demonstrations around the country.

OUR CASE STUDY of the Northwood Theater demonstration illustrates in microcosm an essential factor that has been at the base of all the demonstrations this spring—a rising mood of frustration with previous tactics due to the lack of concrete progress, a sense of frustration that made these communities especially sensitive to the stimulus that came from Birmingham. What occurred this spring is in a way remarkably like what happened in 1960, when the demonstration at Greensboro, North Carolina, sparked a sit-in movement throughout the South, because youth were becoming impatient and disillusioned with older techniques. In practically all of the southern cities where direct action has taken place this spring there has been a history of such action, often of a sustained nature. In Savannah, Georgia, a brilliant campaign conducted by the NAACP that included a fifteen-month boycott, had obtained not only the desegregation of buses, lunch counters, and municipal facilities but also over a hundred new jobs for Negroes as sales clerks and cashiers. But since then little or no progress had been made. In Jackson, following the Freedom Ride, both NAACP and SNCC stimulated nonviolent action there for a brief period (and disagree as to which organization deserved the credit for it), while both SNCC and CORE joined in the voter registration work there. Danville, Virginia, it is true, had had no previous demonstration, but for two years an affiliate of the Southern Christian Leadership Conference (SCLC), had been working unsuccessfully.

The North Carolina communities had a rich history of demonstrations and achievements in 1960–1961, though little had been accomplished recently. In Cambridge, Maryland, there had been a year of bitter conflict with city authorities that began with the Civic Interest Group's Eastern Shore Freedom Ride in the spring of 1962, but intermittent efforts by the Cambridge Nonviolent Action Committee founded at that time had brought no results. In the North, the past three years had witnessed sharply increased agitation over both jobs and de facto school segregation; and frustration there was augmented—as it was in the South—by the serious unemployment problem. Thus, everywhere there was growing disillusionment with methods that seemed to be bringing little in the way of tangible accomplishments. In essence what Birmingham did was transform this disillusionment and frustration into constructive, direct action efforts for social change throughout the nation.

Actually what is going on today is the culmination of efforts under way since the late 1950s. There was a shift in emphasis from legalism to direct action, and a broadening of the scope of civil rights activity. In membership and leadership the civil rights movement became more and more a Negro movement, and more and more a mass movement. The competitive rivalry among civil rights organizations supplied additional impetus. The emerging African states, and their importance in international affairs, gave American Negroes a new self-image. There was the goad of swelling unemployment at the very time that the gradually accelerating pace of change in American race relations, and the embarrassment the American race system was causing in the conduct of the nation's foreign policy, combined to create a revolution of expectations in Negro thinking. All of these are interrelated and interlocking phenomena; but the net result was that here, indeed, was a classic case of a rising class in society, confident of itself and its future, but denied its just place in the social structure, and therefore turning to increasingly radical tactics in order to secure that goal.

TODAY, THE FOUR LEADING civil rights organizations are—in order of historical appearance—the NAACP, the Congress of Racial Equality, the Southern Christian Leadership Conference, and the Student Nonviolent Coordinating Committee. (We omit from the discussion, as being somewhat peripheral to our interests, the Urban League. This, the most conservative of the Negro advancement organizations, is not strictly a civil rights institution, but a cross between that and a social welfare agency.)

A decade ago the NAACP was easily preeminent among civil rights organizations. Often interlocked with it were the voter registration groups that had been formed in the South after the Supreme Court invalidated the white primary in 1944. Called conservative today, the NAACP's program of protest and political and legal action had originally been regarded as radical, in contrast to the accommodating ideology of Booker T. Washington in the ascendancy when the NAACP was founded in 1909. By the mid-fifties the NAACP's legal arm had secured an impressive series of Supreme Court decisions which appeared to guarantee voting rights and set forth a set of legal precepts that unequivocally banned any official support for segregation—whether in transportation, housing, or in publicly owned facilities. During the late fifties the NAACP's southern work consisted largely of litigation against the South's resistance to the school desegregation decision, and fighting the attacks an aroused white South was now making on the organization and its leaders. In the North there was a broadening program, with increasing emphasis on fair housing and especially on employment. The organization's vigorous labor department scored some significant breakthroughs in both the North and the South, most notably the opening up of several hundred jobs at the Lockheed Plant in Marietta, Georgia.

Throughout the country there was major stress on voter registration as the fundamental technique by which to obtain civil rights legislation and the favorable ear of public officials. More recently northern branches have been giving major attention to eliminating de facto school segregation. Prior to 1960, nonviolent direct action was a peripheral NAACP concern, though in 1958 and 1959 NAACP college and youth groups in Oklahoma City and St. Louis engaged in successful sit-ins and elsewhere, as in Louisville and Baltimore, adult branches had sponsored direct action projects.

CORE, a decade ago, was still a small, chiefly white organization, confined to the northern and border states, and lacking even a single paid staff member. Founded in 1942, CORE utilized methods that had been developed over the preceding two or three years by the Fellowship of Reconciliation. This group of religious pacifists had, at the suggestion of A. J. Muste, combined Gandhi's method of satyagraha with the sit-*down* tactics of the Detroit automobile strikers to produce the technique known as the sit-*in*. The synthesis of union methods (including picketing) with Gandhian nonviolence having proved successful as far south as Baltimore and St. Louis, CORE in 1956 hired its first field secretary, and soon thereafter began its southern work in earnest (though actually its first foray in that direction had been the Freedom Ride in the upper South in 1947). CORE's major emphasis throughout the fifties was on public accommodations. Early in the decade, however, it had pioneered in the method—later so effectively employed and popularized by the Philadelphia ministers—of selective buying to obtain employment; and in 1958–1959 it began using direct action to secure desegregation of privately owned apartment houses. Today, in the North, CORE concentrates on employment and housing, with some work in school desegregation; in the South it concentrates on public accommodations and to a lesser extent on voter registration.

CORE pioneered in satyagraha in the United States, but it was the Montgomery bus boycott in 1955–1956 that dramatically brought it to the attention of the nation, and popularized its use among Negroes. And it has been Martin Luther King, catapulted into prominence by the boycott, who has become the leading symbol of this strategy. Before the court decision (obtained by NAACP Legal Defense Fund lawyers) had spelled success for the Montgomery Improvement Association, a similar movement had started in Tallahassee, under the leadership of Rev. C. K. Steele (president of the NAACP branch, and later a vice president of SCLC). Later, similar action was undertaken in Birmingham where, following the state's injunction against NAACP operations, a group of ministers headed by Fred Shuttlesworth had established the Alabama Christian Movement for Human Rights. About the same time, there appeared the Tuskegee Civic Association, which conducted a three-year boycott of local merchants in response to the state legislature's gerrymandering Negro voters out of the town's limits. This campaign attained its object when the Supreme Court ruled the gerrymander illegal in 1960.

The events in Montgomery, Tallahassee, and Tuskegee were widely heralded as indicating the emergence of a "New Negro" in the South—militant, no longer fearful of police harassment, jails, and white hoodlums, and determined to use his collective economic strength to obtain his freedom. Seizing upon the new mood, King in 1957 organized the Southern Christian Leadership Conference—an organization of affiliates rather than a membership organization like the NAACP and CORE. Ideologically committed to a thoroughgoing pacifism of the Gandhian persuasion, SCLC's program includes not only the familiar mass demonstrations, but also citizenship training institutes which prepare local leaders to work on voter registration in their communities.

The NAACP perceived the beginning of the end to the Negro's second-class citizenship in the 1954 Supreme Court decision. Yet, impressive as it was to cite the advances made in the postwar years, in spite of state laws and Supreme Court decisions, something was clearly wrong. Negroes were still disfranchised in most of the Deep South; legal decisions in regard to transportation were still largely ignored there; discrimination in employment and housing was the rule, even in states with model civil rights laws; the Negro unemployment rate grew constantly due to recessions and automation; and, rather than giving in, the South responded with the White Citizens' Councils.

At the very time that legalism was thus proving itself a limited instrument, Negroes were gaining a new self-image as a result of the rise of the new African nations; King and others were demonstrating that nonviolent direct action could be effective in the South; and the new laws and court decisions, the gradually increasing interest of the federal government, and the evident drift of white public opinion developed a new confidence in the future among American Negroes. As a result of this revolution in expectations, Negroes no longer felt that they had to accept the humiliations of second-class citizenship, and consequently these humiliations— somewhat fewer though they now were—appeared to be more intolerable than ever. This increasing impatience accounted for the rising tempo of nonviolent direct action in the late 1950s which culminated in the student sit-ins of 1960. Ironically, the NAACP by its very successes in the courts and legislatures had done more than any other agency to create the revolution in expectations that was to disillusion so many Negroes with the limitations of the NAACP program.

Many date the "Negro Revolt" from the Montgomery Bus Boycott of 1955—and the significance of this event cannot be overemphasized. Yet it seems to me that the truly decisive break with the past came with the college student sit-ins that began spontaneously at Greensboro in 1960. These sit-ins involved, for the first time, the employment of nonviolent direct action on a massive Southwide scale that led to thousands of arrests and elicited the participation of tens of thousands of people. Moreover, a period was inaugurated in which youth were to become the spearhead of the civil rights struggle. And this is still the case—for it has been the youth who have been the chief dynamic force in compelling the established civil rights organizations to revamp their strategy, which they found it imperative to do to retain their leadership in the movement.

The NAACP quickly went into action, and the national office deliberately speeded up the creation of youth councils and college chapters with the specific intent of engaging in demonstrations, while national staff members "knocked heads together" at regional conferences that spring in a vigorous effort to obtain local NAACP participation and support for this type of mass action. In fact, a great deal of the sit-in activity during 1960 and 1961 was carried on by NAACP youth councils and college chapters. Like the NAACP, SCLC sought to get on the student bandwagon, and it sponsored the Raleigh Conference in April, at which the Student Nonviolent Coordinating Committee was founded—though SNCC and SCLC later drifted apart. CORE in 1960 seemed to be a dying organization, its methods appropriated by more enterprising successors. But in 1961, after the Freedom Ride to Alabama and Mississippi, CORE reemerged as the most imaginative and resourceful of the civil rights agencies in the application of the tactics in which it had pioneered.

THUS, EACH OF THE FOUR organizations is now committed to direct action. In other ways also the differences between them appear largely to be differences of emphasis. All four are now engaged in voter registration; all of them have moved energetically into the employment problem; and both CORE and NAACP—the only two with northern operations—are stepping up their activities in regard to de facto school segregation and housing. The NAACP however has eschewed primary emphasis on direct action, regarding it as an extremely useful technique; the others regard direct action as the chief focus of their work and consider legal remedies of distinctly secondary value. This fact should not obscure the importance of the legal work done in support of the direct-actionists, most notably in the Supreme Court decisions secured on behalf of the demonstrators. In fact there is evidence that one reason for the willingness of so many youth to violate southern laws has been the fact that there was a general expectation that the court would rule, as it has done thus far, in behalf of demonstrators convicted of trespass, disorderly conduct, parading without a permit, breach of the peace, and so forth.

Even the differences in emphasis between the NAACP and the other organizations seem likely to disappear in the light of what happened at the NAACP's recent national convention, where militants among the rank and file and the "radicals" on the paid staff triumphed against the more conservative elements. The convention enthusiastically endorsed direct action as the major NAACP tactic for the future. Undoubtedly the 1963 convention will mark a real turning point in NAACP history.

However, there has been one important difference in the way in which direct action is conducted by national NAACP leaders as compared to that of the leaders of other organizations. The NAACP has tended to act on the premise that the "professionals" should not go to jail; while all the others believe that the "professionals" should not only go to jail along with their followers, but they should also stay there with them. Roy Wilkins' arrest in Jackson was thus a highly significant *symbolic* act.

On the other hand, there are differences in style among the three more exclusively action-oriented bodies. King and SCLC appear to be the most cautious and to specialize in a few showy projects. The SNCC people are the most spontaneous. For some of them, demonstrating and going to jail almost appear to have become a way of life. Status is measured by the number of arrests and amount of time spent in jail. More than any of the others the SNCC people are the "true believers."

AS IN OTHER GREAT MOVEMENTS for the advancement of human welfare, the idealistic and egoistic motivations among civil rights leaders become so inextricably intertwined that one often cannot tell where one ends and the other begins. Consequently, it is not surprising that the events of 1960 and 1961 ushered in a period of intense competitive rivalry for power and prestige in the civil rights field. It has been a four-way struggle between SCLC, NAACP, SNCC, and CORE, and even the Urban League has become more aggressive.

Of the four it may be said that SNCC has probably been the most dynamic force closely seconded by CORE. SNCC, theoretically a coordinating committe of affiliated college and youth groups, ordinarily operates through a small group in Atlanta which engages in action of its own choosing and enlists the aid of people in the communities where it decides to work. SNCC has been extraordinarily effective. Though it has the most modest budget of any of the four (its field secretaries, currently reported as numbering about ninety, work on a subsistence basis), and although it has, until very recently, received far less publicity than the other organizations, it can probably be said that it has supplied the major drive for the civil rights movement in the South.

While various SCLC affiliates have taken the lead in nonviolent action in certain communities, especially in NAACP branches dominated by conservative leadership, King himself functions as a symbolic or "spiritual leader." Ordinarily, he moves into situations after they have been started, and then lends the magic of his image to the support of the local movement. King operates effectively in this way both because he is a superb symbolic figure and because he is easily the most effective interpreter of Negro aspirations to white America. Elsewhere there have arisen numerous local organizations, often established by ministers, taking various names and unattached to any national body. Sometimes these are "umbrella" groups, including local units of national bodies; at other times they are independent of, though not necessarily hostile to, the NAACP or other established groups. As the oldest and therefore the most bureaucratic of the civil rights agencies, in many localities dominated by older conservative leaders, the NAACP has quite naturally been on the defensive in a number of cities. Yet, while the NAACP can scarcely take credit for initiating the use of direct-action techniques, it is clearly invalid to stereotype it as run by a conservative black bourgeoisie irrevocably wedded to legalism. Pushed and shoved by the more exclusively action-oriented groups, the NAACP has pretty effectively met the challenge posed by them—though its dominance in the civil rights field, not seriously contested as late as 1960, has been broken. Often, in fact, one gets the impression that rivalry among the different groups is not due so much to differences in philosophy, tactics, or degree of militancy, as much as to a power struggle for hegemony in the civil rights movement. Painful as these conflicts have been, the rivalry of the civil rights groups has actually proved to be an essential ingredient of the dynamics of the Negro protest movement over the past three and a half years. For, in their attempt to outdo each other, each organization puts forth a greater effort and is constantly searching for new avenues along which to develop programs. And despite all rivalries, when the chips are down, the different agencies can and usually do manage to cooperate. Especially significant has been the growing cooperation between CORE and SNCC in the past few months. The best example of this cooperation amidst rivalry is, of course, the fact that all four of these organizations, along with others, are currently working together in sponsoring the March on Washington to take place late in August.

It is impossible to generalize about the NAACP. To arrive at a valid account of the relationship of the NAACP to the nonviolent movement one would have to make a detailed study of the complexities in various local situations, and the policies of the national staff. The patterns of what actually happened seem infinitely varied. Some branches have resisted the direct-action approach; others have embraced it wholeheartedly. In some branches there has been fierce internal fighting. Thus in Philadelphia one faction denounced the branch leaders for being conservative, picketed their homes with signs calling them "Uncle Toms," and having captured the branch offices has subsequently enjoyed an unusual degree of support from the masses of people. In Lynchburg a few years ago, the initiative in civil rights passed to a group of ministers affiliated with the SCLC because the branch leadership there was a conservative group, consisting chiefly of businessmen and school people. (Teachers, because of their vulnerability, have been the most cautious group in the Negro community. When, therefore, the Birmingham teachers openly sided with their demonstrating students it was an event of major significance.) In some instances adult leadership worked well with youth, as in Durham, one of the first action groups in the South to add successful work in the area of employment to its achievements in desegregating places of public accommodation. In Memphis militant NAACP adult leadership maneuvered originally autonomous youth groups into the NAACP, and misunderstanding and some bitterness followed when the adults and youth did not agree on tactics, since the adults did not see the necessity of so many arrests.

In a number of places it was the youth chapters that pushed the adult branches into action. Thus in St. Louis there was also some friction. There adults organized the youth council, then thought the youth were moving too fast and finally when dramatic youth action brought results, they wished to take the credit for the achievement. In Charlotte and Richmond also, the college activists quarreled with adult NAACP leadership over tactics and credit, the students being action-oriented, impatient with negotiating, and intolerant of anything that smacked of compromise. Such personality and tactical conflicts undoubtedly explain why CORE, in the aftermath of its Freedom Highways project in the summer of 1962, has been able to enlist so much support from NAACP people in North Carolina—so much so, in fact, that the state youth conference leaders were tempted to go lock, stock, and barrel over to CORE. In Durham the activists now refer to themselves as NAACP-CORE, and that town's unusually able and dedicated NAACP lawyer, Floyd B. McKissick, was this past June elected National Chairman of CORE. Something of the same order occurred in Savannah, where there was a break between an unusually militant branch president and the youth leader. The upshot was that the NAACP predominance in civil rights activity in Savannah was broken. Both the NAACP branch and the SCLC affiliate there now have vigorous, but independent programs, with some cooperation. However, it is the work of the SCLC affiliate that is currently receiving national attention.

The story of the interaction between the NAACP and the more activist groups is therefore one that defies easy generalization. In at least three cases—Atlanta, Tallahassee, and Nashville—dynamic NAACP branch presidents became heads of local SCLC affiliates. What the NAACP has been aggrieved about is not their direct-action work, but the fact that its leaders' identification with SCLC sub-tracted deserved credit from NAACP. In a Danville project initiated by the local SCLC affiliate, CORE and SNCC sent field workers to assist, and both the local and state NAACP are also cooperating. In Baltimore, the NAACP's effort to dominate the Civic Interest Group led to a bitter quarrel; but the local arrangements for the CIG's Eastern Shore demonstrations in the spring of 1962 were set up by an NAACP field secretary, and on the basis of these demonstrations he was able to establish or reactivate several NAACP branches in the area, to the benefit of the Maryland State NAACP conference, pre-sided over by the head of the Baltimore branch.

In some cases the NAACP's problem seems to be that it is too aggressive, as in Baltimore and Philadelphia. In other cases its problem arises from the fact that it is not aggressive enough. In New York, CORE and NAACP have worked together on picketing the Har-lem Hospital construction site in an effort to secure employment for skilled Negroes in the building trades, but there has been some dis-agreement on who deserves the credit. In Philadelphia, the prob-lem is more serious; but even there, though the fractionalization of leadership has been deplored, analysis of the situation reveals that the nasty rivalry over who is going to do most to secure new employment opportunities in the skilled trades has led both groups to step up their activities more than otherwise anticipated, and has thus led to more rapid progress than would otherwise have been possible. In Jackson, on the other hand, SNCC and CORE people who had been assisting the NAACP in its recent major effort there felt that the NAACP's failure to conduct continuous massive demon-strations was a serious tactical error arising from NAACP timidity and lingering faith in legalism, and eventually they withdrew from the demonstration. The NAACP itself was not unified on the matter; not only were certain local elements anxious to have more vigorous action, but it has been reported that national leaders who were on the scene were not agreed among themselves.

In Louisville, the tension between the NAACP and other organiza-tions operated in quite a different fashion. For some reason the NAACP there was quiescent during 1960, and not until a tiny CORE group led the way at the end of the year was the NAACP galvanized into action. After some bickering, a coordinating committee was organized to run the demonstrations which included the NAACP, CORE and a voter registration group. Under the forcible leadership of the son of the local Negro newspaper publisher, a mass boycott of all downtown Louisville, mammoth parades, mass arrests, and other colorful—if, at the time, rather unorthodox—techniques, resulted in the complete desegregation of downtown Louisville. The campaign cost the local NAACP treasury some $6,000—given under the compulsion of circumstances—and most of the demonstrators happened to be members of the NAACP. But the organization did not get the lion's share of the credit. The NAACP is still bitter about this; Roy Wilkins referred specifically to the Louisville situation in his acid remarks last month about other organizations taking the credit and letting the NAACP foot the bills. Yet the truth in Louisville is a complex one, for youthful dynamism, CORE's prodding, the resourceful leadership of a person on the NAACP executive board who neither spoke for the branch, nor was an officer of it, and NAACP money were *all* essential ingredients of the movement's spectacular and probably unparalleled success.

These questions of finances and credit are touchy ones. Concern with the latter is not entirely unjustified. As responsible officials in both CORE and NAACP have put it to me, it is essential for their respective organizations to receive full credit for what they are doing, since each needs a good image if it is to attract the members and funds necessary to carry on and expand its work. And it is, in fact, in large part this need for a good public image that has propelled the NAACP into more and more direct action throughout the nation, either by itself or in coalition with other organizations. The NAACP, and particularly the NAACP Legal Defense Fund, the two wealthiest civil rights organizations, have played an important role in financing the direct-action movement. The Defense Fund has performed an exceedingly important function in representing activists both in and out of the NAACP in the courts. However, it should be noted that since 1955, the NAACP Legal Defense Fund has been a completely independent organization, legally, administratively, and financially. As for the other groups, CORE and SNCC are in chronic need of funds, while the best-heeled of the more strictly actionist organizations is easily the SCLC. There is a widespread feeling in the civil rights movement that King is able to get a great deal of money because of his excellent public relations image, but that most of it is spent on overhead. His field staff, for example, is small—a half-dozen compared to the dozens that are employed by SNCC, whose annual budget has not been much more than $100,000.

SINCE 1960 THE PUSH from the youth and the competitive rivalry between the various organizations have galvanized the civil rights cause. Organizations and leaders just have to take more dramatic action if they are to maintain their position since arrests numbering fifty or a hundred are scarcely news any longer. Both the NAACP and SCLC, as we have observed, attempted to tie the student movement to its image. But youth have a way of being independent, overthrowing the yoke of their elders. The importance of the work of NAACP youth in 1960 and 1961 was made very evident at the NAACP 1961 convention, when the organization was faced with a serious revolt of its own youth councils and college chapters, which regarded themselves as setting the pace for the adults. They demanded and received greater autonomy and representation on convention committees and on the national board. As one youth was overheard to remark: "We can do without the adults, but they can't do without us." Though in view of the students' dependence upon the adults for financial and legal aid this statement was clearly an oversimplification, it did epitomize the dynamics of the situation. Thus, when CORE recouped itself by the 1961 Freedom Ride, it was the Nashville students who were responsible for continuing it when it bogged down in Alabama. Later, when CORE and SCLC leaders thought it was time to call the whole thing to a halt, the students insisted on continuing to bring Freedom Riders into Jackson.

Student groups have kept things humming ever since. King, the youth tend to say, stays in jail only long enough to obtain the publicity necessary to maintain his symbolic leadership. Especially revealing is an incident reported to have occurred during the recent Birmingham demonstration. The decision to use young children was not King's, but was made by two younger men—one a man on King's staff (and a former leader in the student movement), and the other a CORE representative—while King and other adult leaders were out of the city. By the time King returned the children were ready to move, and at the very moment when King was questioning the tactics at a strategy meeting—so the report goes—the two young men slipped the children out of the church and led them on their way to jail in what probably proved to be the most brilliant tactic of the whole campaign. And just as King, many felt, had to help lead the Birmingham campaign in order to revive his fading image [his reputation had been severely damaged by his two defeats in Albany, Georgia] so it was obvious that the NAACP had to do something. That this something proved to be Jackson was apparently due not only to the external pressures facing the NAACP, but also, in part, to the considerable pressure from the youth groups in Jackson itself for direct action. Similarly the acclaim accorded Paul Zuber for his victory in the New Rochelle school case must have been a major stimulus for the NAACP's all-out attack on educational segregation in the North. As we shall point out below there are several factors that account for the recent burgeoning civil rights activity in the North, but surely the competition between CORE and NAACP is partly responsible for the vigor with which these two organizations are now working on de facto school segregation, job discrimination, and housing. Finally, the pressure of competing organizations was very largely responsible for the turn taken by the NAACP annual convention held in July 1963. Not only did the convention resolve to emphasize direct-action work, but the youth were granted greater autonomy than ever, and the convention recommended to the national board procedures for removing do-nothing conservative branch officials.

TWO OF THE MOST SIGNIFICANT aspects of the civil rights movement since 1960—and essential components of its dynamics—are that it has become increasingly a Negro movement and a mass movement. The two developments are not unrelated, and both of them, of course, had their origins well before 1960. The NAACP membership and branch leadership had always been almost entirely Negro; but at the start, most of the staff and executive board were white liberals. In 1921 the NAACP employed its first Negro executive secretary, James Weldon Johnson; in 1933 its legal staff came under Negro direction when Charles Houston took over; and today only two NAACP staff members are white (though the Legal Defense Fund's chief counsel, Jack Greenberg, is white). Constitutional changes made in 1947 and 1962 have permitted greater membership participation in the selection of the national board; one result has been a decline in the number of whites on it so that today they make up less than one-fourth of its membership. CORE started off as a predominantly white liberal middle-class organization. As late as 1960, perhaps only one-third of its membership was Negro, and at that time its three chief executive officers as well as its national chairman were white. With the selection of James Farmer as national director in 1961, CORE's image in the Negro community changed markedly, and it was thereby able to attract far more Negro support. Today, of CORE's four chief paid executives, two are white and two are Negro. While the majority of northern CORE members are still white there has been increasing Negro participation and in the South CORE's membership is almost entirely Negro. CORE's recent convention, held in June 1963, witnessed two firsts: it was the first time that a majority of the delegates were Negro, and it was the first time that a Negro was elected national chairman. And the southern Negro delegates set the tone for the convention and moved into positions of leadership.

The March on Washington Movement during the Second World War encouraged current tendencies insisting upon an all-Negro membership and leadership; and the same holds true of the Negro American Labor Council formed in 1960, to combat discriminatory trade-union practices within the AFL-CIO. Organizations like SCLC and the various local movements that have sprung up around the country have been Negro organizations from the start. SNCC has avoided any form of union with the predominantly white northern Student Movement for Civil Rights—though it and northern white students generally have been a prime source of SNCC's funds. SNCC has a number of white field secretaries, but it consciously projects itself as a Negro-led organization, and Negroes dominate SNCC's power structure. There has, in fact, been a growing insistence that Negroes must take the initiative and leadership in achieving their freedom, that white liberals tend to be compromisers who cannot be fully trusted, though their financial assistance and their participation in direct action—under Negro leadership—are to be welcomed.

CORE's experience has shown clearly that in order to attract large numbers of Negroes to the civil rights movement Negro leadership is essential. White liberals—and radicals—in the movement have accepted this fact. The NAACP had originally appealed to the elite Negroes, and during the 1930s some of the younger intellectuals like Ralph Bunche criticized it for doing nothing about the problems of the Negro working masses. The association modified its program somewhat, and during the forties and fifties, largely as a result of the energetic work of its labor secretary, made an increasing appeal to working-class people. Actually it would be impossible to make any generalization about the sources of NAACP branch membership and leadership today, since the variations are so great, and since so much depends on local conditions and personalities. In some branches the more elite people in the community set the tone; in others the professional and business people show no interest and blue-collar workers dominate. Thus, suburban New York branches have an elite tone, while the Youngstown, Ohio, branch, for example, is under labor control and has a steelworker for president. At the risk of much oversimplification one may say that, in general, branch leadership today tends to be more middle class rather than either lower class or upper class. For example, the noted work of the Savannah branch was carried out under the leadership of a postal worker.

CORE originally attracted white-collar middle-class Negroes. Since 1960, however, it has found blue-collar skilled and even semiskilled workers joining its ranks, both in the North, where it has started to place major emphasis on the problem of obtaining jobs for working-class Negroes, and in the South. The youthful sit-inners of 1960 and 1961 were chiefly of working-class origins—that is they tended to be upwardly mobile members of the Negro lower-middle and upper-lower classes, though their leadership was more likely to be of middle-class origin. From the beginning the bus boycotts of the South were mass movements, and the same is true of movements like the Albany movement and the selective buying campaigns that appeared in a number of cities, though it should be pointed out that all classes of the community are involved in these efforts and that the upper-middle and even upper classes are disproportionately represented in their leadership.

A RECENT DEVELOPMENT of the highest significance has been the active involvement in the civil rights movement of menial lower-class people, many of whom are chronically unemployed. Apparently it was they who were responsible for the brick and bottle throwing in Birmingham and Jackson. Generally, individuals of this group have heretofore avoided actual participation in demonstrations sponsored by the direct-action groups. I personally remember how in Chestertown, on the Eastern Shore of Maryland, where most of the Negro population is composed of unskilled cannery workers with only seasonal employment, few of the local people attended the mass meetings or participated in demonstrations— but they were ready, more than ready, to fight the white hoodlums who attacked the interracial teams of nonviolent demonstrators. In fact a riot at that time (the spring of 1962) was only narrowly averted. Especially remarkable was the situation in Jacksonville, Florida, a year or so ago, where youthful Negro gangs started to defend the NAACP demonstrators from attacks by white gangs. The NAACP was able to establish contact with the Negro gangs and creatively channeled and coordinated their activity to fit in with NAACP direct-action strategy.

It is exceedingly significant that some individuals from lower-lower-class background have actually begun to demonstrate with nonviolent activists. Unlike the latter, they have not remained nonviolent in the face of provocation from white mobsters, but have become involved in fracases with them in places like Cambridge and Nashville. In the North, people of this class are chiefly concerned with obtaining jobs; in the South, despite a high rate of unemployment, they are becoming involved in the struggle for public accommodations, though this is quite likely a result, at least in part, of the new practice of packaging demands for desegregation of lunch counters and so forth, with demands for jobs. CORE's experiments with direct action to secure improvement of slum housing in Newark and Brooklyn suggest that the major civil rights organizations will soon be deliberately making a bid, through concrete action projects, for the support of this most underprivileged element in the Negro population.

There are those who believe that overt violence on the part of Negro demonstrators will rise, and that in hard-core areas of the South, Gandhian techniques will not work and disillusionment with nonviolence will set in even among those heretofore committed to it. Certainly, few of the demonstrators in CORE or SNCC are philosophically committed to nonviolence. Rather it has been a technique that has proved successful, and has given those who use it a certain sense of moral superiority. But with the increasing police brutality as in Alabama, Danville and elsewhere, the growing frustration at the resistance to change on the part of the white South, and the expanding involvement of lower-class people whose values condone the use of violence, it is likely that the tendency to fight back rather than accept brutality passively, may increase. In retrospect, the incident involving Robert Williams of Monroe, North Carolina, who was suspended as NAACP chapter president in 1959 because he held that Negroes should fight in self-defense when attacked, which at the time seemed to be a unique and relatively inconsequential phenomenon, turns out to be something of a harbinger of the future. Williams later said that only if Negroes fought back would federal intervention on their behalf occur—and recent events in Birmingham suggest that there was an element of truth in this prediction. There are some who believe that rioting and bloodshed are inevitable and could even be of value in compelling the intervention of federal authority and the recognition of the Negro's constitutional rights. Moreover, it is possible that the dire predictions in the daily press about the likelihood of racial violence may act in the nature of a self-fulfilling prophecy. Whether or not extensive racial violence occurs, astute leadership in the civil rights movement will certainly employ its possibility as a device for eliciting quicker action from the white power structure. In any event, the movement is at the point where CORE, SNCC, and many NAACP leaders say that no matter what the risks of violence may be, they cannot stop pressing forward now. The outlook is therefore clearly for more direct action, not less.

One must conclude that there has emerged a real thrust for achieving "Freedom Now" from the working-class and lower-

middle-class people. SNCC, highly critical of both the black bourgeoisie and the white liberals, regards itself as the vanguard of the
Negro masses—and to a remarkable extent that is exactly what the
youthful demonstrators of the years since 1960 have proved to be.
And this pressure from the working class—especially working-class
youth—has been largely responsible for the greater momentum the
civil rights movement has recently attained. It is ironical that what
started out some time ago as a Negro middle- and upper-class and a
white liberal movement, has ended up as a movement where the
largest impetus is coming from the Negro working masses. In fact,
the competition for prestige and power among the major civil rights
organizations is in considerable degree a competition for control
over the masses of working-class Negroes. It is also likely that a large
part of the waxing militancy of middle- and upper-class Negroes is
derived from the new militancy of the working classes. As Bayard
Rustin wrote concerning Birmingham in the June 1963 issue of
Liberation, here was a "black community [that] was welded into
classless revolt. A. G. Gaston, the Negro millionaire who with some
ministers and other upper-class elements had publicly stated that
the time was not ripe for such a broad protest, finally accommodated
himself, as did the others, to the mass pressure from below and
joined the struggle." There is, however, a wide range of patterns.
Thus in Baltimore it has been the example of certain prominent
ministers and the Urban League executive secretary, who were
arrested July 4 at the Gwynn Oaks amusement park demonstration,
that is galvanizing large numbers of adults in the community to a
willingness to participate in direct-action activity.

It has become fashionable in activist circles to criticize the Negro
bourgeoisie and the white liberals as being conservative compromisers, wedded to gradualism and legalism. But this is a gross
oversimplification of the true situation. Much of the leadership in
the civil rights movement comes from the more elite Negroes. Even
the leadership of SNCC, which is most vociferous in its denunciation
of the black bourgeoisie is largely of middle-class origins. From
Cambridge to Albany the leadership of the southern movement is
peppered with members of the middle and upper classes. And the
Birmingham experience suggests that if the businessmen and leaders drawn from the upper strata wish to retain their position they
will have to go along with the tide.

It is as erroneous to stereotype the white liberals as it is to stereotype the black bourgeoisie. "Farewell to the white liberal," has now
become a familiar slogan. And in large part this feeling is justified.
As far back as the middle fifties, Negroes exhibited disillusionment

with many white liberals who thought the NAACP (of all organizations) was going too fast. Liberal labor leaders have temporized on
the issue of trade union discrimination in deference to prejudiced
elements within their unions, especially in the South. Often white
liberals, who ideologically think in terms of gradual change and
compromising where necessary, and whose wide-ranging concerns
sometimes lead them to feel that progress in other areas should not
necessarily be sacrificed for an all-out attack on civil rights (a point
of view that plagued the Kennedy administration during its first
two years and more in office) display what to Negro activists is an
alarming tendency to compromise, if not betray, their cause. Certain white liberals who have entered the establishment since Kennedy became president tend to urge a go-slow approach because
they do not like to see the president placed in a difficult position.

Yet, all liberals are not alike; a significant number are activists
themselves. Faculty members and students from Duke University
and the University of Tennessee, and more recently Vanderbilt
University have participated in direct-action demonstrations, as
have a handful of liberal white professors in the Negro colleges.
White liberals formed an important element in CORE's 1961 Freedom Ride, and CORE still draws largely from the liberal white group
in the North; a very substantial share of the financial support (possibly over half) of SNCC, SCLC, CORE and the NAACP Legal Defense
Fund comes from liberal whites; many hundreds of northern white
liberal college youth have participated in demonstrations in Maryland, and some have worked as field secretaries for SNCC in the
Deep South. Moreover, it seems inevitable that as desegregation
progresses in the South, increasing numbers of southern white
liberal youth will want to participate. If they do so in significant
numbers, the most active ones will certainly wish to participate in
policy making, and thus SNCC will have to reexamine its Negro-
only leadership policy. It is natural that Negroes should want to
discard paternalistic white leadership. But the ironic result is that a
movement for racial equality operates ideologically with the notion
that whites should be subordinate in it to Negroes. Undoubtedly
this is a passing phase; as we approach genuine full citizenship for
American Negroes this sort of anomaly will disappear.

The sharpest censure of liberal whites is of course reserved for
those labor leaders and politicians who, subjected to many cross-
pressures, do not act fully in accordance with their ideals. Southern
union locals, and vested interest groups who do not wish to share
their monopoly of skilled jobs or their power within the unions with
others, resist granting equality to Negro union members. Even

unions that pass resolutions in support of Negro rights significantly compromise the rights of their own Negro members. The situation in the ILGWU, for example, where nonwhites make up a large proportion of the membership is a scandal. There is not a single Negro on the union's general executive board, and though nonwhites make up over 90 percent of the membership of certain locals, all managers are white. Not only are there no Negroes in positions of real leadership in the ILGWU, but Negroes have difficulty in entering the skilled craft local unions. Even the UAW, known for years for its outstanding liberalism on the race issue, has lacked Negro participation in its top circles. Not until the 1962 convention was a Negro elected to the international executive board—and this came about only after a Negro caucus conducted a spirited two-year fight on the floor of the convention. The situation, of course, is far worse in most of the old-line illiberal AFL unions, especially in the building trades, printing and skilled metal crafts. In the South, union locals are sometimes identified with the white supremacists, as in Savannah, Front Royal, Virginia, Lithonia, Georgia, and elsewhere. In the steel center of Birmingham, the most highly unionized town in the South, and in Little Rock, Atlanta and New Orleans, which are all well unionized, organized labor failed to take a stand in behalf of civil rights during the racial crises in those cities. Union leaders have simply abdicated their responsibilities on this issue. All this is not lost on Negro workers. As far as Negroes are concerned, the theory of Negro-labor unity is meaningless. Thus, with few exceptions, labor, which many conceive of as the natural ally of the Negro, is under attack from Negro protest groups.

THE TREMENDOUS PRESSURES generated by the Negro protest movement in recent months have forced the president to finally come out forcefully for Negro citizenship rights on moral grounds and to make some relatively strong legislative recommendations to congress. While pleased with the step forward Kennedy has taken, Negro leaders, even Roy Wilkins, are nevertheless dissatisfied with his proposals. In many ways, they feel that the legislative package could and must be strengthened. They are particularly disappointed that Kennedy's recommendations do not attack the heart of the employment problem, whose solution they are now coming to recognize as the key to the solution of the whole problem of racial discrimination. And there have been strong rumblings of dissatisfaction over the administration's seeming willingness to compromise on the public accommodations proposals. Thus Kennedy is caught between the accelerating Negro demands and the counter-pressures from groups hostile to civil rights. Under the circumstances, whatever he feels able to do will not satisfy the integrationists.

Yet in attacking white liberals, and in making the incontrovertible assertion that Negroes through their own actions have brought about more changes in the past three years than took place in all the preceding fifty, it seems to me that the civil rights activists appear to be taking a somewhat narrow view of social causation. Leaving aside the role of white liberals in creating the climate of opinion which makes more rapid advancement now possible, it should be pointed out that the civil rights movement even now depends a great deal financially upon the contributions of liberal whites. Kennedy acts too late and then too little on civil rights matters, but it is doubtful that if Nixon had won the presidency with southern support there would have been much significant progress. Indeed, undoubtedly the current Negro mood is partly rooted in the expectation that Kennedy would act decisively. Disillusionment set in when he did not.

Some white liberals, no longer regarded as authorities on strategy by Negro integrationists, amazed at some of the demands that Negroes are now making—such as bringing white children into Negro areas for school so as to create racially balanced educational facilities, and giving Negroes preferential treatment on jobs until employment equality is achieved—must feel rather like the Girondists did when overtaken by the Jacobins. Should violence become a common tactic rather than a sporadic reaction, more will find themselves in this position. Thus to some extent, there is a tendency for many white liberals to feel rather alienated from the civil rights movement today. This is true even for those who participate in the movement. They sense the general suspicion of white liberals, the deliberate exclusion of whites from leadership, and their relegation, as whites, to secondary and supporting roles. (I do not intend to suggest that this attitude toward white participation is universal. Baltimore, North Carolina, and probably Nashville would be exceptions. In North Carolina a white Duke University student was elected president of the NAACP state youth conference in 1962; in Baltimore where the NAACP leadership has for years held that "You can't trust any white people," the nonviolent demonstrators in CORE and CIG tend to regard some of the more extreme activists in SNCC as something akin to racists.)

INTERESTINGLY ENOUGH there are signs that the white radicals in the civil rights movement are also somewhat alienated from it.

Radicals of various hues—Socialists, Trotskyites, Russophile Communists, and others—perceived in the student nonviolent movement important implications. They saw it as a potentially revolutionary movement and believed that, given the context of American life in the sixties, in this movement lay the key to a more socialized America. They may yet be right, not because their aims are the aims of the Negro activists, not because they will be able to generate a truly revolutionary movement out of the Negro protest, but because the unemployment problem facing Negro workers is of such serious dimensions that the government may be compelled to take what by American standards would be highly radical steps to solve it. For civil rights leaders are on the road to making employment their chief area of direct action, and it is the area most fraught with the danger of explosive violence in the North. In a sense, the solution to the nation's growing economic problems is a key to the solution of the civil rights question. Integration will be meaningless without jobs, and not very meaningful if the jobs are the old menial ones. In fact, a major source of the very urgency characterizing the Negro protest movement today is the economic deprivation suffered by millions of unskilled and semiskilled Negro workers and their families.

The Socialists, and particularly the more militant revolutionary Marxists saw a golden opportunity in the student movement and the expanding work of SCLC. Superficially their ideas fitted in well enough with the vocabulary of the Negro activists, who were imbued with the mystique of conducting a "revolutionary" movement destined to shake the social structure to its very foundations, and who identified themselves with the Negro masses against the black bourgeoisie. Undoubtedly the white radicals added to the revolutionary, anti-Negro-bourgeois, anti-white-liberal psychology of the movement. Their presence was welcomed by many, though fully understood by only a few, for they seemed sincere, dedicated and uncompromising in their advocacy of civil rights. Attending the SNCC meeting in 1962 was like going to a Popular Front affair in the 1930s.

Lately one can discern some disenchantment on the part of the white radicals. In the winter 1963 issue of *Freedomways*, Ann Braden voiced concern over the second-class position accorded to southern white radicals in the civil rights movement.

More significantly, some of the revolutionary Marxists, both Negro and white, are looking with dismay upon the signs that southern businessmen are coming to terms with the demonstrators since this would deflect the movement from what they believe is its true revolutionary course. They regard it as regrettable that Negroes would be satisfied with the ballot, a home, and a car. But they have really missed the point of the Negro protest movement. After all, the vote, a job, a decent standard of living, the right to come and go like other American citizens are what Negroes are really striving for.

The nonideological activists are not aiming at radical change in the social structure—they simply talk as if they are. In speaking with Negro youth who use the vocabulary of revolution, one soon discovers that the vast majority of them are attempting to *reform* American society. They want to "revolutionize" the system of race relations, and anticipate that in the process the political system of the South will undergo a radical transformation into a two-party system. But they contemplate no change in the basic political and economic structures; at most, some of them talk rather vaguely of the identity of interest between poor whites and poor Negroes. More fundamentally what most of them want is the opportunity to participate fully in American society as it stands.

SINCE THE AMERICAN NEGRO is now an emerging class that demands the opportunity to participate fully in the American social structure, one would expect that, like thwarted emerging classes elsewhere, if the employment situation is not improved, and if unbreakable resistance should persist in the South, or if a period of reaction should reverse the present trends, he might become a genuine revolutionary radical, and reject entirely the American system and what it stands for. But in such an eventuality the trend is not likely to be toward Marxism—which has had practically no impact upon the Negro activists—but toward some form of nationalism. Until recently, in fact, it seemed quite possible that the unskilled, lowest-class urban Negroes might turn to the escapist nationalist ideology of the Black Muslims, for this sect offered a sense of dignity and a hope for the future to those whom the civil rights movement neglected. More than anything else, increasing unemployment joined with the revolution in expectations created a climate in which the Black Muslims thrived. The Black Muslims are simply one of several nationalist movements, but the only one of any size, and though their number is almost certainly below 100,000 they have many admirers. Historically, extreme nationalism of this sort has been usually found among the most dispossessed of the Negro masses (the chief exception being the discouraging decade prior to the Civil War when considerable interest in colonization was to be found among the Negro elite), though there are certain tiny groups of nationalist intellectuals, like the avowedly Marxist

Monroe Defense Committee, and like the Liberation Committee for Africa, which seems to lack any coherent program.

JUST AS THE GARVEY MOVEMENT was the lower-lower-class counterpart of the New Negro of the 1920s, so the Black Muslims are the counterpart of the new "New Negro" of the 1960s. They preach an eschatological vision of the doom of the white devils and the coming dominance of the black man, promise a utopian paradise of a separate territory within the United States in which Negroes will establish their own state, and offer a more practical program of economic accumulation and building up Negro business through hard work, thrift, middle-class morality, and racial unity. Nevertheless, despite the stark contrast between the integrationist aims of the civil rights organizations, and the separatist ideology of the Black Muslims, it is important to recognize that the two have much in common. Both are manifestations of a militant rejection of white discrimination and doctrines of Negro inferiority. Both are essentially a quest for recognition of the Negroes' human dignity. Both reflect the new self-image of American Negroes arising out of the emergence of the new African states. Both exhibit profound dissatisfaction with the traditional Christianity of the Negro masses which offered rewards in heaven rather than a correction of abuses here on earth. Both work for a future in which Negroes lead the life of bourgeois Americans. Both exhibit a skepticism about liberal whites. And both are indications of Negro rejection of the philosophy of gradualism. In part, perhaps because they have sensed the increasing attraction for the masses of the direct-action activists of the civil rights organizations which have been moving more vigorously into the area of employment discrimination; in part, undoubtedly, because they thought the moment opportune to make a bid for leadership of the entire Negro community, since March 1963, the Black Muslims appear to have made a turn to the right. They now give less emphasis to separatism, and place more emphasis on the generalized abstractions of justice and freedom; they even urge support of the programs of the civil rights groups which are working for freedom and justice for the race.

The influence of the Black Muslims on the civil rights movement is somewhat speculative. Negroes of all classes approve of their searing indictment of the American race system, and of their ability to place white men on the defensive. Their renown may have contributed to some extent to the vogue of asserting pride in being black that has enjoyed some popularity among Negro activists in recent years. Their presence has also probably contributed not a

little to the intensified activities of the more traditional organizations like the NAACP and Urban League, and may in fact have
helped alert the civil rights organizations generally to the importance of vigorous action on behalf of the unemployed. This of
course will, in turn, almost certainly undermine the Black Muslims'
appeal. And finally, the fear of the Black Muslims has certainly
accelerated the efforts of influential whites to satisfy the demands
of the civil rights organizations. Ironically, the Black Muslims, by
frightening white people, are putting themselves out of business.

IT IS FAREWELL to the white liberals, and probably also to the white
radicals, and quite likely it will be the same shortly for the Black
Muslims. Prejudice and discrimination have produced strong ambivalences in the psychology of American Negroes. They wish to be
accepted as Americans, and yet are forced to an ethnocentric loyalty
to the black race. Basically they wish to participate in the American
social structure, yet they are forced into revolt against it. But revolutionary radicalism, whether of the nationalist or the Marxist variety,
seems to be an unlikely haven for the majority of Negroes, simply
because, in contrast to the Africans, they are in a minority that is too
small and too dispossessed to obtain freedom and dignity by either
of these methods. But they are numerous enough to be a crucial
factor in national and in many state and local elections; they are
numerous enough to disrupt the normal operations of city life by
demonstrations; and they are numerous enough and prosperous
enough to wield a mighty economic threat through the power of
selective patronage. The future success of the Negro protest movement therefore lies in the use of economic and political pressures,
dramatized by nonviolent demonstrations, that will compel the
politicians and the business community (in the South the so-called
moderates) to accord equal treatment to Negroes in American society. I do not conceive of the politicians or the business community
as allies of the Negroes; rather they are the power blocs most
susceptible to pressures that Negroes are able to exert.

   If, as I think, this will be the likely course of events, we will be
faced with another interesting irony in that certain groups that in
the past have done so much to advance the cause of civil rights will
be the least to benefit from the results. I refer to the Black Muslims
who have advanced civil rights by scaring the white man, and to the
white liberals and radicals who have worked directly for racial
equality. Though one may anticipate that for some time Negroes
will remain a relatively distinct group in view of the ethnic plural-
ism traditional in our society, there will no longer be a base upon

which the Black Muslims can erect a powerful movement although they will continue to appeal to the thousands of disadvantaged people whose problems cannot be solved even if tremendous progress is made. Nor will Negroes have any more cause to be liberals or radicals than Americans generally.

Unless the problems posed by automation prove insoluble within the framework of a capitalist economy, the United States is likely to remain dominated by a middle-class ideology; the routes of upward mobility for Negroes will be the same as those for whites; and Negroes consequently will share in the typical bourgeois values and aspirations of American life.

The new thrust from the Negro masses, the complex patterns of rivalry and cooperation among the civil rights organizations, the increasing power of the Negro vote in the urban centers North and South, the growing realization of the Negro's economic power that he has learned from successful boycotts, the obvious sensitivity of the government to foreign criticism of our racial system, have together resulted in a broadening and intensification of the Negro protest. Year by year and month by month, Negroes have been growing more militant, more immediatist, more fed up with limited successes and tokenism. Paradoxically both the increasing pace of advancement and the growing resistance in the South are leading to greater and greater Negro militance. It is conceivable that a stiffening of southern white intransigence, or large-scale unemployment may complicate matters and encourage the development of a black nationalist revolutionary ideology. But two things are quite certain—Negro militance is bound to grow, and an accelerated tempo of improvement in civil rights appears almost inevitable.

THIRTEEN

The Continuing Quest for Equality

REVIEW-ESSAYS, I have found, are often helpful in evaluating one's thinking and crystallizing one's ideas. Between 1964 and 1968 I composed three such essays for *Social Education*, each of them evaluating a group of recently published and related books. The first of these review-essays, published in 1964 and reprinted here, reflects much of my thinking about the movement during the months following passage of the Civil Rights Act of 1964.

Black Man's America. By Simeon Booker. Englewood Cliffs, New Jersey: Prentice-Hall, 1964.

The New Equality. By Nat Hentoff. New York: The Viking Press, 1964.

A Profile of the Negro American. By Thomas F. Pettigrew. Princeton: D. Van Nostrand Company, 1964.

Race Riot at East St. Louis, July 2, 1917. By Elliott M. Rudwick. Carbondale: Southern Illinois University Press, 1964.

Ten Years of Prelude: The Story of Integration Since the 1954 Supreme Court Decision. By Benjamin Muse. New York: The Viking Press, 1964.

To Be Equal. By Whitney Young, Jr. New York: McGraw-Hill Book Company, 1964.

White and Black: Test of a Nation. By Samuel Lubell. New York: Harper and Row, 1964.

Why We Can't Wait. By Martin Luther King, Jr. New York: Harper and Row, 1964.

Nineteen sixty-three was a turning point in the history of the Negro protest movement. It became a truly mass movement, and the militancy that had permeated southern Negro protest moved North. It became evident that, as Nat Hentoff phrased it, "beyond civil rights" there lay a host of economic problems that would have to be solved if the American Negro was really, to use Whitney Young's words, *To Be Equal*. Above all 1963 was the year in which the whole Negro protest movement was seized with a new quality of imme-

From *Social Education* 28 (December 1964): 481–83.

diatism, which Martin Luther King undertakes to explain in his *Why We Can't Wait*.

Negroes are more militant than ever, but as Thomas Pettigrew points out in his *A Profile of Negro Americans*, there remain "serious limitations to white understanding of the Negro American. The majority of white Americans as yet neither identifies with Negro Americans nor senses the urgency of the present revolution." No more apt words could be used to describe Samuel Lubell's *White and Black*. King wrote his noted "Letter from Birmingham Jail," reprinted in his book under review here, as a reply to a group of white clergymen who, though endorsing Negro goals, believed that King was moving too fast. But the letter might as well have been directed at the noted pollster and professor of journalism. In his letter King

confess[ed] that over the past few years I have been gravely disappointed with the white moderate. I have almost reached the regrettable conclusion that the Negro's great stumbling block in his stride toward freedom is not the White Citizen's Councilor nor the Ku Klux Klanner, but the white moderate, who is more devoted to "order" than to justice; who prefers a negative peace which is the absence of tension to a positive peace which is the presence of justice; who constantly says: "I agree with you in the goal you seek, but I cannot agree with your methods of direct action"; who paternalistically believes he can set the timetable for another man's freedom; who lives by a mythical concept of time and who constantly advises the Negro to wait for a "more convenient season."

Exhibiting the same sentiments, Whitney Young, executive director of the traditionally conservative National Urban League, writes:

Good race relations—race harmony—is more than the absence of conflict, tension, or even war. *It is the presence of justice*. Nothing is more immoral than the suggestion that people adjust to injustice or that we make a god of "timing." The time is always ripe to do right.

Lubell's book offers some interesting insights, but from beginning to end it betrays the earmarks of a journalistic "quickie." The discussion of Negro thought prior to the New Deal is superficial. Lubell is more at home in the New Deal period, and he correctly stresses the benefits it brought to Negroes, who consequently shifted their political allegiance from the Republicans to the Democrats. But he fails to discuss the New Deal policies that were retrogressive in regard to Negroes. Notable among these were the practices of the housing authorities, which did so much to promote the growth of the mammoth northern urban ghettos which Lubell now perceives as the chief threat to racial peace. But Lubell does highlight two important trends underlying the situation which the nation faces today: the breakdown of the Negro-labor coalition forged during the New Deal, and the way in which an almost inevitable clash developed out of the simultaneous growth in southern white resistance and in Negro expectancies that followed the Supreme Court decision outlawing school segregation in 1954. These trends lead Lubell to paint a pessimistic picture. He denounces the Negro militants, because he fears that their work will lead to the shattering of the Democratic party and to serious race conflict between the Negro-dominated cities and the white-dominated suburbs of the North. His solution: good old-fashioned civil libertarianism that sounded so progressive a generation ago. Take discriminatory laws off the books, allow Negroes who can afford it to move unrestrictedly into the suburbs (where, Lubell predicts, they will probably resegregate themselves anyhow, following the pattern of other ethnic minorities), and make it possible for Negroes, through their own exertions, to advance in society in the time-honored manner of the European immigrant nationalities.

Those of the other books under review here which deal with the current racial crisis reveal neither Lubell's pessimism, nor his misreading of the Negro Revolution. Benjamin Muse's useful volume, *Ten Years of Prelude*, which is a careful examination of the history of the struggle over southern school desegregation since 1954, makes it apparent that once desegregation comes, even in the Deep South, it is accepted. Young points out that what happened in 1963 was not that white opposition to Negro advancement increased, but that for the first time white Americans generally could not avoid facing the issue of race discrimination, which the Negro militants now posed so dramatically. Overt expressions of tension and hostility naturally resulted. But as King says, the nonviolent actionists "are not the creators of tension. We merely bring to the surface the hidden tension that is already alive. We bring it out in the open, where it can be seen and dealt with." Young and King, moreover, both refer to the support the movement gained in 1963 from new sources, particularly among clergymen. This is a phenomenon which Lubell fails to take into account in his oversimplified dichotomy of whites vs. blacks.

Simeon Booker, Hentoff, King, Young, and Pettigrew, each in his own way, illuminate the changed mood of American Negroes and the growing emphasis of the protest movement on economic conditions. They explore the roots of the new mood in the revolution of Negro expectations that occurred during the 1950s (especially after the 1954 decision), in the new self-image of American Negroes derived from the rise of the new African nations to independence and power, and in the fact that the pace of change, while notable, did not match up to the higher expectations. Of particular importance was the increasing unemployment among working-class Negroes, especially youth, due to technological change and periodic recessions.

The alienated urban slum dwellers have been stirred by the spirit engendered by the Negro revolt. But the "dream" of which King speaks so eloquently remained for most of them more than ever, as Langston Hughes has put it, "a dream deferred." Raised hopes were met only with the same old bleak prospects of chronic unemployment, rat-infested tenements, and overcrowded and inferior schools. Such conditions provided fertile ground for the youthful rioters who battled with police in certain northern cities last summer. All of the books reviewed here were written too early to deal with the implications of these events. But Elliott M. Rudwick's skillful blending of sociology and history, *Race Riot at East St. Louis,* is a minor masterpiece that should be studied by all concerned with the future of race relations. The disorders of 1964 were not true race riots; and the situation in 1917–1919, when whites mercilessly attacked Negroes in cities across the country from Washington to Chicago, was much different from the one we face now. Yet Rudwick's analysis of the bloodiest race riot in American history makes it evident that the main ingredients of earlier race riots are present today: hot, long summers, inept city officials, competition for jobs, and a new militancy among Negroes.

Pettigrew is almost certainly the most perceptive social psychologist now working in the field of race relations, and the opening and final sections of his volume are an excellent synthesis of what has been learned by studies of changing Negro attitudes, self-conceptions, and aspirations. The result is a scholarly yet lucid explanation of how it happened that patterns of resignation, passivity, and inferiority feelings have been replaced by the growth of militancy, aggressiveness, and pride.

Pettigrew writes with clarity and insight; yet it can be predicted that the essence of what he says will almost certainly be more successfully communicated by King. For in *Why We Can't Wait* King exemplifies the qualities that make him, despite criticism from other civil rights activists, the protest movement's symbol. He articulates better than anyone else the aspirations of the great majority of Negroes, and at the same time he is easily the most effective interpreter of these aspirations to white America. He devotes most of the book to a not very complete, or even entirely accurate, account of the Birmingham demonstrations in the spring of 1963. But the chapter entitled "The Sword That Heals," is a magnificent illustration of the secret of his appeal for countless white Americans. For King, nonviolent, direct action is a weapon with which Negroes battle evil in American society; but in effect what Negroes are doing is not only for their own salvation, but for that of the white man as well. As always King criticizes white Americans; but unlike James Baldwin and other angry young writers, he quite explicitly believes in the likelihood of their redemption.

Hentoff stresses the fact that philosophic dedication to pacifism is not characteristic among the nonviolent direct actionists, and that in the most militant wing of the movement there is disillusionment with the strategy of nonviolence and some talk of the possible necessity of Negroes reacting violently. Hentoff, a white jazz critic, knows certain sectors of the Negro community and of the civil rights movement very well. Thus in a way his book complements Booker's *Black Man's America*. Booker, who is *Ebony* magazine's Washington correspondent, seems to know just about everybody who is anybody in civil rights and the Negro power structure. He gives us a chatty, if poorly organized, account of goings-on on the civil rights front, and nearly every chapter contains illuminating information. Booker, who practically ignores the militant Student Nonviolent Coordinating Committee, which ideologically identifies with the Negro masses, focuses on the Negro elite. Hentoff, on the other hand, has mixed with the Negro masses and the militant mass-based wings of the movement. It is not inappropriate therefore that the volume is dedicated to Bayard Rustin, whose views form the basis for much of what Hentoff says.

It is of singular interest that Hentoff, associated with Socialists like Rustin, should enunciate views very similar to those expressed by Young, often described by activists as a "conservative." Both focus on jobs, housing, health, and schools; both insist that Negroes cannot achieve equality simply by the granting of constitutional rights. Both favor bussing and other devices to eliminate de facto school segregation. Both favor special efforts—crash programs, compensatory treatment—to bring Negroes to the point where they can compete on an equal level with whites. So also do King and Booker and, by implication, Pettigrew. To these men it is useless to argue, as does Lubell, that Negroes should follow the slow upward path of European immigrants. Negroes, they insist, have been here three hundred years, longer than any of the non–Anglo-Saxon peoples; they have been oppressed and prevented from rising in a way the European ethnic groups never experienced. Says Young:

The basic issue here is one of simple logic and fairness. The scales of justice have been heavily weighted against the Negro for over three hundred years and will not suddenly in 1965 balance themselves by applying equal weights. In this sense, the Negro is educationally and economically malnourished and anemic. It is not "preferential treatment" but simple decency to provide him for a brief period with special vitamins, additional foods, and blood transfusions.

Young's book is a cogent argument for a domestic "Marshall Plan"—for a decade of special assistance to the Negro masses, so that real equality can be achieved. Young emerges from the pages of *To Be Equal* as a realistic militant who, without mincing words, effectively interprets the work of the direct-action groups to white businessmen. But as he is once alleged to have said, today it takes courage to be a leader without having gone to jail.

Hentoff, King, and Young suggest that massive federal economic intervention may be necessary to create enough jobs for the elimination of unemployment of both whites and Negroes. Hentoff and Pettigrew believe that it will be impossible to solve this problem without some fundamental structural changes in American society, though they do not spell out what these changes are likely to be. Hentoff and King see the solution to the economic problem as coming through a Negro-labor alliance. Both are as dismayed as Lubell at the disintegration of this coalition. Young, whose emphasis is in many respects similar to Hentoff's, quite naturally is not concerned with this issue. For the Urban League continues, as it did in the past, to base its strategy chiefly on winning over white businessmen. Hentoff is well aware of the difficulties involved in re-creating an effective Negro-Labor coalition; if it comes he believes that it must come through a reshaping of the Democratic party. Hentoff does not say so, but presumably the reshaping will involve the departure of the conservative southerners from the party. Both King and Hentoff write of the probable future importance of partisan political activity as an instrument in the struggle for equality, and indeed this subject is increasingly under discussion in civil rights circles. Lubell on the other hand holds—and in my view correctly—that only limited gains can be obtained through partisan politics. He points out that the Negro vote is to a remarkable degree tied to the big-city machines, which make only minimal efforts to alleviate the misery of the urban slum-dwellers.

But Lubell's advice—both sound and unsound—will go unheeded. The very unanimity with which Hentoff, King, Young, Pettigrew, and Booker agree upon immediatism, upon compensatory treatment, upon the importance of attacking the oppressive economic problems, suggests that Lubell, for all his polling, is sadly out of touch with the mood and needs of the Negro community. His old-fashioned proposals are irrelevant. Negroes simply feel that they no longer have to put up with the legacy of inferiority stemming from three centuries of degradation. Thus, though the Negro protest is not truly a revolutionary movement, it has a revolutionary mystique. It is not a revolutionary movement because as yet few Negroes want to overthrow the American social structure; the vast majority still aim at participation in it. Advocates of varying combinations of nationalism, totalitarian Marxism, and violence are in the wings, ready to act if the nonviolent movement should fail. But thus far, as Whitney Young says:

> This is a revolution peculiarly characterized by a heroic drive and a courageous fight to gain the rights and respect that should be synonymous with the word "American." It is a revolution not by black people against white people, but by people who are right against those who are wrong.

FOURTEEN

Dynamics of Crisis and Unity in the Southern Movement

THIS ARTICLE, composed at the request of the editor of the Socialist periodical *New America*, flows from my experiences, observations, and reading during the high tide of nonviolent direct action in 1963 and early 1964. In the original version submitted, there was a final section, deleted by the editor as being too speculative, about the reasons for the unprecedented kind of unity displayed in the Mississippi Council of Federated Organizations (COFO), 1962–1964. In my analysis this unity was explained as being rooted in two factors. One was the very unusual personalities of the state NAACP president, Aaron Henry; of the head of CORE operations in the state, David J. Dennis; and of the SNCC's leader and COFO's chair, Robert Moses, all of whom were able to put aside the parochial interests of their respective organizations. Second, I pointed to the extreme repressiveness of the situation in Mississippi. I maintained that without the presence of either one of these factors the two-year-long coalition would probably not have occurred.

WRITING OF THE Birmingham demonstrations in the June 1963 issue of *Liberation*, Bayard Rustin noted that here a "black community was welded into classless revolt. A. G. Gaston, the Negro millionaire who with some ministers and other upper-class elements, had publicly stated that the time was not ripe for such a broad protest, finally accommodated himself, as did the others, to the mass pressure from below and joined the struggle."

In numerous other communities also the crisis situation produced by the demonstrations of last spring and summer created a new and dramatic unity in the Negro community.

Generally it can be said that youth are more militant than adults and upper classes. In this article I will describe developments in five cities where I either have observed events personally or have done some field research, in an attempt to analyze the dynamics of how, in a crisis situation, the more militant elements compel the more conservative elements in a community to support their strategy.

The pattern of events can be observed in microcosm in the story of the Northwood Theater demonstration conducted by the Bal-

From *New America*, January 10, 1964, pp. 4–5

timore Civic Interest Group in February 1963, when over four hundred Morgan State College students were arrested in a successful effort to open a theater near a school that had resisted integration attempts for eight years.

Activists among the Morgan students had always been in the minority. By and large the more elite students—honor students, outstanding athletes, and the fraternity crowd—had been conspicuous by their absence among the participants, and student government officials had shown no interest in demonstrations after the early spring of 1960.

Indeed, when in February 1963, CIG officials and student government leaders decided upon a program of deliberate mass arrests in order to compel the theater to change its policy, the response among the students generally was one of apathy and ridicule.

This apathy was largely overcome by getting certain leading campus personalities to be among the first group arrested, though the great majority among the first sixty or seventy to spend a night in jail—the ones who in short made having been in jail a "status symbol"—were drawn from the more obscure elements in the college population.

Even after 150 were arrested on the fourth night of demonstrations—the first night of truly mass arrests—the whole effort might have petered out, if the judge had not charged the students with both trespassing and disorderly conduct and set a punitive high bail of $600 per person, which came to a grand total of $90,000.

Unable to raise the bond money immediately, CIG leaders decided to change their tactics and let the students stay in jail until the theater desegregated; at the same time, stung by the judge's action, the student body closed ranks, and hundreds more offered themselves for arrest—twice as many in fact as actually went to jail, since with the city jail filled to overflowing the police deliberately held back on the number of arrests.

Students who had earlier scoffed at the idea of direct action found themselves first walking on the picket line, then lining up in an attempt to enter the theater, and finally being carted off to jail. For the first time honors students, football players, and large numbers of fraternity and sorority people were arrested.

Under the impact of the crisis, the adults at Morgan and in the city were more deeply affected than they had ever been previously. Some administrative officers openly espoused the cause of the students, and the very bourgeois dean of women, who had heretofore done all she could to thwart direct-action activities, did a remarkable about-face and vigorously supported the student effort.

Over the years, when arrests had been few, the president had taken a benignly hands-off policy toward the demonstrators, holding that they were simply exercising the rights of citizens. Now, however, he told leaders of the movement that the demonstrations had reached such proportions that they were interfering seriously with the school's academic program, and that he was therefore considering disciplinary action, though of a distinctly mild nature.

The number of arrests continued to mount. At a college assembly, the president's advice to discontinue the demonstrations was received with visible discontent. Finally, the afternoon before the theater capitulated, at a conference in the mayor's office, the president militantly informed the mayor that unless the matter was settled promptly, he believed that there would be 2,400 Morgan students in jail by Monday morning.

Adult leadership in the city exhibited varied patterns. The NAACP came out vigorously in support of the students. The chairman of the students' adult assistance committee, who was responsible for raising bail money, was at first upset by the idea of mass arrests—but after a couple of days he urged them to fill the jail.

Because the Baltimore police and judiciary are gubernatorial appointees, the Civic Interest Group, after the judge had set the punitively high bail, appealed to a close political ally of the governor—the Negro state senator—to intercede with him. She declined to do so at first; but two days later, after over 350 youths had been arrested, and it had become clear that the demonstrations were assuming even larger proportions, she announced that she was off to Annapolis at once to speak with the chief executive.

Thus, under student pressure, when the demonstrations became massive enough, adult elements that had been skeptical or lukewarm toward the students' tactics, came to their support.

Orangeburg

Orangeburg, South Carolina, was unusual in 1963, for there adults took the initiative. Since the dramatic but unsuccessful student demonstrations of 1960, Orangeburg had been quiet. But in the wake of its successful campaign in Charleston for desegregation of lunch counters and for jobs in King Street stores, the state NAACP launched a major campaign in Orangeburg, enlisting the assistance of all major adult groups and students under the name of the Orangeburg Movement of the NAACP.

During the summer adults and youth picketed in equal numbers; when Claflin and South Carolina State Colleges opened in the fall, youth participation climbed dramatically, and of the 1,500 arrested the majority were youth. As in Greensboro the preceding spring the example of the students influenced a few of the professors—at Orangeburg a half-dozen of them, including several from the state college, were arrested. And when the NAACP secretary was dismissed from her job in the public schools, students and teachers rallied in a remarkable spontaneous boycott of the public schools that lasted several days. As on the Morgan campus, citizens of Orangeburg spoke feelingly of the newly established unity in the community.

The NAACP in South Carolina has become thoroughly imbued with the value of direct action, but the same cannot be said for Danville and Cambridge.

Cambridge

When the Civic Interest Group initiated the first demonstrations in Cambridge in 1961 and stimulated the creation of the Cambridge Nonviolent Action Committee (CNAC), the nonviolent movement there was complicated by the factional rivalries already existing among the adults. Consequently the NAACP and leading ministers vacillated in their attitude toward the movement.

CNAC leadership centered in the hands of Cambridge's most distinguished old-line upper-class family, but when demonstrations were revived early in 1963 the only source of mass support for this leadership came from the lower classes. At first the only church that would open its doors to the demonstrators was a poverty-striken Baptist church. Only after the demonstrations picked up momentum, and it became clear that they had widespread support, did the leading ministers and the NAACP lend their cooperation to the movement again. And during the crisis of the early summer the movement enjoyed more support in all groups of the community than it had ever done before.

Danville

The story in Danville is an extremely complicated one. At the risk of some oversimplification one may say that the NAACP leadership there generally has been somewhat reluctant to endorse demonstrations. However there is a significant amount of overlapping between the NAACP leadership and that of the local SCLC affiliate, the Danville Christian Progressive Association (DCPA), formed two years ago for the purpose of direct action to desegregate lunch counters.

The DCPA's support is drawn from the working-class Negroes; NAACP support is chiefly from middle- and upper-class Negroes. This year the DCPA and the NAACP had agreed to attempt joint negotiations in order to secure employment in downtown department stores; if these did not succeed it was understood that direct action would follow.

The first negotiations had not been too fruitful, and before the two organizations could jointly decide on the next step, certain of the DCPA leaders spontaneously led youth on the first demonstrations of 1963. SNCC field workers came in at DCPA's request. From the start some of the NAACP lawyers were cooperating in the legal work.

But it was not until the now infamous night of 10 June—with its unprecedented police brutality—that the more elite members of the community became thoroughly aroused.

Teachers and others lent their assistance, cooking food for the demonstrators and doing secretarial chores; the NAACP contributed three thousand dollars to the legal costs; the more prosperous members of the community put up between $250,000 and $300,000 worth of property bonds; and finally, on a demonstration at the end of July, a few members of the upper class—including the bank cashier and the wife of one of the NAACP attorneys—subjected themselves to arrest.

Alabama

In Alabama the NAACP has been banned. In Selma—home of Alabama's first White Citizens' Council—as elsewhere in the Black Belt, where Negroes range from 50 to 75 percent of the population, the resistance to Negro progress is most determined. The focus of protest in these hard core counties is not on public accommodations, but on the even more fundamental right to vote.

SNCC, the most militant of the civil rights organizations, sent field workers into Selma in the fall of 1962. Thoroughly intimidated, only a few adults responded to SNCC urgings to try to register, and SNCC field workers were harassed by police.

Sensing the future trends, however, a group of leading Negro citizens organized the Dallas County Improvement Association, and in the spring of 1963 asked the city's officials to make changes before demonstrations and possible violence occurred. Their overtures were rejected.

Meanwhile the youth had responded to SNCC's overtures—and the result was a sit-in demonstration with mass arrests, police brutality, and even police intimidation of Negroes attending mass meetings. The adults rallied to the aid of the youth; and the Dallas County Improvement Association proved helpful financially and in other ways.

Finally, in October, as a consequence of the demonstration and its repression, hundreds of adults courageously attempted to register, even in the fact of continuing police brutality to sncc field workers.

Unity Temporary

Unity thus achieved does not, unfortunately, necessarily remain when the crisis period is over. At Morgan, despite the momentum given to the student movement by the Northwood demonstration, the great majority of students returned to their customary concerns, and direct action withered.

In Cambridge, after the signing of the "Cambridge Agreement" in Attorney General Kennedy's office, the naacp-ministerial group again split with cnac when the latter held that Negroes should not participate in the referendum on the public accommodations amendment to the city charter.

And in Danville, since the end of the summer, the coalition between naacp and dcpa has been subjected to many strains, and cooperation between the two groups has tended to be spasmodic.

As the examples cited illustrate, under the impact of the demonstrations of last spring and summer, greater unity emerged among the different civil rights groups, and there has been greater adult participation in direct action. While there is now far more cooperation among civil rights organizations than there was a year ago, the evidence would seem to suggest that only in a situation of real crisis is profound unity of spirit and action very likely between the different organizations, between youth and adults, and between the upper and lower classes.

FIFTEEN

Who Are the "True Believers"?—A Tentative Typology of the Motivations of Civil Rights Activists

LIKE THE PRECEDING essay on crisis and unity in the protest movement, this essay is an experimental "think-piece." A colleague at Morgan State had introduced me to Eric Hoffer's discussion of the role of the "true believer" in radical social movements, and in an adapted form his analysis had a considerable influence on my thinking (see Eric Hoffer, *The True Believer*, 1951). The very tentative discussion that follows was prepared in response to a request to read a paper at the meeting of the American Orthopsychiatric Association in March 1965. Composed during my first year at Roosevelt University, it draws upon experiences of the preceding five years. I have always regretted that I was never in a position to do something more on the topic than this very tentative piece.

ABOUT THIS TIME last year there were some disturbing reports emanating from Mississippi. I am not referring to the well-known facts about intimidation and oppression of Negroes in that state, but to a situation known only to those in "the movement" as civil rights activists refer to it. Civil rights workers in Mississippi, especially those connected with the Student Nonviolent Coordinating Committee (SNCC), were engaged in the preliminary preparations for what later became the famous Mississippi Summer Project. At that time northern white activists working in Mississippi found themselves, as they said, being "race-baited." These college youth, taking time out from their studies to work in dangerous Mississippi, found that the southern Negro activists were, to put it with some detachment, ambivalent toward the presence of the whites. The northern white youth discovered that their suggestions were not wanted—were in fact resented. At best the white workers were to be the tolerated followers and foot soldiers, no matter what their qualifications.

Paper read at the March 1965 meeting of the American Orthopsychiatric Association, printed in Joseph R. Gusfield, ed., *Protest, Reform and Revolt: A Reader in Social Movements* (New York, 1970), pp. 473–82.

201

Thus the rising tide of what has been described as Negro "nationalistic" feeling within the civil rights movement—a development that involved criticism of white liberals, and an assertion of the necessity of Negro leadership—appeared to exhibit itself in an aggravated form. Actually, however, I believe that there are other factors involved in what Howard Zinn has described as the "tensions and troubles, antiwhite and black nationalist feelings among Negroes in SNCC, resentment expressed against white kids rushing into the movement, personal piques and gripes and explosions, and, in one setting of high nervous tension, a fistfight" [Howard Zinn, *SNCC: The New Abolitionists* (Boston, 1964), p. 126]. This paper will attempt to describe and explain at least some of these other factors.

What I intend to do is to analyze in very tentative terms the characteristics of the youth, both white and Negro, who become dedicated activists. It has been my observation that the movement has attracted different sorts of people from each racial group. By "the movement" I refer not to the total civil rights movement, but to its direct-action wing—including people in SNCC, SCLC, CORE, and some in NAACP. These are the people who are called activists—that is, they participate in nonviolent, direct-action demonstrations.

Some individuals have only a fleeting and superficial participation in direct action. But those I shall be chiefly concerned with are the highly dedicated ones—the "true believers" who give up jobs, postpone their education, risk physical injury and even death, and at the very least expect to be arrested and to spend some time in jail. These are the people whose life for a period of months, even years, becomes almost entirely oriented to the movement.

While I consider the movement to be a reform rather than a revolutionary movement, it does have a revolutionary mystique; and the dedicated activists would fit Eric Hoffer's definition of the "true believer," those who are completely devoted to a cause, who find meaning in life through their participation in what they esoterically refer to as "*the* movement." I recall one charming white girl with whom I spoke during the course of her month-long stay in the Annapolis, Maryland, jail, where she elected to serve out her term rather than pay a small fine. "I have thought it all over," she said, "and I have decided that I and the movement are one."

The generalizations that I will set forth must of necessity be gross oversimplifications of the complexity of social reality. There are many types of people in the movement, and they enter it for diverse reasons. Obviously all of these will not be subsumed under the model types I suggest. It must be emphasized furthermore that the speaker has not done systematic research on the motivations and social backgrounds of civil rights activists. My generalizations are based in part upon four years (1960–1964) of observation as a participant in direct-action organizations in Baltimore, Maryland, and Newark, New Jersey, and in direct-action demonstrations from Cambridge, Maryland, and Atlanta, Georgia, to Syracuse, New York. In part they are based upon numerous conversations and interviews conducted during the past five years in a number of southern and northeastern cities, in the course of research for a book on the history of the twentieth-century civil rights movement. I do not claim that the people with whom I talked and worked form a representative sample. My conclusions, it must be stressed, are oversimplified and very tentative. I hope, however, to be provocative and suggestive.

When the college student sit-in movement swept the South in 1960 I was teaching at Morgan State College, a Negro institution in Baltimore. Though Morgan does have a few students from elite families, its population is mostly working class. The majority of them come from census tracts in which average family income is $3,000 or less per year. Most of them belong to the first generation in their families to go to college, and for them college is a route of upward mobility. Their parental occupational background would place the majority in the upper-lower class if they were white; but in view of the skewed nature of the Negro class structure, arising out of the lack of economic opportunity within the Negro community, these youth come chiefly from families that function as lower-middle class.

Morgan students have been involved in sporadic direct-action demonstrations for a half-dozen years prior to 1960. Practically every spring the student council would inaugurate a campaign to desegregate the movie theater and one or more of the eating facilities at the shopping center less than a mile from the campus. These efforts, some successful and others not, were ordinarily of a brief duration. Prior to 1960 not one Morgan student had been arrested on any demonstration—though in the early years police were distinctly unfriendly. In short, these student activists had not been "true believers."

Though the revival of Morgan student demonstrations in March 1960 came after the wave of sit-ins had spread through the South, the pattern of previous years was at first followed. But something different soon happened. Three students were arrested for blocking the entrance to the restaurant being picketed. It is perhaps significant that this group did not include any of the college's political or social elite, but did involve an aggressive personality, who was seeking to overturn the student-council leadership of the demonstrations, and who eventually dropped out of school for poor grades. In two or three weeks the student council and fraternity crowd had—with two or three exceptions—retired from active association with the demonstrations. Those students who remained active, those who sat in and walked on picket lines week after week—those, that is, who formed the small group who were the backbone of the movement—consisted for the most part of individuals obscure in campus life. They tended to be rather below average in their scholarship; and in part because their energies were monopolized by the movement, several dropped out of school and others found themselves on probation. They were not the campus leaders, not the members of sororities and fraternities, not the good students, not even the athletes. The leaders who emerged often tended, it is true, to be above-average students, though these became so involved in the movement that their grades fell disastrously. To these youth life's meaning—and their own contribution to society—came not through athletic prowess, social or political distinction in campus life, or high academic achievement, but through attacking social injustice.

This state of affairs was neatly illustrated by the response of Morgan's students to a convocation address by the college president in the fall of 1961. The president recognized the contributions made by the demonstrators, but held that just as important as the "glamorous" sit-ins and arrests that were breaking down the Negro's exclusion from American society was the work of preparing oneself academically to achieve success in the expanding opportunities of an integrating society. His remarks failed to achieve their objective. They served as an effective rationalization for the great majority of students who felt somewhat guilty because they lacked the commitment to become activists. But the president was so far from reaching the activists with his homily that they took his remarks to mean that he opposed demonstrations. Actually, he was very proud of his students' participation in the demonstrations. As he often said, while white students were engaged in panty raids, Morgan students were working for the good of society.

My observations indicate that at other colleges a similar pattern existed—though there were a few exceptions, notably in Atlanta. As the college student movements shifted from the campus to the community and drew high school youth into their activities, they appeared to attract much the same kind of persons. In discussions of this question with a group of student leaders from all parts of the

South at a workshop in Nashville in the summer of 1961, the typical observation was that the participants were youth who came from "the striving lower class." Put in more sophisticated sociological jargon, it would appear that most of the Negro college and high school youth involved at that stage of the movement were of working-class origins, with high upward mobility aspirations. They came from the working-class, church-going "respectables," and an important part of their motivation lay in their religious faith. To them the movement was a natural, practical application of the Christian faith in which they had been reared, and which had been such a vital psychological support for them and their parents. Later, those who remained in the movement were to become increasingly secularized for a number of reasons—among them contact with northern white students, and frustration at the slow pace of social change that the nonviolent method achieved.

But that was to lie in the future. The spirit of the southern Negro activists in the early months of the movement was brought into sharp focus at a conference of northern and southern students sponsored by the National Student Association early in 1961. The northern white students believed that the ideological basis of the movement should be rooted in such statements as the United Nations Declaration of Human Rights. The southern Negro students, however, insisted that it be firmly rooted in Christian writ.

The ranks of these southern Negro youth included few achievers in athletics, in Greek-letter circles, or in scholarship. It would seem, in fact, that the high achiever, especially the high academic achiever, at the southern Negro college pictures himself as advancing both himself and the race not through protest activity but through preparing himself thoroughly for a career. Seldom does it seem possible to reconcile both roles. The upwardly mobile person of lower- or lower-middle-class origins must, in view of both his financial insecurity and cultural deprivation, put all his energies into his studies if he is to succeed by the American standards of success. If he has the inclination to become deeply involved in the protest movement, he lacks the time. And he cannot afford to take a year or two off from his studies and hold his career back while engaging in a financially unremunerative pursuit. On the other hand, those Negro youth of high academic accomplishment who do become deeply involved in civil rights come principally from upper-middle and upper-class families, and ordinarily from the best northern universities. Thus they are financially secure and culturally advantaged. One can, of course, think of many exceptions to these generalizations. At Morgan the ablest leader in the student movement was an extraordinarily gifted young man, who possessed erratic study habits and average grades, and who preferred to be active in the world rather than sit at home with his books.

At this point I should state that during the last couple of years there has been increasing involvement of lower-class youth and young adults, and in times of severe crisis—as at Danville, Virginia, Selma, Alabama, and Birmingham, Alabama—people from all social classes and all ages may become so deeply motivated that they participate in demonstrations and risk going to jail. In Birmingham, in Selma, in Orangeburg, South Carolina, and in certain other places, even the schoolteachers—the most vulnerable, and therefore the most conservative, group in the Negro community—have become involved, as in Selma, where two or three hundred attempted to register. Equally significant has been the growing involvement of lower-class youth and young adults during 1963 and 1964. As a factory worker who became chairman of a CORE chapter in upper New York State put it, "It's in CORE that you find the Holy Spirit."

In my emphasis upon the lower-middle-class and working-class origins of today's activists, I would be remiss if I did not point out that most of the Negroes who were active in CORE in its first years, from 1942 to 1960, were middle-class people. CORE was very tiny then, and the numbers of middle-class Negroes who participated must have been very small indeed, especially in view of the fact that down to 1961 two-thirds of CORE's members were white. The whites in direct action in these years were also middle-class people in terms of their education and occupation. They were usually professional people, highly idealistic, frequently pacifists, and often Socialists as well. Since 1961 the trend has been for CORE to become predominantly Negro and for the Negroes to come more and more from the working class, though there are still CORE chapters in which middle-class Negroes predominate and set the tone. Meanwhile those white pacifists who have not left CORE have been pushed into the background.

My first contact with large numbers of white civil rights demonstrators was in the winter of 1961–1962, when projects sponsored jointly by Baltimore CORE and the Baltimore student nonviolent group brought hundreds, even thousands, of people to demonstrate in Baltimore and on Maryland's conservative Eastern Shore. They came from all up and down the northeastern seaboard. CORE people came from Philadelphia and New York; Negro youth came from Howard University in Washington; and white students came by the hundreds from such elite institutions as Swarthmore and

Brown, Queens College and New York University, Yale and Harvard. I believe that, like the first student demonstrators I knew at Morgan, few of these white youth could have been classed as "true believers." But questionnaires answered by several hundred of these visitors and analyzed by graduate sociology students at Johns Hopkins University did reveal some interesting things about this rather unrepresentative group that could afford to spend up to thirty dollars or more for a weekend trip to Baltimore. It turned out that it consisted largely of upper-middle-class youth and professional people, liberal idealists. My own personal observations with a number of northern college students who came to Maryland that winter and spring of 1961–1962—the winter that witnessed a civil rights revolution in Baltimore, and brought demonstrations to the agrarian old-fashioned Eastern Shore, thus paving the way for the later dramatic movement and tragic denouement in Cambridge in 1963—revealed a group of young people who were from the best colleges, and usually at the top of their classes. They were idealistic, liberal youth, both Jewish and Gentile, who were eager to participate in our demonstrations.

It is doubtful that most of them would have gone farther south. Maryland not only was close enough for a weekend trip, but was a place where one could demonstrate against the sort of public accommodations that were integrated at home, and thus participate in the movement, but without much serious danger of arrest. And if one were arrested—as some hoped to be—there was no danger of police brutality, and bail money was available. The Maryland demonstrations thus tended to attract a type of clean-shaven, highly intellectual, idealistic white youth, whose commitment to direct action involved considerable personal sacrifice in terms of money and time taken from pressing studies, but who were unlikely to engage in Freedom Rides in Mississippi. Some of them did of course remain in the movement and did engage in the most dangerous types of direct action, but these real true believers were a minority.

By way of contrast, earlier, in the summer of 1961, CORE's Freedom Ride to Alabama and Mississippi included a wide variety of people, both white and Negro. Among the whites were old-line CORE pacifists, college intellectuals, bearded "beatnik" types, and revolutionary Marxists. Though it is impossible to indicate precise proportions, perhaps the majority of the dedicated white activists of the period 1961–1963 were radicals and beatnik types. Both were alienated from American middle-class values, and in their rejection of these values turned either to the Marxist critique of capitalist society or, perhaps more often, took on something of the hipster personality. Many of the latter type fitted quite neatly into Norman Mailer's concept of the "white Negro." Alienated from the middle-class conventions of their parents, they glorified the most alienated and outcast group in American society, lower-class Negroes. They accepted the stereotypes whites hold about lower-class Negroes— the stereotypes of personal sloppiness and uninhibited sexuality. Only, instead of considering these qualities bad, they regarded them as the warp and woof of a superior way of life. As one bearded Johns Hopkins graduate student gravely informed me: "Of course Negroes are more promiscuous and uninhibited sexually than whites. I envy them and wish I could be like them." Similarly, the radicals tended to romanticize lower-class Negroes as part of their romanticization of the oppressed and poor of all societies.

Such individuals find in the movement more than a peg on which to hang their alienation and criticism of American life. They find that it also provides a cause with which to identify, a meaning for life, and a sense of purpose for themselves. As one vibrant, well-proportioned lass with long, stringy yellow hair set off against a deliberately pallid complexion said to a group of civil rights workers in Chicago last fall: "The movement means so much to those of us who disagreed with our parents and rebelled against society. In it we have found a home."

To some, the hipster sorts are "kooks." Many of them so reject their identity as members of conventional American white middle-class society that, far from objecting to the "race-baiting" of some of the Negro militants, they either revel in it masochistically or join in similar criticism themselves. A few even fancy themselves "black nationalists." At CORE's 1963 convention one such activist unsuccessfully urged a Negro to run against a white candidate for the organization's National Action council. His reason, succinctly stated, was simple: "We don't want any more of those God-damned white people on the council."

But over the past two years an important change has come about in the kinds of whites involved. As already suggested, from the beginning there were always a few idealistic white liberals and other intellectuals who became deeply dedicated civil rights activists. But the events of 1963 marked a turning point in the kind of white participation, as it did for so many other things in the movement. The key factor here was undoubtedly the formation of the Interfaith Commission on Race in January. Six months later eminent clergymen of all three major faiths were among nearly a thousand arrested in demonstrations that led to the desegregation of an amusement park outside Baltimore. At the end of the summer a quarter million people marched on Washington—an event in which the clerics played a major supporting and symbolic role. Thus by the summer of 1963 the demonstrations that culminated in Birmingham that spring, and the awakened conscience of the supposed guardians of the moral values of the community, had started a moral awakening in America that made civil rights activism fully respectable. The recent events in Selma, and President Johnson's declaration that "We Shall Overcome" and his praise for the Negro activists, are the most recent evidence of this growing trend.

By the spring of 1964 the fruits of this development were evident in the large numbers of white moderates who had become so committed to civil rights that they clamored for the chance to pay the money to enable them to risk their lives in Mississippi during the summer. In using the term "white moderates" I mean to distinguish them not only from the radical Marxists but also from the middle-class liberals, both of whom had been interested in civil rights for years. These moderates differed from all the other types of whites who had heretofore been involved in substantial numbers, because their involvement flowed not from any alienation and rejection of the outlook of conventional Americans, but from commitment to the traditional shibboleths and pieties. I talked to some of these youths in Mississippi last summer, where I was interested to find many of them along with other types. I found them generally to be good students, from stable family backgrounds, not terribly concerned with social issues before they became interested in civil rights. Like the southern Negro youth who first set the tone for the civil rights revolution in the early 1960s, they were good Christians, sincerely motivated by their religious tradition, and some were preparing for the ministry. The examples of the status figures in their churches and the civil rights crisis of 1963 combined to make it suddenly evident to these young men and women that race discrimination was a burning issue. And it was a burning issue to them precisely because it violated the democratic and Christian values which they had been trained to treasure. Certainly, one must look for other personality traits to explain the intensity and dedication that propelled these particular youths, and not others, from conventional apolitical backgrounds to become true believers in the cause of civil rights. The point I am making is that in contrast to the beatniks, the radicals, the pacifists, and even the liberals, the commitment of these youths arose not out of any alienation from American society, but out of a profound attachment to it.

I believe that on the basis of the foregoing analysis we can see that the situation in COFO, described at the opening of this paper, is exceedingly complex and involves far more than Negro "nationalistic" feeling or general Negro distrust of whites. Much of the problem stems from the fact that the northern white youths in the movement—liberal, radical, or moderate—have tended to be intellectuals who stand high in their classes at the best colleges and universities. They are therefore equipped with valuable skills largely lacking among the culturally deprived southern Negro youths in the movement, whose educational background is at best inadequate, and who are very often from the lower half of their college classes, or are not college students at all. As outsiders with superior skills, young northern Negro intellectuals also experience similar resentments from southern youths in the movement. Thus resentments developed and became focused on the racial identity of most of the workers coming from the North, when in fact much of the problem stems from the fact that the movement does not attract the same kinds of people from both races.

To summarize, the movement thus draws from different social types among Negroes and whites. Broadly speaking, the majority of Negro activists appear to come from upwardly mobile people of working-class background. They tend to describe themselves as "striving lower-class" people, though in the context of the Negro class structure it is better to regard them as lower-middle class. More recently some members of the very lowest classes have become involved. Some participants are Negro intellectuals at prestigious northern universities, but for the most part Negro activists either have been youths without a college education or, if they have been to college, have tended to be students who have not distinguished themselves in athletics, scholarship, social life, or campus politics. The leaders, however, often tend to be people of greater versatility, especially in the skills of communication.

White youths, on the other hand, have tended to be college students or recent college graduates, often from outstanding schools, and quite frequently near the top of their class. They tend to break down into two major categories: those who are alienated from American society and those who are not. The former include beatnik sorts, who identify with Negroes as the most alienated group in America, and the radical intelligentsia, ranging from Quaker-type pacifists to Trotskyites and Maoists. This group formed a large proportion of the participants from 1960 to 1963, along with a sprinkling of upper-middle-class idealistic Jews and other liberals. Beginning with the March on Washington, when the civil rights movement gained greater respectability and the support of prominent white clergymen, the movement came to attract more conventional types, motivated not by their alienation from American society but by their deep attachment to its values and ideals. As the recent events in Selma indicate, it is this very important fact which, from the point of view of the historian, suggests that the civil rights movement may well succeed in transforming the racial relations of American society.

SIXTEEN

On the Role of Martin Luther King

As INDICATED in the introduction, this essay was the direct fruit of debates with John Bracey and other students at Roosevelt University during my first year there, and of Martin Luther King, Jr.'s actions in the course of the Selma, Alabama, campaign during my second and final year at Roosevelt. In certain ways of course, its roots go much farther back than that—to the kind of functional analysis with which I became familiar as I pursued my early reading of sociological and anthropological literature more than twenty years before. Also influential on my thinking was Seymour Martin Lipset's discussion of the role of consensus and class conflict in a democratic polity (*Political Man: The Social Bases of Politics* [1960]). Although at least one significant essay would follow, in my judgment this article on King represents the maturation of my views on the "functions of disunity," and the final flowering of the kind of writings I had published in nonacademic media. In retrospect I regard myself as fortunate in having had access to publications like the *Crisis* and *New Politics* since it would have been impossible to present these essays—which did so much to shape my scholarly career—in the learned journals of the historical profession.

THE PHENOMENON THAT IS Martin Luther King consists of a number of striking paradoxes. The Nobel Prize winner is accepted by the outside world as *the* leader of the nonviolent direct action movement, but he is criticized by many activists within the movement. He is criticized for what appears, at times, as indecisiveness, and more often denounced for a tendency to accept compromise. Yet, in the eyes of most Americans, both black and white, he remains the symbol of militant direct action. So potent is this symbol of King as direct actionist, that a new myth is arising about his historic role. The real credit for developing and projecting the techniques and philosophy of nonviolent direct action in the civil rights arena must be given to the Congress of Racial Equality which was founded in 1942, more than a dozen years before the Montgomery bus boycott projected King into international fame. And the idea of mass action by Negroes themselves to secure redress of their grievances must, in large part, be ascribed to the vision of A. Philip

From *New Politics* 4 (Winter 1965): 1–8. (Actually this issue appeared late, not before the late spring of 1965.)

Randolph, architect of the March on Washington movement during World War II. Yet, as we were told in Montgomery on March 25, 1965, King and his followers now assert, apparently without serious contradiction, that a new type of civil rights strategy was born at Montgomery in 1955 under King's auspices.

In a movement in which respect is accorded in direct proportion to the number of times one has been arrested, King appears to keep the number of times he goes to jail to a minimum. In a movement in which successful leaders are those who share in the hardships of their followers, in the risks they take, in the beatings they receive, in the length of time they spend in jail, King tends to leave prison for other important engagements, rather than remaining there and suffering with his followers. In a movement in which leadership ordinarily devolves upon persons who mix democratically with their followers, King remains isolated and aloof. In a movement which prides itself on militancy and "no compromise" with racial discrimination or with the white "power structure," King maintains close relationships with, and appears to be influenced by, Democratic presidents and their emissaries, seems amenable to compromises considered by some a half loaf or less, and often appears willing to postpone or avoid a direct confrontation in the streets.

King's career has been characterized by failures that, in the larger sense, must be accounted triumphs. The buses in Montgomery were desegregated only after lengthy judicial proceedings conducted by the NAACP Legal Defense Fund secured a favorable decision from the U.S. Supreme Court. Nevertheless, the events in Montgomery were a triumph for direct action, and gave this tactic a popularity unknown when identified solely with CORE. King's subsequent major campaigns—in Albany, Georgia; in Danville, Virginia; in Birmingham, Alabama; and in St. Augustine, Florida—ended as failures or with only token accomplishments in those cities. But each of them, chiefly because of his presence, dramatically focused national and international attention on the plight of the southern Negro, thereby facilitating overall progress. In Birmingham, in particular, demonstrations which fell short of their local goals were directly responsible for a major federal Civil Rights Act. Essentially, this pattern of local failure and national victory was recently enacted at Selma, Alabama.

King is ideologically committed to disobeying unjust laws and court orders, in the Gandhian tradition, but generally he follows a policy of not disobeying federal court orders. In his recent Montgomery speech, he expressed a crude, neo-Marxist interpretation of history romanticizing the Populist movement as a genuine union of

black and white common people, ascribing race prejudice to capital-
ists playing white workers against black. Yet, in practice, he is
amenable to compromise with the white bourgeois political and
economic establishment. More important, King enunciates a superficial and eclectic philosophy and by virtue of it he has profoundly
awakened the moral conscience of America.

In short, King can be described as a "conservative militant."

IN THIS COMBINATION of militancy with conservatism and caution,
of righteousness with respectability, lies the secret of King's enormous success.

Certain important civil rights leaders have dismissed King's position as the product of publicity generated by the mass communications media. But this can be said of the successes of the civil rights
nonviolent action movement generally. Without publicity it is hard
to conceive that much progress would have been made. In fact,
contrary to the official nonviolent direct action philosophy, demonstrations have secured their results not by changing the hearts of
the oppressors through a display of nonviolent love, but through
the national and international pressures generated by the publicity
arising from mass arrests and incidents of violence. And no one has
employed this strategy of securing publicity through mass arrests
and precipitating violence from white hoodlums and law enforcement officers more than King himself. King abhors violence; as
at Selma, for example, he constantly retreats from situations that
might result in the deaths of his followers. But he is precisely most
successful when, contrary to his deepest wishes, his demonstrations precipitate violence from southern whites against Negro and
white demonstrators. We need only cite Birmingham and Selma to
illustrate this point.

Publicity alone does not explain the durability of King's image, or
why he remains for the rank and file of whites and blacks alike, the
symbol of the direct-action movement, the nearest thing to a charismatic leader that the civil rights movement has ever had. At the
heart of King's continuing influence and popularity are two facts.
First, better than anyone else, he articulates the aspirations of Negroes who respond to the cadence of his addresses, his religious
phraseology and manner of speaking, and the vision of his dream
for them and for America. King has intuitively adopted the style
of the old-fashioned Negro Baptist preacher and transformed it
into a new art form; he has, indeed, restored oratory to its place
among the arts. Second, he communicates Negro aspirations to
white America more effectively than anyone else. His religious

terminology and manipulation of the Christian symbols of love and nonresistance are partly responsible for his appeal among whites. To talk in terms of Christianity, love, nonviolence is reassuring to the mentality of white America. At the same time, the very superficialities of his philosophy—that rich and eclectic amalgam of Jesus, Hegel, Gandhi, and others as outlined in his *Stride Toward Freedom*—makes him appear intellectually profound to the superficially educated middle-class white American. Actually, if he were a truly profound religious thinker, like Tillich or Niebuhr, his influence would of necessity be limited to a select audience. But by uttering moral clichés, the Christian pieties, in a magnificent display of oratory, King becomes enormously effective.

If his success with Negroes is largely due to the style of his utterance, his success with whites is a much more complicated matter. For one thing, he unerringly knows how to exploit to maximum effectiveness their growing feeling of guilt. King, of course, is not unique in attaining fame and popularity among whites through playing upon their guilt feelings. James Baldwin is the most conspicuous example of a man who has achieved success with this formula. The incredible fascination which the Black Muslims have for white people, and the posthumous near-sanctification of Malcolm X by many naive whites (in addition to many Negroes whose motivations are, of course, very different), must in large part be attributed to the same source. But King goes beyond this. With intuitive, but extraordinary skill, he not only castigates whites for their sins but, in contrast to angry young writers like Baldwin, he explicitly states his belief in their salvation. Not only will direct action bring fulfillment of the "American Dream" to Negroes but the Negroes' use of direct action will help whites to live up to their Christian and democratic values; it will purify, cleanse, and heal the sickness in white society. Whites will benefit as well as Negroes. He has faith that the white man will redeem himself. Negroes must not hate whites, but love them. In this manner, King first arouses the guilt feelings of whites, and then relieves them—though always leaving the lingering feeling in his white listeners that they should support his nonviolent crusade. Like a Greek tragedy, King's performance provides an extraordinary catharsis for the white listener.

King thus gives white men the feeling that he is their good friend, that he poses no threat to them. It is interesting to note that this was the same feeling white men received from Booker T. Washington, the noted early twentieth-century accommodator. Both men stressed their faith in the white man; both expressed the belief that the white man could be brought to accord Negroes their rights. Both stressed the importance of whites recognizing the rights of Negroes for the moral health and well-being of white society. Like King, Washington had an extraordinary following among whites. Like King, Washington symbolized for most whites the whole program of Negro advancement. While there are important similarities in the functioning of both men vis-a-vis the white community, needless to say, in most respects, their philosophies are in disagreement.

It is not surprising, therefore, to find that King is the recipient of contributions from organizations and individuals who fail to eradicate evidence of prejudice in their own backyards. For example, certain liberal trade union leaders who are philosophically committed to full racial equality, who feel the need to identify their organizations with the cause of militant civil rights, although they are unable to defeat racist elements in their unions, contribute hundreds of thousands of dollars to King's Southern Christian Leadership Conference (SCLC). One might attribute this phenomenon to the fact that SCLC works in the South rather than the North, but this is true also for SNCC which does not benefit similarly from union treasuries. And the fact is that ever since the college students started their sit-ins in 1960, it is SNCC which has been the real spearhead of direct action in most of the South, and has performed the lion's share of work in local communities, while SCLC has received most of the publicity and most of the money. However, while King provides a verbal catharsis for whites, leaving them feeling purified and comfortable, SNCC's uncompromising militancy makes whites feel less comfortable and less beneficent.

The above is not to suggest that SNCC and SCLC are responsible for all, or nearly all, the direct action in the South. The NAACP has actively engaged in direct action, especially in Savannah under the leadership of W. W. Law, in South Carolina under I. DeQuincy Newman, and in Clarksdale, Mississippi, under Aaron Henry. The work of CORE—including most of the direct action in Louisiana, much of the nonviolent work in Florida and Mississippi, the famous Freedom Ride of 1961—has been most important. In addition, one should note the work of SCLC affiliates, such as those in Lynchburg, Virginia, led by Reverend Virgil Wood; in Birmingham led by Reverend Fred Shuttlesworth; and in Savannah, by Hosea Williams.

(There are other reasons for SNCC's lesser popularity with whites than King's. These are connected with the great changes that have occurred in SNCC since it was founded in 1960, changes reflected in the half-jocular epigram circulating in SNCC circles that the Student Nonviolent Coordinating Committee has now become the "Non-Student Violent Non-Coordinating Committee." The point is, however, that even when SNCC thrilled the nation in 1960–1961 with the student sit-ins that swept the South, it did not enjoy the popularity and financial support accorded to King.)

King's very tendencies toward compromise and caution, his willingness to negotiate and bargain with White House emissaries, his hesitancy to risk the precipitation of mass violence upon demonstrators, further endear him to whites. He appears to them a "responsible" and "moderate" man. To militant activists, King's failure to march past the state police on that famous Tuesday morning outside Selma indicated either a lack of courage, or a desire to advance himself by currying presidential favor. But King's shrinking from a possible bloodbath, his accession to the entreaties of the political establishment, his acceptance of face-saving compromise in this, as in other instances, are fundamental to the particular role he is playing, and essential for achieving and sustaining his image as a leader of heroic moral stature in the eyes of white men. His caution and compromise keep open the channels of communication between the activists and the majority of the white community. In brief: King makes the nonviolent direct-action movement respectable.

Of course, many, if not most, activists reject the notion that the movement should be made respectable. Yet, American history shows that for any reform movement to succeed, it must attain respectability. It must attract moderates, even conservatives, to its ranks. The March on Washington made direct action respectable; Selma made it fashionable. More than any other force, it is Martin Luther King who impressed the civil rights revolution on the American conscience and is attracting that great middle body of American public opinion to its support. It is this revolution of conscience that will undoubtedly lead fairly soon to the elimination of all violations of Negroes' constitutional rights, thereby creating the conditions for the economic and social changes that are necessary if we are to achieve full racial equality. This is not to deny the dangers to the civil rights movement in becoming respectable. Respectability, for example, encourages the attempts of political machines to capture civil rights organizations. Respectability can also become an end in itself, thereby dulling the cutting edge of its protest activities. Indeed, the history of the labor movement reveals how attaining respectability can produce loss of original purpose and character. These perils, however, do not contradict the importance of achieving respectability—even a degree of modishness—if racial equality is ever to be realized.

There is another side to the picture: King would be neither respected nor respectable if there were not more militant activists on

his left, engaged in more radical forms of direct action. Without
CORE and, especially, SNCC, King would appear "radical" and "irresponsible" rather than "moderate" and "respectable."

KING OCCUPIES A POSITION of strategic importance as the "vital
center" within the civil rights movement. Though he has lieuten-
ants who are far more militant and "radical" than he is, SCLC acts,
in effect, as the most cautious, deliberate and "conservative" of
the direct-action groups because of King's leadership. This permits
King and the SCLC to function—almost certainly unintentionally—
not only as an organ of communication with the establishment and
majority white public opinion, but as something of a bridge between the activist and more traditionalist or "conservative" civil
rights groups, as well. For example, it appears unlikely that the
Urban League and NAACP, which supplied most of the funds,
would have participated in the 1963 March on Washington if King
had not done so. Because King agreed to go along with SNCC and
CORE, the NAACP found it mandatory to join if it was to maintain
its image as a protest organization. King's identification with the
march was also essential for securing the support of large numbers
of white clergymen and their moderate followers. The march was
the brainchild of the civil rights movement's ablest strategist and
tactician, Bayard Rustin, and the call was issued by A. Philip Randolph. But it would have been a minor episode in the history of the
civil rights movement without King's support.

Yet curiously enough, despite his charisma and international
reputation, King thus far has been more a symbol than a power in
the civil rights movement. Indeed his strength in the movement has
derived less from an organizational base than from his symbolic
role. Seven or eight years ago, one might have expected King to
achieve an organizationally dominant position in the civil rights
movement, at least in its direct-action wing. The fact is that in the
period after the Montgomery bus boycott, King developed no program and, it is generally agreed, revealed himself as an ineffective
administrator who failed to capitalize upon his popularity among
Negroes. In 1957, he founded SCLC to coordinate the work of direct-
action groups that had sprung up in southern cities. Composed of
autonomous units, usually led by Baptist ministers, SCLC does not
appear to have developed an overall sense of direction or a program
of real breadth and scope. Although the leaders of SCLC affiliates
became the race leaders in their communities—displacing the established local conservative leadership of teachers, old-line ministers, businessmen—it is hard for an observer (who admittedly has

not been close to SCLC) to perceive exactly what SCLC did before the 1960s except to advance the image and personality of King. King appeared not to direct but to float with the tide of militant direct action. For example, King did not supply the initiative for the bus boycott in Montgomery, but was pushed into the leadership by others, as he himself records in *Stride Toward Freedom*. Similarly, in the late fifties and early sixties, he appeared to let events shape his course. In the last two years, this has changed, but until the Birmingham demonstrations of 1963, King epitomized conservative militancy.

SCLC under King's leadership called the Raleigh Conference of April 1960 which gave birth to SNCC. Incredibly, within a year, the SNCC youth had lost their faith in the man they now satirically call "De Lawd," and had struck out on their own independent path. By that time, the spring of 1961, King's power in the southern direct action movement had been further curtailed by CORE's stunning Freedom Ride to Alabama and Mississippi.

The limited extent of King's actual power in the civil rights movement was illustrated by the efforts made to invest King with the qualities of a Messiah during the recent ceremonies at the state Capitol in Montgomery. Rev. Ralph Abernathy's constant iteration of the theme that King is "our Leader," the Moses of the race, chosen by God, and King's claim that he originated the nonviolent direct-action movement at Montgomery a decade ago, are all assertions that would have been superfluous if King's power in the movement was very substantial.

It is, of course, no easier today than it has been in the past few years to predict the course of the Negro protest movement, and it is always possible that the current state of affairs may change quite abruptly. It is conceivable that the ambitious program that SCLC is now projecting—both in southern voter registration and in northern urban direct-action programs—may give it a position of commanding importance in civil rights. As a result of the recent demonstrations in Selma and Montgomery, King's prestige is now higher than ever. At the same time, the nature of CORE and NAACP direct-action activities at the moment has created a programmatic vacuum which SCLC may be able to exploit. Given this convergence of circumstances, SCLC leaders may be able to establish an organizational base upon which to build a power commensurate with the symbolic position of their president.

It is indeed fortunate that King has not obtained a predominance of power in the movement commensurate with his prestige. For today, as in the past, a diversity of approaches is necessary. Needed in the movement are those who view the struggle chiefly as a conflict situation, in which the power of demonstrations, the power of Negroes, will force recognition of the race's humanity and citizenship rights, and the achievement of equality. Equally needed are those who see the movement's strategy to be chiefly one of capitalizing on the basic consensus of values in American society by awakening the conscience of the white man to the contradiction between his professions and the facts of discrimination. And just as necessary to the movement as both of these are those who operate skillfully, recognizing and yet exploiting the deeply held American belief that compromise among competing interest groups is the best *modus operandi* in public life.

King is unique in that he maintains a delicate balance among all three of these basic strategy assumptions. The traditional approaches of the Urban League (conciliation of the white businessmen) and of the NAACP (most preeminently appeals to the courts and appeals to the sense of fair play in the American public), basically attempted to exploit the consensus in American values. It would of course be a gross oversimplification to say that the Urban League and NAACP strategies are based simply on attempting to capitalize on the consensus of values, while SNCC and CORE act simply as if the situation were purely a conflict situation. Implicit in the actions of all civil rights organizations are both sets of assumptions—even where people are not conscious of the theoretical assumptions under which, in effect, they operate. The NAACP especially encompasses a broad spectrum of strategies and types of activities, ranging from time-tested court procedures to militant direct action. Sophisticated CORE activists know very well when a judicious compromise is necessary or valuable. But I hold that King is in the middle, acting in effect as if he were basing his strategy upon all three assumptions described above. He maintains a delicate balance between a purely moral appeal and a militant display of power. He talks of the power of the bodies of Negro demonstrators in the streets, but unlike CORE and SNCC activists, he accepts compromises at times that consist of token improvements, and calls them impressive victories. More than any of the other groups, King and SCLC can, up to this point at least, be described as exploiting all three tactical assumptions to an approximately equal degree. King's continued success, I suspect, will depend to a considerable degree upon the difficult feat of maintaining his position at the "vital center" of the civil rights movement.

Viewed from another angle King's failure to achieve a position of power on a level with his prestige is fortunate because rivalries between personalities and organizations remain an essential ingredient of the dynamics of the movement and a precondition for its success as each current tries to outdo the others in effectiveness and in maintaining a good public image. Without this competitive stimulus, the civil rights revolution would slow down.

I have already noted that one of King's functions is to serve as a bridge between the militant and conservative wings of the movement. In addition, by gathering support for SCLC, he generates wider support for CORE and SNCC, as well. The most striking example is the recent series of demonstrations in Selma where SNCC had been operating for nearly two years with only moderate amounts of publicity before King chose that city as his own target. As usual, it was King's presence that focused world attention on Selma. In the course of subsequent events, the rift between King and SNCC assumed the proportions of a serious conflict. Yet people who otherwise would have been hesitant to support SNCC's efforts, even people who had become disillusioned with certain aspects of SNCC's policies during the Mississippi Summer Project of 1964, were drawn to demonstrate in Selma and Montgomery. Moreover, although King received the major share of credit for the demonstrations, it seems likely that in the controversy between King and SNCC, the latter emerged with more power and influence in the civil rights movement than ever before. It is now possible that the administration will, in the future, regard SNCC as more of a force to be reckoned with than it has heretofore.

MAJOR DAILIES LIKE THE New York Times and the Washington Post, basically sympathetic to civil rights and racial equality, though more gradualist than the activist organizations, have congratulated the nation upon its good fortune in having a "responsible and moderate" leader like King at the head of the nonviolent action movement (though they overestimate his power and underestimate the symbolic nature of his role). It would be more appropriate to congratulate the civil rights movement for its good fortune in having as its symbolic leader a man like King. The fact that he has more prestige than power; the fact that he not only criticizes whites but explicitly believes in their redemption; his ability to arouse creative tension combined with his inclination to shrink from carrying demonstrations to the point where major bloodshed might result; the intellectual simplicity of his philosophy; his tendency to compromise and exert caution, even his seeming indecisiveness on some occasions; the sparing use he makes of going to or staying in jail himself; his friendship with the man in the White House—all are essential to the role he plays, and invaluable for the success of the movement. It is well, of course, that not all civil rights leaders are cut of the same cloth—that King is unique among them. Like Randolph, who functions very differently, King is really an institution. His most important function, I believe, is that of effectively communicating Negro aspirations to white people, of making nonviolent direct action respectable in the eyes of the white majority. In addition, he functions within the movement by occupying a vital center position between its "conservative" and "radical" wings, by symbolizing direct action and attracting people to participate in it without dominating either the civil rights movement or its activist wing. Viewed in this context, traits that many activists criticize in King actually function not as sources of weakness, but as the foundations of his strength.

Afterword

John H. Bracey, Jr.

IN STRONGLY encouraging August Meier to publish a selection of some of his earlier and less formal pieces and to include some reflections on how they came into being, I was motivated primarily by two concerns. The first was my belief that *Black History and the Historical Profession* was weakened by the lack of a sustained discussion of how Meier had come to play so prominent a role in bringing about many of the changes that he and Elliott Rudwick were analyzing. The second was my growing awareness that the magnitude of Meier's later scholarly achievements has resulted in an almost complete overshadowing of the earlier activist phases of his life and writings. Recent reminiscences by other leading historians in the field often make claims to an activist past decidedly less militant than Meier's. Most of the younger scholars confine their radicalism to the printed page and have little activist instincts or experience. These factors make it all the more imperative that this aspect of Meier's career be made better known. The essays, articles, and reviews speak largely for themselves, and there is little that I would add to Meier's introduction. What I would like to do in this brief afterword is to reverse Meier's "outsider" perspective and say a bit from an "insider" point of view about what is rather unusual and interesting about Meier's experiences, and about how the relative uniqueness of them enabled him to make the impact that he has.

As mentioned by Meier, I was one of a number of black students at Roosevelt University who began in 1963 to step up our agitation to get the history department to hire someone to teach Negro History. I remember quite vividly pouring over a newly bought copy of *Negro Thought in America 1880–1915: Racial Ideologies in the Age of Booker T. Washington* (Ann Arbor: University of Michigan Press, 1963) with Owen Lawson and Newell Brown, and then going to Jack Roth, chair of the history department and asking him to hire the guy who wrote the book. We students of course presumed that the author was black. After all, *Negro Thought in America* displayed an awesome knowledge of the intellectual and social history of that crucial period in Afro-American history; it took the *ideas* of Afro-Americans seriously; the author was teaching at a black school; the author didn't seem to be a Communist. We did have a brief discussion about the name. "August Meier" did not sound very black. But we shrugged that off and made our appeal anyway. We had no knowledge of the other efforts being made on Meier's behalf that he mentions in the introduction. In any case he was hired and came to teach at Roosevelt in fall 1964. Needless to say, Meier wasn't black, but such is life.

The first course that Meier taught had a required reading list of twenty-four books that we thought should have been more appropriately titled "Negro History: A Bibliography for Lifelong Learning." Meier gave a quiz on the reading assignments at the beginning of every class, a midterm, and a final exam. Detailed knowledge was expected, classroom discussions had to be based solidly on the readings, speculations and flights of fantasy were frowned upon. What kept this situation from getting out of hand—tension was building over the lengthy reading assignments and the daily quizzes—was the presence in the class of two white females who had movement experience, one of whom was a good friend of Chuck McDew, a prominent figure in SNCC who visited the class from time to time. They all seemed to know who Meier was. McDew even called him "Augie" rather than Professor Meier. It was clear that in addition to being a historian, Meier was a veteran of the civil rights movement. At that point we felt much more confident in challenging his views and arguing about the way that the class was being conducted without the fear of driving him away because of his misreading our enthusiasm and rhetorical excesses as hostility. In teaching at black colleges or in participating in the movement, you learn quickly the distinction between style and substance or you don't last long or are ineffective.

Another benefit of Meier's movement experience reflected in several of the essays in this volume is the awareness that political and social movements are often quite complicated, confusing, and full of contradictory ideas and actions. Meier's writings on the sit-ins and his assessments of the civil rights movement at various stages still make rewarding reading because they capture with great accuracy some of the complex ambience of those years.

Our awareness that Meier was willing to act in behalf of his beliefs, to "put his body on the line" as we used to say, gave him a level of acceptability among those of us who also had shared those risks during those exciting years of nonviolent direct action. Movement people, we felt, had the right to say and write things that nonmovement people would be castigated or shouted down for. In addition, Meier's reticence about talking about the extent of his involvement, the arrests and so forth, was seen as an appropriate display of humility. Meier's firm hold on his liberal faith, despite the rise of black power and the reemergence of black nationalism, was a further indication of Meier's ability to stand fast regardless of attacks from the right or the left. This tendency, again, is exemplified in many of the essays on the movement contained in this volume.

As I came to know Meier more, I learned that he had rather extensive experience among black intellectuals and scholars and in their institutions. We also shared a number of acquaintances and connections. My sister Connie went to Oberlin College in the late 1950s and engaged in some of the same forms of activism as Meier had done a decade before. In Connie's case the segregated bowling alleys in the towns around Oberlin were often the target. The Fisk connection was that my older cousin Helen Page had attended Fisk during the 1940s, and my younger cousin Helen Harris and her husband-to-be were at Fisk at the time of Meier's tenure and were part of that circle of extremely talented students that Meier writes of. From the late nineteenth through the first quarter of the twentieth century, Tougaloo had been the college of choice for many members of my family including my mother, aunt, grandmother, grandfather, two great-aunts, two great-uncles. In addition, Meier was at Tougaloo at the same time as two close family friends now active among Tougaloo alumnae, who told me stories of how "Gus" was always eager to experience all aspects of black life both in and around the college. That Meier made a conscious decision to teach and live in the Mississippi of the 1940s and to identify with the black population while so doing is still a source of wonder to me. The particularly virulent nature of racial oppression in Mississippi during the jim crow years is well known. I am reminded of Nina Simone's song "Mississippi Goddam."

Martin Jenkins shared an office with my mother, Helen Bracey, in the School of Education at Howard University before he assumed the presidency of Morgan State College. The group of scholars that Meier found to be so warm and supportive was also part of the environment on the Howard campus that I grew up on from the mid-1940s until I left Washington, D.C., in 1961. During my high school years and as a freshman at Howard, I often studied in the Moorland Room in Founders Library, which, as Meier notes, was always virtually empty. I also remember Dorothy Porter taking me back into the stacks to show me rare documents that could be of use in papers I was writing, or just to satisfy my curiosity that some of the more interesting entries in the card catalog really existed.

What this all means is that I had a wealth of shared experiences that enabled me to assess Meier's comments and evaluations of black life, and especially that of the black middle class and academic community. That Meier was asked by other black scholars, and felt confident enough to respond in the affirmative, to a face-to-face discussion with E. Franklin Frazier about *Black Bourgeoisie*, indicates that my view of the depth of Meier's knowledge was shared by others much more qualified than me to make that judgment. It is interesting to note that one consequence of the success of integration, such as it has been, is that it is likely that this current generation of students of black history will never be able to experience to the same degree the interactions in communities of brilliant black thinkers such as those who congregated at Fisk, Howard, and Morgan during those last years before the onset of the civil rights movement. It is difficult to convey the knowledge and insights that one could absorb just listening to discussions between the likes of Charles Thompson, Frazier, John Hope Franklin, Sterling Brown, Merze Tate, Emmett Dorsey, and Robert Martin. My mother was on the editorial board of the *Journal of Negro Education* so her office was often the site of discussions of the contents of forthcoming issues. On my daily trek home from Mott Elementary School or Banneker Junior High I had to check in at Douglass Hall and frequently walked into the middle of such discussions. That Meier would be welcomed into those circles was not all that unusual. The criterion for admission was not skin color, but a level of demonstrated knowledge of and serious interest in the Afro-American experience.

One characteristic that Meier did not share with other liberals of his generation was his interest in black nationalism. From his master's thesis at Columbia, to the early articles in Lorenzo Greene's *Midwest Journal*, to *Negro Thought in America*, Meier was virtually the only liberal scholar to take black nationalism seriously as an ideology and as an important tendency throughout the history of Afro-Americans. He was not an adherent of it, far from it. But the contrast is between his views and those of both someone like E. David Cronon's on Marcus Garvey and the silence of the rest of the historical profession on this subject. Those of us at Roosevelt and in the Chicago movement saw Meier's writings, whatever his intentions, as providing the historical underpinnings of our own developing nationalist views. That Meier focused primarily on secular thinkers made his work much more relevant than the studies of the Nation of Islam by E. U. Essien-Udom (*Black Nationalism: A Search for an Identity in America* [Chicago: University of Chicago Press, 1962]) and C. Eric Lincoln (*The Black Muslims in America* [Boston: Beacon Press, 1961]). That Meier could treat nationalist ideas with both fairness and understanding is one explanation for the rather amazing decision of the black students at Morgan State to choose Meier to debate Malcolm X.

The essays in this volume end several years before I collaborated with Meier and Elliott Rudwick on *Black Nationalism in America* (Indianapolis: Bobbs-Merrill, 1970). It is clear that Meier's willingness to look at the broadest spectrum of opinions emanating from the black community has characterized the way that he later developed a series of historical studies at Atheneum Publishers and the University of Illinois Press. The Atheneum series, "Studies in American Negro Life," included reprints in paperback of such classics as Sterling Spero and Abram Harris, *The Black Worker;* Alain Locke's *The New Negro;* Du Bois's *Black Reconstruction;* Sterling Brown's *Negro Poetry and Drama and the Negro in American Literature,* Horace Mann Bond's *Negro Education in Alabama* and *The Philosophy and Opinions of Marcus Garvey.* It would be difficult, if not impossible, to fashion an ideological net that would snare all those works. The "Blacks in the New World" series of original monographs published by the University of Illinois Press includes titles by authors with equally diverse points of view.

A final point. Meier mentions that much of his fame today is a result of the resurgence of black nationalist concerns in the late 1960s which helped to stimulate a vastly increased interest in Afro-American history. That is probably true. What also is true is that Meier's actions and writings during the period covered by this volume clearly were not aimed at securing a place in the top ranks of the historical establishment. One does not voluntarily take on the demanding teaching responsibilities at Tougaloo, Fisk, and Morgan, choose a dissertation topic that few, if any, white historians knew or cared about, get arrested in demonstrations in Baltimore and Newark, and challenge the racist practices of the Southern Historical Association if one is career building. Of course, in the late 1960s after King's death and the ensuing riots, many of the nation's colleges and universities, more often than not run by white liberals, began to hire teachers of Afro-American history, of course preferring those whom they felt looked like them, shared their values, and would be less likely to pose fundamental criticisms of the ways that those institutions were run. Black liberals were the next choice, and radicals, of any color, were way down the line.

The timing of Meier's acceptance of a position at Kent State University in fall 1967 clearly does not fit this pattern nor can it be seen to have impeded the development of Afro-American history as a field. In fact, black undergraduates from Roosevelt, like Darlene

Clark Hine and Christopher Reed, who had studied with Meier, or knew of his reputation, followed him to Kent State to pursue their doctoral studies.

One does hear that Meier is a harsh taskmaster, a ruthless editor of manuscripts, an unstinting critic. I am not sure why that is bad. Meier takes quite seriously the study of the history of Afro-Americans. He has devoted the vast majority of his adult life to that end. He tends to expect that others in, or entering, the field will share that commitment. He reacts vehemently to weak research, poorly developed arguments, and especially to work that appears to be treating the Afro-American historical experience with insufficient respect. Meier has some standard in his head toward which he pushes himself, and others who choose to work with him are expected to come as close to it as possible. Obviously the entire field of United States history would have been much better off if white scholars had been willing to listen to black scholars such as Du Bois, Woodson, and Wesley decades ago. Then, by now we would have had many years of experience with such a commitment and standards that Meier would not seem so unusual. He would have been just one of a long line of scholars, of whatever color, who studied the black experience as part of their contribution toward achieving a society free from racial oppression. As we now know, and as *Black History and the Historical Profession* has shown us in great detail, things did not work out that way. As a result of a number of factors, both inside and outside of the academy, the study of black Americans has blossomed during the past twenty years to an extent undreamed of in Woodson's day. There are now many excellent scholars—of all colors—teaching and doing research on virtually every aspect of the black experience. What one can conclude from reading these essays and Meier's account of his early career is that the unique combination of his intellectual interests, his experiences at black colleges, his interactions with leading black thinkers, and his active involvement in the civil rights movement placed him in a position from which he was able to make the contributions to the expansion and consolidation of the field of Afro-American history, upon which his current reputation rests.

Index

CONTENTS

Content of the Federal Government's Proposed Changes

How Necessary is Senate Reform?

FOREWORD

From its inception, the Senate of Canada has been a source of controversy and proposals for its reform have never been long absent from the political scene. It was no surprise, therefore, that, in the general election of 2006, such proposals figured prominently in the agenda for democratic reform advanced by the Conservative party led by Stephen Harper. What was surprising was that, rather than endeavouring to proceed by way of constitutional amendment, the government chose to proceed legislatively, evidently assuming that s. 44 of the Constitution provides the requisite authority for Parliament to make the change on its own. Accordingly, the Harper government tabled in the Senate Bill S-4 (to change the tenure of senators from appointment till age seventy-five to an eight-year renewable term) and, in the Commons, Bill C-43 (to conduct consultative elections to identify candidates for appointment by the Prime Minister). Both bills died on dissolution of the session, but C-43 was subsequently reintroduced as C-20, together with C-19, which would restrict a senator to one eight-year term.

Given the evident seriousness of the current federal government's intention to act on Senate reform, and the likely impact of the proposed reforms on the operation of both the Canadian Parliament and federation, the Institute of Intergovernmental Relations was delighted when Dr. Jennifer Smith, Professor of Political Science, Dalhousie University, suggested the Institute host a Senate-reform working-paper series on its website. It was but a short step from there to invite Professor Smith to be the guest editor of the series and, shortly thereafter, when the invitation to submit papers elicited a most enthusiastic and informed response, to edit the collection for publication. We very much appreciate her willingness to undertake both tasks. We would also like to acknowledge the contribution made by Dr. Nadia Verrelli, our post-doctoral fellow, in co-ordinating the work on this project here, at the Institute.

The IIGR is pleased to publish *The Democratic Dilemma: Reforming the Canadian Senate*, and hopes that it will help inform the ongoing debate on whether, and in what manner, the Canadian Senate should be reformed.

Thomas J. Courchene,
Director, IIGR

John R. Allan,
Associate Director, IIGR

NOTES ON CONTRIBUTORS

JANET AJZENSTAT taught public law and political philosophy in the Department of Political Science at McMaster University before retiring in 2001. Her most recent book is *The Canadian Founding, John Locke and Parliament* (McGill-Queen's University Press, 2007). She is currently preparing a new edition of *Documents on the Confederation of British North America*, ed. G.P. Browne (Carleton Library, No. 40). In 2002 she received the Queen's Golden Jubilee Medal.

PETER AUCOIN is Eric Dennis Memorial Professor of Government and Political Science at Dalhousie University. He was Research Coordinator for National Institutions, the Royal Commission on the Economic Union and Development Prospects for Canada, and Research Director of the Royal Commission on Electoral Reform and Party Financing. The former recommended Senate reform; the latter considered campaign finance issues in depth. He has also been an expert witness in several court cases concerning campaign finance law.

LOUISE CARBERT is associate professor of political science at Dalhousie University. Over the past decade, her research has pursued the question of why rural women have been less likely to be elected to public office. Her recent publications include Rural Women's Leadership in Atlantic Canada (UTP, 2006) and "Are Cities More Congenial? Tracking the Rural Deficit of Women in the House of Commons" (ed. Bashevkin, UBC 2009).

DON DESSERUD holds Bachelor and Master's degrees in English and Political Science from Dalhousie University, and a PhD in Political Science from The University of Western Ontario. He has also completed an MA in Creative Writing from the University of New Brunswick. He was recently the recipient of the James R. Mallory research grant from the Canadian Study of Parliament Group for his project "The Separation of Powers and Responsible Government in the Canadian Parliamentary System." He is currently the Associate Dean of Graduate Studies at UNBSJ.

ANDREW HEARD is an Associate Professor in the Political Science Department at Simon Fraser University. His research interests centre on the Canadian Constitution and political institutions. He has authored numerous articles and chapters on parliament, the electoral system, the division of powers, judicial behaviour, and the Charter of Rights. He has also published the only book-length examination of Canadian constitutional conventions.

TOM KENT, a Companion of the Order of Canada, served in wartime intelligence, was an editor and a corporation executive, before becoming in 1963 principal assistant to Prime Minister Pearson. His other positions have included federal deputy minister, crown corporation president, royal commission chairman and university dean. He has written extensively on public policies, is the founding editor of *Policy Options*, a lifetime fellow of IRPP and a fellow in the Queen's School of Policy Studies.

STEVEN MICHAEL MACLEAN received a Master of Philosophy in Humanities from Memorial University of Newfoundland in 1997, specializing in political philosophy. He has been involved in community economic development and local historical projects. His current research focuses on Anglo-Canadian Toryism and Catholic Social Teaching, particularly subsidiarity and the common good. He has been published in *Reformer*, the journal of the Tory Reform Group (UK). Stephen lives in Cape Breton, Nova Scotia.

LORNA R. MARSDEN is currently President Emerita and professor of sociology at York University. Previously, she was a faculty member and administrator at the University of Toronto (1972-92) and President of Wilfrid Laurier University (1992-1997). She was appointed to the Senate of Canada by Prime Minister Pierre Trudeau in 1984 and resigned in 1992. She has authored several books and many articles, including "What Does a Senator Actually Do?" in Paul Fox (ed.) Politics in Canada, 1987.

VINCENT POULIOT is a lawyer and entrepreneur. Following the Quebec Referendum to secede from Canada in 1995, he became Leader of the Libertarian Party of Canada to promote provincial representation in the Senate, as the means to end the conflict of power in our federation. He intervened before the Supreme Court of Canada in the reference regarding the secession of Quebec.

HUGH SEGAL is a senior fellow at the Queen's University School of Policy Studies, and former president of the Institute for Research on Public Policy in Montreal. He was appointed to the Senate by Paul Martin in 2005, as a Conservative, and served on the special committee on Senate reform in the last parliament.

DAVID E. SMITH holds degrees from the University of Western Ontario (Hons BA), Duke University (MA and PhD), and the University of Saskatchewan (DLitt). A past president of the Canadian Political Science Association, he was elected Fellow of the Royal Society of Canada in 1981. His most recent publications include the parliamentary trilogy, *The Invisible Crown: The First Principle of Canadian Government* (1995),*The Canadian Senate in Bicameral Perspective* (2003), and *The People's House of Commons: Theories of Democracy in Contention* (2007). The Senate book was nominated for the Donner Prize in Canadian Public Policy (2004); the Commons book won the Donner Prize (2007).

JENNIFER SMITH is a professor of Political Science at Dalhousie University. She is the author of *Federalism* (2004), a volume in the Canadian Democratic Audit. She writes on a range of subjects associated with Canadian government and politics, including parliamentary government, intergovernmental relations and campaign finance law. She has served on both federal and provincial electoral boundaries commissions for Nova Scotia.

NADIA VERRELLI is a post-doctoral fellow at the Institute of Intergovernmental Relations. Her research looks principally at Canadian federalism, the Supreme Court of Canada, constitutional politics and Quebec politics. Her publications include (with F. Rocher) "Questioning Constitutional Democracy in Canada: From the Canadian Supreme Court Reference on Quebec Secession to the Clarity Act" (in Gagnon et al. (ed.) *The Conditions of Diversity in Multinational Democracies*, 2003. She has edited *The Role of the Policy Advisor: An Insider's Look*, (forthcoming).

RONALD L. WATTS is Principal and Vice-Chancellor Emeritus and Professor Emeritus of Political Studies at Queen's University where he has been since 1955. He was a founding board member of the international Forum of Federations. He has been a consultant to the Government of Canada during constitutional deliberations, most notably 1980-1 and 1991-2, and has been an advisor to governments in a number of other federations. He has written or edited twenty-nine books, monographs and reports and over one hundred articles, chapters and books. His most recent book is *Comparing Federal Systems*, third edition, 2008. He has received five honourary degrees. He became a Companion of the Order of Canada in 2000.

JOHN WHYTE currently holds the Law Foundation of Saskatchewan Chair at the College of Law, University of Saskatchewan. He has taught constitutional law at a number of Canadian universities and from 1987 to 1992 he was the Dean of Law at Queen's University. He also served as Saskatchewan's Deputy Minister of Justice and has held a number of other positions in government including constitutional advisor to Saskatchewan during the patriation process.

1

INTRODUCTION

Jennifer Smith

En premier lieu, dans l'introduction, l'auteur replace dans leur contexte les propositions de réforme du Sénat du gouvernement Harper. Elle établit un lien entre la proposition du Parti réformiste de créer un sénat triple E (élu, égal et efficace), présentée il y a presque 20 ans, et les propositions qui sont devant nous aujourd'hui. Elle décrit brièvement les propositions du gouvernement de raccourcir la durée du mandat des sénateurs et que ces derniers soient élus. Puis, elle passe en revue tous les articles de la collection, et résume les idées principales des auteurs. Elle conclut en citant les leçons à tirer de ces articles et nous fait voir toute la complexité de la réforme du Sénat.

The idea of an elected Senate dates to the Confederation debates. Maritime critics of the proposed Constitution, the Nova Scotian anti-confederate Joe Howe prominent among them, complained bitterly about the idea of a body appointed by a federal government that would necessarily draw most of its support – and bias – from seat-rich central Canada. The idea has bounced about ever since, to no effect, until it was featured prominently in the platform of the federal Reform party.

Established in 1987, the Reform party advocated the so-called "Triple-E" Senate – equal, elected, effective. The proposal gained some traction among the public during the constitutional rounds that preoccupied the country from 1984 to 1992, a version of it – elected and effective – appearing in the Charlottetown Accord that was voted down by Canadians in a referendum in 1992. The idea of an elected Senate remained alive through the transformation of the Reform party into the Canadian Alliance, and then the merger of the Canadian Alliance and the Progressive Conservatives to form the Conservative Party of Canada. That party's general election win in 2006 was the opportunity for it to move on the file. And move it has, although not in the way most might have expected.

It was widely assumed that to change the Senate from an appointed body to an elected one would require an amendment to the Constitution under a process requiring the consent of Parliament and at least two-thirds of the provinces, which together contain at least half the population of the country. By reason of democratic form if not legal requirement, the people might need to be consulted as

well. It was equally widely assumed that such consent would be extremely difficult to gather. Faced with the bleak prospect of Senate reform as a constitutional
matter, the minority Conservative government of Prime Minister Stephen Harper
has developed an alternative strategy based on the assumption that Parliament can
make the change on its own under s. 44 of the Constitution that permits such
action in relation to the executive government of Canada, the House of Commons
and the Senate.

In 2006, in its first legislative session, the government tabled S-4 in the Senate
to change the tenure of senators from appointment to the age of 75 to an eight-
year, renewable term. It also introduced C-43 in the House of Commons to change
the method of appointment from the decision of the prime minister on his own
heft to the decision of the prime minister based on the results of Senate "consultative" elections. Both bills died on the order paper following the dissolution of the
session. In the second session, the government reproduced the bill on the election
of senators, now C-20. It also tabled – this time in the House rather than the
Senate – a slightly amended Senate tenure bill (C-19) that would restrict a senator
to one eight-year term.[1]

Not content simply to let the chips fall where they may on the bills in the
minority Parliament, the government has pursued aggressive strategies to move
along its project. Initially, the prime minister said he would refuse to fill vacant
seats in the Senate by individuals who have not been elected to them. He persisted
in this strategy until, at the time of writing, there now are 18 vacant seats. Then in
December 2008, a scant two months after the general election in which his government was returned to office for a second time with only minority support in the
House, and days after the opposition parties threatened to bring down the government over economic issues, the prime minister changed tack. He announced his
intention to fill the vacancies with individuals who support his plan of reform.
This is a remarkable demonstration of will. It presents the spectacle of a government that is openly toying with a foundational institution of the country in order
to get its way on reform. It should be noted that some senators themselves have
prepared bills to reform the institution. Senator Moore has introduced Bill S-224
in an effort to require the prime minister to fill vacancies in the Senate in a timely
manner. Senator Banks has introduced Bill S-229 to remove the property qualifications that candidates for a Senate appointment are required under the constitution
to fulfill as well as a resolution to amend the Constitution to eliminate the senatorial districts in Quebec.

Legislative committees in the House and the Senate have held hearings on the
bills, and experts and interested parties have appeared before them to offer their
views on the constitutionality and the substance of the proposals. However, to
date the public has not been engaged by the issue. This might reflect the media's
lack of interest in it based on their judgement that nothing much is likely to happen

---

[1] For details on bills S-4, C-43, C-20 and C-19, please see appendix.

unless the Conservatives win a majority government. In the meantime, why waste the effort? On the other hand, given the current government's determined approach to the issue, there is every reason to make the effort. The Senate is a central institution to which the federal government wants to make serious changes – transformative ones. But it is not a stand-alone institution. If it changes, its relationships with other institutions – the House of Commons, the Cabinet, the Crown, the provinces – will change as well. That's the trouble with Senate reform. It is actually a very big issue with complex ramifications for the conduct of Canadian politics. The purpose of this book is to study carefully the government's proposed reforms and to explore the issues they raise for other institutional players in the system as well as Canadians themselves.

The book is organized in four sections. In the first or background section, the authors set the table by writing about the Canadian Senate in particular and upper houses in general. David Smith and Janet Ajzenstat write about the origins of the Canadian Senate. Smith reminds us that the Senate was central to the Confederation agreement. Without the guarantee of regional equality of representation (the 24 seats assigned to Ontario, Quebec and the Maritime provinces), he writes, the Maritime provinces simply would not have agreed to join the federation. He also points out – and Ajzenstat agrees – that the Senate was conceived as the legislative upper house of a bicameral parliament, not a provincially appointed body along the lines of the German Bundesrat.

Pondering the reasons for the difficulty of Senate reform, Smith identifies four, beginning with the longevity of the average term of a senator – about 12 years. Senators outlast their parliamentary competitors who are out to reform them. A second reason is that the existing Senate, the members of which are appointed from the provinces and the territories, has allies in the provinces, most of which have shown no interest at all in reforming the institution. Then there is the constitutional indeterminacy of the function of the Senate, which inevitably leads to enormous variety in people's ideas of reform. Finally, there is the fact that Canada is a constitutional monarchy, which means a system of the Crown-in-Parliament: Crown, Senate, House of Commons. It is not at all certain that the Senate can be treated breezily as an entity apart from the other two.

Ajzenstat, too, writes forcefully about the Senate as a legislative upper house, the members of which are involved in national deliberations on national issues rather than local ones. As she explains, they can bring local perspectives to the deliberations, but they are not there to press local issues. There is a mighty difference between the two standpoints. She arrives at this point by making the case that the Senate is part of an egalitarian and inclusive parliamentary system in which all who live here are represented by the elected members of the House of Commons and the appointed senators. One way or another, she writes, all political positions get an airing in these institutions. The Senate – a body of sober second thought – has a related, additional obligation to resist efforts by the governing party to use its weight in the House to limit discussion of its policy agenda. In this respect it contributes to what she calls the most important factor buttressing the inclusiveness of the system, that is, the lack of finality in decision making.

Even when bills become laws, they are not necessarily permanent laws. Opponents can live to fight another day.

Recalling the effort of Prime Minister Pierre Trudeau to reform the Senate, Nadia Verrelli reminds us that, like the current prime minister, Trudeau pursued the objective in unilateral fashion. Trudeau's reform idea was much more modest. He proposed to maintain an appointed body, but to permit the provinces to appoint half of the senators while the federal government appointed the other half. More importantly, his decision to proceed unilaterally precipitated a legal battle on the role of the provinces in the amendment of the Senate. In its decision on the point handed down in 1980, the Supreme Court of Canada determined that the provinces had a stake in the issue and needed to be involved in the process. The court's decision might well prove critical to the determination of the Harper government's efforts at Senate reform.

In a fitting conclusion to the first section, Ron Watts places two important considerations before us in his comparative analysis of second chambers. One is simply the fact of the variety of second chambers in the national governments of countries throughout the world. There are many ways in which four key factors can be combined in any one of them. These factors are the method of selection of the members; the regional composition of the body; the powers assigned to it; and the roles that the body undertakes. The second consideration is the impact of political processes on second chambers. The process Watts explores is the political-party system. As he points out, political parties can override, or at least mitigate, structural features like the regional differences that are often articulated in second chambers. One cannot leave Watts's analysis without realizing how complex is the task of institutional reform. To those inclined to throw up their hands and opt for abolition in the face of complexity, however, he points out that almost all federations use second chambers to represent regional concerns in their national – that is, shared – institutions.

The second section of the book is focused on the constitutionality of the government's unilateral approach to Senate reform. The authors who addressed the issue regard the approach to be dubious in this respect. Perhaps the most straightforward analysis is authored by Watts, who considers the bill on the election of senators. He refers to the relevant provision of the constitutional amending formula that requires any change to the selection and powers of senators to be supported by Parliament and the provincial legislatures of two-thirds of the provinces that together contain 50 percent of the population of the country – the general formula. By his lights, a change from appointment to election merits the use of this amending provision, even if the elections in question are styled "consultative" rather than definitive. At the very least, he writes, the attempt to pursue change "on the sly through the devious use of ordinary legislation constitutes an anti-constitutional process." Watts himself thinks reform of the Senate is an urgent matter for the health of the federation, but through the hard work of gathering the needed consensus for change, not by taking shortcuts.

Don Desserud shares Watts' dim view of the government seeking indirectly to amend the Constitution when it is forbidden under the Constitution to do so. In

Desserud's case, the analysis is trained on Bill C-19, the gist of which is to institute an eight-year, non-renewable term of office. He employs three arguments, the first of which is a study of the history of s. 44 of the Constitution, the one the government says gives Parliament the green light to proceed unilaterally. According to him, this is a misunderstanding of the restrictive scope of the provision. The second argument rests on s. 42, which requires the use of the general formula for changes to the selection of members of the Senate and their powers. Desserud argues that the proposed change from retirement at age 75 to a fixed term in fact affects the powers of senators. Finally, like Smith, he points to the consequences of Senate reform for so much of the governmental system. His bottom line? The general formula that requires a broad consensus of many players bound to be affected by the issue, he concludes, is the superior way to go.

Andrew Heard also questions the constitutionality of the government's unilateral approach. In Desserud's case, the argument is a historical one that hinges on the history of s. 44 and the implications of it for a change in term. Heard is focused on the use of the unilateral approach to Bill C-20, which would establish a process to elect senators. On his analysis, an elected Senate signifies a radical change in the parliamentary system because it would refashion entirely the relationship between the House of Commons and Senate. He argues that under the amending formula, no such change is possible without the consent of the provinces. John Whyte agrees. He also raises some different issues associated with the government's approach, among them that of the 24 senatorial districts in Quebec. How, he asks, could the Quebec government manage an election from districts that, taken together, do not cover the entire province?

What about the content of the government's proposals? Even if the unilateral process is a constitutional one, is the Senate that the government envisages an improvement over the existing one? Five of the authors address the question, each from a distinct point of view. Stephen Michael MacLean worries about the effects of wholesale Senate change for the parliamentary system. Andrew Heard considers the likely effects of the proposed eight-year term on senatorial behaviour. The other three look at aspects of the election proposal, beginning with Vincent Pouliot's consideration of provincial representation in the election of senators. Peter Aucoin pursues the campaign-finance provisions that would govern aspiring senators who run for office and Louise Carbert analyzes the likely effect on the prospects for women candidates of the electoral system that the government favours for the election of senators.

MacLean takes the position of the traditional conservative who is not inclined to pursue institutional change unless there is near institutional breakdown in store. Obviously that is not the case with the current Senate – or if so, it is the federal government triggering the breakdown by refusing to appoint senators who have not been elected in Senate elections. In any event, MacLean foresees a number of difficulties that an elected Senate portends, an example of which is the fact that under Bill C-20, the prime minister retains the practical constitutional responsibility to advise the Governor General on the appointment of senators. At some point, he says, a prime minister might have very good reason not to appoint a successful contestant in Senate elections. What then?

Looking at the issue of the term of office, Heard argues that in the immediate future the combination of a non-renewable, eight-year term and the end of the mandatory retirement at age 75 (currently serving senators exempted) would privilege current senators over their elected counterparts in such matters as committee chairs. In the long term, he says, the eight-year term – shorter than the current average of 12 years – is likely to weaken the Senate as a chamber of legislative review since it is a slight bar to the demands of party discipline, especially when elected senators are permitted to stand for election to the House of Commons before serving out their Senate term.

On the election front, Pouliot is troubled by the fact that senatorial candidates are not required to live in the province from which they would stand for election and by the prospect that the federal political parties might monopolize senate elections. In other words, there is no guarantee that members of provincial political parties that are not represented at the federal level would find their way into the Senate, thereby diminishing that body's credentials in representing the people in their provincial capacity. Pouliot offers historical evidence that such representation was held to be an important objective of the Senate and he recommends that in a reformed Senate the provinces be authorized to choose their senators as they see fit.

A keen student of women and politics, Carbert is interested in the implications of the preferential vote for the election of women. Will it help? Or will it hinder? She identifies four factors in Bill C-20 that bear on these questions: the preferential vote; the campaign-finance provisions; the slate or panel of nominees; and the district magnitude, or number of senators to be elected from a specified region or province. She finds that the key is the district magnitude. The greater the number of senators to be elected from a district – in other words, the longer the list of nominees – then all others things being equal, the better the chance of women candidates getting elected. Better than under the first-past-the-post system used for elections to the House, in which parties nominate a single standard bearer who in turn competes against a field from which only one winner is chosen. Carbert concludes that the proposed system is promising for women. But then there are the campaign-finance provisions of Bill C-20.

According to Peter Aucoin, these provisions mark a complete change from the campaign-finance regime that Canadians have developed to govern elections to the House of Commons. The Commons regime, which he labels an egalitarian model, attempts to inject fairness into the competition essentially by restricting the amount of money that the candidates and the political parties can spend in the campaign and by supplying them with public money as well. Bill C-20 does neither. Instead, it would establish what Aucoin labels a libertarian model under which candidates can spend as much as they choose and can afford (depending on how much money they raise). The latter is important because, like the Commons regime, the proposed Senate regime maintains strict limits on campaign contributions. Aucoin draws attention to the fact that under Bill C-20, candidates for election to the House of Commons can stand for election to the Senate. He argues that should elections to the two houses coincide, then the Senate campaign-finance regime is bound to diminish the effectiveness of the spending limits still in effect for elections to the Commons.

In the last section of the book, Tom Kent, Senator Hugh Segal and Lorna Marsden offer different views of the need for Senate reform. For Kent it is a matter of some urgency, so much so that he is prepared to overlook the risk that the government's plan entails. It is urgent, he writes, because the national government is in a funk. Whatever its merits, the existing Senate does not contribute to a robust federal government, but instead detracts from it, largely because the chamber's electoral legitimacy long ago opened the door for the provincial premiers to assume a larger role in national affairs than was intended at the outset. Since it is not their brief to think nationally, their local grievances tend to dominate federal-provincial relations at the expense of national concerns. Kent is aware of the problem of an elected Senate with the same powers as the existing chamber. However, he concludes that that is a problem for another day, and that it is important now simply to get the ball rolling on a revitalized second chamber.

Like Kent, Segal thinks it is high time Canadians turn their attention to the transformation of the Senate into a modern, democratic body. He is concerned about the legitimacy of the appointed Senate, particularly in the light of the vast legal powers that it possesses. Conceding that senators are careful not to abuse their powers, he points out that a benign Senate is not a democratic one. Segal argues that under the current amending formula, Senate reform is likely out of the question – just too difficult to do. But accepting that fate, he says, sends out the wrong message – that Canadians cannot make the changes they need to do. His is a vigorous defence of the government's effort to cut the Gordian knot of the amending formula to find a way to an elected Senate.

Marsden is not opposed to Senate reform, although she is dubious about the prospects of it. She counsels reformers to attempt to maintain the existing role of the Senate as a check on the government of the day, a body capable of getting the government to rethink the more doubtful provisions of its proposed bills. She points out that the existing chamber has managed to perform this role – sober second thought – largely because the lengthy terms of many senators allow them to master their role as parliamentarians, including the craft of drafting good legislation. Election, she notes, need not diminish this service if the term of office is long enough, which in her view means ten years at least. Finally, Marsden cautions that an elected Senate is likely to introduce a level of political competition between senators and premiers that Canadians might not understand or appreciate.

The authors in this volume offer intelligent insights on the Conservative government's proposals for Senate reform. Some address the constitutionality of the proposals. Others bring to light features of them that have not yet been analyzed and assess their significance for the conduct of a reformed chamber. They consider whether the objectives of the reformers are likely to be met by these proposals. Or, whether the result will be unintended consequences, some unimportant, others potentially harmful. If nothing else, readers certainly will realize how complicated a subject is Senate reform, full of unexpected twists and turns. Successful reform requires a deep understanding of the country's parliamentary system and culture and a delicate approach to institutional change.

THE SENATE OF CANADA: HISTORICAL BACKGROUND

2

THE SENATE OF CANADA AND THE CONUNDRUM OF REFORM

David E. Smith

Dans cet article, l'auteur s'intéresse à l'énigme que constitue la réforme du Sénat. Il rappelle au lecteur que le Sénat, telle que la Chambre des lords, a été conçu en tant que corps législatif, l'une des chambres d'un parlement bicaméral, et non en tant qu'assemblée composée de bureaucrates ou en tant que conseil formé de politiciens choisis par les provinces. L'autorité législative suprême devait résider entre les mains des deux chambres. Il croit que la réponse à l'énigme de la réforme du Sénat se trouve dans la compréhension que l'entente au sujet de la structure du Sénat était le principe sur lequel reposait l'accord de la Constitution.

The Preamble to the *Constitution Act, 1867*, states that the uniting provinces desire "a Constitution similar in Principle to that of the United Kingdom." The meaning of the phrase is open to dispute, although a persuasive case may be made that it encompasses, for instance, the principles of responsible government and an independent judiciary. Still, additional attributions presumably exist, and it is to one of these that my initial comments on the Senate of Canada and the conundrum of reform are addressed.

There was a time when Canadian commentators on the Senate saw it as an imperfect representation of the House of Lords. Appointment for life was not the same thing as hereditary membership, but the inference critics drew was that the composition of both bodies constrained expression of the popular will in their respective Commons.[1] Nonetheless, despite similarities in form the chambers were not identical, while the function of each was in significant respects distinct. This became clear most recently, when in March 2007 the House of Commons at Westminster voted in support of an elected House of Lords, and the question was

---

[1] In twentieth century Great Britain, life peerages were introduced in 1958, while most hereditary peers ceased to be eligible to sit in the Lords in 1999; in Canada, life appointment to the Senate was replaced by mandatory retirement at age 75 in 1965.

asked in Canada: "If such reform is possible in the Mother of Parliaments, why not here?"

One would have thought that the answer was obvious: however similar "in Principle" the two constitutions, with regard to upper chambers they are far from being the same. The House of Lords is a vestigial institution of historic lineage; the Senate of Canada is neither. It is original, tailor-made – in other words statutorily prescribed – to fit the conditions of a new federal union. That contrast alone should make Canadians wary of following British example when contemplating reform of the upper chamber. A case in point is the proposal by now retired Senator Dan Hays that, among other actions, "the Senate of Canada should emulate the UK example and encourage the government of the day to appoint a royal commission on Senate reform" (Hays 2007, 23).[2]

Arguably, whether the subject is institutions (such as Parliament), or politics (the Cooperative Commonwealth Federation and socialism), or economic doctrine (Social Credit and social credit), British models have always been strongly entertained in Canada. This was true in 1867, when "an essentially atypical second chamber, the House of Lords, [was taken to] represen[t] a basic element of a stable constitution" (Jackson 1972, ix). Yet this was a curious claim when seen through British eyes. The year of Confederation was the year of Great Britain's second reform bill, which further expanded the franchise and confirmed the moral of the 1832 reform bill – that is, the House of Commons was to be Parliament's pre-eminent legislative chamber. Paradoxically, at the very time the Senate of Canada appeared set to follow the British model, a House of Lords problem had begun to appear, and would remain unresolved for some decades – what role was the Lords to have and, depending upon the answer to that question, what was to be its relationship to the House of Commons?

If this seems an indirect way to launch a discussion of the conundrum of Senate reform, I apologize. The point I wish to emphasize is that the Senate – like the House of Lords – was conceived as a legislative body, one chamber of a bicameral Parliament, not a Bundesrat-like assembly of bureaucrats, or an advisory body of provincially selected politicians. If the phrase "a Constitution similar in Principle to that of the United Kingdom" meant anything, it meant this – supreme legislative authority was to reside in two chambers.

Nor was the subject of legislatures and their number of chambers confined to the Parliament of Canada. Embedded within the *Constitution Act, 1867* are the provincial constitutions of Ontario and Quebec, wherein Ontario is given a legislative assembly and Quebec a legislative assembly and a legislative council. It is relevant to the topic of this paper that Ontario, the largest colony of settlement in the British Empire, and loyal to the core, should opt for a unitary legislature and

---

[2] The British royal commission is Royal Commission on the Reform of the House of Lords, *A House for the Future*, London: The Stationery Office, January 2000 (Cm 4534). For an analysis, see Smith 2000; for a personal critique, see Cook 2003.

that Quebec should seek a bicameral legislature, with an upper chamber of appointed members each drawn from one of the province's twenty-four electoral divisions. Those divisions were the same ones from which Quebec's twenty-four senators were to be selected for appointment by the governor general.

As Garth Stevenson has shown in his research on the anglophone minority in Quebec, the requirement that appointments be made from the individual divisions had as its purpose the protection of the religious and linguistic rights of the province's minorities (Stevenson 1997). In one respect that is an obvious conclusion to draw, although it does not detract from the contrast it poses between the Canadian Senate and the House of Lords. At no time, until the report of the Royal Commission on the Reform of the House of Lords (chaired by Lord Wakeham) made it one of its recommendations, did the House of Lords have sectional or minority interests as part of its responsibilities. By contrast, from Confederation onward, protection of these interests was a primary function of the Canadian Senate.

How well the Senate actually performed the task is secondary to the point being made here, which is about legislative structure, in particular bicameralism at the centre and unicameralism in the parts. Quebec retained its upper chamber until 1968, but the other provinces that had upper chambers (Manitoba, New Brunswick, Prince Edward Island and Nova Scotia) abolished them decades earlier, partly on grounds of economy but also on the theoretical grounds that they were redundant.[3] At the Quebec conference, George Brown argued for provincial unicameralism, because the new Senate would "extinguish or largely diminish the Local Legislative Councils" (Pope 1895, 76-7). Almost a century later, Senator Norman Lambert reiterated the point: "Equal representation in the Senate was to be the collective equivalent of the original Legislative Councils of the provinces" (Lambert 1950, 19).

Canada is unusual among federations for the asymmetrical composition of its national and provincial legislatures. It is a contrast that has seldom elicited scholarly comment, although one academic who did reflect on its significance was Harold Innis: "The governmental machinery of the provinces has been strengthened in struggles with the federal government by the gradual extinction of legislative councils" (Innis 1946, 132). Another observation would be that provincial politicians today have no experience of second chambers, and thus neither

---

[3] One of the first occasions for a discussion of Senate reform was the Interprovincial Conference of 1887, called by Honore Mercier, premier of Quebec, and attended by five of the then seven provincial premiers (British Columbia and Prince Edward Island absented themselves). Among the resolutions passed was one (number 4) that recommended the provinces be permitted to choose one half of their senatorial allocation. Another resolution (number 12) advocated the abolition of provincial second chambers because "experience ... shows that, under Responsible Government and with the safeguards provided by the *British North America Act*, a second chamber is unnecessary" (Canada 1951: Minutes Interprovincial Conference, 1887).

understanding nor sympathy for their place in the legislative process. The exception to that generalization is where provinces recognize the value of the Senate as a forum for opposing policies of the federal government. A recent example saw a majority of provinces present position papers to the Standing Senate Committee on Legal and Constitutional Affairs, which either rejected or expressed concern at the Harper government's Bill S-4, "An Act to Amend the Constitution Act, 1867 (Senate Tenure)." In the words of the New Brunswick presentation, term limits (the subject of S-4) would "dilute the independence [of Senators]" and it "would lead to a further marginalization of small Provinces at the federal level" (New Brunswick 2007, 7).

Membership in Canada's upper house is by senatorial region, of which there are four – Ontario, Quebec, the Maritime provinces and the four western provinces (Newfoundland and Labrador and the northern territories are treated as exceptions), each with twenty-four senators. A familiar complaint about this arrangement is that a province such as British Columbia, with close to four million inhabitants, has six senators, while PEI, with a population of less than 150,000, has four.

Standing grievance or not, the inequity has an explanation, and one important to understanding the place of the Senate in the federation. The guarantee of equal (regional but not provincial) representation with the more populous provinces of Ontario and Quebec was responsible for the entry of the Maritime provinces (Nova Scotia and New Brunswick). According to George Brown: "On no other condition could we have advanced a step" (*Confederation Debates* 1865, 88). Regional equity was *essential* to concluding the Confederation bargain; no other issue took so long to resolve.

In consequence of that agreement, it was possible for some decades after 1867 to think of the young Dominion as Christopher Dunkin, minister in charge of Canada's first census, described it in the House of Commons in 1868, that is, as "the three kingdoms"(HOC Debates 8 March 1870, 280). The allusion was to the United Kingdom, which encompassed England, Scotland and Ireland, along with the Principality of Wales, and notwithstanding whose diversity appeared to the Fathers of Confederation the paradigm of a successful nation.

What was missing in this analogy was federalism. Despite talk late in the nineteenth century of imperial federation and of federal solutions to the Irish Question, Great Britain was not a federal system. Canada was a federal union, although on the part of its principal politicians there was little discussion of the theory of federalism. For instance, the Macdonald government had no vision as to how the federation would be expanded, but rather was forced into a response following the rebellion at Red River. When introducing the *Manitoba Act* in 1870, the prime minister told the House that "it was not a matter of great importance whether the province was called a province or a territory. We have Provinces of all sizes, shapes and constitutions ... so that there could not be anything determined by the use of the word" (HOC Debates 2 May 1870, 1287). The postage stamp province of Manitoba that resulted – with its bicameral legislature, official bilingualism and denominational schools – conformed to no blueprint past or future. In the words of David Mills, Liberal journalist and later minister in the Mackenzie government, Parliament but more particularly the Conservatives had failed to do what "the theory of their system required" (HOC Debates, 25 April 1870, 1178). It should be said, however, that an anemic federal idea was not to be confused with weak national purpose, as the National Policy bore witness.

When it came to the Senate, however, the Liberals were no different. In this regard, the Liberal interregnum of 1873–8 is a puzzle. Why did the government of Alexander Mackenzie – who created the Supreme Court of Canada, secured a revised commission and set of instructions for the governor general, proposed ending appeals to the JCPC, and who allowed an expanded provincial franchise to determine the federal franchise – apparently never contemplate reform of the Senate? A perverse explanation for Liberal inactivity on the Senate front is this: more than the Conservatives, the Liberals were provincially minded; more than the Conservatives, they favoured a local and broadened franchise (even in federal elections). Uniting these two proclivities in aid of a reformed (most likely, an elected) Senate would probably have led to the demand for representation by population in the upper house as well as the lower. And this result would strike at the very roots of the Confederation compromise.

Canadians like to contrast their history with that of Americans as evolution versus revolution. This perspective locates the pre-Confederation past on a continuum leading to the post-Confederation era. Here, in George Etienne Cartier's words, was one justification for equal treatment of the Maritime provinces with Ontario and Quebec when it came to Senate membership:

> It might be thought that Nova Scotia and New Brunswick got more than their share in the originally adopted distribution, but it must be recollected that they had been independent provinces, and the count of heads must not always be permitted to outweigh every other consideration. (HOC Debates 3 April 1868, 455)

No longer independent colonies, Nova Scotia and New Brunswick had become provinces of a much larger colony. For this reason as much as for any other, the heavy hand of Maritime history, evident in the original Confederation settlement as regards the Senate, has continued into the present in a remarkably extensive way.

The story begins in 1912, when Parliament added portions of the Northwest Territories to the adjoining provinces of Ontario, Quebec and Manitoba. Why territory was added to existing provinces rather than creating new provinces, as the Northwest Ordinance (1787) had required for expansion of the United States, is a mystery. Nonetheless, it did have the effect of keeping the Senate formula stable. Ultimately, it led to its constitutional entrenchment.

In 1915, a half century after Confederation and following a debate in which no member of Parliament dissented from the principle of senatorial regions, an act of Parliament (*Constitution Act, 1915*) recognized the four provinces of western Canada as the fourth such region. In a "Memorandum on Representation of the Maritime Provinces," the Maritime provinces expressed disquiet at the prospect of these developments and their eventual effect on the composition of Parliament: "Representation by population while accepted as a guiding principle in fixing the representation of each province in the Dominion parliament, was intended to be made subservient to the right of each colony to *adequate* representation in view of its surrender of a large measure of self-government" (Memorandum 1913, ital. in orig.). Echoing Cartier's rationale of fifty years before, the Memorandum continued: "A self-governing colony was something more than the number of its inhabitants."

Sacrifice as well as history was invoked: "[The Maritime provinces] gave their sons and daughters to the west. From Manitoba to the Pacific coast the Maritime Provinces people form an important element of the population who have played no small part in the development of these new lands." Justice too: "[The Maritime Provinces] had as good a right to share in the public demesne of Canada as had those provinces upon which it was bestowed"; and, finally, future prospects: "[The territory added to the three provinces] will increase to a limit not now possible of calculation the representation of these provinces in the federal Parliament." The concern of the Memorandum was to restore the "representation of the Maritime Provinces in the House of Commons ... to the number allowed upon entering confederation upon terms that the same may not in future be subject to reduction below that number."

The federal government responded sympathetically to this request but in a manner not anticipated in the Memorandum. The *Constitution Act, 1915* amended the 1867 Act by the addition of section 51A, which read: "Notwithstanding anything in this Act a province shall always be entitled to a number of members in the House of Commons not less than the number of senators representing such province." The nexus thus created between a province's Commons and Senate seat allocations has had at least two long-term implications for federal-provincial relations. First, it has fixed the attention of small provinces in particular upon the guarantee the nexus provides and strengthened their resolve to resist any change that might threaten it. Secondly, and in company with another amendment to the Constitution's representation provisions, adopted in 1952, which said (s. 51.5) that "there shall be no reduction in the representation of any province as a result of which that province would have a smaller number of members than any other province that according to the results of the then last decennial census did not have a larger population," it has given ammunition to Senate critics who seek equality of provincial representation in the upper chamber comparable to that found in the United States and Australia.[4]

The desire of the Maritime Provinces in 1913 for predictability as to their numbers in Parliament achieved a level of unimagined certainty decades later in the *Constitution Act, 1982* (s. 44), when one of the four specified matters requiring unanimous consent for their amendment—the Crown, the Supreme Court of Canada, the use of English or the French language were the others—was the

---

[4] The story of the politics surrounding this provision is well told by Norman Ward 1952.

guarantee that no province should have fewer members of the House of Commons than it had senators.

Here is a Herculean obstacle to any proposed Senate reform that touches upon the subject of membership numbers. It is also one to whose history reformers would be advised to pay close attention. None of the impediments to reform listed in the preceding paragraphs were original to the *Constitution Act, 1867*. They occurred because of territorial and demographic expansion, and took the form of compensation, largely by the central government, to those who did not expect to grow. (There are parallels here to the history of another fundamental component to Canadian federalism, and now constitutional guarantee – equalization.)

In addition to the representational nexus between the two chambers of Parliament, there is a further parliamentary dimension to the conundrum of Senate reform: Canada is a constitutional monarchy in a system of responsible (cabinet) government. These are important features in a discussion of the Senate. To begin with, constitutional monarchy makes explicable – if not acceptable to some – appointment of senators by the Crown on advice of the prime minister. There is no need to rehearse the arguments against an appointed upper house. They are well known. What can be said is that constitutional monarchy offered a practicable method of selecting senators to the upper chamber at a time when there were few alternatives. Election was not popular in United Canada after the experiment initiated in the mid-1850s, while selection by provincial legislatures of delegates from among their numbers to sit at the centre, as was done in nineteenth- century United States, violated the common sense of Parliament as the supreme legislative power (as in the UK) and the belief British North Americans held that the creation of a national parliament marked an important step to constitutional maturity.

Senate critics have fixed on patronage and partisanship as twin scourges that come from political domination of the appointment process. Political life in Canada after 1867 could not have been predicted from colonial experience. Party discipline and long periods of single party domination of government (and thus a monopoly on patronage) had been unknown in the colonies. Now politics in the Dominion worked to centralize power in the political executive, that is, the Cabinet. The reason why lay in the development of national political parties through the constituencies, a practice that produced local party notables, who in turn personified the provincial party at the centre. These people became cabinet ministers in Ottawa because of a second practice which was quickly treated as a convention of the Constitution – the federalization of the Cabinet. Other influences were at work as well, such as the custom governments of United Canada had had of including within their ranks representatives of significant groups, be they religious, or linguistic, or regional.

The extent to which the cabinet was federalized deprived the Senate from playing a similar, integrative role. The late American scholar Martin Landau wrote about federalism in the United States as a system of redundancies (Landau 1973). One example would be the presidential power shared with the Senate to confirm treaties and key executive and judicial appointments. Such sharing was never possible in a constitutional monarchical system where treaties and appointments are the prerogative of the Crown and made on advice of a single (first) minister. Significantly, for those who look to the Australian Senate as a model for a reformed Canadian Senate, these are not part of its powers either.

Nonetheless, the intrastate argument – that federations require a legislative mechanism to integrate the parts at the centre – remains alive in Canada, where the Senate does not perform this role. Just how well the upper chambers of Australia and the United States fulfill it is another matter. In *Platypus and Parliament: The Australian Senate in Theory and Practice,* Stanley Bach makes clear that the Australian Senate is more accurately described as a house of state parties rather than a house of the states (Bach 2003).

Dunkin's 1868 metaphor of the three kingdoms to describe the original Union was artistic in its historical allusion to the mother country but artfully simplistic in its treatment of the new Dominion's vast geography. Two years later, with the acquisition of Rupert's Land and the North-Western Territory, the physical frame for the "novel" constitution (the adjective was Lord Monck's in the first Speech from the Throne, 1868) quadrupled, creating a challenge for the Canadian federation it has yet to meet. The reason why is part of the conundrum of Senate reform.

Essentially, there are two reasons for experimenting with federal systems: to recognize cultural difference and to incorporate territory. Canada's is a double federation in that both imperatives are present. The *Constitution Act, 1867* is largely about realizing the first, by recognizing French Canada's distinctiveness through its own set of institutions. Note that it was French Canada's and not Quebec's distinctiveness that was at issue, as was confirmed in 1870 by the almost identical terms found in the *Manitoba Act.* But as all who know their Canadian history know, the *Manitoba Act* foundered in the face of the other, "transcontinental" imperative. Because of massive immigration of non-French farmers, French Canadians were to have negligible influence on the future of West, at least for a century, until appointment of the Royal Commission on Bilingualism and Biculturalism, passage of the *Official Languages Act* and entrenchment of the *Canadian Charter of Rights and Freedoms* (Behiels 2004). At the same time, geographic scale and colonial experience delayed realization of the second federal imperative. Instead, the West was seen as another empire, whose constitutional development would recapitulate that of central Canada and the Maritime provinces, that is, it would pass by stages from representative, to responsible, to eventual provincial government. Absent from this imperial persuasion was the federal idea.

Beginning in 1887 and until the present day, territories not yet provinces are represented in Parliament by MPs and senators. What does this membership signify? The *Constitution Act, 1915,* which created the western Senatorial Division, also provided that when Newfoundland entered Confederation, it "shall be entitled to be represented in the Senate by six members." According to the 1911 census, Saskatchewan had a population of 492,432; Newfoundland had less than half that number (242,619). What larger reasoning dictated this future allocation? Whatever the answer, it helps explain, perhaps, the comment by Canada's high commissioner to Newfoundland almost thirty later that Newfoundlanders "really [do not] appreciate or understand the workings of the Federal system of Government" (Canada. External Affairs, 16 November 1943, 87).[5]

The central government's view of the Prairie West as its empire, as testified to in its retention of the natural resources of Manitoba, Saskatchewan and Alberta until 1930 and in the use of these resources as in the case of land for national purposes, such as building the transcontinental railroads, contributed to a sense of regional grievance that no amount of good fortune afterward appeared able to moderate. Twenty-five years after the addition of section 92A to the *Constitution Act, 1867*, intended to affirm the provinces' jurisdiction over the exploration, development and transportation of non-renewable natural resources, distrust of the centre on this matter continued. Consider Peter Lougheed's prediction in a speech to the Canadian Bar Association in August 2007 that federal environmental and provincial resource development policies are on a collision course and that the discord will be "ten times greater" than in the past (Makin 2007).

The tension between the centre and the parts, particularly the western part of the country, is evident in both cultural and economic spheres. The questions of denominational schools and of language have roiled relations for over a century. This happened by making those subjects, which had been at the core of the original Confederation settlement, matters that were seen to trespass on provincial rights (Lingard 1946, 154). The effect was to slow down the rounding out of Confederation. The same tension, but cast in economic terms – the tariff, freight rates, the National Energy Policy, the Canadian Wheat Board are examples – goes a long way toward explaining the regional decline of national parties on the prairies and the rise and perpetuation of third-party opposition from the West in Ottawa. Here is another factor that contributes to Canada's Senate being different from its counterparts in Australia and the United States. Many, maybe most, of the best known politicians of western Canada have been from neither of the major national parties. Even if it were the ambition of reformers to make the Canadian Senate like Australia's – using Bach's language, a house of provincial parties – how could this be done, given the manner of senatorial selection and the condition of national parties, in some instances almost vestigial, in the provinces?

The effect of the frontier was to increase federal power. Since acquisition of Rupert's Land and the North-Western Territory in 1870, this has been evident in economic matters. If, however, frontier is more liberally construed to mean the

---

[5] If there was a shallow understanding of federalism one reason might be inadequate preparatory information. Despite its title, "Some Notes on the Constitution and Government of Canada and on the Canadian Federal System" (A Reference Paper Prepared for the Information of a Delegation from the National Convention of Newfoundland), prepared in Ottawa in June 1947, four (of 43) paragraphs dealt with "division of powers as laid down in the *BNA Act*," while five described "provincial governments" in terms of their legislatures (unicameral), adult franchise and office of lieutenant governor. Parties and inter-governmental relations receive no mention. (NAC 1947)

new and the unknown, as with the Charter and its interpretation by the courts, it applies as well to the Constitution, law and rights. This is a subject where the Senate has a claim to some expertise and experience. Its great advantage is that it has nothing to do with numbers, either equal or fixed. There is a Canadian penchant for using fixed numbers to offer protection: 65 MLAs each for Canada East and Canada West after 1840; 65 MPs from Quebec after 1867, all other representation to be proportionate; an irreducible 75 MPs today; and, as already noted, s. 41 of The *Constitution Act, 1982*, which guarantees that no province shall have fewer senators than it has members of Parliament.

The belief that more means better is not borne out in Senate experience. The Senate is a chamber of the people but it is not a representative body. A motion by Senators Lowell Murray and Jack Austin in 2006, to create a fifth Senatorial Division comprised solely of the province of British Columbia, with twelve senators, presupposed otherwise (Canada. Senate 2006). (The same motion envisioned a new prairie region with twenty-four seats – seven each for Saskatchewan and Manitoba, and ten for Alberta). Implicit in the motion is the assumption that the Senate is deficient as an institution of intrastate federalism and that increasing the number of senators from a particular region, as well as the total number (in this case from 105 to 117), will begin to remedy that condition. Whether British Columbia is a "region" distinct from the Prairie provinces is open to debate. For instance, such designation runs counter to intra-regional developments in western Canada in the last twenty-five years that treat the four western provinces as an entity with common but not identical economic and regulatory interests in its relations with the federal government. Even if British Columbia has distinct public policy interests in its relations with the federal government, it begs the question whether the Senate is the forum and senators the voice for their effective expression.

Increasing numbers in one region does not deal with the criticism of inequity elsewhere, a reality the federal government confronted also in the House of Commons in 2007 with its Bill C-56, "An Act to Amend the Constitution Act, 1867 [Democratic Representation]." In part this is the other, or Commons, side of the "senatorial floor" guarantee adopted as a constitutional amendment in 1915. The upper house ceiling on Commons representation for a province amounts to a continuing distortion to the principle of rep-by-pop. John Courtney, who is the authority on this matter, has shown that, for example, "if on the basis of the 2001 census Ontario had been awarded one seat for every 33,824 people (as was the case for Prince Edward Island), it would send 337 MPs to Ottawa—a larger delegation than the current House of Commons"(Courtney 2007, 11). The Harper Government's way of dealing with this matter is the way of past governments – to increase the total size of the chamber. That would be the outcome of the Murray/Austin motion for the Senate too. To guarantee protection Canadian politicians favour fixed numbers for representation; to recognize growth they opt for additional seats. As a result, no province loses. Thus the distortion of the principle of rep-by-pop mounts, and the quest for equality proves fruitless and without historical justification.

Although elected politicians took the decisions, it was the unelected Senate which provided the keystone for modern Canada's structure of representation. A maze of compromises, deals and agreements, its architecture is central to the conundrum of Senate reform. Central but inadequately acknowledged, since debate seldom strays from the tried and true. Should the Senate be appointed or elected, and, in either case, should this be done at the centre (nationally) or in the parts (provincially)? Should the tenure of senators be limited to terms, of whatever length, as opposed to a mandatory retirement age? When it comes to function, should the Senate be limited to a delaying or suspensive veto only, like its Westminster counterpart, or should weighted voting be introduced for measures in specific categories (for example, use of the federal spending power), or double-majority voting on measures of "special linguistic significance," or should the Senate be given power to approve order-in-council appointments as well as consent to treaties?

Proposed reforms come and go, and come again, but always with the same outcome – no change. Why is institutional and constitutional change in the matter of Canada's upper chamber – whether major, in the form of the Meech Lake and Charlottetown Accords, or minor, in the form of the Harper Government's Senate Tenure Bill, which the government described as incremental, so difficult to achieve? Is stasis in this matter any different from the half-century search for a constitutional amendment formula in Canada or the eighty-eight year hiatus in Great Britain between the introduction of the suspensive veto in 1911, as a first step to Lords reform, and the next, the severing of the hereditary peers from membership in the Lords, in 1999?

Part of the explanation lies in the longevity of senators – appointed for life until 1965 and until age seventy-five since then. Although that provision may lead to extraordinarily long tenure, generally it does not: the average length of office is almost twelve years (Smith 2003). Still, this is far longer than the parliamentary career of most MPs, and, more particularly, of cabinet ministers who pilot reform through Parliament. Moreover, the overlap of generations in the Senate is more pronounced than in the Commons.[6] Nor is it immaterial that senators are at the end of their political careers. There is no political uncertainty or calculation as to their future. Time is on their side.

Part of it lies in the composition of the Senate, where despite specified senatorial divisions senators are allocated among the provinces. In the eyes of each province, their senators – or, better still, their number of senators – belongs to them. Proposed reforms that would affect the numbers or the function of senators are carefully scrutinized by the provinces (as in the case of Bill S-4, noted above). Thus, the Senate never stands alone. The Senate has allies who, regardless of party complexion, usually come to its aid.

---

[6] On the matter of overlap and, more generally, temporality in politics, see Pierson 2004 and Smith 2005.

Another part of the explanation can be found in the constitutional indeterminacy of the Senate's role and function. One reason there are so many different proposals for its reform is that there is great latitude, even ambiguity, about what the chamber might be expected to do. Although it may be a factually incorrect statement, almost everyone agrees that the job of the House of Commons is "to make laws that are acceptable to the public." In a bicameral Parliament, the Senate is a legislative chamber but with one important limitation on its activities: Section 53 of The *Constitution Act, 1867*, states that appropriation measures must originate in the House of Commons. Otherwise, the Senate's powers are those of the Commons, with the conventional limitation that it shall not act in a manner to thwart the will of the people as expressed by their elected representatives. Here is "the space," if you will, for sober second thought, even sober first thought – the Senate as an investigative and deliberative chamber, bringing to bear on public policy the weight of long experience and broad knowledge.

In 1980 the Supreme Court of Canada was asked by the federal government to give its opinion on the authority of Parliament to amend the constitution unilaterally as regards the Senate (Canada. Supreme Court of Canada, 1980). At issue was the Trudeau government's constitutional reform package of 1978 – Bill C-60, the Constitutional Amendment Bill, which among other matters provided for a House of the Provinces, in place of the Senate, with members indirectly elected by provincial legislative assemblies and the House of Commons. The details of that proposed reform of thirty years ago are immaterial, except for the long reach of the Court's opinion in two respects. First, it said that "it is clear that the intention [of the Fathers of Confederation] was to make the Senate a thoroughly independent body which could canvass dispassionately the measures of the House of Commons" (77). Further, it stated that "the Senate has a vital role as an institution forming part of the federal system …Thus, the body which has been created as a means of protecting sectional and provincial interests was made a participant of the legislative process" (56).

"Thoroughly independent," and "an institution forming part of the federal system ... [as well as] a participant in the legislative process." These phrases have come to severely test proposals for Senate reform. Unlike the general procedure for amending the Constitution, as set down in s. 42 (that is, support from seven provinces with 50 percent of the population) and which applies to the powers of the Senate, the method of selecting senators and the numbers of senators to which a province is entitled, threats to independence are less easy to calculate, although not to imagine. At the same time, the 1982 advisory opinion made clear that the Senate was already a part of the federal system and an actor in the legislative process. Schemes to alter the upper chamber in a manner that could be said to weaken these judicially ascribed characteristics face informed opposition from their outset. For instance, would Triple_E with its emphasis on representation undermine the dispassionate contemplative role envisioned for the Senate by the Supreme Court? Or again, are senatorial terms compatible with "thorough independen[ce]"?

Senators may hold office until age 75; with the hereditaries gone, members of the Lords (for the time being) are appointed for life. What conclusion is to be drawn from these facts? That Canada is not a democracy? That Great Britain has never been a democracy? If the questions sound extreme, they are meant to, for they underline an essential aspect of the conundrum of Senate (and Lords) reform: there is no popular will, no popular movement to make it happen, because there is insufficient discontent with the status quo. Attempts at Senate reform have no staying power. Triple-E, which had some claim to a popular component, although regionally concentrated, appears to be fading.

Everybody, when asked, will dismiss an appointed Senate, but nobody, when left alone, will do anything about changing the Senate. Senate reform is a preoccupation of academics and bureaucrats. Of 24 relatively recent proposals on the subject, 15 are the product of governments, royal commissions or legislatures. Three others come from political parties. Concern about strengthening the mechanisms of intra-state federalism or institutionalizing intergovernmental relations through a recast Senate have no popular appeal, or understanding. It is an incomprehension proponents of such schemes do little to dispel (Canada. Library of Parliament. Stilborn 1999).

Increasingly, debate about Senate reform has less to do with maintaining the tapestry of federalism (the focus of reform activity in the last quarter of the last century), than it has with an evolving sense of constitutionalism which, as the Supreme Court of Canada opinion of 1980 demonstrates, preceded the adoption of the *Canadian Charter of Rights and Freedoms* but which has been reinforced by it. Proponents of term limits for senators or of advisory elections to determine the nominee for appointment by the governor-in-council find the debate that results from this change in register conducted at a level of constitutional abstraction distant from the object they seek. Thus the frustration evident in Mr. Harper's remark to the Australian Senate – that Canadians suffer from "[Australian] Senate envy" (Galloway 2007).

The irony of recent debates on Senate reform is hardly subtle – that the unelected, retirement-at-75 upper house might have a role to play redressing the "democratic deficit" attributed to all-powerful prime ministers, and that any reform that would politicize its members and make them more subject to partisan direction is to be avoided.

Far easier in Great Britain, one might think – no nexus to bind the distribution of members in one chamber to the distribution in the other; no federation of provinces and territories who look to the upper house to articulate regional, sectional, and minority interests; no double federation, of cultures and provinces; no federalized cabinet; no written constitution with a difficult amending formula to discourage formal change – and yet the same outcome. Robin Cook, Leader of the House of Commons at Westminster between 2001 and 2003, was in charge of the Blair government's initiatives on reform of the House of Lords. He supported the elective principle, his leader (when pressed) the appointive principle. Cook makes clear that Tony Blair's indecisiveness was a crucial, but not determinative, factor in explaining lack of movement on Lords reform. Everyone had a view of what a future Lords should look like. More important, however, everyone had a priority of legislative objectives, and for many on the government side Lords reform was not their most paramount concern.

The object of reform should not be confused with a priority for reform. In this last respect the Blair Government was exceptional for introducing a period of constitutional inquiry not seen in Great Britain for nearly a century. The same might be said of the initiatives of the Trudeau Government in Canada, which led to bargaining with the provinces that culminated in the *Constitution Act, 1982*, except that for most of the twentieth century Canada had been preoccupied with constitutional questions, either as it sought autonomy in its relations with the imperial power or as it confronted sovereignist sentiment within its boundaries after 1960. Yet despite the promising and accommodative language, in neither country did upper chamber improvement have the same political or popular bite as, for instance, devolution and local government reform in Britain or the advent of the Charter in Canada.

In part, the conundrum of Senate reform is that it has had more popular competitors. More fundamental still, is that reform of the Senate in terms of the selection of its members, or in the redistribution of their number among the provinces, according to some standard of equity, have immediate implications for the other two parts of Parliament – the senatorial floor to provincial representation in the Commons and the prerogative power of appointment possessed by the Crown. The unity of the Crown-in-Parliament and the theory that sustains it – that there is no constituent power outside of that tripartite institution – acts as an original and powerful disincentive to articulating and initiating reform of the Senate, and then carrying it through to a successful conclusion.

The OED gives as one definition of conundrum the following: "a riddle, especially one with a pun in its answer." (A second definition is: "a hard or puzzling question.") In the context of the subject of this paper, any attempt to follow this injunction will not equal Churchill's memorable description of the Soviet Union – a riddle wrapped in a mystery inside an enigma. A best effort results in something more prosaic – a phonetic anagram of the word itself, "cum round"; and that, admittedly, is an approximation. This is a strained way of saying that the answer to the conundrum of Senate reform lies not in myriad prescriptions for change but in understanding that agreement on the structure of the Senate was the principle on which the Confederation accord rested. Central to that accord was the idea of balance – "the three kingdoms." With the arrival of a new transcontinental federation, balance gave way to concern for protection, achieved not through the Senate alone but by creating a senatorial floor for representation of the provinces in the Commons. Over time that guarantee became constitutionally entrenched. The last step in that development occurred with adoption of the *Constitution Act, 1982*. The 1980s and succeeding decades witnessed a constitutionalization of federalism far beyond old concerns about the division of powers. It is a re-constitution of federalism according to norms distinct from those evoked by the preambular phrase, "a Constitution similar in Principle to that of the United Kingdom," that further deepens the conundrum of Senate reform.

REFERENCES

Bach, S. 2003. *Platypus and Parliament: The Australian Senate in Theory and Practice.* Canberra: Department of the Senate.

Behiels, M. 2004. *Canada's Francophone Minority Communities: Constitutional Renewal and the Winning of School Governance.* Montreal and Kingston: McGill-Queen's University Press.

Canada. 1868–71. House of Commons Debates.

— 1951. Dominion Provincial and Interprovincial Conferences from 1887 to 1926. Ottawa: King's Printer.

— 1951. King's Printer. *Parliamentary Debates on Confederation of* the *British North American Provinces.* (Reprint) Quebec: Hunter, Rose & Co., Parliamentary Printers, 1865.

— 1984. Department of External Affairs. *Documents on Relations between Canada and Newfoundland: Vol. 2, 1940–49, Confederation, Part 1.* ed. P. Bridle. Ottawa: Supply and Services Canada.

— 1999. Library of Parliament. J. Stilborn, "Comments on Twenty-Four Senate Reform Proposals Provided for Analysis," 5 July.

Reference re: Legislative Authority of Parliament in relation to the Upper House. 1 S. C. R. 54.

Courtney, J.C. 2006. "The Conundrum of Electoral Districting in Canada." Festschriftkonferenz in Honor of Paul Weiler. Harvard University, Cambridge, MA. 27p.

Cook, R. 2003. *The Point of Departure.* London: Simon and Schuster UK.

Galloway, G. 2007. "PM Launches Blow at Liberal-dominated Senate," *The Globe and Mail,* 11 September, A 11.

Hays, Senator D. 2007. "Renewing the Senate of Canada: A Two-Phase Proposal," 25 May. Unpublished paper, 42p.

Innis, Harold A. 1946. "Political Economy in the Modern State," in *Political Economy in the Modern State,* ed. H.A. Innis. Toronto: Ryerson Press: 103-44.

Jackson, W.K. 1972. *The New Zealand Legislative Council: A Study of the Establishment, Failure and Abolition of an Upper House.* Toronto: University of Toronto Press.

Lambert, Senator N. 1950. "Reform of the Senate: Historical Justification," in *The Winnipeg Free Press,* 15 April.

Landau, M. 1973. "Federalism, Redundancy and System Reliability," *Publius* 3 (2): 173-96.

Lingard, C.C. 1946. *Territorial Government in Canada: The Autonomy Question in the Old North-West Territories.* Toronto: University of Toronto Press.

Makin K. 2007. "High Stakes Battle Looms over Oil-Sands Pollution," *The Globe and Mail,* 15 August.

Memorandum on Representation of the Maritime Provinces. Canadian Sessional Papers, 1914, no.118a, pp.1-3, reprinted in *Constitutional Issues in Canada, 1900-1931,* ed. R. MacGregor Dawson. Toronto: University of Toronto Press, 1933, 173-5.

National Archives of Canada. 1947. MG 26 L, vol. 36, Newfoundland National Convention and Canada. Government Meetings 1947, Part 1.

New Brunswick. 2007. Position Paper of the Government of New Brunswick: Bill S-4-An Act to Amend the Constitution Act, 1867 (Senate Tenure). Presented to the Standing Senate Committee on Legal and Constitutional Affairs, 20 April, 12p.

Pierson P. 2004. *Politics in Time: History, Institutions, and Social Analysis.* Princeton and Oxford: Princeton University Press.

Pope, Sir Joseph, ed.1895. *Confederation: Being a Series of Hitherto Unpublished Documents on the British North America Act.* Toronto: Carswell.

Senate of Canada. 2006. Special Senate Committee on Senate Reform. "Report on the Motion to Amend the Constitution of Canada (western regional representation in the Senate)."

Smith D. E. 2000. "A House for the Future: Debating Second Chamber Reform in the United Kingdom." *Government and Opposition,* 35(3): 325-44.

— 2003. "The Improvement of the Senate by Non-Constitutional Means," in *Protecting Canadian Democracy: The Senate You Never Knew.* ed. Serge Joyal. Montreal and Kingston: McGill-Queen's University Press. 229-70.

— 2005. "Path Dependency and Saskatchewan Politics," in *The Heavy Hand of History: Interpreting Saskatchewan's Past,* ed. G.P. Marchildon. Regina: Canadian Plains Research Center. 31-50

Stevenson, G. 1997. "A Long Farewell: The Declining Representation of Quebec Anglophones in Parliamentary Institutions since 1867," *National History: A Canadian Journal of Inquiry and Opinion* 1(1): 22-34.

Ward, N. 1953. "The Redistribution of 1952," *Canadian Journal of Economics and Political Science* 19(3):341-60.

3

HARMONIZING REGIONAL REPRESENTATION WITH PARLIAMENTARY GOVERNMENT: THE ORIGINAL PLAN

Janet Ajzenstat

Les Pères de la Confédération ont désigné le Parlement du Canada, incluant le Sénat, pour délibérer sur des questions politiques touchant tous les gens de la même manière au sein de la nation, et ce sans exception. Quant aux questions touchant certains groupes en particuliers, surtout les questions liées à la religion et au pays d'origine, elles devaient relever des provinces. Bien que, de nos jours, il y ait des raisons de vouloir réformer le Sénat, nous devrions éviter d'introduire de nouvelles mesures, telle la représentation ministérielle, qui réduiraient les pouvoirs du Sénat en tant qu'organe délibérant à part égal et de manière inclusive.

The people

> could never be safe nor at rest, nor think themselves in Civil Society, till the Legis-
> lature was placed in collective Bodies of Men, call them Senate, Parliament, or what
> you please. By which means every single person became subject equally with other
> the meanest Men, to those Laws, which he himself, as part of the Legislative had
> established. (Locke 1690, para. 94)

Following the British legal tradition familiar from Locke, the Fathers of Canadian Confederation "placed" the legislative power in a Parliament consisting of three "Bodies of Men": the political executive, and two legislative houses; today, Cabinet, Senate, and Commons. They intended that "every single person" would be "subject equally with other the meanest Men, to those Laws which he himself, as part of the Legislative had established." The general legislature of the federation was to be egalitarian and inclusive.

There are features of the *Constitution Act, 1867* that might be taken to call in question this assertion. One is that the members of the Senate were appointed for life on a property qualification. Another is that *regional* representation in the Senate breaches the idea of provincial equality and the principle of representation by population. Ontario and Quebec were given twenty-four senators each; the three

Maritime provinces together were to have an additional twenty-four. Thus although the regions were represented equally, the provinces were not. Each of the smaller provinces had fewer representatives in the upper house than did the giants of the heartland, Upper and Lower Canada, but more representatives than population warranted. I will argue nevertheless that the Fathers indeed believed that the general legislature of the federation would be egalitarian and inclusive, and that the Upper Chamber they designed would reinforce those characteristics.

They had two tasks. Making the national legislature was the first. The second was to determine the division of legislative powers. From the American example the Fathers learned *that* a division of powers could be reconciled with parliamentary government and the rule of law. But they did not propose to follow the American scheme to the letter. They assigned the general government, including the Upper Chamber, a different role.

MAKING PARLIAMENT

They understood well that the general legislature represented "every single person," that is, everyone subject to the legislature's edicts. In the debates on Confederation in the Province of Canada, Joseph Cauchon argues that "Each representative, although elected by one particular *county* [region, electoral constituency], represents the *whole country*, and his legislative responsibility extends to the whole of it" (Cauchon, Canadian Legislative Assembly, 6 March 1865, in *Canada's Founding Debates* 448; my emphasis).[1] The Parliament of Canada still today, including the Senate, represents not merely the majority party, not merely the electorate, but every last child, woman and man in the land, from sea to sea.

The fact that a senator speaks for both region and *nation* enables him or her to bring local perspectives into national debates and, by the same token, to bring to bear on regional perspectives the national concerns that are the federal Parliament's responsibility. Parliamentary debate is not characterized by a head-butting confrontation in which members speak exclusively for a particular interest or region. Parliament is, as I have said, an *inclusive* institution; parliamentary deliberation must satisfy Locke's requirement that no person be excluded.

The Fathers and the legislators like Cauchon, who were called on to ratify the federation proposal in their provincial legislatures, knew as well as we do that in the Westminster system, majority-party and government leaders dominate the legislative process. They were experienced parliamentarians and intimately familiar with this aspect of procedure. Some had themselves been involved in the overthrow of the colonial oligarchies and the introduction of parliamentary democracy in 1848; all knew the story. My point is that no one at Confederation – or

---

[1] Quotations from the Confederation debates are taken from Janet Ajzenstat, Paul Romney, Ian Gentles, and William D. Gairdner, eds., *Canada's Founding Debates* (Toronto: University of Toronto Press, 2003); hereafter, CFD.

very few – believed that majority decision-making is incompatible with Parliament's inclusiveness. On the contrary, they regarded it as the mark of an inclusive institution.

The single most important factor securing the necessary inclusiveness, I would argue, is that Parliament's decisions are not final. If we are to live together in peace, Parliament must reach decisions and those decisions must have the force of law. But there is no requirement that measures will have effect once and for all time. Laws can be repealed. Defeated issues and arguments spring to life in subsequent parliamentary sessions. Discussion continues in the extra-parliamentary arena. Majorities erode; new majorities form; minorities join coalitions or swell to majority proportions. The process will often seem imperfect; it will never satisfy the impatient. Yet it is difficult to imagine one that does more to include all voices and to give all political perspectives an equal chance.

In short, the Lockean idea of human equality underpins not only the process of making a constitution but also the process of parliamentary deliberation on statute law. Consider this statement by John A. Macdonald:

> [We] ... enjoy the privileges of constitutional liberty according to the British system ... We will enjoy here that which is the great test of constitutional freedom – we will have the rights of the minority respected. In all countries the rights of the majority take care of themselves, but it is only in countries like England, enjoying constitutional liberty and safe from the tyrannies of a single tyrant or of an unbridled democracy that the rights of minorities are regarded. (Macdonald, Canadian Legislative Assembly, 6 February 1865; CFD 209)

By "the minority," and "minorities," Macdonald means the political groups and parties that disagree with the government of the day – dissenters in the government caucus, perhaps, and individuals and parties on the opposition benches.

The Senate is a vital part of the scheme. It must stall or veto legislation when a prime minister attempts to use his majority in the Commons to ride roughshod over the opposition's questions and complaints. The importance that Macdonald attached to the Senate's obligation is shown by his reluctance to countenance appointment of additional senators to break a deadlock between the legislative houses.

In the Quebec Resolutions there was no provision for appointment of additional senators and Brown and Macdonald had a lively exchange on the subject when the Resolutions came before the Canadian assembly. Brown hinted at the idea that he had been inclined originally to approve of appointments to break a deadlock but was dissuaded by the realization that such a measure might upset the scheme of regional representation in the upper house. Macdonald perhaps cared less about regional representation. What alarmed him was the idea that governments might use the appointing power to push through measures in the face of determined and principled opposition.

> No ministry in Canada in future can do what they have done in Canada before – they cannot, with the view of carrying any measure or of strengthening the party, attempt

to overrule the independent opinion of the upper house by filling it with a number of its partisans and political supporters (Macdonald, Canadian Legislative Assembly, 8 February 1865; CFD 79-80).

When he said this, Macdonald was the leader of the majority party in the provincial assembly. He was in his prime. He could expect to lead the Conservatives, the province, and if all went as expected the new country for years to come. Yet here he is defending the rights of the opposition parties, that is, the Independents, the Liberals, and the Rouges. He wants the new nation to have an effective Parliament including an effective upper house, with powers secured by the law of the Constitution.

To sum up: Parliament's inclusiveness is ensured by the outstanding features of the Westminster system: first, that members (including senators) must not forget either local or national perspectives in a process of political deliberation that protects the political opposition and brings dissenting views into the open; and second, that the Upper Chamber has an additional obligation: to resist attempts by the party in office to use its clout in the Commons to limit deliberation.

THE DIVISION OF LEGISLATIVE POWERS

I turn to the framers' second task. Parliament, including the Senate, was not intended to debate all political issues. The Fathers gave each level of government its "list" of powers. Indeed they adhered to what comes to be called the doctrine of "water-tight compartments." The most helpful spokesmen on the division of powers are George-Etienne Cartier, H.V. Langevin, and George Brown.

Brown describes the Fathers' intentions and difficulties at length: the "framers of this scheme ... had the prejudices of race, language and religion to deal with; and we had to encounter all ... the jealousies of diversified local interests" (Brown, Canadian Legislative Assembly, 8 February, 1865; CFD 115). As he tells the story, the Fathers of Confederation took away from the general legislature the power to entertain debate on the contested issues of race, language and religion. "The questions that used to excite the most hostile feelings among us have been withdrawn from the general legislature" and "thrown over onto the provinces" (ibid., 289).

My argument to this point has been that Parliament's inclusiveness enables senators to bring local perspectives into national deliberations. I am now amplifying this assertion. The senators bring a local perspective, but not local *issues*. Neither the Senate nor the Commons was intended to bring into the national legislature substantive matters that were of exclusive interest to one province or region. Thus: French-speaking senators would not introduce matters of importance to French Canadians alone. Their task rather as representatives of a French-Canadian region was to ensure that the English-speaking majority in Parliament did not entertain measures to curtail the rights of French-speakers or demote their status as equal subjects of the Crown.

It is hard to imagine a bolder argument on the division of powers than Brown's:

> We are endeavouring to adjust harmoniously greater difficulties than have plunged other countries into all the horrors of civil war. We are attempting to do peacefully and satisfactorily what Holland and Belgium, after years of strife, were unable to accomplish. We are seeking by calm discussion to settle questions that Austria and Hungary, that Denmark and Germany, that Russia and Poland, could only crush by the iron heel or armed force. We are seeking to do without foreign intervention that which deluged in blood the sunny plains of Italy. We are striving to settle for ever issues hardly less momentous than those that have rent the neighbouring republic and are now exposing it to all the horrors of civil war. (ibid., 14)

Is there anyone in Canada today who claims to have the one and sovereign remedy for civil strife and the contestation of what we now call "identities"? Brown is contending that the Fathers of Confederation found a remedy for what is perhaps the greatest political ill of modern regimes, a remedy that had eluded Europe and eluded the United States.

Note that he was not proposing to rely on civility or enlightened attitudes as means to forestall strife. He was certainly not saying in the manner of today's multiculturalists merely that individuals should be polite or that groups should get to know one another better. He believed that civility had failed utterly in the united Province of Canada. He spoke of "agitations in the country" (the Province of Canada), "fierce contests" in the Legislative Assembly, and "the strife and the discord and the abuse of many years" (ibid., 285). The remedy that he and the French Canadians devised was wholly institutional. To repeat: the proposal was to allocate to the general government, that is, the Parliament of Canada, the issues of concern to everyone in the federation without exception and to relegate exclusive and particular matters to the provinces.

Cartier presents the complementary argument. Forbidding the general legislature power to deliberate on particular issues would strengthen the provincial legislatures, better enabling them to preserve provincial particularities:

> Some parties pretended that it was impossible to carry out federation, on account of the differences of races and religions. Those who took this view of the question were in error. It was just the reverse. It was precisely on account of the variety of races, local interests etc., that the federation system ought to be resorted to and would be found to work well (Cartier, Canadian Legislative Assembly, 8 February 1865; CFD 285).

H.V. Langevin makes the same point: "Under the new system ... our interest in relation to race, religion and nationality will remain as they are at the present time. But they will be better protected" (Langevin, Canadian Legislative Assembly, 21 February, 1865; CFD 235). He then continues, supporting Brown's contention: in the legislature of the general government of the federation, "there will be no questions of race, nationality, religion, or locality, as this legislature will only be charged with the great, general questions which will interest alike the whole federacy and not one locality only" (ibid., 297-8). The better protection for particularity at the *provincial* level depends on the exclusion of particularity from the federal Parliament. Langevin, Cartier, and Brown are as one on this point. It is a pleasure to see them, political enemies of old, working so deftly together to secure approval for the union resolution. Here is another passage from Brown's speech:

> Mr. Speaker, I am ... in favour of this scheme because it will bring to an end the sectional discord between Upper and Lower Canada. It sweeps away the boundary line between the provinces so far as regards matters common to the whole people – it places all on an equal level – and the members of the federal legislature will meet at last as citizens of a common country. The questions that used to excite the most hostile feelings among us have been taken away from the general legislature and placed under the control of the local bodies. No man hereafter need be debarred from success in public life because his views, however popular in his own section, are unpopular in the other – for he will not have to deal with sectional questions; and the temptation to the government of the day to make capital out of local prejudices will be greatly lessened, if not altogether at an end (Brown, Canadian Legislative Assembly, 8 February, 1865; CFD 288-9).

The hope was that because the general legislature dealt with – and dealt only with – matters concerning everyone, it would make of the various colonial populations, one country. And it was because the federation was to be one country in the civic sense that it could allow and protect expression of separate cultural loyalties at the provincial level. I hardly need to say that other speakers raised objections: many wanted to know what Cartier and his colleagues had to say about the "racial" minorities *within* the provinces. How would they fare? And I hardly need to say that the Canadian constitutional division of legislative powers has undergone changes in the years since Confederation, some initiated by constitutional amendment, some brought about by the courts, and some, it appears, the more or less unanticipated result of ongoing political pressures. The elegant scheme defended by Cartier, Langevin, and Brown has been severely battered.

CONCLUSION: PROPOSALS FOR REFORM

The Senate was intended to be an arena of national deliberation on the matters that affect everyone in the country equally, and was expected to use its status as arena of national deliberation to resist attempts by the House of Commons to trespass on the rights of the political opposition and the rights of the provinces. But Canadians no longer understand the Fathers' prescription. The time has come for reform.

There are good reasons today for increasing the numbers in the Senate. There are reasons to consider the election of senators and limits on the term of office. These are measures that are appropriate in the twenty-first century. They are also measures that will not impair the Senate's traditional roles and may indeed enhance them.

We cannot return to the original plan in all its details. But we can do much to avoid measures that would further erode the Senate's powers as an inclusive and equalitarian deliberative body. If we take our cue from the Fathers of Confederation we will not set aside seats in the upper house for particular interests and groups. The role of the Senate is not to drag into national politics matters that would be better left in the private sphere, or better looked after by provincial and local governments. The role of the Senate – let me repeat – is to deliberate on the issues that affect equally every last person in the nation without exception, because such deliberation is our best security that government will not resolve itself into a gang of bullies that protects the politicians of the majority and the government's favourites against the ordinary citizen.

REFERENCES

Ajzenstat, J., P. Romney, I. Gentles and W. D. Gairdner, eds. 2003. *Canada's Founding Debates*. Toronto: University of Toronto Press.

Locke, J. 1690. "Second Treatise of Government," in *Two Treatises of Government*, ed. P. Laslett. Cambridge: Cambridge University Press, 1988.

4

FEDERAL SECOND CHAMBERS COMPARED

Ronald L. Watts

Dans cet article, l'auteur effectue une analyse comparative de secondes chambres au sein de différentes fédérations. Il souligne quatre aspects principaux : (1) la relation entre le bicaméralisme et le fédéralisme; (2) une comparaison entre les différentes méthodes de nomination, la composition, les pouvoirs et les rôles des secondes chambres législatives fédérales; (3) l'influence des partis politiques sur le fonctionnement des secondes chambres fédérales; et (4) la question de savoir si les secondes chambres fédérales facilitent ou limitent les processus démocratiques. Malgré les différences d'une fédération à l'autre, les contrôles effectués par les secondes chambres fédérales ont habituellement eu un effet positif sur la démocratie de « consensus », et les secondes chambres ont contribué à la vitalité et à la reconnaissance du caractère distinct des différents groupes dont elles font partie.

INTRODUCTION

This paper attempts to provide a broad outline of the main comparative features of second chambers in a wide range of federations to provide a context for the discussion of Senate reform in Canada. This paper is in four parts: (1) a brief consideration of the relation of bicameralism to federalism; (2) a comparative outline of the methods of appointment, composition, powers and roles of federal second legislative chambers in a variety of federations; (3) the impact of political parties on the operation of federal second chambers; and (4) whether federal second chambers constrain or enhance democratic processes. An overall theme of the paper is to emphasize the variety of federal second chambers and the importance of examining not only structures but equally, political processes, in understanding the nature of federations.

BICAMERALISM WITHIN FEDERATIONS

Most federations have adopted bicameral federal legislatures. This has led to the notion held by some that bicameral federal legislatures are *by definition* a characteristic feature of a federation (see, for instance, King 1982, 44; Davis 1978, 142; Amellier 1966, 3). Amellier (1966, 3) for instance, argued a priori that "In federal states no choice [between unicameral and bicameral systems] is open because [federations] are *by definition* two-tier structures."

If such statements are meant to argue that only federations instance a bicameral legislature, then this is clearly mistaken. As King (1982, 94) notes, a great many non-federal states have featured legislatures divided into two or more bodies. For instance, the British, French, Dutch and Japanese Parliaments are just a few of the many non-federal states that are bicameral or multicameral (see also Megan Russell 2000).

If the point of Amellier's statement is to argue that all federations have bicameral legislatures, then clearly this too is mistaken. Indeed, of the some 24 current federations generally so identified (see Griffiths 2005), five do not have bicameral legislatures: these are the United Arab Emirates, Venezuela, and the small island federations of Comoros, Micronesia, and St. Kitts and Nevis. Until its recent division, Serbia-Montenegro also had a unicameral federal legislature. Earlier, prior to the secession of Bangladesh, Pakistan also had a unicameral federal legislature in which the two provinces were equally represented. Even where there has been a federal second legislative chamber the principle of equality of representation of the constituent units of a federation in a second federal chamber has not been universally applied. Among the many exceptions are Canada, Germany, Austria, India, Malaysia, Belgium and Spain. It would seem, therefore, that it is inappropriate to regard a bicameral federal legislature as a definitive characteristic of federations.

Nevertheless, it has to be noted that the principle of bicameralism has been incorporated into the federal legislatures of most federations. Most federations have found a bicameral federal legislature to be an important institutional feature for ensuring the entrenched representation of the regional components in policy making within the institutions of "shared rule" that are an important element for the effective operation of a federation.[1]

In establishing bicameral federal institutions, subsequent federations have been influenced by the example of the precedent of the United States. Debate over whether representation in the federal legislature should be in terms of population

---

[1] Following Elazar (1987), the essence of federations has often been described as a combination of "shared rule" and "self-rule." The concept of "shared rule" has been open to some ambiguity, however. As Elazar used the term, the combination referred to institutions and processes by which citizens in different territories related directly to the common institutions for dealing with shared problems, while retaining self-rule on other matters through the governments of the constituent units. Some commentators have interpreted "shared rule" to refer, not to the citizens, but to the constituent governments. The latter, however, would infer a form of confederal governance in which the common institutions relate to the member governments rather than directly to the citizens.

or in terms of the constituent states was intense at the time of the creation of the first modern federation in the United States. The clash between the proponents of these two positions had brought the Philadelphia Convention to a deadlock, and this impasse was finally resolved only by the Connecticut Compromise whereby a bicameral federal legislature was established with representation in one house, the House of Representatives, based on population, and representation in another house, the Senate, based on equal representation of the states with the senators originally elected by their state legislatures. This, it was believed, ensured that differing state viewpoints would not be overridden simply by a majority of the federal population dominated by the larger states.[2]

Since then, most (though not all) federations have found it desirable to adopt bicameral federal legislatures. But while most federations have established bicameral federal legislatures, there has been in fact an enormous variation among them in the method of selection of members, the regional composition, and the powers of the second chambers, and consequently of their roles. The next four sections of this paper will deal with those four aspects, which are also summarized in two tables. Table 1 sets out the varieties of these elements that have existed in various federations, and table 2 summarizes the particular combination of elements in each of the federal second chambers in a representative selection of ten federations and quasi-federations. It should be noted that the Latin American federations have generally followed the pattern of the United States, with senators directly elected, states equally represented but by three senators each (with some additional senators nationally elected in Mexico), and strong veto powers. What stands out in these tables is the enormous degree of variation elsewhere.

SELECTION OF MEMBERS OF FEDERAL SECOND CHAMBERS

There is considerable variety in the ways in which members of federal second chambers are elected or appointed. In three federations, Australia since its inception in 1901, the United States since 1913, and Switzerland (by cantonal choice but eventually in all the cantons), members of the federal second chamber are directly elected by the citizens of the constituent units. A feature unique to Switzerland is the provision enabling cantonal legislators to sit concurrently in a federal legislative house. In practice about one-fifth of the members of each federal house concurrently hold seats in a cantonal legislature thus providing a channel for cantonal views to influence federal policy making. Originally in the US (from 1789 to 1912) members of the federal second chamber were indirectly elected by the state legislatures. This is currently the case in Austria and India for most members of the federal second chamber. In Germany, the members of the Bundesrat are

---

[2] It should be noted that in some federations (e.g. Canada and Spain) the principle of representation by population in the first chamber has been partially modified to take some account of territorial representation.

TABLE 1

Variations in Selection, Composition, Powers and Role of Second Chambers in Selected Federations

Selection	Composition	Powers	Role
1. Appointment by federal government (no formal consultation) (e.g. Canada term until age 75, Malaysia 63% of seats)	1. Equal "regional" representation (e.g. Canada for groups of provinces)	1. Absolute veto with mediation committees (e.g. Argentina, Brazil, Mexico, Switzerland, USA)	1. Legislative chamber only (e.g. Argentina, Australia, Brazil, Canada, India, Malaysia, Mexico, Switzerland, USA)
2. Appointment by federal government based on nominations by provincial governments (e.g. Canada: Meech Lake Accord proposal)	2. Equal state representation (e.g. Argentina, Australia, Brazil, Mexico, 37% of Malaysian senate, Nigeria, Pakistan 88% of seats, Russia, South Africa, USA)	2. Absolute veto on federal legislation affecting any state administrative functions (e.g. Germany, South Africa)	2. Combined legislative and intergovernmental roles (e.g. Germany, South Africa)
3. Appointment ex officio by state government (e.g. Germany, Russia 50% of seats, South Africa 40% of seats)	3. Two categories of cantonal representation (e.g. Switzerland: full cantons and half cantons)	3. Suspensive veto: time limit (e.g. Malaysia, South Africa (except above), Spain)	3. Ultimate interpretation of the constitution (e.g. Ethiopia)
4. Indirect election by state legislatures (e.g. US 1789–1912, Austria, Ethiopia, India, Pakistan, Malaysia 37% of seats, Russia 50% of seats, South Africa 60% of seats)	4. Weighted state voting: four categories (e.g. Germany: 3, 4, 5 or 6 block votes)	4. Suspensive veto: matching lower house vote to override (e.g. Germany for some)	
5. Direct election by simple plurality (e.g. Argentina, Brazil, Mexico 75% of seats, US since 1913)	5. Weighted state representation: multiple categories (e.g. Austria, India)	5. Deadlock resolved by joint sitting (e.g. India)	
6. Direct election by proportional representation (Australia, Nigeria, Mexico 25% of seats)	6. Additional or special representation for others including aboriginal (e.g. Ethiopia, India, Malaysia, Pakistan)	6. Deadlock resolved by double dissolution then joint sitting (e.g. Australia)	
7. Choice of method left to cantons (e.g. Switzerland: in practice direct election by plurality)	7. A minority of regional representatives (e.g. Belgium, Spain)	7. Money bills: brief suspensive veto (e.g. India, Malaysia) or no veto (Pakistan)	
8. Mixed (e.g. Belgium, Ethiopia, Malaysia, Mexico, Russia, South Africa, Spain)			

TABLE 2
Selection, Composition, and Powers of Some Federal Second Chambers

Argentina	Senate: elected by direct vote; one-third of the members elected every two years to a six-year term; absolute veto.
Australia	Senate: direct election (by proportional representation); equal state representation; absolute veto (but followed by double dissolution and joint sitting).
Austria	Bundesrat: elected by state legislatures; weighted representation (range 12:3); suspensive veto (may be overridden by simple majority in lower house, the Nationalrat).
Belgium	Senate: combination of directly elected (40), indirectly elected by linguistic Community Councils (21), and co-opted senators (10); variable representation specified for each unit; equal competence with House of Representatives on some matters but on others House of Representatives has overriding power.
Brazil	Senado Federal (Senate): 3 members from each state and federal district elected by a simple majority to serve eight-year terms; one-third elected after a four-year period, two-thirds elected after the next four-year period; absolute veto.
Canada	Senate: appointed by federal government; equal regional representation for 4 regional groups of provinces (Ontario; Quebec; 4 Western provinces; 3 Maritime provinces) plus 6 for Newfoundland and one each for the 3 territories; absolute veto (legally) but in practice weakened legitimacy.
Ethiopia	House of Federation (Yefedereshn Mekir Bet): 71 members (63%) appointed by regional bodies and 41 (27%) appointed based on population and ethnicity. This body serves as the supreme constitutional arbiter. Members serve five-year terms. For members selected by states, directly or indirectly elected according to decision of state councils.
Germany	Bundesrat: state government ex officio delegations; weighted voting (3, 4, 5 or 6 block votes per state); suspensive veto on federal legislation overridden by corresponding lower-house majority, but absolute veto on any federal legislation affecting state administrative functions (60% of federal legislation reduced to about 40% by reforms in 2006); mediation.
India	Rajya Sabha (Council of States): elected by state legislatures (plus 12 additional representatives appointed by the President for special representation); weighted representation of states (range 31:1); veto resolved by joint sitting.
Malaysia	Dewan Negara (Senate): 26 (37%) elected by state legislatures plus 44 (63%) additional appointed representatives for minorities; equal state representation (for 37% of total seats); suspensive veto (six months).
Mexico	Camara de Senadores (Senate): 128 seats in total; 96 (3 per state) are elected by popular vote to serve six-year terms and cannot be re-elected; 32 are allocated on the basis of each party's popular vote; absolute veto.
Nigeria	Senate: each state has three seats while one senator represents the Federal Capital Territory. A total of 109 senators are directly elected for a four-year term; absolute veto (except taxation and appropriation bills resolved by joint sitting) with joint committees to resolve deadlocks.

... continued

TABLE 2
(Continued)

Pakistan	Senate: 100 seats indirectly elected by provincial assemblies to serve 4-year terms. Of the 22 seats allocated to each province, 14 are general members, 4 are women and 4 are technocrats. Federally Administered Tribal Areas (FATAs) and the Capital Territory fill seats through direct election, with 8 seats given to the FATAs and 4 for the Capital Territory; no veto on money bills, budget, borrowing or audit of federal accounts
Russia	Federation Council (Soviet Federatsii): Asymmetry of length of term and method of selection depending on the republic or region. Each unit has 2 representatives in the Federation Council, one elected by of the constituent unit legislature, the other appointed by the governor; dispute resolution by joint committee which may be overridden by two-thirds majority in lower house.
South Africa	National Council of Provinces (NCOP): 90 seats, consisting of 54 representing provincial legislatures and 36 representing provincial executives; equal provincial representation (6 legislators plus 4 executives per province); veto varied with type of legislation.
Spain	Senate: 208 directly elected members and 51 appointed by parliaments of 17 Autonomous Communities; categories of 4, 3 or one directly elected senator(s) per provinces (sub-units of Autonomous Communities) supplemented by representation of one or more (related to population) appointed by each autonomous parliament; suspensive veto (2 months).
Switzerland	Council of States: in practice direct election (direct election by plurality; method chosen individually by all cantons); 2 representatives for full cantons and 1 for half cantons; absolute veto (mediation committees).
United States	Senate: direct election since 1913 (by simple plurality); equal state representation (six-year terms with one-third elected every two years); absolute veto (mediation committees).

delegates of their Land cabinets, holding office in the federal second chamber ex officio as members of their Land executive and voting in the Bundesrat for each Land in a block on the instructions of their Land government. In Canada, senators are appointed by the federal prime minister and currently hold office until their retirement at 75. Although appointed to represent regional groups of provinces, they have as a result of the method of appointment tended to display little accountability to regional interests, and to vote instead generally on party lines. The federal second chambers in Malaysia, Belgium and Spain have a mixed membership. In Malaysia, only 38 percent of the senate seats are filled by indirect election by the state legislatures, the remaining 62 percent being central appointees. The Spanish senate has 204 directly elected members and 55 regional representatives. In Belgium, 40 senators are directly elected, 21 indirectly elected by the Flemish, French and German Community Councils and 10 are co-opted (appointed by the directly elected senators).

In those federations where the members of the federal second chamber are directly elected, generally they are representative of the interests of the regional electorates. Where they are indirectly elected by state legislatures they are also generally representative of regional interests although regional political party interests also play a significant role. Where, as in the German case, they are ex officio instructed delegates of the constituent governments, they represent primarily the views of the dominant parties in those governments and only indirectly those of the electorate. Where senators are appointed by the federal government, as in Canada and to a large extent in Malaysia, they have the least credibility as spokespersons for regional interests, even when they are residents of the regions they represent. Federal appointment does, however, provide a means for ensuring representation of some particular minorities and interests who might otherwise go unrepresented. It was for that reason that the Indian constitution specifically provided for 12 such appointed members out of an overall total of 250 members in the Rajya Sabha and the Malaysian constitution currently provides for 43 out of 69 senators to be appointed by the federal government. The mixed basis of selection of senators in Spain and Belgium represents political compromises intended to obtain the benefits of the different forms of selection for members of the federal second chamber.

BASIS OF REGIONAL REPRESENTATION IN COMPOSITION OF FEDERAL SECOND CHAMBERS

It is often assumed that equality of state representation in the federal second chamber is the norm in federations. In only nine of the federal second chambers in the federations specifically referred to in tables 1 and 2 are the states strictly equally represented, however. These are the United States, Australian, Argentinean, Brazilian, Mexican, Nigerian, Pakistani, Russian and South African senates. In most other federations where there is not equality of constituent unit representation, there is, however, some effort to weight representation in favour of smaller regional units or significant minorities. On the other hand, account has also been taken of the unequal consequences of equal state representation (for an analysis of the consequences of equal state representation in the US Senate see Lee and Oppenheimer (1998)). Switzerland basically has equal cantonal representation in the Council of States although "half cantons" are distinguished: these have only one member instead of two. In the Malaysian senate the seats filled by indirectly elected senators are equally distributed among the states, but the substantial proportion that are filled by centrally appointed senators have not followed a consistent pattern of balanced state representation, thus the net effect has been one of considerable variation in state representation. In most other federations the population of the units is a factor in their representation in the federal second chamber, although generally this has been moderated by some weighting to favour the smaller units. There have been various degrees of weighting. In Germany, the constitution (article 51) establishes four population categories of Länder having three, four, five or six block votes in the Bundestrat. In India, Austria and Spain the range of state representation is wider: for example, 31:1 in India and 12:3 in Austria. In Belgium the differential representation of each Community and Region in the senate is specified in the constitution, but for some especially significant issues the constitution (art. 43) requires majorities within both the French-speaking and Dutch-speaking members in the Senate (as well as within the House of Representatives). Canada, as is the case with so much about its Senate, is unique among federations in basing senate representation on regional groups of provinces with the four basic regions having 24 seats each, plus an additional 6 for the province of Newfoundland and Labrador and one each for the three Territories.

POWERS OF SECOND CHAMBERS RELATIVE TO
THE FIRST CHAMBERS

Where there is a separation of powers between the executive and the legislature, as in the U.S.A., Switzerland, and the Latin American federations, normally the two federal legislative houses have had equal powers (although in the USA the Senate has some additional powers relating to ratification of appointments and treaties). Where there are parliamentary executives, the house that controls the executive (invariably the chamber based on population) inevitably has more power. In these federations the powers of the second chamber in relation to money bills are usually limited. Furthermore, in the case of conflicts between the two houses provisions for a suspensive veto, for joint sittings where the members of the second chamber are less numerous, or for double dissolution have usually rendered the second chamber weaker (see table 1, column three, for examples). This has sometimes raised questions within parliamentary federations about whether their second chambers provide sufficient regional influence in central decision making. This concern is reinforced by the usually greater strength of party discipline within parliamentary federations. Nonetheless, some of the federal second chambers in parliamentary federations, such as the Australian senate and the German Bundestrat, have been able to exert considerable influence. The particular membership of the German Bundestrat and the fact that its constitutional absolute veto over all federal legislation involving administration by the Länder has in practice applied to more than 60 percent of all federal legislation, have been major factors in its influence. Concerns about the resulting deadlocks have led to currently proposed reforms intended to limit this.

RELATIVE ROLES OF FEDERAL SECOND CHAMBERS

The primary role of most of the federal second chambers in the federations reviewed in this study has been legislative: reviewing federal legislation with a view to bringing to bear upon it regional and minority interests and concerns. By contrast with the others, the German Bundestrat performs an additional and equally important role of serving as an institution to facilitate intergovernmental cooperation and collaboration. It is able to do this because, unlike the other federal second chambers, as already noted, it is composed of instructed delegates of the Land governments and because its suspensive veto power over all federal legislation and absolute veto over federal legislation affecting state legislative and administrative responsibilities has given it strong political leverage. This model heavily influenced the South Africans in the design of their national second chamber in the new constitution adopted in May 1996, although some significant modifications were made to include representation of both executives and legislators from the provinces in the National Council of Provinces (NCOP). From time to time during the past two decades the reform of the Canadian Senate has been suggested, but while most Canadians agree that the Senate should be reformed, disagreement about the model that would be appropriate has left it unreformed. Nevertheless, in the Speech from the Throne, 16 October 2007, the Harper government announced that it "will continue its agenda of democratic reform by reintroducing important pieces of legislation from the last session, including direct consultations with voters on the selection of Senators and limitations on their tenure."

How are we to account for this enormous variety among federal second legislative chambers? One factor has been the different circumstances at the time each federation was created. In some notable cases such as Germany and Canada, historical precedents were significant. In Germany in 1949 a Senate was considered, but in the end the Bundesrat created in 1949 owed much to the earlier model of the Bismarkian Empire. In Canada, the Senate was a major issue in the deliberations at the Quebec Conference, 1864, taking up more time than any other issue. The adoption of an appointed Senate was a conscious rejection of an elected second chamber which had existed previously under the *Act of Union, 1840* and which had caused so many difficulties in combination with cabinets responsible to the lower chamber. It should also be noted that the operation of federal second chambers has frequently proved significantly different from the expectations of the founders, often due to the operation of political parties (see below). This has often led to subsequent pressures for reform of federal second chambers and of their role, but once institutionalized, efforts to reform them in practice have proved extremely difficult. The repeated failure of efforts at Senate reform in Canada illustrate this. More recently, efforts to modify the blocking role of the German Bundesrat have achieved some success, but only after protracted negotiations.

While the European Union is a hybrid of federal and confederal institutions, it is worth noting that it too has bicameral legislative institutions. Both the Parliament, representing the citizens, and the Council, representing constituent governments, have co-decision powers. The Council has an intergovernmental character and there is weighted voting on many matters. In this sense the Council has corresponded to the second chambers in federations, although playing a stronger role than many of them.

THE IMPACT OF POLITICAL PARTIES

An important factor affecting the operation of any federal second chamber is the character and role of the political parties. As Friedrich (1966) has noted, an examination not only of structures but of political processes is fundamental to understanding the very nature of federations. The interaction of political parties with federal structures is, therefore, particularly important. Political parties tend to be influenced by both institutional characteristics, particularly the executive-legislative relationship and the electoral system, and by the nature and characteristics of the diversity in the underlying society. There are four aspects of political parties that may particularly affect their operation within a federation: 1) the organizational relationship between the party organizations at the federal level and provincial or state party organizations, 2) the degree of symmetry or asymmetry between federal and provincial or state party alignments, 3) the impact of party discipline upon the representation of interests within each level, and 4) the prevailing pattern for progression of political careers.

In terms of party organization, the federal parties in the United States and especially Switzerland have tended to be loose confederations of state or cantonal and local party organizations. This decentralized pattern of party organization has contributed to the maintenance of non-centralized government and the prominence in their federal legislatures, and particularly their second chambers, of regional and local interests. Nevertheless, in recent years the voting pattern in the US Senate has tended to be more dominated by party interests than state interests. In the parliamentary federations, the pressures for effective party discipline within each government, in order to sustain the executive in office, have tended to separate federal and provincial or state branches of parties into more autonomous layers of party organization. This tendency appears to have been strongest in Canada. The ties between federal and regional branches of each party have remained somewhat more significant, however, in such parliamentary federations as Germany, Australia and India. In the case of Belgium, the federal parties have in fact become totally regional in character, with each party based in a region or distinct linguistic group.

In virtually all of these federations there is a degree of asymmetry in the alignment of parties at the federal level and the alignments of parties within different regional units. Within different regions, the prevailing alignment of parties in regional politics has often varied significantly from region to region and from federal politics. These variations in the character of party competition and predominance in different regional units have usually been the product of different regional economic, political and cultural interests, and these regional variations in prevailing parties have contributed further to the sense of regional identification and distinctiveness within these federations.

The presence or absence of strong party discipline in different federations has also had an impact upon the visible expression of regional and minority interests within the federal legislatures and particularly their second chambers. Where parliamentary institutions have operated, the pressure has been to accommodate regional and minority interests as far as possible behind closed doors within party caucuses so that the visible facade is one of cabinet and party solidarity. This contrasts with the shifting alliances and visibly varying positions much more frequently taken by legislators in federal legislatures where the principle of the separation of powers has been incorporated. Regional and minority concerns are more openly expressed and deliberated in the latter cases, although that has not necessarily meant that they are translated any more effectively into adopted policies.

Here, it is clear that there has been considerable variation among federations in the impact of political parties on the operation of their federal second chambers. Whether due to the pressures for party discipline within parliamentary federations, or the emphasis upon party representation in proportional representation electoral systems, or the combined effect of both, party considerations have tended to override regional differences (although not totally) within federal second chambers. This has especially been the case where party representation has differed between the two houses. A particularly notable example of clashing party representation between the two federal legislative chambers in recent years has been the operation of the German Bundesrat. Indeed, this tendency there has led to pressures for reform. Even in federations where the separation of powers exists between executive and legislature resulting in less pressure for strict party discipline, there has been an increasing tendency for polarization along ideological rather than regional lines, as has become apparent within the US Senate. Generally, the net effect of the impact of the operation of political parties has been to moderate (although not eradicate) the role of federal second chambers as a strong voice for regional interests in federal policy making.

An area that illustrates the contrasting representational patterns in different federations is the differences in the normal pattern of political careers. In some federations, most notably the United States and Switzerland, the normal pattern of political careers is progression from local to state or cantonal and then to federal office. Presidential candidates in the US, for instance, have usually been selected from among governors or senators rooted in their state politics. By contrast, in Canada, few major federal political leaders have been drawn from the ranks of provincial premiers, and it is the norm for Canada's most ambitious politicians to fulfill their entire careers solely at one level or the other, either in federal or in provincial politics. The political career patterns in most of the other parliamentary federations fall between these extremes, examples of the links between provincial experience and filling positions of federal office being more frequent in such federations as Germany, Australia and India than in Canada.

DO FEDERAL SECOND CHAMBERS CONSTRAIN DEMOCRACY?

In addressing this question, it should be noted at the outset that much will depend on our definition of democracy, a concept whose definition has over the years been much debated. Modern democracy may be about rule of, by and for the people, but as Scott Greer (2006, 262-6) has noted, different interpretations have given primary emphasis to "participation," "accountability," or "group self-government."

Critics of federalism who emphasize the majoritarian essence of democracy as "rule by the *demos*" have noted particularly that most federations have established bicameral federal legislatures weighted in differing degrees to favour the smaller constituent units, thus violating a cardinal principle of democracy based on one-person-one-vote. Consequently, they characterize such federal second chambers as "demos-constraining" (Riker 1964, 1982 and Stepan 2004a, b, c). For instance, to take just one example, in the United States Senate, a single vote in Wyoming counts 65 times more than its equivalent in California. Such contrasts are replicated in many other federal second chambers.

But an important point that Stepan (2004, a, b, c) and Tsebelis (1995, 2002) note is that among federations there are variations in the position and strength of the federal second chamber as "veto player" and as "demos-constraining" or "demos-enhancing" in character. One might quarrel with the factual basis on which Stepan characterizes the impact of particular federal second chambers, but fundamentally he is correct in noting the enormous variation in the role and powers of federal second chambers in different federations. Earlier in this paper it has already been noted that there has been considerable variation in the weight given to territorial representation and to the methods of selection, composition, powers and consequent roles of federal second chambers. For instance, although virtually all federations give some weighting to favour smaller constituent units, they range from equal representation in the US, Australia and the Latin American federations and the virtually equal representation in Switzerland, to the strongly weighted (Germany) and lightly weighted (Austria and India) representation in the territorial chamber for smaller constituent units. In some cases such as Belgium and Spain, regional representatives are in fact only a minority of the members of the second chamber. In Canada, the composition of the Senate was originally based on equal representation, not of provinces, but for regional groups of provinces with varying numbers of provinces in these regional groups. As we noted previously, there have been variations too in the methods of appointment: by direct election, by indirect election by state legislatures, by state executives, by appointment by the federal government, or by a mixture of these. Furthermore, there is considerable variation in the relative powers of these federal second chambers as "veto players," and hence in the degree to which they are "demos-constraining." Second chambers in parliamentary federations, where the federal cabinet is responsible to the popularly elected house, have normally been weaker (although in Germany and Australia these have had some special or significant veto powers), while those in non-parliamentary federations, such as the United States, Switzerland and the Latin American federations have had at least equal powers and hence have been in a stronger position as "veto players." It is these variations that led Stepan to place federations on a continuum in terms of their "demos-constraining" or "demos-enhancing" character, based on the varied role of their federal second chambers as "veto players."

While discussing the degree to which federations are "demos-constraining" or "demos-enhancing," some further points should, however, be noted. It can be argued that while federal institutions may place some limits upon majoritarian democracy, democracy more broadly understood as liberal democracy may actually be expanded by federalism. Democracy and governmental responsiveness are enhanced by federalism because multiple levels of government maximize the opportunity for citizens' preferences to be achieved (Pennock 1959), establish alternative arenas for citizen participation, and provide for governments that are smaller and closer to the people. In this sense federalism is "demos-enabling" and hence might be described as "democracy-plus."

From a liberal-democratic point of view, by emphasizing the value of checks and balances and dispersing authority to limit the potential tyranny of the majority, federal second chambers contribute to the protection of individuals and minorities against abuses (*Federalist Papers*, No. 9). Furthermore, as Lipjhart (1999) has noted, the checks on democratically elected majorities imposed by federal second chambers have often pushed these federations in the direction of "consensus" democracy, contributing to the accommodation of different groups in multinational federations. Indeed, as Burgess (2006, 206) comments, the acceptance in most federations of the need for federal second chambers points to the vitality and recognition in these federations of the distinct *demoi* in their various constituent units.

Switzerland, with its extensive application of the processes of direct democracy in relation to legislation both at the cantonal and the federal levels, represents a special case. These processes give the citizens in relation to both levels of government the opportunity to accept or reject constraints, and the operation of direct democracy has had an important impact upon the operation of political parties in both federal legislative houses.

CONCLUDING SUMMARY

While bicameral federal legislatures are not a definitive characteristic of federations, most federations have found it desirable to establish bicameral federal legislatures to provide an entrenched institution for the representation of distinct territorial *demoi* in federal policy-making. A review of second federal legislative chambers makes it clear, however, that there is an enormous variety among federations in the methods of appointment, composition, powers and hence roles of these bodies in different federations, particularly differentiating those in parliamentary and non-parliamentary federations. Furthermore, political party systems have also often affected the operation of federal second chambers, frequently limiting their role as "regional chambers." As a result of these variations, federal second chambers fall along a broad continuum in terms of their role as "veto players" and "demos-constraining" in relation to democratic processes as defined in terms of rule by simple majority. But from a liberal-democratic point of view, the checks and balances provided in processes of federal policy making through the operation of federal second chambers have often enhanced "consensus" democracy and contributed to the vitality and recognition of the distinct *demoi* in their various constituent units.

REFERENCES

Amellier, M., ed. 1966. *Parliaments*. London: Inter-Parliamentary Union by Cassell.

Burgess, M. 2006. *Comparative Federalism: Theory and Practice*. Abingdon: Routledge.

Davis, S.R. 1978. *The Federal Principle: A Journey through Time in Quest of a Meaning*. Berkeley: University of California Press.

Elazar, D.J. 1987. *Exploring Federalism*. Tuscaloosa, AL: University of Alabama Press.

Friedrich, C.J. 1968. *Trends of Federalism in Theory and Practice*. New York: Praeger.

Greer, S.L., ed. 2006. *Territory, Democracy and Justice: Regionalism and Federalism in Western Democracies*. Houndsmills, Basingstoke, Hampshire: Palgrave Macmillan.

Griffiths, A.L., ed. 2005. *Handbook of Federal Countries, 2005*. Montreal and Kingston: McGill-Queen's University Press for the Forum of Federations.

King, P. 1982. *Federalism and Federation*. London and Canberra: Croom Helm.

— 1993. "Federation and Representation," in *Comparative Federalism and Federation: Competing Traditions and Future Directions*, eds. M. Burgess and A.-G. Gagnon. Hemel Hempstead: Harvester Wheatsheaf.

Lee, F.E. and Oppenheimer, B.I. 1998. *Sizing up the Senate: The Unequal Consequences of Equal Representation*. Chicago: University of Chicago Press.

Lijphart, A. 1999. *Patterns of Democracy: Government Forms and Performance in Thirty-Six Countries*. New Haven: Yale University Press.

Madison, J., A. Hamilton, and J. Jay. 1987. *The Federalist Papers, 1787-8*. New York: Penguin Books.

Pennock, J.R. 1959. "Federalism and Unitary Government – Disharmony and Reliability," *Behavioural Science* 4(2): 147-157.

Riker, W.H. 1964. *Federalism: Origin, Operation and Significance*. Boston: Little Brown.

— 1982. *Liberalism against Populism: A Confrontation between the Theory of Democracy and the Theory of Social Choice*. Prospect Heights: Waveland Press.

Russell, M. 2000. *Reforming the House of Lords: Lessons from Overseas*. Oxford: Oxford University Press.

Stepan, A. 1999. "Federalism and Democracy: Beyond the US Model," *Journal of Democracy* 10(4): 19-34.

— 2004a. "Toward a New Comparative Politics of Federalism, Multinationalism, and Democracy," in *Federalism and Democracy in Latin America*, ed. E.L. Gibson. Baltimore: Johns Hopkins Press.

— 2004b. "Electorally Generated Veto Players in Unitary and Federal Systems," in *Federalism and Democracy in Latin America*, ed. E.L. Gibson. Baltimore: Johns Hopkins Press.

— 2004c. "Federalism and Democracy," in *Federalism and Territorial Cleavages*, eds. U.N. Amoretti and N. Bermeo. Baltimore: Johns Hopkins Press.

Tsebelis, G. 1995. "Decision-Making in Political Systems: Veto-Players in Presidentialism, Parliamentarism, Multicameralism and Multipartyism," *British Journal of Political Science* 25: 289-325.

— 2002. *Veto Players: How Political Institutions Work*. Princeton: Princeton University Press.

Watts, R.L. 1999. *Comparing Federal Systems*, 2nd ed. Montreal and Kingston: McGill-Queen's University Press.

— 2003. "Bicameralism in Federal Parliamentary Systems," in *Protecting Canadian Democracy*, ed. S. Joyal. Montreal and Kingston: McGill-Queen's University Press.

5

HARPER'S SENATE REFORM:
AN EXAMPLE OF OPEN FEDERALISM?

Nadia Verrelli

Cet article compare les efforts fournis par le Premier ministre Harper en ce qui a trait à la réforme du Sénat aux efforts fournis par le Premier ministre Trudeau en 1978. Selon cet article, bien qu'Harper essaie de se distinguer des premiers ministres qui l'ont précédé en prônant l'idée d'un fédéralisme ouvert, ses méthodes, ainsi que celles de Trudeau sont toutefois des exemples de fédéralisme « fermé ». Les deux n'accordent aux provinces aucun rôle à jouer dans la réforme du Sénat. Cet article suggère qu'en plus de prendre en considération l'élément constitutionnel de la proposition d'Harper, il faut également tenir compte de l'aspect fédéraliste, en particulier du rôle des provinces au sein de la fédération.

Upon entering office in 2006, Prime Minster Stephen Harper quickly professed that his new government would engage in a policy of "open federalism" in an attempt to address the apparent democratic deficit in Canadian federal governance. Briefly, open federalism is the idea that the federal government should strive for open negotiations and equal relations with the provinces on key intergovernmental issues. Accordingly, Prime Minister Harper offered Senate reform as a crucial way to achieve this end. The government proposed two changes to the Canadian Senate, asserting that both could be enacted through the federal legislative process: Bill C-19, which seeks to limit the term of senators to eight years; and Bill C-20, under which senators would be appointed after having been elected by the people of each region. The government argued that these reforms would enable the provinces and the electorate to play an ongoing role in the selection process of the senators, thereby rendering the Senate independent, efficient, effective and, most importantly, fully democratic. But is the process through which the government intends to enact these changes really an example of "open federalism"?

Though Prime Minister Harper speaks of practising open and transparent federal governance – thereby attempting to distinguish himself from his predecessors, most notably Jean Chrétien and Pierre Trudeau – his government's proposed amendments to the Canadian Senate are arguably indicative of a more "closed" view of federal relations in that the provinces are being actively shut out of the process of institutional reform. In fact, despite Harper's intention to achieve a greater openness in the federation by encouraging the active involvement of the provinces, his preferred method of pursuing reform is symptomatic of an arrogant, if not rogue, government that believes it can circumvent and disregard its constitutional obligations in order to realize its desired agenda. So, while the passage of Bill C-19 and Bill C-20 might result in a Senate that is indeed more democratic, independent, efficient and effective, the means through which Harper wishes to achieve this end is far from "open."

In fact, and perhaps ironically, Bills C-19 and C-20 closely resemble Trudeau's own Senate reform proposal of 1978. As with the Trudeau proposal, Harper's plan has the ultimate aim of rendering the Senate more legitimate by opening the door for the provinces and the electorate to play a significant role in deciding its future makeup. In attempting this, both governments – the Liberals under Trudeau and the current Conservative government under Harper – have ignored past practices, constitutional obligations and a consultative role for the provinces in redefining the selection process and the tenure of senators.

Given the incredibly contentious nature of Senate reform and the repeated failure of past governments to achieve it, an analysis of Harper's novel methods of reform is required. Accordingly, this paper deals with the specific legislative procedures through which the Harper government is advancing its proposals and highlights how closely they parallel Trudeau's own failed attempt to change the structure of the Canadian Senate in 1978. The paper does not address the merits of the issue itself, or deal with the broader question of whether or not the Senate, as it currently exists, is even in need of reform. Nor does it discuss whether the current proposals will achieve the ends that Harper claims they would.

The paper begins by briefly reviewing the historical sentiments that have fuelled the desire for Senate reform in order to contextualize the Harper scheme. It then proceeds to connect the idea of reform to Harper's notion of open federalism, which allegedly sets his government apart from its predecessors. In this way, the paper argues that, although Harper attempts to separate himself from previous prime ministers by championing the idea of open federalism, both his and Trudeau's methods are actually examples of a "closed" federalism, both excluding the provinces from having any role in helping to reform the Senate. Furthermore, the necessity of such a role has been consistently recognized by past governments and by the Supreme Court of Canada in *Reference: re Authority of Parliament in Relation to the Upper House*, (Supreme Court, 1980, 54) (in this reference, the Trudeau government referred the constitutionality of its own proposal to the Supreme Court).

WHY SENATE REFORM

The fundamental composition and function of the Senate in the Canadian federation has long been a source of contention amongst western and, to a lesser degree, eastern politicians. First arising during the debates concerning western settlement, then in the constitutional debates from the 1970s through the 1990s, the issue persists today. In fact, as Roger Gibbins and Loleen Berdhal argue, "support for Senate reform, is a staple of western Canadian political discourse" (2003, 53). The core issue in this protracted debate has been the need to secure equal and effective regional representation in Canada's federal centre, with proponents of Senate reform viewing the need to transform the institution into one that offers regional perspectives on federal policies.

But how much credence should we give to those who argue that the Canadian Senate, as an institution originally intended to represent regional interests and identities, is a failure? According to proponents of reform, the way in which the system operates now – with twenty-four senators per region, plus six assigned to Newfoundland and Labrador and one for each of the Northwest Territories, Yukon and Nunavut, appointed by the prime minister to serve until the age of seventy-five – does not reflect the political reality of contemporary Canadian federal relations. This, coupled with the fact that senators almost always accept the policies produced by the federal government of the day, calls into question the Senate's independence from the House of Commons and, in turn, its function and role of exercising sober second thought. As a result, many question the democratic legitimacy and effectiveness of the Senate. Gibbins and Berdhal (2003, 54-55), amongst others, argue that

> ... the Senate makes a mockery of federal principles. Senators are neither elected by citizens nor appointed by provincial governments; they are appointed at the sole discretion of the prime minister and retain their seats until reaching 75 years of age. The number of Senate seats per province is based on the math of Confederation, which bears little resemblance to today's demographic or federal realities [...] From the perspective of federalism or regional representation, the Senate can most charitably be described as wasted institutional space.

Since the late 1980s, the desire for reform has crystallized into a platform that calls for a Triple-E Senate: elected, effective and efficient. This model of the Senate made its way onto the mainstream Canadian federal agenda mainly upon the insistence of political leaders from the West. Indeed, in this time, two constitutional packages aimed at amending the Constitution, the 1987 Meech Lake Accord[1] and the 1992 Charlottetown Accord,[2] included provisions for Senate

---

[1] Had Meech Lake been ratified by all ten provinces and the federal government, vacancies in the Senate would have been filled not on the initiative of the federal government alone; rather, "Ottawa would [have had to] choose from a list of names submitted by the government of the provinces in question." This, of course, was to be a temporary solution until a new formula vis-à-vis Senate reform was agreed upon by the political leaders. A similar formula was also proposed for the reform of the Supreme Court of Canada. (McRoberts 1997, 94)

[2] A Triple-E Senate was in fact proposed in the 1992 Accord in which, had it been ratified, the Senate would have been comprised of an equal number of elected senators

reform aimed at appeasing the growing unrest of political players in the West. Both these attempts to amend the Constitution, however, eventually collapsed.[3] Irrespective of these failures or maybe in spite of them, regional discontent embodied in the demands for institutional reform in general and Senate reform in particular, persists, and alleviating it remains a high priority on the political agenda of the Harper government. In light of this, it is not surprising that the federal government is pursuing Senate reform.

In his attempt to deal with the issue of federal accountability, Harper speaks of engaging in a kind of open federalism that "refers to divided sovereignty between regional and general governments" (Young 2006, 7). Robert Young has listed six core elements contained of this principle:

1. Rectitude and order in the process of federal-provincial relations
2. Strong provinces
3. "Strict constructionism"
4. Quebec is special
5. Fix the fiscal imbalance
6. Municipalities are provincial (ibid., 8-9)

For the purposes of this paper, the first element is most pertinent. Open federalism "is about collaboration – with every level of government – and about being clear about who does what and who is responsible for it" (Harper 2006a). In its essence then, as Peter Leslie states, "open federalism is about procedure or practice in the conduct of intergovernmental relations: a commitment to collaborative federalism." (Leslie 2006, 39) Given this, the "closed federalism" supposedly practised in the past could be described as a type of federal relations dominated by Ottawa – in effect discouraging collaboration with the provinces in restructuring key features of the Canadian federation.[4] According to Harper, his "open federalism" should be viewed as a clear break from the past. Indeed, in his own words, open federalism is "the very opposite of the centralist philosophy espoused

---

from each province, two from each territory and representatives from the aboriginal community (the number to be determined at a later date). The new Senate would have been effective as its powers to delay or veto a bill would have increased. (McRoberts 210) (For more detail on this proposed Triple-E Senate, see McRoberts, *Misconceiving Canada*, Russell, *A Constitutional Odyssey*).

[3] For the causes and reasons for the failure of these two Accords see McRoberts, *Misconceiving Canada*, Russell, *A Constitutional Odyssey*.

[4] It should be noted that Harper's contention that past governments practiced closed federalism is debatable. Indeed, Lester B. Pearson as prime minister was accommodating to the demands of Quebec, and, to a lesser extent, the other provinces. Brian Mulroney and other prime ministers, though notorious for practicing executive federalism, did engage in open negotiations with the provinces. Arguably though, John A. Macdonald and Wilfrid Laurier did engage in what can be referred to as closed federalism in their attempts to undermine the provinces.

by successive federal Liberal regimes, from Mr. Trudeau right up to his current successor, Mr. Dion" (Harper 2007). However, considering Harper's preferred approach to Senate reform, we are quickly reminded of a Trudeau-style of governance that dismissed the provinces as equal players in the Canadian federation when he attempted to reform the Senate.

TRUDEAU AND HARPER COMPARED

On 20 June 1978, the federal government under Trudeau tabled *A Time for Action*, which included a proposal to abolish the current Senate. Under this proposal, the existing Senate would be replaced by a new House of the Federation made up of 118 senators – half of whom were to be chosen by the federal government following a federal general election and the other half by the provincial governments following their respective provincial elections. Furthermore, the proposal was to be enacted under Parliament's unilateral constitutional amending authority.

The similarities between the Trudeau and the Harper proposals are evident. Both attempt to restructure the Senate so as to correct its commonly held inadequacy in representing regional interests and identities. According to the Trudeau government, the Canadian federation needed a "second chamber that will function as a politically effective regional forum" (Lalonde 1978, 3). In a similar vein, the Harper government has argued that "Canada needs an upper house that provides sober second thought [... and] gives voice to our diverse regions with democratic legitimacy" (Harper 2006b).

The procedures by means of which both governments intended to push through their proposals also closely resemble one another: Trudeau favouring a unilateral amendment to the Constitution itself, and Harper attempting to push through his amendments via the federal legislative process. According to the Trudeau government in the arguments it submitted to the Supreme Court of Canada in *Reference re: Authority of Parliament in Relation to the Upper House*, s. 91(1) of the *British North America Act, 1867* (now s. 44 of the *Constitution Act, 1982*) authorizes it to make changes unilaterally to the Senate. Section 91(1), enacted in 1949, gave the federal government the power to amend unilaterally the Constitution of Canada where the amendments did not affect federal-provincial relations (amongst other exceptions including the provision that there be one session of Parliament at least once a year). Here, Trudeau held that since the Senate is included in the phrase "the Constitution of Canada" found in s. 91(1), and since s. 91(1) clearly stipulates that the federal power under this section is absolute except for the specified limitations (a list that does not include the Senate), the federal government could affirm that Parliament did have the exclusive jurisdiction under s. 91(1) to modify the Senate. According to the Harper government, because neither Bill C-19 nor Bill C-20 affects the constitutional provisions vis-à-vis the Senate, a constitutional amendment is not required. Rather, the reforms are held to be within the normal legislative powers of the federal Parliament and necessitate no resort to the amending formulas that require the consent of the provinces. Ordinary legislation is sufficient.

It may seem that Trudeau was much bolder in his attempt to reform the Senate by asserting an ability to do so under s. 91(1) of the *British North America Act, 1867*. Yet Harper, by preferring to pursue reform through legislation passed by Parliament, would achieve a very similar end result: the exclusion of the provinces from the reform process and a repudiation of the long-established principles of constitutionalism and federalism in Canada. Indeed, the approaches of both the Trudeau and Harper governments ignore a role for the provinces in the federation by denying them a voice in determining how the federalism principle of *regional representation at the centre* should continue to be realized.

In *Reference re: Authority of Parliament in Relation to the Upper House (1S.C.R. 56 at p. 71)*, the Supreme Court of Canada adopted Lord Sankey's understanding of Canadian federalism and the original federal bargain:

> Inasmuch as the Act embodies a compromise under which the original Provinces agreed to federation, it is important to keep in mind that the Preservation of the rights of minorities was a condition on which such minorities entered into the federation, and the foundation upon which the whole structure was subsequently erected.

The Court understood the federal bargain and Canadian federalism as a consensus among the constituent units in which the Senate, securing and ensuring regional representation at the centre, is a key feature. In fact, in the original negotiations that took place prior to Confederation, the less populated provinces had insisted upon securing regional representation at the centre before agreeing to join the new country. As such, the Court's ruling recognized the fundamental role played by the provinces in the original makeup of the Senate and the process of selecting senators. Furthermore, it acknowledged that there was a role to be played by the provinces if the provisions of the original contract, including the Senate, were to be changed. In this reference, then, the Supreme Court found that the provinces ought to be consulted and their consent obtained if fundamental changes are to be made to the Senate. Moreover, it concluded that the federal government was not authorized to change unilaterally the selection process of senators.

Emerging from the Supreme Court's opinion in *Reference re: Authority of Parliament in Relation to the Upper House* is the idea that the Senate continues to play an important role in the federation because it secures regional representation at the centre. As such, any changes to the makeup of the Senate cannot be effected unilaterally by the federal government; doing so would negate the idea of a distinctly "regional voice" being expressed independently of the central government. In order to change the Senate, then, the federal government must acknowledge that the provinces need to be consulted and their consent obtained. Though Harper's proposal does not directly change the selection process – as senators will continue to be appointed by the Governor General on advice from the Prime Minister – it does so covertly by introducing elections into the selection process. In effect then, Bills C-19 and C-20 do affect the constitutional provisions relating to the Senate: Bill C-19 by limiting the tenure of senators to eight years, and Bill C-20 by ultimately transforming the Senate from an appointed upper house into an essentially elected one.

Four of the ten provinces – Ontario, Quebec, New Brunswick, and Newfoundland and Labrador – have already openly voiced objections to the manner in which Harper is proceeding with Senate reform, arguing that, as with Trudeau's failed proposal, a constitutional amendment endorsed by the provinces is required. Quebec has even gone so far as to state that it is prepared to challenge in court Harper's plans to reform the Senate. It appears that Harper, by ignoring the objections of the provinces as well as the spirit of the Supreme Court opinion rendered in *Reference re: Authority of Parliament in Relation to the Upper House*, is not only circumventing constitutional principles and past constitutional practices, but is also ignoring the proper role the provinces ought to play in the federation.

The ultimate effect of both Trudeau's and Harper's proposed actions are similar: push aside the provinces and ignore the vital position they hold within the federation. Though the Senate is a part of Parliament, its role is not limited to federal matters. This was affirmed by the Supreme Court of Canada in *Reference re: Authority of Parliament in Relation to the Upper House (1 S.C.R. 54 at p.56)* when it pointed out that the Senate was created "to afford protection to the various sectional interests in Canada in relation to the enactment of federal legislation." (Reference, para. 10). If the federal government alone can determine and alter the selection process of the Senate, and if it alone can establish the tenure of senators, then this undermines the role of the provinces in actualizing the notion of regional representation at the centre. It negates a crucial role entrenched by a century of constitutional deliberations between the federal and provincial governments that culminated in the signing of the *Constitution Act, 1867* and the *Constitution Act, 1982*, a role recognized and respected by the government of Brian Mulroney in its own attempt to reform the Senate through the 1987 Meech Lake Accord and the 1992 Charlottetown Accord.

The negotiations that led to the signing of the *Constitution Act, 1867* included the establishment of a Senate, because it was insisted upon by delegates from New Brunswick, Nova Scotia and Lower Canada (Quebec) in order to ensure a healthy respect for their sectional interests and identities at the centre. In 1982, during the negotiations leading up to the patriation of the Constitution, political leaders agreed that the powers and selection of senators, if they were to be altered, required an amendment to the Constitution by way of the general amending formula. In both the Meech Lake Accord and the Charlottetown Accord, the provincial premiers and the prime minister agreed that the proposals to reform the Senate along Triple-E lines could only be put into effect after the unanimous consent of the provinces was obtained (the Charlottetown Accord was first put to the electorate in a national plebiscite). In all these cases, the provinces were actively and equally engaged in the negotiation process, and indeed, in the last thirty years there have only been two instances in which the federal government chose not to consult the provinces or obtain their consent when pushing through their proposals for Senate reform. In these two instances, the governments of Trudeau and Harper chose to ignore the long-established principles of Canadian federal relations by minimizing the role of the provinces in the federation.

When discussing Harper's Senate proposals, then, in addition to considering the constitutional element of the proposal, we must also consider the federalism factor. Harper describes himself as a proponent of open federalism. Yet, despite this, the attempts of the Mulroney government to reform the Senate appear to be more "open" than Harper's as they included a provincial voice through federal-provincial negotiations. Harper's approach contradicts the way Canadian federalism vis-à-vis Senate reform has evolved over the past two decades, and ignores the authoritative understanding of the relationship between the Canadian federation, the Senate, and the federal government rendered by the Supreme Court in 1980. In a similar fashion to Trudeau, then, Harper is attempting to circumvent constitutional practices and obligations. And as with Trudeau, there is little indication that employing a strategy that circumvents the established mechanisms for reform will produce a more open federalism.

REFERENCES

Gibbins, R. and L. Berdhal. 2003. *Western Visions, Western Futures: Perspectives on the West in Canada*. Peterborough: Broadview Press.

Harper, S. 2006a. Conservative Party of Canada. *Prime Minister Harper Outlines his Government's Priorities and Open Federalism Approach*. 20 April. Accessed online at http://www.conservative.ca/EN/1004/42251

— 2006b. Office of the Prime Minister. 7 September. *Senate Reform*. Accessed online 11 July 2008 at http://www.pm.gc.ca/eng/media.asp?id=1306

— 2007. *Prime Minister's remarks to the Rivière-du-Loup Chamber of Commerce*. Office of the Prime Minister. 7 December. Accessed online 11 July 2008 at http://pm.gc.ca/eng/media.asp?id=1938

Lalonde, M. 1978. Honourable Minister of State for Federal-Provincial Relations. *Constitutional Reform: House of the Federation*. Ottawa: Government of Canada.

Leslie, P. 2006. "The Two Faces of Open Federalism." In *Open Federalism: Interpretations, Significance*. Kingston: Institute of Intergovernmental Relations, p. 39-66.

McRoberts, K. 1997. *Misconceiving Canada: The Struggle for National Unity*. Toronto: Oxford University Press.

Russell, P.H. 1993. *Constitutional Odyssey: Can Canadians Become a Sovereign People?* 2nd ed. Toronto: University of Toronto Press.

Reference re: Authority of Parliament in Relation to the Upper House, [1980] (The Senate Reference)1 S.C.R. 54.

Young, R. 2006. "Open Federalism and Canadian Municipalities." In *Open Federalism: Interpretations, Significance*. Kingston: Institute of Intergovernmental Relations, p. 7-24.

CONSTITUTIONALITY OF THE FEDERAL GOVERNMENT'S APPROACH TO CHANGE

6

BILL C-20: FAULTY PROCEDURE AND INADEQUATE SOLUTION
(TESTIMONY BEFORE THE LEGISLATIVE COMMITTEE ON BILL C-20, HOUSE OF COMMONS, 7 MAY 2008)

Ronald L. Watts

Cet article remet en question la validité du projet de loi C-20 sur le plan constitutionnel. L'auteur soulève deux problèmes au sujet de ce projet de loi sous sa forme actuelle : premièrement, la procédure législative, et deuxièmement, l'absence de contexte en ce qui a trait à la relation entre le processus d'élection proposé et la nature, les fonctions et le rôle du Sénat au sein du Parlement. Selon lui, une réforme complète et immédiate du Sénat est nécessaire au bien-être du Canada en tant que fédération, et pour pouvoir réformer le Sénat, il faut modifier la Constitution. Le projet de loi C-20 ne va pas assez loin. De plus, il comporte des risques et des dangers dans le sens qu'il ne tient pas compte de l'effet probable qu'il aura sur le rôle et les pouvoirs du Sénat si l'on modifie seulement le mode de sélection.

I wish to draw attention to two concerns about Bill C-20 in its present form. The first has to do with the *legislative procedure,* and the second with the *lack of context* in terms of the relation of the proposed election process to the character, functions and role of the Senate within Parliament.

The first concern relates to the use of ordinary legislation to effect what is in substance a constitutional amendment. The explicit objective outlined in the Preamble to Bill C-20 appears to be to replace patronage in the appointment of senators by a more democratic electoral element in the process of selection. Bill C-20 appears to have been very carefully crafted to ensure constitutionality by creating a procedure which neither contradicts nor purports legally to alter in any way the governor general's constitutional power of appointment or the prime minister's right of advising the governor general. But it violates the spirit of the *Constitution Act, 1982,* which explicitly states in section 42(1) that "an amendment to the Constitution of Canada in relation to the following matters may be made only in accordance with section 38(1)," and lists in section 42(1)(b) specifically: "the powers of the Senate and the method of appointing Senators." Section 38(1) requires for this not only a resolution of the Senate and House of Commons, but of resolutions in two thirds of the provinces that have in aggregate at least fifty percent of the population of all provinces for such amendments.

The purpose of the amendment procedure outlined in section 38(1) is to ensure a broad consensus for amendments to the basic features of our constitutional structure. Difficult as this may make amendments, nevertheless this requirement is fundamental to the operation of Canadian federal democracy. The effort to avoid this procedure by reforming the Senate on the sly through the devious use of ordinary legislation constitutes an anti-constitutional process. It purports to seek a democratic objective by resorting to a non-constitutional and hence ultimately anti-democratic process. The Supreme Court in 1978 declared that "To make the Senate a wholly or partially elected body would affect a fundamental feature of that body," and the Supreme Court provided clear and unanimous guidance that Parliament could not unilaterally alter "the fundamental features or essential characteristics of the Senate." No matter how democratic the objectives of Bill C-20 may be, and no matter how attractive an alternative unilateralism is to the difficult process of constitutional amendment, those objectives should be pursued by the appropriate constitutional process rather than in the devious manner proposed by Bill C-20.

A second concern arises from the proposal in Bill C-20 to alter the appointment process for senators without relating these alterations to the broader context of the role, representative basis, functions and powers of the Senate as a part of the parliamentary structure. Any reform of the Senate must take account of three factors that are *interrelated*: (1) the representation of the regions and provinces, (2) the mode of possible election, and (3) the powers of the second chamber.

To consider just one of these aspects without its relation to the others in a piece of discrete legislation is likely to create unintended consequences in the relationship between the Senate and the House of Commons. For instance, if the current powers of the Senate – equal to those of the House of Commons except for the introduction of money bills – remain for a Senate whose members gain the legitimacy of an electoral base, this could produce a serious challenge to the principle of House of Commons primacy and of cabinets responsible to it. It is no accident that in virtually all federations elsewhere that have parliamentary institutions (even in those parliamentary federations with relatively strong second chambers such as Australia and Germany), the constitutional powers of the second chamber have been more limited. It is only in federations with separated executives and legislatures, such as in presidential-congressional systems, that directly electoral, equally powerful second chambers have proved sustainable. Of the seven federations in which all the members of the second chamber are directly elected, only Australia has a parliamentary form of institutions, and there, ultimately, the Senate can be overridden by the much larger House of Representatives in a joint sitting. Of the other eight parliamentary federations, not including Canada, the second chambers consist of members elected by state legislatures, appointed by state governments, or selected by a variety of processes. In Canada, despite the almost equal formal constitutional powers of the Senate, in practice its lack of electoral legitimacy – in contrast to the democratic legitimacy accruing to the House of Commons – has induced senators to play a secondary role on most occasions. Would a Senate, composed of ambitious politicians with an ultimately electoral base and with their individual importance enhanced by a smaller chamber than the House of Commons, willingly eschew exercising their full constitutional powers? There is a very real risk that senators with an ultimate electoral mandate but without modification of their current formal powers would exercise those powers they have not dared to exercise in defiance of the House of Commons when they were unelected. Here we might note our pre-Confederation history in the United Canadas. In 1856, with John A. Macdonald's support, an elected second chamber was adopted. But after eight years of its assertiveness complicating the operation of responsible cabinet government, Macdonald admitted that the elective system "did not fully succeed in Canada as we expected." Consequently, in 1864 it was he who introduced into the conference at Quebec the resolution for appointment of members of the Senate (MacKay 1963, 31).

Does this mean that I support the status quo and am opposed to reform of the Senate? Not at all. First of all, my own comparative study of some 25 federations throughout the world has convinced me of the importance of an effective federal second chamber to the effectiveness of federations including parliamentary federations. To those in Canada who would argue for abolition of the Senate, I would point out that of 25 federations in the world today, only five do not have federal second chambers: these are the United Arab Emirates, Venezuela, and the three small island federations (each with less than a million in total population) of Comoros, Micronesia, and St. Kitts and Nevis. Virtually all the others, although in varied forms, have found a federal second chamber desirable for at least two functions: legislative review and the inclusion of distinctively regional views in the federal decision-making process. For information on this federal experience elsewhere, I am leaving for the Committee copies of a recent paper of mine entitled "Federal Second Chambers Compared."

As far as the function of independent legislative review and related activities such as investigative reports are concerned, the Canadian Senate has in fact (as pointed out in many of the contributions to the book edited by Serge Joyal, *Protecting Canadian Democracy*) provided a very useful complement to the House of Commons. Indeed, individual senators such as, to name a few, Hugh Segal, Lowell Murray and Michael Kirby, have made a superb contribution to the work of Parliament.

But as to the second major function of second chambers in federations generally, providing a channel for the involvement of distinctly regional viewpoints in policy making within institutions at the federal level, the Canadian Senate's lack of political legitimacy has meant that, by comparison with other federations, it has fallen short in performing these functions of a second chamber in a federation. These are the functions that Canadian political scientists have come to refer to as "intrastate federalism." That these functions are important has been recognized by the Canadian Supreme Court when it declared in 1978 that "the Senate has a vital role as an institution forming part of the federal system ... thus, the body which has been created as a means of protecting sectional and provincial interests was made a participant of the legislative process." Given the current weakness of the Senate in performing this federal role, Senate reform is in fact *important* and *urgent*.[1] Reform is needed to make more effective the federal coherence of Canada. As one of the most decentralized federations in the world, we need not only provincial autonomy, but federal institutions that bring provincial views more inclusively into federal decision making rather than depending solely on the processes of executive federalism. Reform to achieve this may require elections to the Senate by a different electoral process than that used for the House of Commons, *but also* a more rational basis of representing regional and provincial interests, and an adjustment of the Senate's constitutional powers to avoid deadlocks (possibly along the lines proposed in the Charlottetown Agreement). This is not the place to go into prescriptive detail, but reform requires looking not only at the method of selecting senators, but relating this to the role, functions and powers of the Senate within Parliament.

While such full reform is urgent for the welfare of Canada as a federation, it will require constitutional amendment, difficult as that may be, to redefine not only the method of selecting senators but also the basis of representation and powers of the Senate. Piecemeal reform by stealth and unrelated to the broader functions of the Senate, such as proposed by Bill C-20, not only does not go far enough, but is even risky and dangerous in so far as it does not take into account its likely impact upon the relative role and powers of the Senate.

REFERENCES

MacKay, R.A. 1963. *The Unreformed Senate of Canda*. Toronto: McClelland and Stewart.
Joyal, S. ed. 2003. *Protecting Canadian Democracy*. Montreal and Kingston: McGill-Queen's University Press.

---

[1] Here I would draw attention to the paper by Tom Kent, "Senate Reform as a Risk to Take, Urgently," in the Special Working Paper Series on Senate Reform 2007–8 of the Institute of Intergovernmental relations, Queen's University http://www.queensu.ca/iigr/working/senate/papers.html

7

WHITHER 91.1? THE CONSTITUTIONALITY OF BILL C-19: AN ACT TO LIMIT SENATE TENURE

Don Desserud

Les propositions de réforme du Sénat sont mieux régies sous la formule d'amendement général du paragraphe 38(1) de la Loi constitutionnelle de 1982, selon lequel il est nécessaire d'obtenir le consentement du Parlement et d'au moins 7 provinces dont le total des populations doit représenter au moins 50 pourcent du total des populations de l'ensemble des provinces. Pour affirmer ceci, l'auteur s'intéresse à l'article 44 de la Loi constitutionnelle de 1982, à l'obligation du gouvernement fédéral imposée par l'article 42, et aux conséquences de la réforme du Sénat sur le système gouvernemental. La tentative du gouvernement fédéral de réformer le Sénat en se servant de loi ordinaire peut être perçu comme une violation du principe légal que les gouvernements ne doivent pas essayer de faire de manière indirecte ce qu'ils ne peuvent pas faire de manière directe.

It's supposed to be hard. If it wasn't hard, everyone would do it. The hard ... is what makes it great.

Tom Hanks as Jimmy Dugan in the film *A League of Her Own*

INTRODUCTION

Prime Minister Stephen Harper's Conservative government wishes to reform the Senate. However, the government is clearly aware that constitutional change is a tedious process in Canada, particularly when the provinces become involved, and so hopes to accomplish some of its reforms unilaterally. Bill C-19, "An Act to amend the *Constitution Act, 1867* (Senate tenure)" would abolish a senator's mandatory retirement at age 75 and limit tenure to an eight-year, non-renewable term. The Government maintains that section 44 of the *Constitution Act, 1982*, which gives Parliament the exclusive power to "make laws amending the

Constitution of Canada in relation to the executive government of Canada or the Senate and House of Commons," provides sufficient amendment authority for these reforms.

However, were C-19 enacted, the changes to the Senate could be broad, far-reaching and have the potential to affect provincial interests. As such, these reforms are more properly conducted under the amending formula found in section 42, under which an amendment to the constitution in relation to "the powers of the Senate and the method of selecting Senators" must be "made only in accordance with subsection 38(1)." Amendments made under section 38.1 require, in addition to the approval of Parliament, the consent of at least seven provinces (or two thirds), with an aggregate population of 50 percent or more of the provincial total. That the government has chosen not to take this admittedly more cumbersome route for the proposed reforms will deprive the country of an opportunity to fully assess their merits, and prevent the provinces from having a say in changes to an institution in which they have an important stake. Indeed, the government's attempt to avoid the restrictions imposed by section 42 can be seen as a violation of the constitutional principle that governments must not attempt to accomplish indirectly what they are constitutionally forbidden to do directly.[1] At least, such will be my argument.

LEGISLATIVE BACKGROUND

The government began this latest round of Senate reform with Bill S-4, also titled "An Act to amend the *Constitution Act, 1867* (Senate tenure)," and which received first reading in the Senate on 30 May 2006. Like C-19, S-4 would abolish mandatory retirement at age 75, and senators would serve an eight-year term. However, under S-4, this term would be renewable. On 28 June 2006, S-4 was referred to a hastily assembled Special Committee on Senate Reform for a "pre-study" of the "subject matter" of the Bill. The Special Committee was also to consider Senate reform in a wider context, including whether representation from western Canada should be increased. After conducting hearings in September 2006, the Special Committee delivered its report in which it agreed with the government that the proposed limitations on senator tenure were within the powers assigned to Parliament under section 44.

---

[1] This principle is known as "colourability." See Albert S. Abel, "The Neglected Logic of 91 and 92," *The University of Toronto Law Journal* 19, no. 4. (1969): 487-521 (494, n.18), and Bora Laskin, *Canadian Constitutional Law: Cases, Text and Notes on Distribution of Legislative Power*, 3rd ed. (Toronto: Carswell, 1969), 189-191. See also Peter Hogg, *Constitutional Law of Canada: 2001 Student Edition* (Toronto: Carswell, 2001), 369; and Dale Gibson, "Founding Fathers-in-Law: Judicial Amendment of the Canadian Constitution," *Law and Contemporary Problems* 55(1) (1992): 261-284 (269).

After receiving second reading 20 February 2007, S-4 was then referred to the Senate's Standing Committee on Legal and Constitutional Affairs. After concluding its hearings, the Standing Committee reported that the constitutional implications for S-4 were unclear and undetermined. So, when the Standing Committee tabled its report on 12 June 2007, it made the sensible recommendation "[t]hat the bill, as amended, not be proceeded with at third reading until such time as the Supreme Court of Canada has ruled with respect to its constitutionality" (Spano 2007, 10). Otherwise, the Standing Committee accepted limited terms in principle but recommended they be increased from 8 years to 15 and made non-renewable. They also wished to reinstate the mandatory retirement age of 75 years.

The government, however, declined to consult the Supreme Court on the constitutionality of the legislation, and instead on 13 November 2007 introduced a modified version of S-4 in the House of Commons. This was Bill C-19. The probable strategy in reintroducing what is almost the same bill in the House of Commons rather than the Senate is that it will likely receive strong support in the lower house, making it then difficult for the Senate to reject the bill. In any case, the new bill does incorporate the Senate's recommendation that senatorial terms be non-renewable, thereby answering one of the concerns raised by the Standing Committee that the Senate's independence would be compromised were serving senators to become preoccupied with their term renewal. However, except for sitting senators, the bill did not retain mandatory retirement nor did it accept the recommendation that terms be set at 15 rather than eight years. Under C-19, then, current senators would continue to serve until they reached age 75, while senators appointed after the act came into effect would serve until they completed eight years of service regardless of their age. Finally, subsection 29.2 of the proposed amendment would provide for interrupted terms. This would allow a senator to leave the Senate to serve as an MP, but then complete the remaining years of his or her Senate term at a later date.

Supplementing C-19 is Bill C-20, "An Act to provide for consultations with electors on their preferences for appointments to the Senate," introduced in the House of Commons the same day. Under C-20, Elections Canada would be authorized to run elections or, more accurately, plebiscites, in provinces with Senate vacancies. These plebiscites would run concurrently with a general election, and the victorious government would then be expected to nominate the successful senatorial aspirants to fill the vacancies.[2] The two bills are, as Prime Minister Harper told the Special Senate Committee on Senate Reform, "yet another step in fulfilling our commitment to make the Senate more effective and more democratic" (Harper 2006).

Constitutionally, however, C-20 is a very different bill than C-19. While both are designed to provide, ultimately, for an elected senate, Bill C-20 neither commits nor forces the government or the governor general (nor could it) to choose

---

[2] C-20 is the same bill as C-43, introduced in the first session of the 39th Parliament.

the winner as a senator. The bill merely provides for a "consultation." In spirit and intent, this bill certainly violates section 42, under which changes in the method of selecting senators require the use of section 38. However, since it does not attempt to force the governor general to accept the results of these plebiscites, C-20 – technically anyway – is not a violation of section 42. Bill C-19, however, does not allow for such a technicality. Were C-19 merely to encourage senators to serve for only eight years, perhaps by providing for a significant compensation if a senator were to then retire, it would not change then the character of the Senate or its appointments. Senators could ignore the incentive, just as under C-20 the government and the governor general could ignore the preference of a province's electors for a Senate appointment.[3]

GOVERNMENT'S ARGUMENT

The government maintains that limiting Senate tenure falls within its exclusive powers to amend the Constitution provided by section 44 of the *Constitution Act, 1982*. It justifies this claim with three arguments.

The first is that all amendments to the Senate must fall under sections 41, 42 or 44 of the *Constitution Act, 1982*. Section 44 states: "Subject to sections 41 and 42, Parliament may exclusively make laws amending the Constitution of Canada in relation to the executive government of Canada or the Senate and House of Commons." Sections 41 and 42, then, are exceptions to, or restrictions on, section 44. The government maintains that the amending powers found under section 44 are general and residuary. As the term "Senate tenure" is not to be found under either section 41 or 42, it must by default be found under section 44.

The government's second point is found in the preamble to C-19 (fourth clause), which reminds us that Parliament has previously limited Senate tenure when it passed the *Constitution Act, 1965* changing the tenure of senators from life to age 75. This was done with neither provincial consent nor involvement, and was accomplished under the authority given to Parliament under section 91.1, which

---

[3] It is possible, however, that C-20 is in fact a stalking horse. Critics of C-19's predecessor, S-4, noted that changing Senate tenure might well affect, as Professor John McEvoy has put it, "the office of Governor General by altering the nature of the office to which she can summon qualified persons. If so, Bill S-4 is subject to the unanimity formula of section 41." (*Proceedings of the Standing Senate Committee on Legal and Constitutional Affairs*, Issue 23 - Evidence, 22 March 2007). The argument here is that the constitutional powers held by the governor general to summon someone to the Senate are linked to the character of that chamber, and so changes to the character affect not only the powers of the Senate, but also the office of the governor general itself. It may be that by proposing C-20, the government hopes to deflect such a claim being levelled against C-19. Since C-20 is clearly designed to affect the summoning of senators, then C-19 must be about something else. Let C-20 fail; but in doing so, similar criticism of C-19 will be mitigated.

was an amendment to the *BNA, 1867* through the *BNA, 1949 (2)*. However, the *Constitution Act, 1982* repealed the *BNA, 1949 (2)*, and the government argues that with this repeal section 91.1 was (mostly) replaced by section 44.[4] Specifically, the powers that accrued to section 44 certainly included the power to limit Senate tenure, as was used to impose retirement at age 75 with the *Constitution Act, 1965*. The government acknowledges that section 44 does not expand the powers provided under 91.1. But, as the 1965 Act showed, section 44 doesn't need to because 91.1 provided sufficient power to limit Senate tenure.

Finally, the government argues that changing the term of a senator affects neither the powers nor the method of selecting senators, as described under section 42. Senators will still be "summoned" by the governor general on the recommendation of the prime minister. The length of their tenure does not legally affect this summons, or any associated processes. As well, whether a senator serves for eight years or until retirement does not affect the constitutional position of the Senate, or, more specifically, its legal powers. The Senate's approval would still be needed before legislation could become law, and so forth. Besides, under the current system, senators are often appointed just shy of their seventy-fifth birthdays, and so often serve for much shorter terms than eight years. This is not thought to affect the powers of Senate. Hence, the length of a senator's term cannot be a characteristic of the constitutional identity or character of the Senate.

RESPONSE

In this section of this paper, I attempt to counter these arguments. In the first section, I will maintain that justifying Parliament's right to make unilateral amendments to the Senate, based on what was in fact a temporary authority provided under *BNA,1949 (2)*, misunderstands the circumstances under which 91.1 came into being. Furthermore, such an argument ignores the subsequent negotiations to rectify what many, including (and especially) the provinces, believed was an unwarranted power grab by the federal government. The *Constitution Act, 1982* succeeded, finally, in restoring a federal-provincial balance to the amending power, and so whatever amending powers it gave Parliament, they are fewer than the powers Parliament had held under section 91.1.

My second argument looks at the intentions of the framers in writing the amending formulas as revealed by the structure and layout of the formulas themselves as well as the context in which they were drafted. The several amending formulas strike a balance between parliamentary power, flexibility and provincial

---

[4] The government is not alone in this interpretation; in fact, it is rather widely held. See, among others, Hogg, *Constitutional Law of Canada*, 96, and Luc Tremblay, *Rule of Law, Justice, and Interpretation* (Montreal: McGill-Queen's University Press, 1997), 263. Of course, agreeing that section 44 received all the powers granted to Parliament under 91.1 still leaves open the question of just what powers were so granted.

involvement. But in striking such a balance, the framers demoted Parliament's unilateral power to amend the constitution from its former status as residuary and general. The general formula is now found instead under section 38, where amending powers are shared with the provinces.

In the final section of the paper, I will argue that the Senate's place in the Canadian Constitution is complicated and varied, and so even what appear to be minor changes to the Senate have the potential to affect a wide range of constitutional matters. As well, the effects of the length of a senatorial term are themselves fundamentally ambiguous, and lend themselves too easily to slippery-slope arguments. For both these reasons, changes to Senate tenure are better left under the general formula, a place designed for just such constitutional ambiguities.

CONSTITUTIONAL HISTORY

Much of the history of Canada's quest for a patriated[5] Constitution has been a struggle between the federal and provincial governments over who should be able to amend what and how.[6] The federal government, speaking on behalf of Parliament, tried to guard or enhance what it believed was its unilateral and residuary right to amend much of the Constitution, including institutions such as the Senate. However, the provinces, albeit usually more concerned with cultural or economic issues, nevertheless worried that a disempowered Senate would lose whatever powers it had to protect provincial interests. In the end (that is, by 1982), the provinces secured this important victory: they wrestled the general amending power away from Parliament, and narrowed the scope of Parliament's unilateral amending power. Parliament retained its veto: its approval, save for amendments to a province's own constitution, is still required for any amendment. Nevertheless, Parliament's amending powers as now contained in the *Constitution Act, 1982* are the most restricted of all the various proposals over the years. As Stephen

---

[5] "Patriated" is not as anachronistic a term as it might seem. In 1963, Laskin used the term to describe the "sporadic attempts to eliminate the need for formal resort to the United Kingdom Parliament" that had taken place "for over three decades." Bora Laskin, "Amendment of the Constitution," *The University of Toronto Law Journal* 15, no. 1. (1963), 190-4 (191).

[6] For the early history of Canada's attempts to agree on an amending formula, see Paul Gérin-Lajoie, *Constitutional Amendment in Canada* (Toronto: University of Toronto Press, 1950); E.R. Alexander, "A Constitutional Strait Jacket for Canada," *The Canadian Bar Review* 43, no. 2 (1965), 262-313; Bayard William Reesor, *The Canadian Constitution in Historical Perspective: with a Clause-by-Clause Analysis of the Constitution Acts and the Canada Act* (Scarborough, Ont.: Prentice-Hall, 1992), 126-46; James Ross Hurley, *Amending Canada's Constitution: History, Processes, Problems and Prospects* (Ottawa: Canada Communication Group, 1996), and J.R. Mallory, *The Structure of Government in Canada,*(Toronto: MacMillan of Canada, 1971), 370-408.

Scott wrote in 1982, "[t]he language of section 44 creating the unilateral federal procedure is framed in terms distinctly narrower than those of its predecessor, section 91.1 of the amended 1867 Act" (Scott 1982, 277, n. 94). I would go so far as to say that the amending formulas should be seen not just as the repeal of the powers granted to Parliament under the *BNA,1949 (2)*, but their refutation. Any argument that suggests that under the 1982 formulas Parliament retained the amending powers formerly found under 91.1 must acknowledge that the provinces never accepted that 91.1 was a legitimate power under a federal system, and would not have agreed (and did not agree) that such power should stand.

In 1949, the British Parliament amended the *BNA, 1867* with an Act titled the *British North America Act (2) 1949*, which supplemented the powers granted to the federal government under section 91. Under this subsection, named 91.1, Parliament was granted power over "the amendment from time to time of the Constitution of Canada," except over those areas under the exclusive jurisdiction of the provinces (so section 92 of the *BNA, 1867*), the use of French and English, and the extension of Parliament beyond five years.[7] When the *BNA, 1949 (2)* was enacted, constitutional scholars at the time assumed that under this amendment Canada now had most of the power it needed to amend its own constitution, with Great Britain retaining, in F.R. Scott's words, only a "ghostly presence" in Canadian constitutional affairs (Scott 1950, 204). Most regarded the *BNA, 1949 (2)* as the penultimate step in patriating the Canadian Constitution; clearly Canada was moving steadfastly towards "a normal responsibility of nationhood" (Brady 1963, 493-94).[8] Furthermore, the *BNA, 1949, (2)* was seen as complementing the

---

[7] The text of 91.1 reads: "The amendment from time to time of the Constitution of Canada, except as regards matters coming within the classes of subjects by this Act assigned exclusively to the Legislatures of the provinces, or as regards rights or privileges by this or any other Constitutional Act granted or secured to the Legislature or the Government of a province, or to any class of persons with respect to schools or as regards the use of the English or the French language or as regards the requirements that there shall be a session of the Parliament of Canada at least one each year, and that no House of Commons shall continue for more than five years from the day of the return of the Writs for choosing the House; provided, however, that a House of Commons may in time of real or apprehended war, invasion or insurrection be continued by the Parliament of Canada if such continuation is not opposed by the votes of more than one-third of the members of such House." The use of French and English is now covered under the *Constitution Act, 1987*, section 133, and *Constitution Act, 1982*, section 16 through 20, while the provision allowing Parliament to extend its term in times of emergency is covered by *Constitution Act, 1982*, section 4.1.

[8] Brady quotes Prime Minister Louis St. Laurent: "The United Kingdom authorities, I will not say resent, but do not like the position in which they are placed of having to rubber-stamp decisions for Canadians, made by the representatives of Canadians, and having to do it because no other procedure has yet been devised in Canada for implement-

Canadian Citizenship Act, 1947, the new Letters Patent outlining the power of the governor general – now issued under the Great Seal of Canada (1947)[9] – as well as the 1947 JCPC decision that would give birth to the *Supreme Court Act, 1949*.[10] Also worth mentioning is the *BNA, 1949 (1)*, which brought the colony of New-foundland into Confederation, completing Canada's dominion over the northern half of North America. All that remained was a comprehensive amending formula and the last piece of the constitutional puzzle would be put into place.

While for many a welcome step towards full independence,[11] the sweeping powers that 91.1 gave Parliament nevertheless alarmed both the provinces and constitutional scholars (Favreau 1965, 25). Rowat (1952, 11) claimed "that the federal Parliament has for the time being assumed a power of unilateral amend-ment which does not accord with the principle of federalism." F.R. Scott's criticisms were stronger. He worried over the vagueness of the phrase "the Constitution of Canada," a phrase he referred to as "novel" and unknown under "Canadian con-stitutional law." The phrase could conceivably encompass every aspect of the Canadian political and legal system, and as such might provide Parliament with near-limitless amending powers. In any case, wrote Scott, the provinces were left out and clearly the "compact theory of Confederation" was now dead (Scott 1950, 202-3, 207).

The provinces were indeed left out. Prime Minister Louis St. Laurent had not consulted them before moving the joint address requesting the British Parliament amend the *BNA, 1867* (apparently, he saw no point, as he was sure that Quebec premier Maurice Duplessis would never agree) (Cairns 1992, 140). This lack of provincial consultation did not go unnoticed, even in Great Britain. But St. Laurent assured all concerned that the new powers afforded Parliament by *the BNA, 1949 (2)* were not meant to be permanent. All that was needed were "general over-all

---

ing these decisions. I believe we must recognize that either Canada is a sovereign state or she is not. If the former is true, then Canada must act as an adult nation and assume her own responsibilities." *Debates of the House of Commons, 2nd* Session, *1949*, I, *832*, quoted in Alexander Brady, "Constitutional Amendment and the Federation," *The Canadian Jour-nal of Economics and Political Science* 29, no. 3 (1963): 486-94 (493-4). See also Alain Cairns, *Charter versus Federalism: The Dilemmas of Constitutional Reform* (Montreal: McGill-Queen's University Press, 1992), 21.

[9] W.P.M.K., "The Office of Governor-General in Canada," *The University of Toronto Law Journal* 7, no. 1 (1947): 474-83 (474).

[10] Frederick Vaughan, *Canadian Federalist Experiment: From Defiant Monarchy to Reluctant Republic* (Montreal: McGill-Queen's University Press, 2003), 118. See also W.R. Lederman, "Notes on Recent Canadian Constitutional Developments," *Journal of Comparative Legislation and International Law* (3rd Ser.) 32, no. 3/4 (1950): 74-7.

[11] Although not welcome to those who saw Canada's move towards independence from Great Britain as a loss of a valuable British identity. See Philip Buckner, *Canada and the End of Empire*, (Vancouver: UBC Press, 2004), 50.

amending procedures." Were the federal and provincial governments able to agree on such procedures, "the federal power granted by the 1949 amendment would be *ipso facto* subject to re-definition and could be limited to its *true intent* by more precise terms" (emphasis added).[12] So in 1950, St. Laurent convened a dominion-provincial conference on the Constitution to do just that.

The context for the discussions concerning the new amending formula was to be a proposal offered by "a sub-committee of experts" back in 1936.[13] The 1936 proposal had been a somewhat tentative response to the Statute of Westminster (1931), under which the British Parliament renounced any further legal power over its former colonies, "the Dominion of Canada, the Commonwealth of Australia, the Dominion of New Zealand, the Union of South Africa, the Irish Free State and Newfoundland." The intention of the Westminster statute was that these colonies, now equal members of the Commonwealth, would attend to their own constitutional affairs by adopting or using exclusively[14] their own amending formulas. However, the Canadian provinces protested that in the absence of an agreed-upon amending formula, the statute would provide Parliament with far-reaching and comprehensive amending powers (Mallory 1982, 58). So, the British Parliament agreed, for the time being, to act as "a legislative trustee" for Canada (Laskin 1963, 190).[15]

The 1936 proposal did not succeed. While some provinces embraced it, others did not. Nor did the federal government. And then the Depression, followed by the Second World War, intruded on the constitutional reform process. However, the 1936 proposal contained several remarkable features which would inform the 1950 negotiations, particularly (for our purposes) the negotiations pertaining to the Senate. Under the 1936 proposal, Parliament would have the unilateral right to make changes to, among other subjects, the qualifications of senators (with an exception made for Quebec), the "Summons of Senators," resignation and disqualification of senators, the choice of Senate Speaker, quorum and voting in Senate and the rule prohibiting senators also holding a seat in the Commons (Gérin-Lajoie 1950, 306). However, the proposal contained another formula under which amendments would require the consent of Parliament and the legislative assemblies of two-thirds of the provinces whose aggregate population was 55 percent of the total. Subject to this amending formula would be changes to the number of senators, provincial representation in Senate, the addition of senators and reduction to normal number, the maximum number of senators and the "Tenure

---

[12] Lederman, "Notes on Recent Canadian Constitutional Developments," 76. See also Gérin-Lajoie, *Constitutional Amendment in Canada*, xxv.

[13] Gérin-Lajoie, *Constitutional Amendment in Canada*, xxxvi, 248, 301. See also Alexander, "A Constitutional Strait Jacket for Canada," 271, and Mallory, *The Structure of Canadian Government*, 378-9.

[14] Australia, for example, already had an amending formula for its constitution.

[15] Laskin is quoting Ivan Cleveland Rand.

of place in Senate" (ibid., 310). Also included was a provision for a joint session to override Senate intransigence, revealing that those who drafted the proposal anticipated that reforms made under it would affect, but might not be accepted by, that chamber.

Even with the 1936 proposal available as a draft, the 1950 conference failed to find agreement on a new formula, the provinces themselves disagreeing on how flexible the amending formula should be (Alexander 1965, 274).[16] It would not be until 1960 before another patriation formula would emerge. This was the Fulton formula, named after Prime Minister John Diefenbaker's minister of justice, E. Davie Fulton, and it was clearly a reaction to the fear that section 91.1 gave Parliament far too much power. But the Fulton formula swung the pendulum too far towards provincial power by insisting all amendments require, in addition to Parliament, the support of all ten provinces. So Fulton's successor, Guy Favreau, was given the task of finding a compromise. The result was the Fulton-Favreau formula, which emerged in 1964. This formula maintained the general and residuary amending power of Parliament, but limited the "scope of Parliament's exclusive authority." As well, the proposal established the principle that the provinces had a stake in any constitutional reforms that were either "linked to or identified with the federal nature of Canada (e.g., the Senate)"(Meekison 1982, 115-16). This expanded the previous principle that only those matters directly affecting the provinces should require provincial approval. As well, under the Fulton-Favreau formula a qualifying phrase was added to the unilateral amending powers of Parliament. Now, Parliament's powers to amend "the Constitution of Canada" were clarified to mean "in relation to the executive Government of Canada, and the Senate and House of Commons." Finally, the restrictions on this exclusive power were expanded to include several provisions affecting the Senate.[17] Amendments to such matters would now require the consent of "two-thirds of the provinces representing at least fifty per cent of the population of Canada according to the latest general census."

The Fulton-Favreau formula came very close to being ratified, but in the end was not. The next attempt at an agreement over patriation would not come until June 1971, when the federal and provincial governments agreed to a constitutional amendment package named the Victoria Charter. Just like the negotiations which eventually brought forth the Fulton-Favreau formula, the discussions prior to the writing of the Victoria Charter focused on "limiting the scope of Parliament's exclusive authority to amend parts"(Meekison 1982, 116). Under the Victoria Charter's article 53, Parliament retained its right to "exclusively make laws from time to time amending the Constitution of Canada," but the Fulton-Favreau's restriction remained as well, that is, such power was again clarified to

---

[16] See also Laskin 1963.

[17] The text of the Fulton-Favreau formula and proposed amendments is widely available. See Favreau, *The Amendment of the Constitution of Canada.*

mean specifically "in relation to the executive Government of Canada and the Senate and the House of Commons." As well, the previous article, no. 52, allowed the provinces to initiate amendments, something they had not been permitted previously (save for amending their own constitutions). Parliament's veto remained; however, with this new provincial power to initiate amendments, Parliament would no longer be able to simply ignore provincial calls for constitutional reform. To borrow a classic phrase in parliamentary history, the provinces had seized (some of) the constitutional initiative.

The Victoria Charter also allowed for considerable flexibility: no provisions, not even the offices of the Queen or Governor General, required unanimous provincial consent. Instead, amendments would be made under an amending formula that provided for a balance of provinces and population. Article 55 specified what areas would fall under the general formula, three of which were Senate related: "(4) the powers of the Senate; (5) the number of members by which a Province is entitled to be represented in the Senate, and the residence qualifications of Senators; [and] (6) the right of a Province to a number of members in the House of Commons not less than the number of Senators representing the Province" (Hurley 1996, Appendix 4). Also significant, the Senate's power over constitutional amendment was reduced to a ninety-day suspensory veto.

The Victoria Charter, however, also failed to be ratified. In 1978, undoubtedly frustrated by such continual failures, Prime Minister Pierre Trudeau put forth a bold constitutional amendment package known as Bill C-60.[18] The 1978 initiative was one of, if not *the*, most ambitious and far-reaching constitutional proposal in Canadian history, indeed much more ambitious than what finally took place in 1982. In addition to adding a Charter of Rights and amending formulas, C-60 would have entrenched the Supreme Court, defined and limited the powers of the prime minister and Cabinet and provided for House of the Federation in place of the Senate whose members would be "elected" jointly by the House of Commons and the appropriate provincial legislatures. Just as they did after the Statute of Westminster and the *BNA, 1949 (2)*, the provinces reacted with alarm and they pressed upon the federal government to first request a ruling from the Supreme Court on the constitutionality of the proposed reforms, specifically those affecting the Senate. This time the federal government agreed, and the result was "Reference re: Authority of Parliament in Relation to the Upper House (1979)," commonly known as the Upper House Reference.[19]

Bill C-60 never did get implemented; it died on the order paper as a federal election was held in 1979, one in which the PCs under Joe Clark gained a minority government. However, the Court's decision was delivered before the election

---

[18] See Gregory Brandt, "The Constitutional Amendment Act (Bill C-60)," *University of Western Ontario Law Review* 17 (1978-1979): 267-94.

[19] See David E. Smith, "Empire, Crown and Canadian Federalism," *Canadian Journal of Political Science*, 24, no. 3 (1991): 451-73.

and remains the subject of some discussion today. In its decision, the Court ruled that while not all limits on Senate tenure were necessarily *ultra vires* Parliament, neither did Parliament have the unilateral right to impose such limitations. "At some point," said the Court, "a reduction of the term of office might impair the functioning of the Senate in providing what Sir John A. Macdonald described as 'the sober second thought in legislation'" (Reference re: Authority of Parliament, 76). Furthermore, Parliament's unilateral power to reform the Senate was restricted to "mere housekeeping" changes.[20] The Court ruled that the provinces had a stake in the integrity of the Senate and its ability to function, and so any changes that touched on the Senate's constitutional role required some level of provincial consent (Smith 1991, 468). Furthermore, the Court excluded from section 91.1 those matters that could affect "the federal-provincial relationships in the sense of changing federal and provincial legislative powers," as well as "certain sectional and provincial interests such as the Senate" (Tremblay 1997, 263).

At this point, it would be useful to recap. Over many years of constitutional negotiations, the provinces achieved several victories. While these victories were not constitutionally entrenched (a patriation agreement having yet to be achieved), they nevertheless provided the basis for what would be accomplished in 1982. These victories were (1) the scope of Parliament's unilateral amending power was clarified and restricted so that it applied only to its own institutions; (2) the Senate was now acknowledged as a special case, that is, a federal institution in which the provinces had a stake. Therefore some level of provincial consent was needed before amendments affecting the Senate could be made, save for "mere housekeeping" matters. And, finally, (3) the principle that some combination of provinces representing the regions of the country as well as the population should form the basis for a comprehensive amending formula. In the next chapter of constitutional negotiations, beginning in 1978 and culminating in the patriation of the Constitution in 1982, this last principle would become entrenched as the new general amending formula.

PATRIATION OF THE CONSTITUTION – INTENTIONS OF THE FRAMERS

If, in the wake of the 1978 initiative, the provinces needed any more evidence that the Trudeau government was quite prepared to patriate the Constitution unilaterally, they certainly found it in 1980, when the Liberals returned to power and

---

[20] Changing the number needed for quorum is commonly cited as an example of a "housekeeping matter." In any case, the Court's decision in the Upper House Reference was criticized by several legal scholars, including Hogg ["Comment," *Canadian Bar Review*, 58, no. 3 (1980): 631-45], who maintained that the Parliament of Canada did indeed have the right to make radical changes to the Senate under 91.1, including its abolishment.

Trudeau to the prime minister's office. Trudeau had followed his advisors' recommendations that he leave constitutional issues out of the 1980 campaign, and
the ploy seemed to work: the Liberals won a substantial majority. However, during the campaign preceding Quebec's referendum on separation (20 May 1980),
he was not so circumspect, and boldly promised a renegotiated constitution if
Quebec voters rejected the sovereignty-association vote. That ploy worked too,
the "no" votes totalling just under 60 percent. So Trudeau promptly threatened to
unilaterally request that the British Parliament amend the British North America
Acts to allow for an entrenched charter of rights and a Canadian amending formula. The provinces were, once again, alarmed (Russell 1993, ch. 8).

The conflicts and controversies, not to mention drama, surrounding the constitutional negotiations which followed have been well told by others,[21] and won't
be repeated here. My interest at this point in the paper is in discussing the consequences of the federal-provincial negotiations over the various amending formulas
for Senate reform.

Of course, much of what ended up in the *Constitution Act, 1982* was the result
of compromise. What, then, did the provinces get in 1982 and what did they give
up, concerning Senate reform? For that matter, what did the Senate itself get?
Here the compromise is interesting. Stephen Scott explains that in the earlier
drafts of what became the *Constitution Act, 1982*, written at a time when the
federal government stood very much alone in its decision to patriate the Constitution unilaterally, the Senate's role in future constitutional amendments was
significant: "In the revised proposal of April 24, 1981, the Senate had full coordinate power in *all* cases. A beleaguered federal government was in no position to
press forward to Westminster, not only against the opposition of eight provinces,
but without the concurrence of the upper house in the traditional joint address to
the Queen. Coordinate power for the Senate was in effect to be the price of the
Senate's cooperation" (Scott 1982, 265).

However, this changed when the federal and provincial governments (without
Quebec) agreed on a new constitution in November 1981. No longer needing the
Senate's support (at least not so much), the federal government then inserted provisions for overriding Senate intransigence, in particular over its own reform. The
compromise for the provinces was section 42. By involving the provinces through
the general formula, section 42 could now "provide the Senate with a substantial
degree of entrenchment" (ibid.). On the one hand, then, the Senate actually lost
power with the *Constitution Act, 1982*. It had been an equal partner in constitutional amendments, but now it could be overruled. On the other hand, the provinces
gained power over amendments affecting the Senate, providing a measure of constitutional protection for that body. Therefore, one consequence of *Constitution*

---

[21] For example, Keith Banting and Richard Simeon, eds, *And No One Cheered: Federalism, Democracy, and the Constitution Act* (Toronto: Methuen, 1983), and Russell,
Constitutional Odyssey.

Act, 1982 was a shift of power over Senate reform away from Parliament to the provinces, thereby buttressing the provinces' claim that they had a constitutional stake in the function and position of the Senate.

The second compromise benefiting the provinces was the promotion of the formula now found in section 38. In all previous proposals, the listing of the amending powers began with a general statement under which Parliament was acknowledged as having the power to amend the Constitution. Parliament's power in this regard was accepted and assumed to be general and residuary. Over the history of these constitutional negotiations and the proposals associated with them, the scope of the general power was narrowed as more restrictions were imposed (although sometimes removed again). Soon, however, a principle emerged: the provinces had a general stake in much of the constitution, including certain federal institutions, such as the Supreme Court and, more specifically for our purposes, the Senate. Amendments affecting such institutions, then, should involve the provinces at some level. Rather than add a long and growing list of restrictions to Parliament's general power, a new general power was created. This became entrenched with the *Constitution Act, 1982* as the general authority for amendment under section 38, the formula which requires, in addition to Parliament, the consent of two thirds of the provinces with 50 percent aggregate population (note that this is 50 percent of the total provincial population, and not the country as a whole). It is no accident that Part V, the amending formulas of the *Constitution Act, 1982*, begins with section 38, nor is it a coincidence that section 38, and it alone, is referred to as the "general formula" by the gloss.

But what of the general language still contained in section 44? Here we can turn again to the context in which this section was written. The intention of section 44 was clearly explained to the 1981 Special Joint Committee on the Constitution by then-minister of justice, Jean Chrétien. Clark's former minister for Indian and Northern Affairs, the Honourable Jake Epp, was a member of the 1981 Special Joint Committee, which examined earlier drafts of what would become the *Constitution Act, 1982*. Epp expressed concerns about the powers to amend the Senate that were provided to Parliament under (what would become) section 44. Therefore, Epp introduced an amendment to remove the words "the Senate" from the clause "in relation to the executive government of Canada or the Senate and House of Commons." In doing so, Epp maintained that "[t]his amendment would assure that the role and scope of the Senate could not be changed simply through the House or a federal initiative." However, Epp was satisfied with the assurances provided by Chrétien, who suggested that the amendments to the Senate foreseen by the framers of this section were well in keeping with the "housekeeping" measures insisted upon by the Court in the Upper House Reference, such as, in Chrétien's own example, changing quorum (Canada 1980–1981).[22]

---

[22] I am indebted to Professor John McEvoy, whose testimony before the Senate Standing Committee on Legal and Constitutional Affairs, pointed me to this reference (22 March 2007).

AN ENTANGLED SENATE

We come now to the section of the paper in which I argue that the Senate's constitutional position, as befitting a federal body, is a complicated one and cannot easily be altered without affecting many other parts of the Constitution, not all of which are immediately apparent. Furthermore, the specific effects of changing Senate tenure from its present form to eight years are difficult to determine. This is why such changes should be conducted under section 42. Consider, for example, the *Senate and House of Commons Act*, which governs "the privileges, immunities, and powers of the Senate and House of Commons and their members," and which includes provisions for resignations. As it was enacted under the authority found in section 18 of the *BNA, 1867*, some constitutional experts wonder whether the *Senate and House of Commons Act* is therefore a part of the Constitution of Canada. Given that the authority under which it was enacted was a constitutional head of power, I would argue that it is. But as such, any changes to those privileges, etc., are constitutional changes that can only be amended "in accordance with the procedures prescribed in section 38(1)" (Scott 1982, 257). A change in tenure, surely, is a change in a senator's privileges.

Or consider the amending formulas themselves. Amendments to the amending formula can only be made under the unanimity formula found in section 41. But with the exception of section 45 and the exceptions provided by the override procedures in section 47, all amendments to the Constitution require the approval of the Senate. Indeed, the Senate can initiate amendments. What, then, is the Senate as it is defined under the Constitution, specifically in relation to amendments? More specifically, would changing the Senate constitute a change to some of the amending formula? If so, such a change could require the unanimous consent of the provinces.

However, this cannot be right. If it were, then no amendments affecting the Senate could be made except with the unanimous approval of Parliament and the provinces; the other amending formula would be redundant and impossible to use. Yet surely this is precisely why section 42 is there. It anticipates that changes to the Senate may affect other parts of the Constitution. It recognizes that those effects are not always clear or apparent. Under this clause the provinces have an opportunity to consider whether their interests are affected, as does the public at large. Rather than impose an impossibly rigid formula, though, section 42 provides a compromise.[23]

---

[23] It's worth noting that unlike section 38, section 42 does not allow for a province to opt out, nor does it require section 38.2: "Majority of members; An amendment made under subsection (1) that derogates from the legislative powers, the proprietary rights or any other rights or privileges of the legislature or government of a province shall require a resolution supported by a majority of the members of each of the Senate, the House of Commons and the legislative assemblies required under subsection (1)."

I am arguing here that section 42 is specifically designed to deal with such amendments, the effects of which are fundamentally difficult to determine. The question of the impact of an eight-year, fixed Senate tenure compared to (say) a one-year tenure or a 15-year tenure, provides a good example to make my point. Consider one of the criticisms levelled against the eight-year term: that such a length corresponds too well to the normal parliamentary cycle of four years. With eight-year senatorial terms, a government would only have to win two successive majorities in order to have the opportunity to recommend the appointment of every single senator, probably from its own party. Of course, after winning two successive elections, a party in power might well lose the third. But then the new government would find itself facing a Senate in which they had no members, an equally unpalatable option.

This poses an interesting partisan question that the Constitution does not address, and from which constitutional law shies away. From a constitutional standpoint, a senator is an independent decision maker and legislator, just like an MP. The constitution provides no check on one party dominating or even winning every seat in the House of Commons, as happens at the provincial level, my own province of New Brunswick being an example. I doubt a constitutional challenge would be successful were it argued that the single-member, simple-plurality electoral system currently practised in Canada is unconstitutional because it allows for one party to win every seat, thereby undermining the adversarial nature of opposition politics and therefore responsible government (though the suggestion intrigues!).

Nevertheless, what if the reduction in term were to one year, as several critics of the proposal have suggested, and that the Supreme Court itself pondered in the Upper House Reference? Surely a one-year term, for reasons different than those outlined above, would place serious constraints on the Senate's ability to do its job. A one-year term would certainly not provide sufficient opportunity for the Senate to fulfill its duty to be a chamber of sober second thought. It must be true, then, that limitations on terms can affect the Senate's ability to perform its duties as expected by the Constitution. The question becomes one of degree. If not one year, what about two? What about three? And so on. This is not a frivolous point. Drawing an absolute line between when a term limit is too short and acceptably short is impossible. Therefore, constitutions find other means for dealing with such questions. One is to avoid answering the question and instead substitute a process for the answer. No, we don't know how long an optimal term for a senator is, so instead we will force any changes to such terms through a complex process. Then, by the time the process is over, we can at least be assured that most, and maybe all, of the contingencies will have been discussed and incorporated in whatever decision emerges.[24]

---

[24] On vagueness in law, see Dorothy Edgington, "The Philosophical Problem of Vagueness," *Legal Theory,* 7, no. 4 (2001): 371-8, and Timothy Endicott, "Law is Necessarily Vague," *Legal Theory,* 7, no. 4 (2001): 379-85.

We do not know what effect an eight-year term will have. The debate so far seems to be caught up in trying to decide whether the effect of an eight-year term would be deleterious. It is quite possible that eight-year terms are salubrious. But this is not the point. The point is that limiting the term to eight years constitutes a change warranting careful consideration, and is of such a nature as to possibly involve provincial interests. Furthermore, Senate reform is a complex affair, so that changes to tenure affect many other aspects of it, including the powers of the Senate itself. The effects are unpredictable. However, this is precisely why any attempts at Senate reform should be governed by the general formula. That is, I repeat, one of the reasons why the general formula is there: to give all interested parties a chance to consider hitherto unforeseen effects of proposals for constitutional change.

CONCLUSION

Constitutional change in Canada is a complicated, tedious and, at times, impossible affair. However, the rules governing amendments are there precisely to ensure that changes made to the Constitution are pursued with the appropriate level of public consultation. The amending formulas found under Part V of the *Constitution Act, 1982*, are not perfect. Some are probably too strict; perhaps others are too lenient. But they provide a balance between the expedience of unilateral powers of amendment and the rigidity of unanimity. Section 38 provides that compromise, and section 42 enhances it.

I do not claim that the case I have made here against unilaterally imposing eight-year terms on the Senate is airtight. I doubt such a case could be concocted. And were the government restricted to choosing between unilateral amendment and unanimity, then I might sympathize with the unilateral argument. However, the *Constitution Act, 1982* provides a third option. It is there to provide a sensible compromise between those two extremes. To circumvent these sections is to undermine the federal integrity of the Constitution.

REFERENCES

Abel, A.S. 1969. "The Neglected Logic of 91 and 92," *The University of Toronto Law Journal* 19(4): 487-521.

Alexander, E.R. 1965. "A Constitutional Strait Jacket for Canada," *The Canadian Bar Review* 43(2): 262-313.

Brady, A. 1963. "Constitutional Amendment and the Federation," *The Canadian Journal of Economics and Political Science* 29(3): 486-94.

Cairns, A.1992. *Charter versus Federalism: The Dilemmas of Constitutional Reform* Montreal and Kingston: McGill-Queen's University Press.

Canada 1981–1982. Parliament. House of Commons. Special Joint Committee of the Senate and of the House of Commons on the Constitution of Canada. *Minutes of Proceedings and Evidence, 6 Nov. 1980 - 13 Feb. 1981*, 53:50.

Favreau, G. 1965. *The Amendment of the Constitution of Canada*. Ottawa: Queen's Printer.

Gérin-Lajoie, P. 1950. *Constitutional Amendment in Canada*. xxxvi, 248, 301. Toronto: University of Toronto Press.

Gibson, D. 1992. "Founding Fathers-in-Law: Judicial Amendment of the Canadian Constitution," *Law and Contemporary Problems* 55(1): 261-284.

Harper, S. Office of the Prime Minister. 2006. 7 September. *Senate Reform*. Accessed online at http://www.pm.gc.ca/eng/media.asp?id=1306

Hogg, P. 2001. *Constitutional Law of Canada: 2001 Student Edition*. Toronto: Carswell.

Hurley, J.R. 1996. *Amending Canada's Constitution: History, Processes, Problems and Prospects*. Ottawa: Canada Communication Group.

Laskin, B. 1963. "Amendment of the Constitution," *The University of Toronto Law Journal* 15(1):190-94.

— 1969. *Canadian Constitutional Law: Cases, Text and Notes on Distribution of Legislative Power*, 3rd ed. Toronto: Carswell.

Mallory, J.R. 1982. "The Politics of Constitutional Change," *Law and Contemporary Problems* 45(4): 53-69.

Meekison, J.P. 1982–83. "The Amending Formula," *Queen's Law Journal* 8: 99-122.

Reference re: Authority of Parliament in Relation to the Upper House (1979), [1980] 1 S.C.R. 54, 76.

Rowat, D.C. 1952. "Recent Developments in Canadian Federalism," *The Canadian Journal of Economics and Political Science* 18(1): 1-16.

Scott, F.R. 1950. "The British North America (No. 2) Act, 1949," *The University of Toronto Law Journal* 8(2): 201-7.

Scott, S. 1982. "The Canadian Constitutional Amendment Process," *Law and Contemporary Problems* 45(4): 249-81.

Smith, D.E. 1991. "Empire, Crown and Canadian Federalism," *Canadian Journal of Political Science* 24(3): 451-73.

Spano, S. 2007. 21 November. *Legislative Summary: Bill C-19*. LS-580E. Parliamentary Information and Research Service. Ottawa: Library of Parliament.

Russell, P. 1993. *Constitutional Odyssey: Can Canadians Become a Sovereign People?* 2nd ed. Toronto: University of Toronto Press.

Tremblay, L. 1997. *Rule of Law, Justice, and Interpretation*. Montreal and Kingston: McGill-Queen's University Press.

8

CONSTITUTIONAL DOUBTS ABOUT BILL C-20 AND SENATORIAL ELECTIONS

Andrew Heard

Cet article examine les aspects les plus importants des rôles et de la composition du Sénat dans le système politique canadien. L'article se penche sur le rôle du Sénat qui consiste à fournir « une réflexion sereine » et se demande si des mandats de courte durée (comparé à la durée moyenne actuelle des mandats) auraient une influence négative sur ce rôle. Cet article entreprend une analyse empirique du comportement sénatorial. Finalement, l'article examine en détail les conséquences possibles du projet de loi C-19 dans trois contextes : le remplacement de l'âge de retraite obligatoire par des mandats de durée limitée pour les nouveaux sénateurs; les conséquences possibles des pratiques relatives à l'ancienneté au Sénat; et la question de savoir si les sénateurs dont la durée du mandat est limitée ont tendance à agir de manière plus indépendante que ceux en place pour une période de temps plus longue.

Bill C-20 represents a novel attempt at Senate reform that deserves substantial attention. Unfortunately, serious questions arise about whether C-20 is within the legislative powers of Parliament.

Proponents of C-20 argue that it does not disturb the relevant provisions of the *Constitution Act, 1867* and therefore does not require a constitutional amendment. Furthermore, they argue that the Supreme Court of Canada's opinion in the *Upper House Reference* (1979) was rendered moot by the *Constitution Act, 1982.* Therefore, in this case, we need not consider the relevance of the Court's finding that Parliament cannot legislate direct elections to the Senate. Bill C-20's critics, on the other hand, contend that it is indeed unconstitutional. They assert that the *Upper House Reference* still stands and that the election of Senate nominees amounts to an invalid scheme to create an elected Senate. In short, the government is attempting to do indirectly what it cannot do directly.[1] These different

---

[1] The principle has been developed since *A.G. Ontario v. Reciprocal Insurers*, [1924] A.C. 328.

sides of the debate need to be weighed against each other, to determine whether C-20 is in fact within the powers of Parliament. In undertaking this analysis, it is important to bear in mind that the constitutionality of any particular process for Senate reform is very much independent of the merits of the reform.

All participants in the debate have generally agreed that there are only minor conflicts between the provisions of Bill C-20 and the wording of the relevant sections of the Constitution. C-20 does directly conflict with the *Constitution Act, 1867* in specific details relating to the qualification of senators; these conflicts relate to citizenship, residency, and financial assets.[2] Curiously, C-20 does not ensure that those who stand as candidates in the senatorial nominee elections are in fact qualified to sit as senators.[3] Individuals could run in the elections without satisfying all of the criteria in the *Constitution Act, 1867*. In particular, they do not need to be residents in the province for which they would hold a seat. In

---

[2] The qualifications to be a senator are found in s. 23 of the *Constitution Act, 1867*:

(1) He shall be of the full age of Thirty Years;

(2) He shall be either a natural-born Subject of the Queen, or a Subject of the Queen naturalized by an Act of the Parliament of Great Britain, or of the Parliament of the United Kingdom of Great Britain and Ireland, or of the Legislature of One of the Provinces of Upper Canada, Lower Canada, Canada, Nova Scotia, or New Brunswick, before the Union, or of the Parliament of Canada, after the Union;

(3) He shall be legally or equitably seised as of Freehold for his own Use and Benefit of Lands or Tenements held in Free and Common Socage, or seised or possessed for his own Use and Benefit of Lands or Tenements held in Franc-alleu or in Roture, within the Province for which he is appointed, of the Value of Four thousand Dollars, over and above all the Rents, Dues, Debts, Charges, Mortgages, and Incumbrances due or payable out of or charged on or affecting the same;

(4) His Real and Personal Property shall be together worth Four thousand Dollars over and above his Debts and Liabilities;

(5) He shall be resident in the Province for which he is appointed;

(6) In the case of Quebec he shall have his Real Property Qualification in the Electoral Division for which he is appointed, or shall be resident in that Division.

[3] The qualifications for candidates in the consultative elections are found in s. 18 of Bill C-20:

Any citizen of Canada who has attained the age of 30 years may be a nominee in a consultation being held in a province, except (a) the Chief Electoral Officer and the Assistant Chief Electoral Officer;

(b) a consultation officer or an election officer;

(c) a nominee in a consultation being held in another province; and

(d) a person who was a nominee in a previous consultation and for whom a return, report, document or declaration has not been provided under subsection 451(1) of the Canada Elections Act, as applied by section 96 of this Act, if the time for providing it and any extension have expired.

theory it is even possible for someone to run in an election in one province but be later appointed to a Senate seat for another province where they do meet the residency requirements. Neither are there requirements that candidates possess real property in the province for which they are appointed, are solvent and have a net financial worth of over $4,000.[4] Bill C-20 also appears to run afoul of the Charter's right to equality; only Canadian citizens may run as candidates, although any "natural-born subject of the Queen" or naturalized citizen of the UK or Canada may take a seat in the Senate. While these conflicts are substantive, they could be easily eliminated without disturbing the overall thrust of the Bill. On the broader details of the election of nominees, there are no substantial conflicts with the wording of relevant constitutional provisions. More importantly, Bill C-20 does not conflict with any of the constitutional provisions relating to the actual appointment of senators.

However, the constitutional validity of legislation hinges on much more than an absence of manifest conflicts between the wording of an act and that of the Constitution. Fatal conflicts can also involve a clash with judicial decisions that add crucial content to the bare bones of the specific wording of constitutional documents. For example, the *Constitution Act, 1867* does not explicitly state that only federally appointed superior courts may possess the powers of those courts, nor does the Act provide any list of what those powers may be. And yet, the Supreme Court has blocked several provincial attempts to empower provincially appointed courts and tribunals with powers the Court has ascribed to s. 96 courts. The courts have created a list over the years of the powers of so-called "s. 96 courts," even though the powers of those courts varied from one province to another at the time of Confederation. So, the most relevant area of inquiry is whether C-20 conflicts with past judicial decisions about the Senate. Much uncertainty and controversy hinge on this question.

Potential problems for Bill C-20 arise principally from the Supreme Court of Canada's opinion in the *Upper House Reference*. In December 1979, the Court responded to a series of questions put to it by the federal government about Parliament's legislative authority to alter or abolish the Senate. While the Court refused to answer some of the questions in the absence of specific legislative proposals, it did answer others, and in the process of doing so articulated clear positions on them. The Court held unanimously that Parliament could not unilaterally alter any of the "essential characteristics" of the Senate, and neither could Parliament legislate direct elections for the Senate. Therefore, fundamental questions that

---

[4] In reality, many individuals appointed to the Senate only meet the property requirements after they have been chosen by the government for recommendation to the governor general. This is particularly true of senators from Quebec who must hold property in one of the 24 divisions in that province; many have had no connection with their official division until that time. Thus, C-20's failure to require candidates to meet the property and residence qualifications is not a substantial concern.

need to be resolved are whether the *Upper House Reference* still applies and, if so, whether C-20 conflicts with it.

In order to answer these questions, this paper will explore several related issues in turn. First, the paper will review the existing constitutional provisions that govern the appointment of senators, as well as the different constitutional amendment processes for altering those provisions. Second, the Supreme Court's decision in the *Upper House Reference* will be discussed in order to reveal the potential challenges it poses to Bill C-20. Next, the debate over the continued applicability of this decision will be analyzed, with specific attention to whether the subsequent enactment of s. 44 of the *Constitution Act, 1982* has rendered it moot. Particular consideration at this stage needs to be given to whether the exceptions to Parliament's unilateral powers of amendment are exhaustively covered by sections 41 and 42. If these sections are not the sole limitations on those powers then the principles of the *Upper House Reference* may well apply to Bill C-20. With this backdrop in mind, the ultimate question can be examined: whether the "consultative" nature of the elections under Bill C-20 is enough to save the Bill or whether they do indeed constitute real elections that would doom the Bill.

CONSTITUTIONAL PROVISIONS RELATING TO THE SENATE

The constitutional provisions relating to the qualifications, tenure, and method of appointment of senators are found in the *Constitution Act, 1867* and the current processes for amending these provisions lie in the *Constitution Act, 1982*. Section 23 of the *Constitution Act, 1867* contains the qualifications needed to take a Senate appointment. Potential senators must be 30 years of age, reside in the province for which they are appointed, meet stipulations for holding real property, and have a personal wealth of over $4000.[5] Senators used to serve for life, mirroring the British House of Lords, but a mandatory retirement age of 75 years came into effect on 1 June 1965 for senators appointed after that date (Canada 1965, c. 4). The actual appointing power is set out in section 24: "The Governor General shall from Time to Time, in the Queen's Name, by Instrument under the Great Seal of Canada, summon qualified Persons to the Senate; and, subject to the Provisions of this Act, every Person so summoned shall become and be a Member of the Senate and a Senator." Section 32 also stipulates: "When a vacancy happens in the Senate by Resignation, Death or otherwise, the Governor General shall by Summons to a fit and qualified Person fill the Vacancy." The actual choice of senator is made by the prime minister, although his power is purely a matter of constitutional convention and is not mentioned anywhere in the Constitution.

---

[5] Appointees must hold real estate with a net worth of $4,000 and have a personal net worth of at least $4,000; Quebec senators must also hold property within the specific region to which they have been appointed.

The various constitutional amending formulas now in place are found in Part V of the *Constitution Act, 1982*. Only three provisions specifically mention the process to be followed for making amendments relating to the Senate:[6]

> 41. An amendment to the Constitution of Canada in relation to the following matters may be made by proclamation issued by the Governor General under the Great Seal of Canada only where authorized by resolutions of the Senate and House of Commons and of the legislative assemblies of each province:

> (b) the right of a province to a number of members in the House of Commons not less than the number of Senators by which the province is entitled to be represented at the time this Part comes into force;

> 42. (1) An amendment to the Constitution of Canada in relation to the following matters may be made only in accordance with subsection 38(1):

> (*b*) the powers of the Senate and the method of selecting Senators;

> (*c*) the number of members by which a province is entitled to be represented in the Senate and the residence qualifications of Senators...

> 44. Subject to sections 41 and 42, Parliament may exclusively make laws amending the Constitution of Canada in relation to executive government of Canada or the Senate and House of Commons.

The debate about the validity of Bill C-20 revolves around whether it falls within Parliament's normal legislative powers or whether it should be enacted through the "7 & 50" process under s. 42(*b*).

THE UPPER HOUSE REFERENCE

The constitutional doubts about C-20 centre on the continued applicability of the *Upper House Reference*. In December 1979, the Supreme Court of Canada delivered its opinion on a series of questions put to it by the federal government concerning the authority of Parliament to pass legislation to alter or abolish the Senate. This reference followed the publication of Bill C-60, *The Constitutional Amendment Bill*, introduced into the House of Commons in June 1978. This bill contained proposals to replace the Senate with a new House of the Federation; one half of the 118 members would be selected by the House of Commons and the other half by the legislatures of the provinces following each provincial election.[7] Faced with a wide degree of concern about the constitutionality of Bill C-60, the Trudeau government put the following questions to the Supreme Court:

---

[6] While Section 41(*b*) protects the "senatorial floor" for provincial representation in the Senate, an amendment affecting this measure relates more in essence to the House of Commons, than to the Senate.

[7] See sections 62 and 63 of Bill C-60.

1. Is it within the legislative authority of the Parliament of Canada to repeal sections 21 to 36 of the *British North America Act, 1867*, as amended, and to amend other sections thereof so as to delete any reference to an Upper House or the Senate? If not, in what particular or particulars and to what extent?

2. Is it within the legislative authority of the Parliament of Canada to enact legislation altering, or providing a replacement for, the Upper House of Parliament, so as to effect any or all of the following:

(a) to change the name of the Upper House;

(b) to change the numbers and proportions of members by whom provinces and territories are represented in that House;

(c) to change the qualifications of members of that House;

(d) to change the tenure of members of that House;

(e) to change the method by which members of that House are chosen by

(i) conferring authority on provincial legislative assemblies to select, on the nomination of the respective Lieutenant Governors in Council, some members of the Upper House, and, if a legislative assembly has not selected such members within the time permitted, authority on the House of Commons to select those members on the nomination of the Governor General in Council, and

(ii) conferring authority on the House of Commons to select, on the nomination of the Governor General in Council, some members of the Upper House from each province, and, if the House of Commons has not selected such members from a province within the time permitted, authority on the legislative assembly of the province to select those members on the nomination of the Lieutenant Governor in Council,

(iii) conferring authority on the Lieutenant Governors in Council of the provinces or on some other body or bodies to select some or all of the members of the Upper House, or

(iv) providing for the direct election of all or some of the members of the Upper House by the public; or

(f) to provide that Bills approved by the House of Commons could be given assent and the force of law after the passage of a certain period of time notwithstanding that the Upper House has not approved them? If not, in what particular or particulars and to what extent?

The main issue common to all these questions was the extent of Parliament's ability to amend the then *British North America Act, 1867* using the powers gained in 1949 and embodied in s. 91(1):

The amendment from time to time of the Constitution of Canada, except as regards matters coming within the classes of subjects by this Act assigned exclusively to the

Legislatures of the provinces, or as regards rights or privileges by this or any other Constitutional Act granted or secured to the Legislature or the Government of a province, or to any class of persons with respect to schools or as regards the use of the English or the French language or as regards the requirements that there shall be a session of the Parliament of Canada at least once each year, and that no House of Commons shall continue for more than five years from the day of the return of the Writs for choosing the House: provided, however, that a House of Commons may in time of real or apprehended war, invasion or insurrection be continued by the Parliament of Canada if such continuation is not opposed by the votes of more than one-third of the members of such House.

The Court noted that Parliament's powers under s. 91(1) allowed it to amend the "Constitution of Canada," which it held to mean matters relating to "the constitution of the federal government in matters of interest only to that government" (*Reference* [1980], 71). In answering question 1, essentially relating to the abolition of the Senate or its replacement with another body, the Court held that s. 91(1) described a power held by a Parliament constituted of three elements: "There shall be One Parliament for Canada, consisting of the Queen, an Upper House styled the Senate, and the House of Commons" (*Constitution Act, 1867*, s.17)." Thus, Parliament's legislative powers did not extend to replacing any of its constituent elements (*Upper House Reference*, 74-5). The result of the Court's position is that the Senate could have only been abolished by legislation passed by the British Parliament. In reaching this position, the court also stressed the unique federal character of the Senate: "A primary purpose of the creation of the Senate, as a part of the federal legislative process, was, therefore, to afford protection to the various sectional interests in Canada in relation to the enactment of federal legislation" (ibid., 67).

The Court chose to answer only a sub-set of specific issues posed in question 2, but several answers are relevant to Parliament's power to pass Bill C-20.[8] The Court's partial or complete responses to some of the issues in question 2 reveal a central theme of protecting the essential characteristics or features of the Senate. The Court held that regional representation was such an essential feature: "Without it, the fundamental character of the Senate as part of the Canadian federal scheme would be eliminated" (*Upper House Reference*, 76). Similarly, the Court's answers to question 2(*e*) disapproved of legislation that would permit any direct provincial appointing power or direct election by the public. The Court cast doubt

---

[8] Of interest, but not directly relevant to Bill C-20, is the Court's answer to 2(*f*) was that the Senate could not be excluded from the legislative process; thus Parliament could not have enacted legislation providing the Senate with only a suspensive veto. Since 1982, however, a suspensive veto could only be achieved through an amendment under the 7 & 50 process, as required by s. 42(*b*) of the *Constitution Act, 1982*.

on whether provincial legislatures or lieutenant governors could select senators, because this "would involve an indirect participation by the provinces in the enactment of federal legislation" (ibid., 77). Although the court refused to provide a definitive answer about amending the qualifications of senators in the absence of a specific proposal to change qualifications, it did say:

> Some of the qualifications for senators prescribed in s. 23, such as the property qualifications, may not today have the importance which they did when the Act was enacted. On the other hand, the requirement that a senator should be resident in the province for which he is appointed has relevance in relation to the sectional characteristic of the make-up of the Senate.

Thus, Parliament may have been able to abolish the property qualifications, but not the residency requirements, because provincial residence is more central to the character of the Senate. After the enactment of the *Constitution Act, 1982*, only the residency requirement and not the financial requisite would now have to be amended through the 7 & 50 process of s. 38. Financial qualifications, however, may still possibly fall within Parliament's purview under s. 44. Further relevant details emerge from the Court's general conclusion to the issues in question 2:

> Dealing generally with Question 2, it is our opinion that while s. 91(1) would permit some changes to be made by Parliament in respect of the Senate as now constituted, it is not open to Parliament to make alterations which would affect the fundamental features, or essential characteristics, given to the Senate as a means of ensuring regional and provincial representation in the federal legislative process. The character of the Senate was determined by the British Parliament in response to the proposals submitted by the three provinces in order to meet the requirement of the proposed federal system. It was that Senate, created by the Act, to which a legislative role was given by s. 91. In our opinion, its fundamental character cannot be altered by unilateral action by the Parliament of Canada and s. 91(1) does not give that power.

For the purposes of Bill C-20, the most germane issue raised in the *Upper House Reference* was whether ordinary federal legislation could provide for direct elections. The Court ruled this out because of the change it would bring to one of the Senate's "fundamental features":

> The substitution of a system of election for a system of appointment would involve a radical change in the nature of one of the component parts of Parliament. As already noted, the preamble to the Act referred to "a constitution similar in principle to that of the United Kingdom," where the Upper House is not elected. In creating the Senate in the manner provided in the Act, it is clear that the intention was to make the Senate a thoroughly independent body which could canvass dispassionately the measures of the House of Commons. This was accomplished by providing for the appointment of members of the Senate with tenure for life. To make the Senate a wholly or partially elected body would affect a fundamental feature of that body.

The Court ascribed central importance to the existence of an appointed Senate with members serving terms long enough to preserve a character similar to that of the House of Lords. Thus, there are indeed serious questions about Parliament's ability to pass Bill C-20, if the *Upper House Reference* continues as a determining precedent. Bill C-20 may be *ultra vires* Parliament if it alters the fundamental or essential characteristics of the Senate. The Court's denunciation of legislation to implement direct elections also requires an examination of whether the "consultations" provided for by C-20 are tantamount to proscribed elections.

However, it is crucial to understand that the *Upper House Reference* dealt with Parliament's powers under the former s. 91(1) of the *Constitution Act, 1867*, which was repealed and replaced by the new s. 44 of the *Constitution Act, 1982*:

> Subject to sections 41 and 42, Parliament may exclusively make laws amending the Constitution of Canada in relation to the executive government of Canada or the Senate and House of Commons.

There is some debate about how substantially changed is Parliament's power under s. 44 of 1982, compared to the old s. 91(1). Undoubtedly, the s.44 provision is substantively different from the former s. 91(1), and the crux of the matter is how s.44 relates to the other amending procedures. As Justice Department lawyer Warren Newman told the Special Senate Committee on Senate Reform:

> There has been much written in the scholarly community about the extent to which the amending procedures are exclusive, because when you read section 44, for example, it says "subject to sections 41 and 42." It does not say "subject to section 38." It reads that Parliament may exclusively make laws amending the Constitution of Canada in relation to the executive government of Canada or the Senate and the House of Commons.

From one perspective then, Parliament alone is empowered to make any amendment relating to the Senate that is not reserved under s. 42 for the 7 & 50 formula. This would cover any amendments except those dealing with "the powers of the Senate and the method of selecting Senators" and "the number of members by which a province is entitled to be represented in the Senate and the residence qualifications of Senators."[9] Furthermore, it would not be valid to pass other amendments relating to the Senate through the s. 38 process, under which the Senate has only a six-month suspensive veto. The 1984 Molgat-Cosgrove committee believed that a limited term could be achieved by Parliament acting alone.[10] This interpretation appears to be a sound one based on a literal reading of s. 44.

---

[9] The only aspect of the Senate that requires unanimous consent is the "senatorial floor" which entitles provinces to have at least as many representatives in the House of Commons as it had in the Senate; only in a very few scenarios would such an amendment relate to the Senate rather than to the House of Commons.

[10] Parliament of Canada, *Report of the Special Joint Committee on Senate Reform*, 1984, p. 36.

From another perspective, however, s. 44 may be read as permissive. Parliament *may* pass amendments relating to the Senate not reserved by section 41 and 42, but any amendment directly relating to the Senate could also be passed through s. 38 or 41, as the case may be (Canada 1984, 36). The exclusivity referred to in Section 44 may be intended to protect Parliament's legislative jurisdiction from incursions by provincial legislation, not from other amendment processes. It is also quite conceivable for the Supreme Court of Canada to draw from the *Upper House Reference* and place some limits on Parliament's power under s. 44. Such restrictions would arise from the previous acknowledgement that the creation of the Senate was an essential part of the Confederation agreements; the Senate should not, therefore, be unilaterally altered in any significant manner by Parliament acting alone. In this reading of s. 44, the *Upper House Reference* would still be relevant in its prohibition against Parliament acting alone to alter essential characteristics of the Senate or of Parliament as a whole.[11]

The controversy over the continued application of the *Upper House Reference* essentially turns on whether it has been rendered moot by the *Constitution Act, 1982*. When the Supreme Court examined the issues in the *Upper House Reference*, the relevant powers of Parliament were then found in s. 91(1) of the *Constitution Act, 1867*. This section declared that Parliament could amend the Constitution of Canada with five exceptions: the powers of the provincial legislatures, the "rights and privileges" of the lieutenant governors and provincial governments, the use of the French and English languages, the requirement that there be an annual session of Parliament, and that no Parliament can normally last more than five years. Read literally, s. 91(1) would appear to have granted Parliament the power to alter or abolish the Senate, because it is not mentioned in the five exceptions to Parliament's unilateral powers of amendment. Nevertheless, the court ruled that the essential characteristics of the Senate were beyond the powers of Parliament.

Several legal authorities have argued that the repeal of s. 91(1) and its replacement by s. 44 have rendered the *Upper House Reference* inapplicable. For example, Peter Hogg believes that s. 44 should be read as codifying those "essential elements" of the Senate that cannot be amended unilaterally:

> I do not think a court will say that subtracted from the power under section 44 are not only the four matters listed in section 42, but also fundamental or essential changes. That would be an odd way of reading the provisions, I think. What I am saying is that since 1982, the matters listed in section 42 are the fundamental or essential features that cannot be changed unilaterally. (Canada 2006, 37)

---

[11] David Docherty, for example, asserts that the institution of fixed terms for senators would require the use of s. 38; David C. Docherty, "The Canadian Senate: Chamber of Sober Reflection or Loony Cousin Best Not Talked About," (2002) *Journal of Legislative Studies*, 8(3) Autumn, 27-48, p. 45.

This is a strong argument based on a principle of statutory interpretation which holds that the repeal and replacement of a provision normally indicates that the legislative drafters intended the new provision to displace the jurisprudence predicated on the repealed provision. However, further scrutiny of the connection between the old s. 91(1) and the new s. 44 may not sustain that assumption.

If the new amendment processes entrenched in 1982 completely replaces s. 91(1), then one should find a satisfactory accommodation of the matters found in the old provision. However, only two of s. 91(1)'s exceptions to Parliament's unilateral powers are explicitly accounted for in the new amending formulas. Language rights and the office of the lieutenant governor are both explicitly listed among the subjects that now require unanimous consent for any future amendment. None of the other s. 91(1) exceptions are explicitly referred to in the 1982 amending formulas. The legislative powers of provincial legislatures, the "rights and privileges" of provincial legislatures and governments, educational rights, the requirement for an annual meeting of Parliament and the five-year limit on the life of a Parliament are not explicitly listed in sections 41 or 42 as matters requiring either unanimity or the general "7 & 50" process.[12] Instead those amendments could fall within any of the other three processes (s. 43, s. 44, or s. 45), depending upon the content of the amendment. If one focuses simply on the subjects most relevant to s. 44, some troubling problems arise. The provisions ensuring an annual meeting of Parliament and setting a five-year maximum term for Parliament are now found in sections 4 and 5 of the Charter of Rights. But there is no explicit reference in the amending formulas that indicates which process should be used for amendments to the Charter.

If one accepts the argument that the only limitations on Parliament's powers under s. 44 are those exceptions found in sections 41 and 42, then Parliament must be able to legislate unilaterally any other amendments "in relation to the executive government of Canada or the Senate and House of Commons." Parliament should then, logically, be able to repeal its requirements for an annual meeting and a five-year lifespan. Furthermore, Parliament would have the power to alter or repeal the right found in s. 3 of the Charter for citizens to vote and stand for office in elections to the House of Commons. Indeed, Parliament should even be able to amend s. 32(1) of the Charter to say that it no longer applies to the executive government of Canada or the Senate and House of Commons. In short, the Charter would only apply at the federal level to legislation passed by Parliament.

---

[12] S. 38(2) does mention that *if* an amendment relating to the rights and privileges of the provincial legislatures or governments is undertaken through s. 38(1), then resolutions must be authorized by a majority of the membership of the relevant legislatures; resolutions to approve amendments dealing with other subjects only need a majority of those voting. But, that stipulation does not in itself require that amendments relating to the rights and privileges of provincial legislatures and governments can only be approved through s, 38(1).

Such a conclusion about the unilateral powers of Parliament, however, is plainly absurd. No court would support the argument that sections 3, 4, 5 and 32 of the Charter are subject to unilateral legislative amendment when those sections are not even subject to the temporary suspensive effects of the notwithstanding clause.

The exceptions to the s. 44 powers of Parliament must, therefore, be more than just those found in sections 41 and 42. This conclusion is actually consistent with the exact wording of s. 44. Peter Hogg and others who favour the complete and exhaustive displacement of s. 91(1) by s. 44 would require section 44 to be read in practice as "subject only to sections 41 and 42." However, there is no definitive reason why the actual wording, "subject to sections 41 and 42," precludes other possible exceptions. The wording of s. 44 literally may only ensure that sections 41 and 42 are necessary, not unique, exceptions.

The limitations on Parliament's power to legislate on the Senate were read into s. 91(1) by the Court when no such restrictions relating to the Senate were present in that section; they were read into it or drawn from the preamble to the *Constitution Act, 1867*. Those characteristics have not been changed by the enactment of the *Constitution Act, 1982*. Since the Supreme Court did not hesitate to add new exceptions to the apparently definitive list in s. 91(1), there is a clear precedent for adding exceptions to s.44 as well.

Another determinative aspect of the *Upper House Reference* is likely to persist into judicial considerations of s. 44, regardless of its technical applicability. As part of the analysis of the powers of Parliament under s. 91(1), the Court had to decide what the objects of that legislative power were. In the end, it gave quite a narrow definition to the range of matters Parliament could legislate upon. In particular, the Court said: "In our opinion, the power of amendment given by s. 91(1) relates to the constitution of the federal government in matters of interest only to that government." The Supreme Court may well conclude that the powers of Parliament under s. 44 are similarly focused on matters of interest only to the national government. The stipulation that amendments relating to the method of appointing senators can only be achieved through s. 38 clearly demonstrates that this is a matter that concerns both levels of government. The provinces would apparently have as much interest as the federal government in whether senators are directly elected or appointed following a nomination election, especially since the effect of both processes may be the same: the effective transformation of the Senate into an elected chamber.

INVALID ELECTION OR VALID CONSULTATION?

As interesting an issue as the continued application of the *Upper House Reference* is, the ultimate question that must be resolved is whether the indirect nature of the "consultation" process saves C-20. Clearly, legislation to institute direct elections would run afoul of both the *Upper House Reference* and s. 42(1)(*b*) of the *Constitution Act, 1982*. Whether elections for Senate nominees are permissible hinges on how literal an approach one takes to constitutional jurisprudence. Some argue that Bill C-20 is constitutional because of the absence of a direct conflict with the legal powers and discretion of the governor general in sections 24 and 32 of the *Constitution Act, 1867*. However, there is considerable evidence that Supreme Court of Canada would not take such a literal, black-letter approach.

The history of Bill C-20 and its predecessor C-43 clearly shows that the pith and substance of the bill is to achieve an elected Senate. When trying to establish the true nature of legislation, the courts have often asked what deficiency the legislature was trying to remedy. In the case of Bill C-20, numerous government statements plainly declare that the problem they wish to address is the unelected nature of the Senate. Prime Minister Harper has made it clear that he wishes to avoid any more appointed senators. By mid-2008, he had allowed 14 vacancies to accumulate among Senate ranks. His commitment to waiting for elections is underscored by the serious imbalance between the Liberals and Conservatives in the Senate; new Conservative senators are sorely needed.[13] The ability of voters to indicate their choice of new senators would convey democratic legitimacy to those new senators and to the Senate as an institution. In essence, the remedy provided in C-20 could hardly be any different if direct elections were instituted.

Bill C-20 does provide legal discretion on two key matters that supporters of the measure claim are crucial to its constitutionality: there is no legal obligation for a government to hold an election for Senate nominees, and there is no legal obligation to appoint any nominee once they have been declared winners. One can point to the history of senatorial elections in Alberta for evidence that governments might decide not to recommend that the governor general select elected nominees for the Senate: Jean Chrétien and Paul Martin ignored the winners of Alberta's senatorial elections for eight Senate appointments from Alberta between 1996 and 2005.

However, prime ministers may well not be able to ignore C-20 once enacted. First of all, it makes a tremendous difference that this election process would be enacted by the Parliament of Canada and not by a provincial legislature venturing out of its usual legislative domain. Secondly, a question arises as to how the courts would react to a suit brought by a nominee, elected under the C-20 process, who was overlooked for a Senate appointment. Clearly, the courts would not issue a writ of mandamus requiring the governor general appoint the nominee; there simply is no legal obligation under Bill C-20 to enforce the electoral outcome. However, there is every likelihood that the courts would not leave the matter there. In the *Quebec Secession Reference*[14] the Supreme Court could have simply stated that Quebec does not have a right to secession under either Canadian or international law. Instead, the court went on to declare that the Government of Canada would have a moral obligation to negotiate separation if a clear majority of Quebec

---

[13] As of 23 June 2008, the party standings in the Senate were as follows: Liberals 60, Conservatives 22, others 9, vacancies 14. Parliament of Canada, "Standings in the Senate," available at: http://www.parl.gc.ca/common/senmemb/senate/ps-e.htm, (Accessed June 23, 2008).

[14] *Reference re: Secession of Quebec*, [1998] 2 S.C.R. 217.

voters had agreed to secession in a clearly worded referendum question. Also, in the *Patriation Reference*,[15] the Supreme Court could have simply said that the federal government can in law unilaterally request changes to the Constitution that affected provincial powers. Yet, it went on to declare that substantial provincial consent was required by convention. Thus, it is highly probable that the Supreme Court of Canada would also comment on the government's political obligations to respect the peoples' wishes under the C-20 regime.

The Supreme Court is highly unlikely to endorse the view that a prime minister is free to ignore the results of even "consultative" elections and recommend some other individuals to the governor general. In the *Quebec Secession Reference*, the Court was faced with arguments about the implications of a referendum vote in favour of separation. Legally, the results of such a referendum are just as "consultative" and non-binding as the results of a consultative election held under C-20. However, the Court underlined the importance of the democratic principle of Canada's constitution and declared that the government of Canada would have a moral obligation to negotiate the terms of separation if a clear majority voted in favour of a clear question on Quebec's separation. In this light, it is highly probable that the Court would again point to the democratic principle and say that the government is under a moral obligation to respect the outcome of an election for Senate hopefuls.

Given this, it would indeed be all but impossible for a government to ignore the clear wishes of the people in a nominee-election process conducted with all the seriousness and substance of a regular election for members of the House of Commons. If Bill C-20 were enacted, it would not take long for a constitutional convention to be established that prime ministers should only recommend elected nominees for selection to the Senate. The democratic principle would impose a moral and political obligation from the outset. In the end, then, the theoretical discretion left to the prime minister and governor general in C-20 may quickly prove to be a mirage.

The "consultation" process in C-20 is in every sense of the word an election. It would be held under conditions as stringent as those for elections to the House of Commons. These elections would be waged by candidates and political parties at the same time as elections for members of the House of Commons or provincial legislatures. From the voters' perspective, there is nothing to distinguish their involvement in the Senate elections from their involvement in electing other legislators.[16] In all instances, they will have listened to the campaign promises of a field of individual candidates and their parties before making a trip to the polling station to cast a ballot for their preferred candidates. Once the ballots are counted, the winning senatorial candidates will be officially "selected as nominees," rather than declared "elected," but the end of both types of elections comes with the

---

[15] *Reference re: Resolution to Amend the Constitution*, [1981] 1 S.C.R. 753.

[16] There will, of course, be a different ballot for the senatorial elections, since the STV system will be used in place of the usual single member plurality system.

chief electoral officer officially publishing the results in the *Canada Gazette*. In the case of the senatorial elections, the chief electoral officer also directly informs the prime minister of the results. In the case of elections for the House of Commons, the chief electoral officer sends certificates of election to the clerk of the House with the names of the candidates declared elected for each seat. Surprisingly perhaps, the winning candidates do not automatically take their seats in the House of Commons. They can only do so after taking the oath of office, and they may be barred from the House and the seat declared vacant if they refuse the oath (Marleau and Montpetit 2000, 180-81). Thus, there still remains an element of personal discretion to be exercised, even in the normal election process, between the declaration of a candidate's victory and their taking a seat in the legislature. In theory at least, two extra levels of personal discretion are added in the case of senatorial elections: the discretion of the prime minister to recommend the selected nominees to the governor general and the discretion of the governor general to make those appointments. As noted above, however, the reality of these elections means that the prime minister would in fact be obliged to recommend the winning nominees, just as the governor general would be obliged to appoint them to the Senate. In the end, there will be little in substance or form to distinguish the "direct" election process for choosing MPs from the process for choosing senators. In short, the "consultations" of Bill C-20 really do constitute direct elections.

The long-term effects of elections under Bill C-20 must also be considered. Based on current retirement dates, as early as 2013, a majority of senators will have taken their seats after having won nomination elections. There can be no doubt that they will think of themselves as elected members who possess an electoral mandate to achieve their policy objectives. Such an empowerment has great potential for disturbing the current balance of power between the Senate and the House of Commons. The election of senators would result in fundamental changes to the institution's character and behaviour. As an appointed chamber, the Senate currently exercises considerable restraint relative to the legal powers it possesses under the Constitution. Since 1994, the Senate has amended only nine per cent of the bills passed by the House of Commons and explicitly rejected only two out of 465 (Heard 2008, 5). A Senate with a majority of elected members will undoubtedly flex its powers much more often, leading to potentially serious deadlock between the two houses of Parliament. In past discussions of Senate reform, academics and politicians alike have accepted that any substantive change to the selection process requires a concomitant revision of the powers of the Senate or provision of a clear process for resolving deadlock between the two houses.

CONCLUSION

For all intents and purposes, Bill C-20 creates an electoral process to transform the Senate from an appointed body into an elected chamber. Bill C-20 represents an attempt to alter radically the essential characteristics of the Senate as it was created and has operated since 1867. The chosen method for this drastic reformulation is also intended to exclude the provincial governments whose consent would be required if this reform were proposed through a formal amendment.

Bill C-20 attempts unilaterally to privilege the Parliament of Canada in a decision that provincial legislatures were supposed to have a constitutional right to participate in and to veto. Constitutional amendment processes are meant to protect more than just the black letter of the law. The courts have proven many times that they intend to protect the substance of the institutions and principles that are given life by the Constitution. There is a reason why the powers of the Senate and the method of selecting senators are mentioned in the same line in s. 42 (1)(*b*) of the *Constitution Act, 1982*: the two go hand in hand. A successful transformation of the Senate into an elected body would radically transform the workings of Parliament and disturb the balance of powers between the House of Commons and the Senate. The government's recent attempt to extend a test of confidence into the currently structured Senate's consideration of a bill is only a precursor of the institutional battles that would lie ahead (CTV News 2008). Provincial governments would also demand a review of the distribution of seats within the Senate if it were to exercise more effective powers. The Senate was a foundational institution in Confederation over which considerable debate was expended in order to create this country. In 1982, the first ministers agreed that amendments to the powers and methods of selecting senators should only be done through the general amending formula. As such, the Senate is not something for the national Parliament to radically reform without the consent of the provinces.

REFERENCES

Canada. 1965. *Constitution Act, 1965*, Statutes of Canada, 1965, c. 4.

— 1984. Parliament of Canada. *Report of the Special Joint Committee on Senate Reform*. Ottawa: Queen's Printer.

— 2006. Parliament of Canada. Special Senate Committee on Senate Reform. "Proceedings," Issue No. 4, 20 September 20. Ottawa: Queen's Printer.

— 2008. Parliament of Canada, "Standings in the Senate," Accessed online 23 June 2008 at: http://www.parl.gc.ca/common/senmemb/senate/ps-e.htm

CTV News. 2008. "Tories Threaten to Force Election Over Anti-Crime Bill." 7 February. Accessed online 23 June 2008 at http://www.ctv.ca/servlet/ArticleNews/story/CTVNews/20080207/tories_liberals_080207/20080207/

Docherty, D.C. 2002. "The Canadian Senate: Chamber of Sober Reflection or Loony Cousin Best Not Talked About," *Journal of Legislative Studies*, 8(3) Autumn: 27-48.

Heard, A. 2008. "Assessing Senate Reform Through Bill C-19: The Effects of Limited Terms for Senators." Working Paper 2008-12. Kingston: Institute of Intergovernmental Relations, Queen's University.

Marleau, R. and Montpetit, C. 2000. *House of Commons Procedure and Practice*. Montreal: Chenelière/McGraw-Hill.

Reference re: Authority of Parliament in Relation to the Upper House, [1980] 1 S.C.R. 54; 1979.

Reference re: Secession of Quebec, [1998] 2 S.C.R. 217.

9

SENATE REFORM: WHAT DOES THE CONSTITUTION SAY?

John D. Whyte

Le Premier ministre Harper a décidé que les barrières formelles faisant obstacle aux changements constitutionnels en ce qui concerne la réforme du Sénat ne devaient pas empêcher de très importantes réformes qui, selon lui, allaient avoir un effet bénéfique sur le Parlement canadien et la démocratie canadienne. Il n'a pas adopté la tactique de l'homme politique fort et utilisé ses pouvoirs politiques pour déroger à la constitution, mais il a soigneusement préparé des réformes qui lui permettent d'éviter certaines restrictions liées à l'autorité fédérale unilatérale pour amender la Constitution. Cette stratégie se base sur de petites distinctions textuelles, lesquelles, cependant, l'emporteront sur des motifs constitutionnels de base. Cet article examine la loi constitutionnelle relative à ce débat et suggère que le Premier ministre n'a pas bien évalué les règles constitutionnelles qui s'appliquent aux propositions de réforme du Sénat en matière d'élections et de durée des mandats au Sénat.

Beyond question, the present composition of the Parliament of Canada is anomalous. It is a bicameral legislature, the members of one of its chambers – the Senate – being appointed by the government and holding office until the end of the normal working life (age 75). The absence of both popular selection and periodic accountability to electors for a group of national legislators represents a failure of timely Canadian constitutional reform – a nagging sign of the country's weak capacity for self-determination.

In the context of Canada's founding and the emerging state of democratic practices in that period, it is not altogether surprising that the members of one of the chambers in a bicameral legislature would not be elected but, rather, selected by a specially empowered institution of the state – its executive government – on the basis of one form or another of social and political privilege. Nor is it surprising that the representative role of this class of legislators would be directed to interests that are narrower than those of the general electorate. After all, democratic majorities were, it was believed, likely to make decisions ruinous to interests vital to the state's political and economic stability. It is in the nature of all constitutional design to hedge against any particular political principle, especially principles like democracy that reflect emerging values, gaining unchecked ascendancy and thereby producing an unwelcome revolution in the state.

However, states come to accept new political paradigms. They learn the many ways that emerge in the political culture to ameliorate dominance by a single idea. The ideas about which there have been constitutional anxiety – rights, federalism, provincialism, legalism, democracy – cease to threaten state functioning and become basic principles within the context of competing political needs and values. As this happens we tolerate less and less the constitutional mechanisms designed to control them – the trumping instruments of declaration and veto.[1] In this way, the early Canadian arrangement of placing legislative power in two chambers, one with elected members and one with appointed members, and the consent of both chambers being required to enact laws, became anomalous. We have moved past the time when fear over the risk to state well-being of majorities prevailed over notions of democratic legitimacy. One might think that any nation with a normal and healthy capacity to modernize its constitution would have found by now a way to tie comprehensively the democratic principle to the national legislative process.

Possibly, however, this instance of failed self-determination is sensible for Canada. After all, few political realities are better understood than the virtual impossibility of constitutional reform, including reform that might be considered nothing more than constitutional modernization. Perhaps, also, the failure of Senate reform has been tolerated because the Senate generally exercises power in a way that reflects its lack of a democratic license to exercise independent legislative authority. In fact, the lack of legitimacy may have become a positive factor of Canadian legislative efficiency. In the potentially difficult relationship between bicameralism and responsible government, one of the mediating conditions seems to be that the Senate, acting under the condition of a weak political warrant, acts cautiously with respect to frustrating the government's legislative agenda.

However, an insipid legislative role for the Senate, while responsive to both democracy and structural concerns, is not responsive to other bases for the existence of a second legislative chamber. There are sound reasons of constitutional design for having a bicameral legislature that will permit legislative considerations beyond those that engage members of the Commons.[2] None of the

---

[1] For a discussion of constitutional "safety valves" and how they grow superfluous, see John D. Whyte, "Sometimes Constitutions Are Made in the Street: the Future of the Charter's Notwithstanding Clause" (2007), 16 Constitutional Forum 79, 80-81.

[2] While concerns for class, identity, provincial interests or deeper legislative reflection could justify bicameralism, in truth, as David Smith has pointed out, Canada has no developed theory of bicameralism. See David E. Smith, *The Canadian Senate in Bicameral Perspective* (Toronto: U of T Press, 2003) 3-21.

representation needs that could be met by a second chamber – enhanced representation for minority communities, coordinated representation for the sub-national political communities of the federation, a legislative voice for various economic estates, protection of distinct religious, ethnic and language estates minorities, simply a second review of legislative initiatives, or others – is well served through executive appointment of members. None of them offers a compelling case for anything but establishing legislative membership through elections.

Prime Minister Stephen Harper believes that a non-elected Senate is an affront to democracy. He also seems to believe that the national legislature should be structured to allow its work to be more driven by ideas of, if not provincial interests, at least provincial identities. He is determined to remedy the constitutional obsolescence of an appointed Senate through instituting Senate elections and, it seems, channelling Senate legislative participation along the lines of provincial concerns – not just general provincial concerns but, through province-wide elections, each province's specific perspectives and interests.

Notwithstanding the coherence of these goals, the first of his three initiatives in Senate reform revealed only unclear purposes.[3] This proposal was to establish an eight-year term limit on Senate appointments. He did not make clear whether appointments would be renewable.[4] As a result, it is difficult to know the exact ideas of political efficacy and legitimacy that were sought by this reform. He could have had in mind the advantage of hastening the process of legislator renewal which one would think would exacerbate Senate obstinacy flowing from the conditions of no prospect of re-appointment and no reason to nurture long term political capital. Or, if appointments were renewable, he could have had in mind the doubtful advantage of creating a structure of senator accountability to the appointing government. But given the constant uncertainty about who will be governing some years hence, this would work for only a part of the Senate at any given time. The Harper proposal is, in fact, so resistant to purposive analysis that one is tempted to see it as an instance of "jump ball" reform – putting up a proposal to see what happens to it politically and, if it produces confusion, hope that this will somehow lead to reform with more significant and more intelligible purposes. The Special Senate Committee on Senate Reform in October 2006, however,

---

[3] Prime Minister Harper did believe, however, that term limits on senators would in itself enhance the legitimacy of the Senate. He characterized it as "a modest but positive reform." Senate of Canada, *Report on the Subject-matter of Bill S-4, an Act to amend the Constitution Act, 1867 (Senate tenure)*, (October, 2006), 11.

[4] At the 7 September 2006 session of the Senate Committee on Senate Reform, senators several times asked the prime minister his intentions with respect to the renewal of term appointments. He stated that "[t]he government can live with it either way." He also said, "I will be frank in saying that I tend to think of the future Senate in terms of being an elected body. For that reason I tend to [think] that renewability is desirable." See Special Senate Committee on Senate Reform, *Evidence*, 1st Sess., 39th Parl., 7 September 2006.

saw a purpose to the term limit reform. It endorsed the idea on the basis that this would "re-invigorate the Senate with a constant flux of new ideas" (Canada 2006b, 29). Implicit in this purpose, it seems, is the notion that there would be a steady flow of new senators and, hence, might prefer that appointments be non-renewable. In fact, the report seems to endorse renewable terms (ibid., 30-31).[5]

It seems that the general discomfort with the current Senate, the apparent political barriers to open, broadly considered constitutional reform, the strong appeal to democratic values and the general (although, I believe, mistaken) sense that the Senate is not significant to the national legislative process, have all worked to license constitutional reform that may seem valuable, or appealing, but is unintelligible. Equally important, its constitutionality is highly doubtful and the government seems adamant in its refusal to seek authoritative resolution of the constitutional doubts. This aspect of the term limit initiative ought to concern us a great deal, both as a matter of honouring the rule of law and as a matter of leaving us with a clearly valid legislative structure.

The proposal to create term limits on Senate appointments through simple Parliamentary enactments is of doubtful validity for these reasons. Part V of the *Constitution Act, 1982*, sets out the procedures for amending the Constitution. Section 44 in that part gives the Parliament of Canada unilateral power to amend the Constitution in relation to the executive government of Canada and the Senate and House of Commons. Provinces have a similar unilateral amending power. These provisions relate to the internal basic organization and operation of both orders of government. When section 44 says that the Constitution may be amended with respect to the Senate it is not the case that all elements of Senate reform can be achieved through ordinary legislation. First, the section 44 amending power is subject to section 42 of Part V. That section identifies four elements of Senate reform – powers of the Senate, the method of selecting senators, the number of senators from each province and the residence qualification for senators. These matters can be amended only through the general amending formula which requires the consent of the House of Commons, the Senate and legislatures of two-thirds of the provinces so long as they represent 50 percent of the population of all provinces. (This general amending rule is popularly known as the 7/50 formula.)

When Prime Minister Harper spoke to the Special Committee on Senate Reform on 7 September 2006, he claimed that the constitutional amending formula "says that the Constitution of Canada in respect of the Senate can be amended by the Houses of Parliament with four exceptions, and [the current proposal] is not one of them" (Canada 2006a). The Department of Justice lawyer who appeared before the Special Committee immediately following the Prime Minister appears to have reiterated this position. It is noteworthy, however, that in his testimony he

---

[5] The Report, however, is far from clear and conflicts over this issue within the Special Senate Committee were, it seems, not fully resolved.

was careful not to claim explicitly that the implication of the identification in section 42 of specific exceptions to Parliament's section 44 entitlement to make amendments is that the section 44 power is otherwise comprehensive. He noted that the amending power is labelled as an *exclusive* power but that this characterization of Parliament's power does not tell us anything about its scope, only that, whatever its scope, it will displace other amending procedures. The lawyer made no claims with respect to section 44's actual reach (ibid.).[6] Arguably, the "exclusive" power designation used in section 44 (and also commonly present in the 1867 constitutional allocation of legislative jurisdictions) conduces to a narrower reading of the scope of the authority since placing matters within the scope displaces what the framers wanted as the general amending process. This careful strategy is has been evident in the interpretation of "exclusive" federal and provincial legislative powers listed in the *Constitution Act, 1867.*

There are two basic questions. The first is whether the term limit proposal for Senate appointments falls within the matters in section 42 that require use of the general amending formula (the 7/50 formula). The second is, if the proposal does not fall within section 42, does it then, as Prime Minister Harper claimed, fall within Parliament's unilateral amending power under section 44. As to the first question of whether altering the term of a Senate appointment falls within the categories of amendment listed in section 42, it might seem that none of the section 42 amendments are engaged by imposing a term limit. However, it is not unreasonable to entertain the possibility that "method of selection" includes the length of time of an appointment on the basis that the purpose for making an appointment (to create a life appointment or to create a term appointment) bears on the method of appointing. Both the purpose and effect of an appointment are significantly altered by changing the term from "until age 75" to a term of eight years. Selection practices will change to reflect this. Different considerations will be in play and it seems likely that different considerations will require different methods. For one thing, if term limits for senators strengthens the importance of provincial interest representation, as it might do, the method of appointing will change to better reflect provincial sensibilities.

One might buttress this argument through reading purposively the requirement for provincial consent for "method of selection" amendments. Amendments that alter the federal-provincial relationship, or alter the institutions that mediate that relationship (even slightly), should fall within the categories of constitutional change that require provincial consent – the changes that are caught in sections 38 and 42 of Part V (and elsewhere). A change that affects provincial interests

---

[6] This witness did say that enacting very short terms for senators would not fall within Parliament's power under s. 44 because this change would undermine the effectiveness of the Senate. Establishing term limits would, of course, alter the political dynamics of the Senate, but he felt that that degree of change did not require resort to the general mending formula.

properly belongs in the category of amendments requiring consent from both orders of government and, therefore, should, if linguistically possible, fall within
the language of section 42.

However, if it is assumed that length of tenure does *not* fall within "method
of selecting" under section 42, the claim of the Harper government is that
Parliament can unilaterally make this change in the term of Senate appointments. This claim arises from a general presumption of statutory interpretation
that by specifically naming particular members or topics within a general class,
legislators mean to exclude from the general class all other particularities.
But this is only a presumption, and will be displaced when to do so makes
better interpretive sense. There are a number of reasons for believing that the
naming in section 42 of some categories of Senate amendments (and thereby
subjecting them to the general amending procedure) does not mean that every
other type of Senate amendment falls to the unilateral federal amending power
under section 44. The first reason is that sometimes particularities within a
class are named not to exclude implicitly all other instances but simply to
ensure that named instances are brought within the class. This reasoning is
particularly applicable in constitutional drafting and interpretation. Drafters
must frequently capture the very specific trade-offs or resolutions of competing interests that have come up in the constitutional negotiation process. Parties
insist that these specific concessions and agreements be reflected expressly in
the text. This inclusion cannot sensibly lead to distorted readings of general
provisions or underlying constitutional structures.

Second, one can see that listing in section 42 matters that require use of the
general amending formula under section 38 has an important effect on federal-
provincial relations with respect to proposed amendments. Matters listed in
section 42(2) are rendered immune from provincial opt-outs from a constitutional amendment while the general class of amendments under section 38 is
amenable to provincial opt-outs. One of the explicit effects of the section 42
list, therefore, is to avoid the particular opt-out mechanism for some specific
amendments. Of course, it could be argued that many instances of provincial
opting out from Senate amendments (beyond those listed in section 42) could
be undesirable (or irrelevant) and, consequently, this is a weak argument. But
insofar as some amendments relating to the Senate can trigger a provincial
claim to opt out, it is intelligible to claim that the purpose of the section 42
list was to forestall opting out with respect to some amendments. The basic
point is that there are textual readings that make it unlikely that section 42's
real purpose was to place every other sort of Senate amendment within the
unilateral power of Parliament.

Third, if one considers the many sections of the *Constitution Act, 1867* that
relate to the Senate, it defies sense to say that any change to them, save the four
changes named in section 42, can be implemented unilaterally by the federal level.
To make this claim would mean that Parliament, without provincial consent, could
amend the 1867 Constitution with respect to the distribution of Quebec senators

according to the twenty-four electoral divisions, the age qualification of senators, their citizenship qualification, the property and wealth qualifications, the power to add supernumerary senators, the requirement to reduce Senate representation when supernumerary senators are appointed, the total number of senators allowed, the conditions for the removal of senators and the replacement of senators. These are important elements of the national legislative condition and most, if not all of them, impact on how provincial and regional representation will occur in the Parliament of Canada. It is not sensible, from the perspectives of sustaining the federal relationship and constitutional integrity, to conclude that the framers of the 1982 constitution believed that these vital features of Canada's Senate could all be altered by unilateral parliamentary enactment.

Furthermore, there is no sound argument that all Senate reforms (other than those under section 42) must fall within section 44 in order for that section to have purpose or meaning. There are other constitutional provisions relating to how the Senate does its business – and how it relates to the work of the Commons – that that are clearly part of Parliament's internal constitution and, hence, can be amended under section 44.

Finally, The Supreme Court of Canada in the *Reference re: Authority of Parliament in relation to the Upper House* (1980, 54) limited Parliament's authority to amend the Senate to changes that neither impaired the second sober thought in legislation nor changed the essential character of the Senate. Two issues arise from this. Do the standards established by the Supreme Court prior to the constitutionalization of a formal amending procedure in 1982 have any bearing on how the terms of that new procedure are to be interpreted and, second, if they do, does changing a Senate appointment to an eight year term alter the essential character of the Senate. If the Court were to accept the proposition that section 44 allows full unilateral amending capacity, apart from the four section 42 exceptions, its earlier decision would be irrelevant. If it decided that the section 44 power required a limited reading in order to preserve interests of the federal structure, the *Senate Reference* would be highly relevant. Of course, in making this decision – in deciding whether section 44 is exhaustive of Senate amendment authority – the Court is likely to be influenced by the conception of federalism interests that it adopted in *Reference re: Authority of Parliament in relation to the Upper House* in describing limits to unilateral federal authority. And of course, these fundamental federalist conditions were underscored by the Supreme Court's in its decision in *Reference re: the Secession of Quebec* (1998, 217). It seems very unlikely that the Supreme Court in adjudicating a dispute over as foundational an issue as the meaning of the amending formula would not draw on its decisions that touch on the basic conceptions of Canadian statecraft. It is likely that the Court would be at pains to ensure that those judicially endorsed conceptions were reflected in its interpretations.

As for the second question, if the *Upper House* decision were to be considered relevant, the Court is bound to see the change in the term of a Senate appointment as altering the functioning and essential character of the Senate – not necessarily for the worse, but, nevertheless, a significant alteration in the character of the Senate.[7] As we know from many state design contexts, the term of office inevitably shapes the character of the office and that idea is clearly expressed in the Constitution.

There is one further prudential argument of, perhaps, weaker legal significance. If the current proposal to limit senatorial terms to eight years can be implemented under section 44, it must take the form of a parliamentary enactment, which means that it will require the consent of the Senate. But if such an amendment required provincial consent because it fell under section 38 (the general amending formula), lack of Senate could not block the reform beyond 180 days from the date of a House of Commons resolution to amend he Constitution. As a matter of rational constitutional design, it is likely that the amending procedures would contain the restriction on the Senate veto with respect to reforms to the Senate, especially when such reforms are very likely to weaken the political role or legitimacy of sitting senators. It is, however, not clear whether this sort of prudential analysis bears on judicial disposition, at least not unless there is legislative history that suggests that the framers of the provisions had made this very calculation. The very complicated provenance of the *Constitution Act, 1982* makes any discernment of the intentions of the framers virtually impossible.

The second reform proposal of Prime Minister Harper is to hold Senate elections. In the course of Special Committee hearings on the Term Limit Bill, the prospect of senatorial elections was raised. In particular, it was asked that if the government felt that it could only proceed with reforms to the Senate that can be implemented by Parliament under section 44, why had it announced an intention to initiate an election process for choosing senators. At the conclusion of the Senate committee hearing on 7 September 2006, an official from the Privy Council Office suggested that the government would avoid this constitutional difficulty through a parliamentary enactment that would establish an "… elections type consultative type bill that would provide other guidance to the Prime Minister in that appointment process" (Canada 2006a). A Department of Justice lawyer then assured senators that it is always possible to "temper" the effect of constitutional restrictions through "… various legislative and other techniques" (ibid.). When some senators suggested that governments and legislatures should not attempt to do indirectly what they cannot do directly, the Justice lawyer explained his position by saying that that principle is honoured in the breach rather than in the observance. He buttressed his somewhat cynical claim by pointing to the constitutional prohibition against legislative delegation between orders of government which was sidestepped, he said, by the delegation of administrative authority

---

[7] The Court in this case observed that the unilateral predecessor parliamentary power to amend the Constitution as it was stated prior to 1982 and s. 44, was limited to "housekeeping matters" and did not extend to altering the structure of the federal Parliament. (Ibid., 66). Placing term limits on Senate appointments is not "housekeeping."

between jurisdictions (ibid.). This comparison was misleading. The difference between legislative delegation and administrative delegation is significant. The barrier to the former is grounded in the idea of preserving the integrity of the allocation of legislative authority, a central feature of Canada's constitutional structure. Placing amendment of this structure beyond unilateral provincial legislative authority was an essential element of having governments rule according to law and the constitution. Administrative delegation does not alter the constitutional arrangement, but produces co-ordination efficiencies as regulatory programs begin to overlap. In any event, it is wrong to suggest that governments were able to find a way to persist in their unconstitutional plan with respect to legislative delegation. The legislative inter-delegation prohibition has restrained governments and, to this day, they are prevented from engaging in this back-door form of constitutional amendment to the division of powers. In short, it is simply not credible that the clever manipulation of words and concepts that the Justice lawyer seemed to recommend will lead to judicial authorization for an alteration to a constitution's cornerstone – the process by which constitutional terms come into being.

Fourteen months after this exchange the government did, in fact, introduce in the House of Commons a bill which would provide for "the consultation with electors on their preferences for the appointments of Senators." Apart from the preamble, the entire Bill is a reproduction of the *Canada Elections Act* (2000 chap. 9) with the same officers, the same structures, the same restrictions, the same offences and the same processes (other than the Bill contemplates the possibility of the election taking place in the context of a provincial election, as well as in the context of a federal election – an alternative, one assumes, that will prove to be an administrative nightmare, electorally confusing and not likely used).

As an initial observation, one doubts that calling elections consultative or advisory will persuade courts to overlook the lack of provincial consent for substantive constitutional reform relating to Senate appointments. Only if a court were to believe that the new voting process did not materially change the government's actual appointment practices and that, even after a vote, there would be no loss of the government's discretionary room with respect to appointments, would it conclude that there had been no alteration of the constitution. In fact, it is not to be believed that a government would initiate a non-binding electoral scheme for the Senate. This would fly directly in the face of the accountability and legitimacy principles that justify Senate appointment reform in the first place and it would create a corrosive level of electoral cynicism. It is not unreasonable to assume that the Court would share this incredulity over the claim that Senate elections would not constrain completely the discretionary power of governments with respect to appointments. The Supreme Court of Canada seeks to apply constitutional norms to real contexts and to actual practices, and elections for Senate appointments implemented under section 44 would, therefore, be in constitutional jeopardy. It cannot be the case that those seeking to justify an initiative to democratize the Senate can find constitutional justification for their reform through promising never to be bound by the democratic process that they so badly want and that they claim to be so uniquely legitimate.

There are four reasons why the plan to seek electoral advice on who to appoint to the Senate is a change in the method of selecting senators which, if implemented through ordinary legislation, would result in constitutional breach. First, section 42(b) refers to the method of *selecting* persons for appointment, not the means of appointment. The method of selection will now be that governments will consider – and under the normal imperatives of electoral success – only those who win elections to determine who should be selected for Senate appointment. The electoral process is nothing other than a new and crucial component of the method of senator *selection.*

Second, by section 32 of the *Constitution Act, 1867,* the discretion to determine who is a fit and qualified person to be appointed to the Senate is assigned to the federal Cabinet. The new Bill has constructed an electoral mechanism to advise the government as to who should be appointed. A clear constitutional responsibility specifically assigned to a particular agency of government will be eroded or constrained by another element of public government – the electors. In administrative law we say of this situation that the statutory decision-maker has declined its jurisdiction, or has submitted to dictation or has fettered its discretion. The constitutionally recognized decision maker has altered the constitutional plan for making appointments. These actions are *ultra vires.* Of course, it may be claimed that the consultation process and its results will not curtail Cabinet discretion and that the consultation is not designed to limit the list of those considered for appointment but only to add names to a larger list – one that contains names not resulting from election. If one reads the Bill it is simply not believable that consultation will not determine for the Cabinet who is to be selected. The size of the electoral process, the context of a general election, the visibility of the election, the political energy and the higher public attention paid to province-wide votes all preclude any possibility of cabinets disregarding these electoral results. The saving clause of the Bill – this process is to ascertain the preferences of electors on appointments to the Senate "within the existing process of *summoning* senators" (italics added) – cannot save the Bill's constitutionality. This attempt to appear to be preserving the constitutional *status quo* is disingenuous. The precise process of *summoning* is, of course, not altered. It is the method of selecting senators that the reform bill alters and that is exactly what section 42(b) states must be accomplished only through the general constitutional amending process.

Third, the electoral process in the Bill does not satisfy the specific requirements relating to appointing senators from Quebec. The Quebec situation is unique in that the twenty-four Quebec senators must be appointed – one from each of the twenty-four electoral divisions. One doubts that this has the same salience that it had in 1867, but the rule persists. The election bill does not accommodate this peculiarity. Arguably, the Cabinet could overlay the electoral process with the constitutional restraint that all Quebec appointments will match the electoral districts but, in province-wide elections this is unlikely to be possible unless the decision is made to ignore the election results. This, however, could not occur. Quebec would not tolerate a voting system of relative insignificance, one that was uniquely irrelevant and one that would produce Quebec senators who did not reflect the popular preferences and who, as a result, operated with less electoral legitimacy than other senators.

Finally, courts do not treat the Constitution as if it were a tax code. They require fidelity to the Constitution's structures, its relationships, its design and its principles. The proponents of the amendment have admitted that they are unable to institute an election process since they have taken what is clearly an election process, kept all of its attributes but labelled it a "consultation." The process they call consultation is, in fact, an election in everything but name. It would bring Parliament into disrepute, and it will do grave damage to the Constitution and the rule of law if Parliament attempts by such an obvious and self-confessed sleight of hand to amend the Constitution in contravention of amending provisions. A telling experiment to decide if "consultation" is simply a semantic alternative to Senate elections is to replace the word "consult" with the word "elect" wherever it occurs – if the words are interchangeable without affecting the process, this is a strong indication that there is no difference. Section 2(2) of the Bill states: "Words and expressions in this Act have the same meaning as the *Canada Elections Act* unless a contrary intention appears." No contrary intention appears.[8]

The Harper government has sought to justify its Senate election proposal by pointing to the decision of the Judicial Committee of the Privy Council's 1919 decision in *Reference re: The Initiative and Referendum Act* in which a Manitoba plan to have amendments to the provincial constitution put into effect on a majority vote of all electors was ruled unconstitutional. The Judicial Committee saw this plan as abrogating the legislative role of the lieutenant governor. (Of course, it also abrogated the legislative role of the provincial legislature, but the Judicial Committee focused on the constitutional role of giving royal assent.) The defenders of the Senate election bill point out that in that case the Manitoba Act expressly stripped away a legislative role, whereas the current reform leaves intact the Cabinet's role (described, of course, in the 1867 Act as the governor general) to make appointments once the election has been held. Again, defenders of reform take a

---

[8] When Senator Bert Brown appeared before the Legislative Committee on Bill C-20 on 18 June 2008, he spoke in defence of Senate elections. Brian Murphy MP (Liberal) asked him why he chose to speak of the prime minister's commitment to Senate elections when the Bill before the Committee seemed to deal with a consultative process. He reminded Senator Brown of Professor Peter Hogg's testimony about the importance of the distinction – that only if the selection prerogatives of the Cabinet in Senate selection were left unaltered in any way could Bill C-20 be constitutional. Senator Brown replied: "To go back to your question about whether the Prime Minister is committed to the idea of the election of Senators, I would have to answer with an unequivocal yes because he has told me that himself, but with a time-limited offer to provinces. If they hold Senate elections, he will recognize the outcome of those elections." (Legislative Committee on Bill C-20, *Evidence*, No. 10, 2nd Sess., 39th Parl. (June 18, 2008), 1550. Of course, the prime minister's clear political purposes and the electoral scheme of Bill C-20 are not necessarily the same.

constitutional prohibition and infer from it a constitutional licence for everything else. This is simplistic interpretation. It is true that the Judicial Committee was not dealing just with a *de facto* alteration of constitutional power but also with formal alteration. However, its decision that what Manitoba was attempting was unconstitutional does not carry any implication that when in a substantive – and substantial – change of constitutional power the formal process is left intact there is no constitutional violation. The case is no authority in situations like the present in which there is a significant alteration to constitutional powers and processes. The test the Judicial Committee actually applied to the Manitoba proposals was that the Manitoba plan "intended seriously to *affect* the position of [the constitutional power-holder]" (italics added). That particular test of unconstitutionality is, of course, met in the current proposal relating to Senate elections.

Prime Minister Harper's final "reform" initiative has been implicit and is a further instance of "jump ball" reform. It consists of the simple decision not to fill Senate vacancies (apart from bringing a defeated candidate for a Commons seat into his first Cabinet and appointing a person elected under Alberta's experiment with holding elections for filling Senate vacancies from that province) (*Globe and Mail* 2008, A4). One purpose of this is to produce the sense that something urgently needs to be done to reform the Senate.[9] The failure to appoint is also a type of reform in that its effect is to erode the legitimacy of the Senate in two ways. First it expresses disdain for the practice of appointment and, hence, disdain for the Senate generally and the role it performs in the national legislative process. Second, through not filling vacancies the constitutional scheme of representation (as badly skewed as it already was) has been destroyed. Currently, for instance, New Brunswick has three times as many senators as British Columbia and approximately one-sixth the population producing an eighteen-fold over-representation. Certainly the allocation of seats provided by the Constitution produces discrepancies, but not at this scale. This conduct of the Prime Minister is clearly unconstitutional. Appointing senators is not a prime ministerial prerogative but a constitutional requirement placed on him and his Cabinet in section 32 of the *Constitution Act, 1867*, which identifies a duty to "summon qualified Persons to the Senate." Whatever discretionary room may exist in this power, it does not extend to an exercise of it that destroys the element of governmental structure the preservation and functioning of which is the purpose behind the granting of the power. Constitutions do not assign authorities with the idea that they will be used to defeat the Constitution. Certainly, no Canadian government would be allowed to attack and erode the judicial branch through a decision not to fill judicial vacancies. This situation is no different.

---

[9] Senator Bert Brown, a promoter of the prime minister's plan for "elections" has identified the prime minister's decision not to make Senate appointments as designed to push the provinces "to come on side" with Senate elections. See, "Saskatchewan plans to elect senators" The Globe & Mail (Toronto) 19 May 2008 at A1. Senator Brown spoke of the prime minister's plan only in terms of Senate *elections*.

Prime Minister Harper has decided that political barriers to constitutional reform should not stand in the way of reforms that his government sees as having high national value. He has not adopted the political strongman's tactic of improving the Constitution through amendment by decree, or by the less oppressive, but equally improper, device of legislative decree. Instead, he is proposing changes to the Senate that he believes do not violate any of the Constitution's terms and that he is proceeding in accordance with the constitutional order. I believe that he has miscalculated the constitutional constraints that apply to his Senate reform proposals.

It needs to be acknowledged that intergovernmental constitutional reform of the sort required by sections 38 and 42 is very likely to be held up by traditional demands. From Quebec will come proposals for amendment that could lead to Quebec's acceptance of the 1982 Constitution that will have to be dealt with prior to any other reforms. Aboriginal organizations will demand for the right to participate in constitutional discussions and the right to special inclusion in any reformed governmental institutions. Both sets of claims reflect compelling ideas of national justice. Neither claim should be ignored if we are seeking to create a peaceable state. These political conditions will hold up parliamentary reform and this gives rise to the belief that there must be some route for legislated Senate reform under section 44. But there isn't. We need to be nation enough to conduct the inconvenient and difficult intergovernmental discussions that Part V of the *Constitution Act, 1982* has identified as being essential to our sustained nationhood. We might benefit from them.

REFERENCES

Canada. 2006a. Special Senate Committee on Senate Reform. *Evidence*, 1st Sess., 39th Parl. 7 September.

— 2006b. Senate of Canada. *Report on the Subject-matter of Bill S-4, an Act to amend the Constitution Act, 1867 (Senate tenure)*. October.

— 2008. Legislative Committee on Bill C-20. *Evidence*, No. 10, 2nd Sess., 39th Parl. 18 June.

Curry, B. and B. Laghi. 2008. "Saskatchewan plans to elect senators," *The Globe and Mail*, 19 May, A1.

Reference re: Authority of Parliament in relation to the Upper House, [1980] 1 S.C.R. 54.

Reference re: Secession of Quebec, [1998] 2 S.C.R. 217.

Reference re: The Initiative and Referendum Act, [1910] Appeal Cases 935 (Judicial Committee of the Privy Council).

Smith, D.E. 2003. *The Canadian Senate in Bicameral Perspective*. Toronto: University of Toronto Press.

The Globe & Mail. 2008. "Empty seats: Saving taxpayer dollars one vacant Senate seat at a time," 19 May, A4.

Whyte, J.D. 2007. "Sometimes Constitutions Are Made in the Street: The Future of the Charter's Notwithstanding Clause," *Constitutional Forum* 16(2): 79-88.

CONTENT OF THE FEDERAL GOVERNMENT'S PROPOSED CHANGES

10

ANTICIPATING THE CONSEQUENCES OF BILL C-20

Stephen Michael MacLean

Le projet de loi C-20 – Loi sur les consultations concernant la nomination des sénateurs – et le projet de loi C-19, sont désavantageux pour le Sénat. S'intéressant surtout au projet de loi C-20, l'auteur énumère les désavantages de ce projet de loi, entre autres le fait que si le Sénat était « élu », il serait une copie de la Chambre des communes, et non son complément (tel que c'est le cas maintenant); ce projet est, selon lui, un affront aux intentions des Pères de la Fédération, et il trouve le processus de consultation ambigu. Il conclut en affirmant que le Sénat actuel joue le rôle qui lui a été donné.

We wished at the period of the [Glorious] Revolution, and do now wish, to derive all we possess as *an inheritance from our forefathers.* Upon that body and stock of inheritance we have taken care not to inoculate any cyon alien to the nature of the original plant. All the reformations we have hitherto made, have proceeded upon the principle of reference to antiquity; and I hope, nay I am persuaded, that all those which possibly may be made hereafter, will be carefully formed upon analogical precedent, authority, and example.

Edmund Burke, Reflections on the Revolution in France

While the Conservative Party of Canada has often been accused of trying to ape the Republican Party of the United States, there is a marked contrast between them with respect to their attitudes toward constitutional practices. Republicans eschew innovation by an appeal to the "intent of the Framers" and to a strict constructionist ("originalist") interpretation, whereas Canada's Conservatives advocate a radical re-interpretation and adaptation of the *British North America Act, 1867* (in contemporary usage, the *Constitution Act, 1867*).

Nowhere is this "new" Conservative bent and ideological fixation upon "the principles of modern democracy" (C-20, Preamble) more in evidence than in Senate reform. The government has introduced two bills in this area: C-19 (Senate tenure), which introduces a non-renewable eight-year term for senators, and C-20 (Senate Appointment Consultations Act), which encourages public recommendations of senatorial appointments.

While few would deny the salutary benefits of Senate reform – e.g., increased representation from other political parties, more *independent* senators without political party affiliation, a greater diversity of professions and employments ("walks of life") represented, and a more equitable representation of regions the better to reflect Canada's growing population – it is here asserted that this particular reform of Senate Appointment Consultations (SAC) is detrimental to the Senate.

Bill C-20 (as indeed C-19) threatens the organic nature of the Parliament of Canada as it has evolved: an elected House of Commons and an appointed Senate; the former principally of legislative function, the latter deliberative in nature or, in the clichéd phrase, a chamber of "sober second thought." Convention reflected this tension between accountability and legitimacy: the Commons is privileged (*de facto* if not *de jure*) as the pre-eminent *confidence* chamber, the Senate a *complementary* chamber of scrutiny and amendment.

Traditional Conservatives would not undertake constitutional reform were there no obvious breakdown in the system of government that threatened paralysis and chaos. They would instead rely upon a Burkean reverence for prejudice, the belief that "individuals would do better to avail themselves of the general bank and capital of nations, and of ages" (Burke 1790, 183). It is such prejudice, based on the fundamentals of the *Constitution Act, 1867* and the legacy of the Fathers of Confederation, upon which this critique is formed.

I will briefly address the reform of the Senate contemplated in C-20.

DUPLICATION

Upper houses historically have stood apart from their lower house counterparts; ideally, their function is not to oppose, but to complement; not to duplicate, but to augment. Upper houses justify their existence by the promise to provide a political service not fulfilled by lower houses and to provide a fresh perspective and insight on public policy issues – a uniqueness manifest in the fact that their members are selected differently than lower-house members. Canada's appointed Senate is fairly true to this upper house model. A reformed, elected Senate is not, since it merely duplicates the function of the Commons. What's the point of imitation?

SLIPPERY SLOPE

If the idea of senators appointed by an elected prime minister – to a chamber that by convention assumes a complementary role to the Commons – is such an affront to democratic sensibilities, requiring the remedy that C-20 proposes, what is the effect on the credibility of the judiciary and other appointed public offices?

INTENTIONS OF THE FATHERS

By introducing a consultative process, C-20 contravenes the intentions of the Fathers of Confederation. With the British and American examples before them, they devised an upper house to act primarily as a deliberative, secondary body. Only an irresponsible government would set out upon the path of Senate reform with so little regard for what the Fathers of Confederation achieved, and with so little apprehension of what lies ahead, unmindful of "precedent, authority, and example."

CONSULTATION PROCESS

How efficiently will the actual process of consultation work? How will candidates/nominees come forward? What assurances are proffered that "qualified Persons" (*Constitution Act, 1867*, s. 24), different from those elected to the House of Commons, will be nominated to provide sober second thought? And what is the legal and political status of public consultations if constitutional responsibility ultimately remains with the prime minister?

RAISED EXPECTATIONS

Must the prime minister always defer to the recommendations of the voters? Though C-20 leaves him free to exercise his own judgment, the pressure for him to enact the public's choice will be great. What will be the public's response, and its perception of probity and accountability, if the prime minister rejects the nominee(s) provided and, at his own discretion, appoints someone else?

SENATORIAL CONSTITUENCIES

Will the consultative process lead to "senatorial constituencies" in much the way that MPs represent ridings? While senators currently sit for regional districts (with greater geographic specificity in Quebec), they serve no constituents *directly* as MPs do, and can thus focus on national issues and not on the individual needs of their constituents. This distinctiveness is conducive to the independence and objectivity of the upper house and acts as a foil to parochial interests.

PROVINCIAL SPOKESMEN

Though some provincial premiers advocate elected senators in theory (as consultation implies), they might well change their minds when confronted with the establishment of such political rivals. Elected senators, representing provincial interests at the national level, will inevitably supplant the premiers' prestige and their depiction as statesmen to their constituents, a characterization of which they are naturally jealous. Quebec premiers, by virtue of the *deux nations* theory of

Confederation and as the self-appointed representatives of French-speaking rights in the country, are adamantly protective of their special stature. Will premiers relinquish to senators their power and authority to take on Ottawa – as the sole official speakers for provincial interests – without a fight?

HYBRID CHAMBER

If C-20 becomes law, then the short-term prospect includes both appointed and "elected" senators who will sit in the red chamber. If C-19 also receives royal assent, there will be the added ingredient of senators who will sit until the present mandatory retirement age of 75 and those with fixed, non-renewable eight-year terms. With such a mélange of mandates, will senatorial colleagues truly respect each other as peers?

CLASH OF COMPETING CHAMBERS

Were C-20 to be enacted and found to be constitutional, how would the inevitable clash between competing "elected" chambers be resolved? Since the Senate is *co-equal* with the Commons save for money bills, how will a "red veto" be over-turned?

REVERSAL OF FORTUNES

The ultimate poetic justice of C-20 would be the reversal of the pre-eminence of the two chambers in Parliament. With "elected" senators-at-large enjoying both a larger constituency yet fewer provincial peers-*cum*-rivals vying for public atten-tion (in contrast to most MPs); with longer terms to build up public confidence and trust; with traditional politicians polling low numbers for public respect; and with the *Constitution Act,1867* investing the Senate with virtually equal powers to the House of Commons (excepting revenue legislation), may not all these fac-tors tilt public esteem in the Senate's favour?

As the foregoing comments indicate, in my view the Senate reform bills are fraught with more disadvantages than the sought-for remedy or the hopeful folly of benefits-to-be-received. "It is what we prevent, rather than what we do," William Lyon Mackenzie King once observed, "that counts the most in government" (quoted by Reynolds 2007, B2). More aptly, to borrow a British expression, the present Senate of Canada is still "fit for purpose."

REFERENCES

Burke, E. 1790. *Reflections on the Revolution in France*, C.C. O'Brien, ed. Harmondsworth: Penguin Books, 1986.

Reynolds, N. 2007. "Bring back the mighty ship Labrador," *The Globe and Mail*, 14 Feb-ruary, B2.

11

ASSESSING SENATE REFORM THROUGH BILL C-19: THE EFFECTS OF LIMITED TERMS FOR SENATORS

Andrew Heard

Cet article revoit les clauses constitutionnelles au sujet des nominations au Sénat et les différents processus pour les modifier. L'article examine également la décision de la Cour suprême du Canada dans l'Upper House Reference pour voir si elle pose problème au projet de loi C-20. Puis, le débat se poursuit afin de déterminer si cette décision est toujours valable ou si l'amendement ultérieur, l'article 44 de la Loi constitutionnelle de 1982, lui a fait perdre sa raison d'être. L'article conclut en se demandant si la nature consultative des élections dans le cadre du projet de loi C-20 suffira à le sauver, ou s'il s'agit effectivement de vraies élections et que le projet de loi est voué à l'échec.

After some years in the hinterland, Senate reform has again edged its way to the fore of the national political agenda. Many proposals for significant reform were made in the last decades of the twentieth century, culminating in the Charlottetown Accord signed by all first ministers in 1992. This agreement would have replaced the current appointed Senate with one composed of an equal number of elected members from each province; the Accord, however, suffered fatal wounds at the hands of the voters in the referenda organized by the Quebec and Canadian governments in October 1992.

Little appetite remained after that for national constitutional debates; even the narrow results of the 1995 Quebec referendum failed to inspire Canadian politicians to engage in broad federal-provincial negotiations for constitutional renewal. Instead, the federal government reacted with non-constitutional, legislative measures: the regional veto formula embodied in the *Constitutional Amendments Act, 1996* and the *Clarity Act* passed in 2000.

This lower-key approach to unilateral legislative innovation has continued with the minority Conservative government elected in January 2006. Their first concrete government action on Senate reform came only a few months into the first session of Parliament, with the introduction of Bill S-4 into the Senate on 30 May

2006. Instead of dealing with Senate elections, this bill would have ensured that any new senators would serve no more that eight years in office; this term of office dovetailed with proposals introduced that same day in the House of Commons to limit the life of a parliament to a maximum of four years (Canada 2007). Bill S-4 was substantially amended in June 2007 by the Senate after two rounds of committee hearings. At report stage, the Senate adopted committee recommendations that the eight-year tenure of new senators be increased to fifteen years, that a senator could not be reappointed to another term, and that mandatory retirement at 75 be restored. In addition, the Senate effectively killed the bill by agreeing that it would proceed no further until the Supreme Court had ruled on its constitutionality.

Parliament was prorogued not long afterwards, in September 2007, and the government chose to reintroduce the measure into the House of Commons in November 2007 as Bill C-19. Embodying most of the original provisions of S-4, Bill C-19 left out the one provision which had generated the most concerns about the constitutionality of S-4: the ability of the prime minister to reappoint senators to subsequent eight-year terms. As the Senate deliberations on S-4 revealed, this power of reappointment could have undermined the Senate's fundamental independence by inducing some senators to curry favour with the government in the hopes of securing a second term in office.

Although Bill C-19 lacks the major constitutional weakness of S-4, it is still important to consider the effects of introducing an eight-year limit to the tenure of new senators. During the Senate's consideration of Bill S-4, a number of senators and committee witnesses raised concerns that unilateral federal legislation to set eight-year term limits may run afoul of a 1979 reference decision of the Supreme Court of Canada which indicated that federal legislation could not alter the "essential characteristics" of the Senate.[1] While it is beyond the scope of this paper to analyze the legal debate over whether the *Upper House Reference* continues to apply in light of the new amending formulas in the *Constitution Act, 1982*, the main issue of impact on the essential characteristics of the Senate remains a useful perspective for analyzing Bill C-19.

This paper will briefly identify the most important aspects of the Senate's composition and roles in the Canadian political system. Particular attention will be paid to the Senate's role of providing "sober second thought" and whether short-term senators might be less effective in this regard. Rather than relying purely upon abstract considerations, this paper will include empirical analysis of senatorial behaviour. The potential effects of Bill C-19 will be examined in detail in three contexts: the replacement of the mandatory retirement age for new senators with the fixed eight-year term, the possible effects that the seniority practices of the Senate may have on new short-term senators working among many other longer-term senators, and whether short-term senators act less independently than others

---

[1] *Reference re: Authority of Parliament in Relation to the Upper House*, [1980] 1 S.C.R. 54 (hereinafter referred to as the *Upper House Reference*).

with longer terms. A much richer perspective on Bill C-19 can be gained from the combined insights of these three perspectives, and firmer conclusions on its likely effects on the work of the Senate can be drawn.

BILL C-19: CONTENTS AND EFFECTS

The terms of Bill C-19 are very succinct and would change the term of newly appointed senators to a limit of eight years. It would also abolish mandatory retirement for newly appointed senators while preserving it for current senators. The main clause of the Bill would replace section 29[2] of the *Constitution Act, 1867*, with the following:

29. (1) Subject to sections 30 and 31, a person summoned to the Senate shall hold a place in that House for one term of eight years.

(2) If that term is interrupted, that person may be summoned again for the remaining portion of the term.

(3) Notwithstanding subsection (1) but subject to sections 30 and 31, a person holding a place in the Senate on the coming into force of the Constitution Act, 2007 (Senate tenure) continues to hold a place in that House until attaining the age of seventy-five years.[3]

------

[2] The original text of s. 29 is as follows:

29. (1) Subject to subsection (2), a Senator shall, subject to the provisions of this Act, hold his place in the Senate for life.

(2) A Senator who is summoned to the Senate after the coming into force of this subsection shall, subject to this Act, hold his place in the Senate until he attains the age of seventy-five years.

[3] The preamble to Bill C-19 is rather lengthy but provides good insights into the motivation for its enactment:

WHEREAS it is important that Canada's representative institutions, including the Senate, continue to evolve in accordance with the principles of modern democracy and the expectations of Canadians;

WHEREAS the Government of Canada has undertaken to explore means to enable the Senate better to reflect the democratic values of Canadians and respond to the needs of Canada's regions;

WHEREAS the tenure of senators should be consistent with the principles of modern democracy;

WHEREAS the Parliament of Canada enacted the *Constitution Act, 1965*, reducing the tenure of senators from life to the attainment of seventy-five years of age;

WHEREAS, by virtue of section 44 of the *Constitution Act, 1982*, Parliament may make laws to amend the Constitution of Canada in relation to the Senate;

AND WHEREAS Parliament wishes to maintain the essential characteristics of the Senate within Canada's parliamentary democracy as a chamber of independent, sober second thought...

Short-term Senate appointments are not new, indeed short-term appointments are more common than the extra-long appointments that fuel animosity towards the Senate. Since 1867, only 60 (6.9 percent) of 873 Senate terms have been for more than 30 years, while 246 (28.0 percent) senators served for less than 8 years; another 6 current senators will have to retire within eight years or less of their appointment.[4] It is important to note that most of those short-term Senate careers ended prematurely because of death; 146 senators died having served less than eight years. Table 1 shows that, since the 75 year age limit came into force on 1 June 1965, 46 of 276 (16.7 percent) appointments have been given to individuals who had less than eight years to serve.

TABLE 1: Appointment of Short-Term Senators since Mandatory Retirement in effect in 1965

Prime Minister	Total Appointments	Appointments of Less than 8 Years	Short-term as % of Appointments
Harper	2	1	50.0
Martin	17	2	11.8
Chrétien	75	28	37.5
Mulroney	57	5	8.8
Turner	3	1	33.3
Clark	11	1	9.1
Trudeau	81	5	6.2
Pearson	30	3	10.0
Total	276	46	16.7

Source: Library of Parliament

While short-term senators are not a new phenomenon in Canada, Bill C-19 would mark a fundamental change because all appointments would be for a maximum of eight years. A small minority of short-term senators sitting at any one time is quite different from the ultimate goal of ensuring that the entire membership is appointed to an eight-year term.

Limited terms have also been recommended in other proposals for Senate reform. The Beaudoin-Dobbie Report suggested that senators should have renewable terms "of no more than six years in length," and that they be elected (Canada 1982, 44-49). The Molgat-Cosgrove Report favoured electing senators to non-renewable terms of nine years; the committee believed that without adopting

---

[4] There have actually been 876 appointments to the Senate, but three individuals named to it in the 1867 Royal Proclamation declined their appointments. These data were calculated from the individual biographies of senators, as of 9 September 2006, available from: "Senators – 1867 to date – by name," Acessed 28 February 2008 at http://www2.parl.gc.ca/parlinfo/lists/senators.aspx?Parliament=&Name=&Party=&Province=&Gender=&Current=False&PrimeMinister=&TermEnd=&Ministry=&Picture=False

elections, the Senate would benefit from the nine-year term for appointed senators (Canada 1984, 26-27). The Charlottetown Accord provided for elected senators
who would face elections at the same time as MPs.[5]

With this backdrop in place, an assessment of the impact of Bill C-19 can be
undertaken. The next two sections of this paper explore the work of the Senate
and the independence of its members in an effort to identify the salient characteristics that may need protection. Then the paper will analyze 1) the replacement of
the mandatory retirement age for new senators with the fixed eight-year term;
2) the possible effects that the seniority practices of the Senate may have on new
short-term senators working among many other longer-term senators; and
3) whether short-term senators may act less independently than others with longer
terms.

THE WORK OF THE SENATE

The Senate is an insufficiently studied institution in Canadian politics. Scholarly
works usually refer to the Senate as having been designed with two functions in
mind. The role as a forum for regional representation is stressed by those who
point to the lengthy debates over the relative representation of the different
provinces during the Confederation negotiations. As a counter-balance to the general principle of representation by population in the House of Commons, the Senate
was designed to provide equal representation of "regions"; originally this allowed
the Maritime provinces to collectively have representation equal to that which
Ontario and Quebec each had. As has been widely noted, however, the Senate has
not actually operated as a chamber in which distinctive regional interests are championed. Virtually from the start, the main forum for effective regional representation
has been the Cabinet, bolstered by the in-camera debates in the governing caucus
and the House of Commons in public session.[6] In recent decades, the provincial
premiers and other officials have taken a central place in representing provincial
and regional interests. It has become *de rigueur* for many modern advocates of
Senate reform to assert that the Senate must be remade to perform this initial
function effectively, and this motivation underlies the Triple-E ideas spawned in
western Canada in the 1980s.

---

[5] With the exception of any senators that would have been selected by provincial
legislatures.

[6] Paul G. Thomas is one author who believes that the view that the Senate has failed in
regional representation is "not altogether persuasive." See his comments in "Comparing
the Lawmaking Roles of the Senate and House of Commons," in Serge Joyal (ed.), *Protecting Canadian Democracy: The Senate You Never Knew*, Montreal-Kingston:
McGill-Queen's University Press, 2003, 206-9. For an opposite view see Paul G. Weiler,
"Confederation Discontents and Constitutional Reform: The Case of the Second Chamber," (1979) *University of Toronto Law Journal* 29(3): 253-283.

The Senate's role to provide "sober second thought" to precipitous actions in the Commons is the other original function that the founders of Canada felt necessary. Modelled on the British House of Lords, the Senate was envisioned as a bastion to represent propertied interests distinct from the interests of the masses that might be championed by MPs in search of re-election. The qualifications for appointment to the Senate contained in the real property and financial net-worth requirements were substantial at the time of Confederation.[7] Some have argued that the Senate has been too successful in this role of defender or promoter of the interests of capital (Campbell 1978). The Senate's purpose in acting as a counterweight to the Commons, however, is certainly much broader than this. From the beginning, the Senate assumed the roles of scrutinizer of legislative proposals coming from the Commons and of initiators of legislation dealing with more technical and less partisan issues. The Senate provides detailed revision of clauses that are glossed over in the hurly burly of the Commons, and it takes some of the burden off the Commons by giving careful consideration to bills initiated in the Senate on non-controversial matters. In a larger sense, the Senate was meant to act as one of the checks and balances in Canada's parliamentary form of government and as one of the limits on government power essential to liberal democracy (Ajzenstat 2006, 5; Ajzenstat 2003, chap. 1).

In the decades since Confederation, the Senate has demonstrated a varied record in revising legislation from the House of Commons. While the percentage of Commons legislation amended by the Senate dropped over the course of the twentieth century, it still remains at meaningful levels.[8] Indeed, as table 2 shows, the proportion of Commons bills amended by the Senate has actually grown from the early 1960s. It is also important to note that the Senate has an absolute veto over legislation coming from the Commons. Although I have argued elsewhere that a constitutional convention had appeared to have developed by the late 1980s that the Senate should not exercise its outright veto, Senate activity since then has shown an increase in the number of bills rejected by the Senate; little outcry from the general public accompanied any of the defeats of Commons bills since the late 1990s (Heard 1991, 89-98).

The Senate is also able to prevent Commons legislation from being passed in more subtle ways than, for example, an outright defeat on second or third reading. A bill may be processed at treacle-like speeds or be delayed by lengthy and sporadic

---

[7] Those appointed to the Senate must hold real estate worth a minimum of $4000 above any loans or liens, and the appointee's net financial worth must also be at least $4000; these requirements are found in s. 23 of the *Constitution Act, 1867*.

[8] For excellent, recent discussions of the Senate's legislative roles, see C.E.S. Franks, "The Canadian Senate in Modern Times," in Serge Joyal (ed.), *Protecting Canadian Democracy: The Senate You Never Knew*, Montreal-Kingston: McGill-Queen's University Press, 2003; David Smith, *The Senate in Bicameral Perspective*, Toronto: University of Toronto Press, ch. 6; and Thomas 2003.

TABLE 2: Senate Treatment of Commons Bills, 1958–2007

Parliament	Commons Bills Introduced in the Senate	Commons Bills Amended in the Senate	% of Commons Bills Amended	Commons Bills Rejected by the Senate	Senate Prestudy of Commons Bills	No Royal Assent of Commons Bills in the Senate	Bills Amended by Senate and Agreed to by Commons	Bills Amended by Senate and Not Agreed by Commons	Senate Amendments Insisted on by Senate	Further Commons' Amendments Agreed by Senate
2006–2008	88	9	10.2	-	-	20	2ᵃ	3ᵃ	-	1
2004–2005	50	3	6.0	-	-	-	3	-	-	-
2001–2004	131	14	10.7	1ᵇ	1	26	9	2	1	1
1997–2000	122	10	8.2	1	-	6	10	-	-	-
1994–1997	169	14	8.3	1	-	6	10	3	1	1
1988–1993	229	8	3.5	2	9	3	4	3	1	-
1984–1988	248	18	7.3	-	75	7	11	5	2	1
1980–1984	202	1	0.5	-	37	1	1	-	-	-
1979–1979	7	0	0.0	-	3	1	-	-	-	-
1974–1979	221	9	4.1	-	23	4	8	-	-	1
1973–1974	64	1	1.6	-	4	-	-	1	-	2
1968–1972	178	12	6.7	-	1	-	10	2	-	-
1966–1968	113	5	4.4	-	-	-	3	-	-	1
1963–1965	92	3	3.3	-	-	1	2	1	-	-
1962–1963	18	0	0.0	-	-	-	-	-	-	-
1958–1962	211	15	7.1	2	3	3	1	1	-	-
TOTALS	2,143	122	5.7	7	153	78	76	21	5	8

Notes: ᵃWith Bill C-2 and Bill C-31, the House of Commons agreed with some Senate amendments to the bills but objected to or amended others; ᵇBill C-10 was split into 2 bills, C-10A and C-10B; C-10 is counted as a rejection by the Library of Parliament. However, it can be argued that this was really an amendment rather than a defeat.

Source: Library of Parliament

consideration at committee stage. As a result, many bills simply fail to emerge from the Senate by the time a session is prorogued or Parliament dissolved. Granted, some bills are passed on to the Senate from the Commons too late for any effective deliberations in the Senate. However, the fact that decisions are indeed made to not proceed with the passage of certain bills is highlighted by the expeditious treatment of other bills in the dying days of a session. Numerous bills are introduced and passed in perfunctory fashion within a few days of the close of a session, while many other bills introduced weeks or months earlier are simply left to expire. Occasionally these "indirect vetoes,"[9] are made publicly and loudly, such as when the liberal-dominated Senate decided in 1988 that it would not proceed with the original Free Trade Agreement legislation until after a general election had provided a mandate for the policies enshrined in the FTA. Thus, the impact the Senate has on the legislative process is felt beyond the most visible exercises of amending or formally rejecting Commons bills. Table 2 shows a growth through the 1980s and 1990s in the number of Commons bills that fail to make it through the Senate and receive royal assent.[10]

The independence of the Senate is not just revealed in its treatment of legislation passed by the House of Commons, because it can and does reject government bills initiated in the Senate. In doing so, the Senate is directly opposing the Cabinet of the day. The Senate's treatment of Bill S-4, in the 2006–7 Session, is a prime example. The Senate not only fundamentally altered the bill, but effectively killed it by accepting the committee recommendation that the bill not be proceeded with until the Supreme Court of Canada has ruled on its constitutionality.

Almost invisible, but substantive, contributions are also made when Senate committees study the content of bills while they are still formally before the House of Commons. In this process of "pre-study," senators examine the bills in detail and offer suggestions for amendment that are then considered and often adopted by the House of Commons before the legislation ever formally is introduced into

---

[9] This phrase is taken from Smith 2003, 115-6.

[10] Note that the column headed "No Royal Assent of Commons Bills in the Senate" includes bills also listed in the column headed "Commons Bills Rejected by the Senate," as well as Commons bills amended by the Senate without a final agreement with the House of Commons over those amendments before the end of the session. The data in Table 2 are complied from various tables prepared by the Library of Parliament: "Bills introduced in the House of Commons and amended in the Senate," accessed 28 February 2008 at http://www2.parl.gc.ca/Parlinfo/Compilations/HouseOfCommons/Legislation/HOCBillsAmandedBySenate.aspx?Language=E; "Pre-study of House of Commons bills by the Senate, 1971 to date, accessed 28 February 2008 at http://www2.parl.gc.ca/Parlinfo/compilations/HouseOfCommons/Legislation/PreStudyBySenate.aspx?Language=E; "House of Commons bills sent to the Senate that did not receive Royal Assent, 1867 to date," accessed 28 February 2008 at http://www2.parl.gc.ca/Parlinfo/compilations/HouseOfCommons/legislation/billsbyresults.aspx?Language=E&Parliament=&BillResult=03d93c58-f843-49b3-9653-84275c23f3fb

the Senate.[11] In these instances, the official record shows that the bills have passed through the Senate unaltered, when in actuality the Senate's suggested amendments may have already been incorporated. Senate leaders have decided in recent years to engage in pre-study on much fewer occasions. A decision to stop pre-study was reached in the late 1980s because the Liberal leaders in the Senate believed they had been simply helping the Conservative dominated House of Commons to improve its legislation; the reluctance to use pre-study continued even after the Liberals gained control of both houses in the late 1990s, because Senate leaders believed that the Senate was not getting public credit for the work it was doing.[12] With the decline in pre-study in the late 1990s and 2000s, there has also been a corresponding increase in the number of Commons bills amended and not receiving royal assent.

Thus, the information in table 2 should be read together with these caveats in order to understand the actions of the Senate in reviewing legislation passed by the House of Commons. As Ned Franks has written, the ineffective and largely idle "Imaginary Senate" caricatured in the media and much political discussion is quite different from the "Actual Senate" (Franks 2003, 182-85).

In reviewing Commons legislation, the Senate's role has also changed somewhat since Confederation. Rather than being a champion of business interests, Franks notes that much of the Senate's activities have arisen out of the Senate's efforts to defend broad consumer or citizen interests (ibid., 183). In a previous statistical analysis of the Senate's legislative activity between 1958 and 1988, the only robust variable to show strong correlations to the level of Senate amendments to Commons legislation was the size of the governing party's majority in the House of Commons; the Senate is more likely to amend Commons bills when the government has a large majority and can expedite measures through the House of Commons with dispatch (Heard 1991, 91). Some confrontations between the two houses definitely are ignited by pure partisan interests when different parties control the two houses; opposing camps clashed memorably during the GST debacle in 1990 and the battle over the Pearson airport contracts in the mid-1990s. However, the Senate's active treatment of Commons legislation in the late 1990s and early 2000s, for example, came at a time when Liberals controlled both houses.[13]

---

[11] The pre-study of bills is sometimes referred to as the Hayden Formula, after Senator Salter Hayden who began the practise in 1971 while chair of the Senate Committee on Banking, Trade and Commerce; Thomas 2003, 203-4.

[12] Once the Conservatives wrested control of the Senate with the appointment of eight extra s. 26 senators, they revived pre-study between 1991 and 1993, reviewing nine bills mainly dealing with banking and other financial industries. The only instance of pre-study since that time occurred with the *Anti-Terrorism Act* in 2001–2. (Library of Parliament, "Pre-study of House of Commons bills by the Senate, 1971 to date," accessed 28 February 2008 http://www2.parl.gc.ca/Parlinfo/compilations/HouseOfCommons/Legislation/PreStudyBySenate.aspx?Language=E

[13] The rivalry between the Chrétien and Martin camps may explain some Senate activity prior to Chrétien's resignation as Liberal leader.

Perhaps the most widely respected work of the Senate occurs in its committees, both when reviewing legislation in detail and when conducting investigations in specific issues of public policy. Proceedings in Senate committees are usually significantly less partisan than their Commons counterparts. The Senate also benefits greatly from the wide range of professional, business and political experience of its members. Of the 870 individuals who have served in the Senate since 1867, 3 former prime ministers and 22 former premiers have been appointed to the Senate, 305 have served as MPs, and 416 senators had been elected to municipal office.[14] The actual percentage of sitting senators who have previously held public office varies from time to time; for example, between 1970 and 2000 this percentage varied from 75 percent to 48 percent (Nagle 2003, 327-29). The Senate also has had significant numbers of individuals with previous careers in business, the professions, academe, and the arts. This rich range of pre-Senate experience is then further built upon by the often lengthy periods that senators serve. The result is an accumulation of institutional memory, collegiality and expertise.

Harnessing this experience in investigative studies by Senate committees has led to a number of impressive policy reports.[15] These policy investigations are one of the most widely credited aspects of the Senate's work (Franks 2003; Thomas 2003). Significant studies in recent decades have included reports on the banking and financial industries, the fisheries, national security, and health care. The so-called Kirby Report on Health Care, produced by the Standing Committee on Social Affairs, Science and Technology in 2003 is perhaps the most recent report

---

[14] While 875 appointments have been made to the Senate, 3 individuals refused to accept their appointments, and 2 individuals resigned and were reappointed for a total of 5 terms between them. Data compiled from the Library of Parliament: "Senators – 1867 to Date – By Name," http://www2.parl.gc.ca/parlinfo/lists/senators.aspx?Parliament= &Name=&Party=&Province=&Gender=&Current=False&PrimeMinister=&TermEnd= &Ministry=&Picture=False; "Senators – Prime Ministerial of Premiership Experience – 1867 to Date," http://www2.parl.gc.ca/Parlinfo/Lists/PrimeExperience.aspx?Language= E&Menu=SEN-Politic&Section=Senators&ChamberType=; "Senators – 1867 to Date – Previously Members of the House of Commons," http://www2.parl.gc.ca/Parlinfo/compilations/Senate/PreviouslyMembers.aspx; "Senators – Municipal Experience – 1867 to Date," http://www2.parl.gc.ca/Parlinfo/Lists/MunicipalExperience.aspx?Language= E&Section=b571082f-7b2d-4d6a-b30a-b6025a9cbb98&Chamber=b571082f-7b2d-4d6a-b30a-b6025a9cbb98&Parliament=0d5d5236-70f0-4a7e-8c96-68f985128af9&Name= &Party=&Province=&Gender=&MunicipalProvince=&Function= (All accessed 28 February 2008).

[15] The Library of Parliament has compiled a selective list of the more influential reports: "Major Legislative and Special Study Reports by Senate Committees, 1961–2003," available at http://www.parl.gc.ca/37/2/parlbus/commbus/Senate/com-E/pub-E/directorate-e.htm (Accessed 28 February 2008).

with a high public profile (Canada 2003). David Smith notes that this report was produced by a panel that contained experienced health care professionals, while the Romanow Commission on Health Care had to hire experts (Smith 2003a, 178). This influential Senate report was produced for a total cost of about $500,000 while the royal commission headed by Roy Romanow had a budget of $15 million (Canada 2006a). Senate committees have been actively engaged in studying policy matters, producing 91 separate policy reports since 2000; the House of Commons, with almost three times the membership of the Senate, issued 165 in the same time period.[16]

Another noted characteristic of the Senate is its role in representing non-territorial groups in Canadian society. Because prime ministers make deliberate choices for the individuals to be appointed to the Senate, they can ensure that certain population groups do get representation. By contrast, the social groups represented in the House of Commons are subject to the vagaries of constituency-level battles and the electoral system. As a result, women and aboriginal members form a higher proportion of the members in the Senate than in the House of Commons. Currently, women constitute 34 percent of the upper house and 21.1 percent in the lower house; First Nations members are 7.7 percent of the upper house and 1.3 percent of the lower.[17]

---

[16] These figures cover reports tabled by 6 June 2006 of committee investigations on substantive public policy issues, excluding consideration of bills, estimates, public accounts, auditor general's reports or matters of internal organization and processes of either House; multi-volume reports issued on the same day are counted as one report, but multi-volume reports issued on different dates are counted as separate reports. The data are calculated from: Library of Parliament, "Substantive Reports of Committees – House of Commons," http://www2.parl.gc.ca/Parlinfo/Compilations/parliament/SubstantiveReports .aspx?Menu=SEN-Procedure&Language=E&Parliament=&Chamber=de833414-75db-4dc9-8855-73b0faf3e5db&CommitteeType=&TextSearch=; Library of Parliament, "Substantive Reports of Committees – Senate," http://www2.parl.gc.ca/Parlinfo/Compilations/parliament/SubstantiveReports.aspx?Menu=SEN-Procedure&Language= E&Parliament=&Chamber=de833414-75db-4dc9-8855-73b0faf3e5db& CommitteeType=&TextSearch= (Accessed 28 February 2006).

[17] Data calculated from Parliament of Canada: "Women - Party Standings in the House of Commons," http://www2.parl.gc.ca/Parlinfo/lists/PartyStandings.aspx?Language= E&Section=03d93c58-f843-49b3-9653-84275c23f3fb&Gender=F; "Women – Party Standings in the Senate," http://www2.parl.gc.ca/Parlinfo/lists/PartyStandings.aspx? Language=E&Menu=SEN-Politic&Section=b571082f-7b2d-4d6a-b30a-b6025a9cbb98&Gender=F ; "Members of the House of Commons, Current List, Inuit, Metis or First Nations Origin," http://www2.parl.gc.ca/Parlinfo/Compilations/Parliament/ Aboriginal.aspx?Language=E&Menu=HOC-Bio&Role=MP&Current= True&NativeOrigin=; "Senators – Current List – Innuit, Metis or First Nations Origin," http://www.parl.gc.ca/information/about/people/key/Aboriginal.asp?Language= E&Hist=N&leg=S: (All accessed 28 February 2008).

INDEPENDENCE AND PARTISANSHIP IN THE SENATE

Two key, and interrelated, characteristics of the Senate emerge throughout its work on considering legislative proposals or conducting policy investigations. The first is the collection of experienced members who usually conduct their business with much less partisanship than is seen in the House of Commons. The second is a degree of relative independence from both Cabinet and the House of Commons. While the Senate is a partisan chamber and operates through organized party caucuses, there is a much higher degree of collegiality and much more of a tradition of independent voting among its members than among MPs. The independence of the Senate, collectively, is ultimately founded upon the individual independence of its members to vote as they think best, whether following the whip or not.

There is very little detailed research on senatorial voting patterns, so an analysis of each senator's voting record in the 37th and 38th Parliaments was undertaken. This analysis reveals a degree of independence from the caucus whip that would be the envy of most MPs. In the period covered by the lives of the two parliaments, 2001–5, senators voted in a total of 125 formal divisions and many showed a strong inclination to either record a formal abstention or even vote against the position of their caucus leaders.[18]

The record of these divisions is interesting from a number of perspectives, especially since they reveal a much higher average turnout than the caricatured "Imaginary Senate." The average turnout in recorded divisions over the life of the two Parliaments was 62 senators – about two-thirds of the membership, given vacancies and illnesses at any given moment. Of particular interest to this study are the 7732 votes cast by 122 members of the two main caucuses, as the test for independence used here is the degree to which members of organized caucuses are willing to cast their votes independently of their caucus.[19] It must be noted

---

[18] A formal abstention is counted in this study as voting independently of a caucus position, as it is a clear expression of a senator's desire not to directly support the party line. An abstention, of course, may be motivated either by a senator's belief that the matter is too controversial to be reduced to either a yea or nay vote; it may also indicate that senators wished to vote against their caucus position but did not want to directly confront it. In either case a senator would dissent, in the sense of thinking differently, from their caucus leaders.

[19] The creation of the new Conservative Party of Canada created a situation unique to the Senate. While the bulk of the members of the Progressive Conservative Party formally listed themselves as members of the new Conservative Party in time for the start of the 3rd Session of the 37th Parliament, a few members did not; three continued to sit as PC senators while a fourth sat as an independent. Two other senators appointed after the creation of the new Conservative Party chose to sit as PC senators; one switched later to sit as a Conservative in 2006. Another senator crossed the floor from the Liberal to Conservative

that these recorded divisions provide just a partial view of Senate activities, since formally recorded votes, the standing votes, are a minority of all the votes held in the Senate; many more votes are settled informally by a voice vote. But they are important in providing the only solid evidence of senators' individual voting record. Any dissent in formal divisions is all the more noteworthy since the fact a senator did not show solidarity with his or her caucus mates is recorded for posterity.

Perhaps the most remarkable statistic to emerge is that the majority of the formal divisions, 62.4 percent, involved one or more senators either voting against their caucus leader's position or registering an official abstention. The collective record of caucus members' voting also revealed a strong degree of independence, with 65.6 percent registering one or more formal abstentions or votes against their caucus position; conversely, only 34.4 percent always voted with their caucus leaders. These statistics only reflect the 2000–2005 period, and lifetime rates of dissent would likely show even fewer senators always voting faithfully with their caucus. In the 37th and 38th Parliaments, 156 formal abstentions were recorded for 55 (45.1 percent) senators, and 69 (56.5 percent) voted directly against their caucus position 291 times; 42 (33.6 percent) senators had done both. Almost a third had dissented by either means in over 5 percent of their recorded division votes, and, remarkably, 18 (14.8 percent) senators had recorded dissents in 15 percent or more of their votes; the most frequent dissenter did so in 37 percent of their recorded votes. Figure 1 provides an insight into the large numbers of senators who voted against their party position during the life of the 37th and 38th Parliaments, and the distribution of senators into groups according to their rate of dissention.

Clearly, party discipline is not as strong in the Senate as it is in the House of Commons.[20] The relatively greater independence of senators may be explained by several factors, including the fact that no Senate votes involve a test of confidence, senators do not need to seek re-election or re-appointment, and institutional cultural beliefs shared by senators support a degree of independence. In order to

---

caucus in early 2005. Ironically perhaps, this study excludes Independent and latter-day Progressive Conservatives from the analysis of independent voting, as they lacked the same formal caucus groupings as the two main parties. Five other senators died or resigned before casting a vote in any of the recorded divisions. The presence of seven Independent senators during the period of study should also be noted. The Independent senators were not a major factor during this period of study since their votes never tipped the balance between one caucus or another winning a vote. However, Independents did have a more important role during 1995 to 1997 when neither the Liberals nor Progressive Conservatives controlled an absolute majority of seats in the Senate.

[20] For discussions of party discipline in the Canadian House of Commons, see: David C. Docherty, *Mr. Smith Goes to Ottawa: Life in the House of Commons*, Vancouver, UBC Press, 1997, ch.7; C.E.S. Franks, *The Parliament of Canada*, Toronto: University of Toronto Press, 1987.

FIGURE 1: Rates of Senate Dissent, 2001–2005

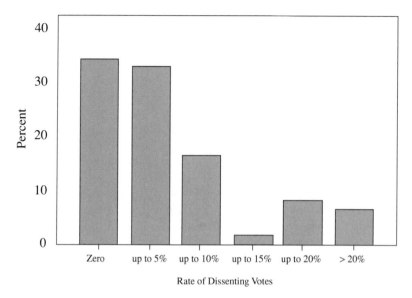

Note: Percent senators grouped by rate of dissent
Source: Senate Journals, 37th & 38th Parliaments

probe for some other explanatory variables for the levels of individual autonomy in the Senate, the rate of overall dissension and the proportion of votes cast directly against the caucus position were both tested for relationships with the specific party caucus a senator belonged to, how many votes the senator cast (as a surrogate for personal levels of experience and engagement), as well as whether the senators had been appointed to terms which had to expire within eight years (to test for the effects of Bill C-19).[21] The only correlation to meet statistical tests of significance was the dummy variable for belonging to the Liberal or Conservative caucus; the Pearson correlation of Liberal caucus membership with the rate of voting directly against the caucus position was a relatively feeble 0.198.[22] The greater propensity of Liberal senators to dissent may reflect the larger caucus size or some fallout from the party's leadership succession battles.[23]

---

[21] The only variable to pass tests of significance was a dummy variable for belonging to the Liberal caucus.

[22] 2-tailed significance: 0.030. The variables were tested for bivariate relationships and then in multiple regression models. In the latter test, the R^2 value was a low 0.057, and the Liberal dummy variable scored an adjusted Beta score of 0.202 and significance or 0.079 with rates of directly voting against the caucus as the dependent variable.

[23] In the period studied, there are 86 senators who sat with the Liberals and 36 with the Conservatives (including one senator who crossed the floor).

A more rounded picture of the Senate emerges from a review of its legislative role, the policy reports of its committees, and the frequency with which many senators vote differently from their caucus leaders. The relative independence of the Senate emerges as an essential characteristic that pervades much of its work. Collective independence is seen in the chamber's moves to substantively amend, reject, or informally bury government legislation that has already passed the House of the Commons. This collective independence may depend on several factors: if different parties control the two houses; if members of the government caucus in the Senate break ranks and support opposition motions to amend or reject bills from the House of Commons; and, theoretically at least, if the governing party's Senate caucus decide to take a different collective position than that desired by the party leadership or their Commons caucus mates. It has been noted that the Senate is most active in times of large government majorities in the House of Commons, regardless of the partisan balance in the Senate. In the end, the collective independence of the Senate depends upon the individual independence of its members, particularly in the governing party, to decide to vote against either their party leaders' positions or those endorsed by a majority in the House.

EFFECTS OF BILL C-19

While the most immediate effect of Bill C-19 is to limit new senators' appointments to a maximum of eight years, the bill will also end mandatory retirement at age 75 for future appointees. The effects of Bill C-19 will now be examined to see how they conflict with the *Upper House Reference*, and for ways in which the bill may be strengthened to better serve the Senate.

Mandatory Retirement

Currently all senators must retire when they turn 75 years old but, as PCO official Matthew King told the Special Committee on Senate Reform, Bill S-4 "effectively removes the requirement" that new senators must retire at 75 if their eight-year term of office has not been completed (Special Senate Committee 2006). One effect of the new section 29 is that new senators can be appointed at any age older than the floor level of 30 years imposed by section 23(1) of the *Constitution Act, 1867*; they could theoretically be appointed at the age of 90. Perhaps this was done as part of a trend in some circles towards ending mandatory retirement. It is ironic that Bill C-19 is intended to breathe new life into the Senate, but it abolishes the very reform of the Senate that did manage to achieve meaningful change in that regard.

The proposed eight year limit may have the effect of reinforcing the unfortunate trend in the last fifteen years of appointing older and older senators. The average age of new senators appointed since 1990 is 60, while the average during the 1970s and 1980s was 55. Shorter-term Senate appointments may end up being accepted by older individuals, as those in their fifties might view an eight-year

Senate appointment as a damaging interruption to their career rather than the career-capping appointment it should perhaps be.

It is true that life expectancy rates continue to lengthen as people live longer and remain in better health for longer than they did in decades past. For example, in 1950–52, the average life expectancy at birth was 66 years for men and 71 for women. However, by 2002 the average life expectancy at birth was 77 years for men and 82 for women (St-Arnaud, Neaudet and Tully 2005, 43). Moreover, men aged 65 in 2003 could expect to live another 17.4 years on average, while women could enjoy another 20.8 years (Statistics Canada 2003). These facts are relevant fodder in arguments about the most common age of mandatory retirement in Canada, at 65.

However, the removal of any upper age limits from new Senate appointees does raise concern about the effect of death rates and late-life infirmity on the Senate's effectiveness as an institution. The reality of average life expectancy numbers is that a large portion of the population is already dead by that age, while many others suffer debilitating infirmities and illnesses. The actual mortality rates among senators may underline the wisdom in maintaining the mandatory retirement age. Of the 276 senators appointed since the 75 year retirement age became mandatory in 1965, 91 are still in office and 101 have died at an average age of 76; and 65 of those deaths occurred at or before age 80. Since 1965, 22.5 percent of individuals appointed to the Senate have died in office before they reached 75. Appointment of senators whose eight-year term stretches into their late seventies or eighties will lead to even shorter terms as some of those die before their term expires. Instead of breathing new life into the Senate, new eight-year terms without retirement at 75 have the potential to increase absenteeism due to late-life illness and turnover due to death.

Effects of Seniority on Limited-Term Senatorial Careers

It is important to consider how the appointment of only limited-term senators in the future would have an impact on the work of the Senate and the degree to which these limited term senators are integrated into the Senate's work along with those current members who will continue to hold office until age 75. Unfortunately there has been little detailed study of many aspects of the internal processes of the Senate to reveal the existence and effects of seniority on the careers of senators. There is a wide-spread consensus in the academic literature looking at elected legislatures that there is a rookie or novice period for most new members that lasts several years. Academic writers generally argue that MPs become most effective only in their second term (Docherty 1997).[24]

---

[24] Note that Docherty's survey of MPs found that their own estimation of their learning period is much shorter, about a year. There may be a difference, however, in an academic's view of full effectiveness, and the MPs view of "learning the ropes," and those two notions could involve quite different lengths of time.

An examination of the current members of the Senate reveals some clear patterns of a seniority system, however informal, which may have an impact on the appointment and performance of limited-term senators in the future. In early 2008, 39 of the 91 sitting senators had less than 8 full years of service.[25] Of these less experienced senators, 26 (66.7 percent) never held a formal position other than being members of committees. For the purposes of this study, "formal position" covers those for which extra remuneration is provided.[26] Senators who have not held a formal position have only participated as ordinary members of Senate committees. The progressive incorporation of new senators into leadership positions is clearly shown in the following table.

TABLE 3: Senators' Leadership Involvement by Years of Service

Years of Service	% Have Never Held Office	% Have Held Office	% Currently Holding Office
0-4 (N=19)	68.4	31.6	26.3
5-8 (N=20)	65.0	35.0	35.0
8-12 (N=12)	33.3	66.7	41.7
12+ (N=40)	7.5	92.5	60.0

Source: Library of Parliament[27]

Table 3 shows clear evidence of a seniority system at work, which favours senators who have served more than eight years. While there is a steady integration of senators into leadership positions during their first eight years in office, only about a third of those who have served between five and eight years have ever held a leadership position. There is a dramatic shift after eight years of service which demonstrates that leadership positions are disproportionately held by the most senior senators. Indeed, those with more than 12 years of service occupy more than 58 per cent of current offices.

Based on the evidence of informal seniority dynamics in the Senate, most senators appointed to eight year terms would not be well integrated into the life of the Senate, particularly into leadership positions. Because of the retirement schedule of current senators, new limited-term senators may continue to play a less involved role in the Senate for some time to come. It will take until 2014 for half of

---

[25] As of 29 February 2008.

[26] In addition to Cabinet ministers, this list includes the Speaker, the Speaker Pro Tempore, the caucus leaders, deputy leaders, and whips, as well the chairs and deputy-chairs of Senate or join committees.

[27] These data were calculated from the individual biographies of senators, as of February 29, 2008, available from: "Senators – 1867 to date – by name," accessed 9 September 2006 at http://www.parl.gc.ca/information/about/people/Senate/SenIdx.asp?Language=E&Hist=Y

the current senators to have been appointed to eight year terms.[28] By this time, the other half of the Senate would have an average of over 14 years of service and eventually retire with an average 22 years of service.

If senators were appointed to a limited term of longer duration, perhaps 12 years, they would be much more thoroughly integrated. A twelve-year term would have the advantage of covering the life of three parliaments under the new reform legislation, limiting the life of a Parliament to four years, and it is roughly the average Senate term held since 1867. David Smith has also noted that a 12-year term is long enough to permit the Senate to continue to act as an effective repository of experience in both parliamentary process and specific areas of public policy; such experience is particularly needed when contrasted with the short careers of many members of the House of Common (Smith 2003b, 259).

Effects on Senate Independence of Eight-Year Terms

Bill C-19 could well weaken the independence of the Senate if an eight-year term were not sufficient for new appointees to absorb the institution's cultural beliefs in independence, particularly the ethos of independent voting. The possible restriction of the independence of individual senators would, if widespread, necessarily mean a decline in the relative independence of the Senate, collectively as an institution.

In order to assess the potential impact of shorter terms in office, data from all the recorded divisions in the 37th and 38th parliaments of 2001–5 were analyzed to see if there were discernable differences between voting patterns for those senators who were appointed within eight years of mandatory retirement and those who were appointed to potentially longer terms.[29] The aim with this analysis is to test the hypothesis that individual senators are more likely to develop a sense of

---

[28] The timing may be advanced somewhat because of deaths prior to retirement.

[29] None of the tables survived tests of significance for the distribution of results among the cells of the table. The lack of statistically significant relationship in these tables was also borne out when regression analysis was used to test the length of service and rates of dissent; the length of potential term was tested against the percentage of abstentions, votes cast against caucus, and total dissenting votes; tests against dummy variables for terms of less or longer than eight years was also conducted. Several caveats must be made about extrapolating from the results of this study into predictions of future behaviour: the votes may be a result of particular partisan dynamics in play during the period studied; this period of analysis only covers a small portion of the careers of long-term senators; independence may be a function of age, which was not tested for; and, the fact that short-term senators in 2001–5 did not vote in remarkably different patterns from their longer-term colleagues does not mean that future short-term senators will act the same. A more rigorous analysis would also have been possible if the actual length of a senator's service at the time of each vote cast could have been used as a variable, rather than testing for the senators; potential term in office.

personal autonomy if they know they have a secure, long-term tenure in office. This data set provides an admittedly limited snapshot of senatorial behaviour from only this period, but it is useful in providing some concrete evidence of how individual senators behave.

Table 4 shows how senators with different lengths of term at the time of their appointment fit into categories based on the rate at which they recorded formal votes directly against the position of their caucus leaders.

TABLE 4: Senators' Rate of Votes against Caucus by Length of Potential Term

	Maximum Term at Appointment		
% Votes Directly Against Caucus	*Up to 8 Years*	*More than 8 Years*	*Total*
Zero	6	47	53
up to 5	6	37	43
up to 10	2	13	15
up to 15	1	4	5
up to 20	0	4	4
> 20	0	2	2
Total number of senators	15	107	122

Several interesting points emerge from this table. Even senators appointed to shorter terms demonstrate a clear willingness to vote against their caucus; more than half voted against their caucus positions at least once. There is little difference between the two groups in the proportion of those who faithfully supported their caucus in all votes. However, the senators appointed to a longer term include a small group who dissented very much more frequently than any of the short-term senators.

Senators can also dissent from their caucus positions by recording a formal abstention, an option that does not exist in the House of Commons. Interestingly, abstentions were far less popular than formal votes opposing the caucus position; at an intuitive level, one might have expected abstentions to be more popular. Table 5 does reveal that longer-term senators were more likely to abstain than their shorter-term colleagues: note that one senator with a term of less than eight years abstained 33 percent of the time; that person had only participated in three recorded votes in the period of time studied.

When abstentions are added together with votes cast directly against the caucus position, a more complete view of a senator's rate of public dissent emerges. Table 6 shows a significant independence of mind among all senators, as only about a third of either group had never abstained or opposed their caucus. While there are more long-term senators in absolute numbers who are frequent dissenters, the difference is not remarkable when considering the proportions involved.

The results of this analysis show that, during the period of the study, short-term senators appear to have readily acquired the cultural beliefs in personal autonomy

TABLE 5: Senators' Rate of Abstentions by Length of Potential Term

	Maximum Term at Appointment		
Abstentions as % of Votes	*Up to 8 Years*	*More than 8 Years*	*Total*
Zero	9	58	67
up to 5%	3	36	39
up to 10%	2	8	10
up to 15%	0	1	1
up to 20%	0	4	4
> 20%	1	0	1
Total number of senators	15	107	122

TABLE 6: Senators' Rate of All Dissenting Votes by Length of Potential Term

	Maximum Term at Appointment		
Rate of All Dissenting Votes (%)	*Up to 8 Years*	*More than 8 Years*	*Total*
Zero	5	37	42
up to 5	5	35	40
up to 10	2	18	20
up to 15	0	2	2
up to 20	2	8	10
> 20	1	7	8
Total number of senators	15	107	122

and independent voting held by their more senior colleagues. While some longer-term senators were clearly more likely to directly oppose their caucus, most of their more junior colleagues were also prepared to dissent publicly in significant numbers. As a result, the move to adopt shorter periods of tenure for future senator may only slightly weaken rather than threaten the Senate's independence.

CONCLUDING ASSESSMENT OF BILL C-19

These discussions have provided a variety of perspectives on Bill C-19. It is clear that there would be significant changes felt in the Senate with its passage. There are two principal changes the bill would make: new appointees would be limited to an eight year term, and future appointees would not have to retire at age 75.

The removal of the mandatory retirement age may not bring sufficient consequences to change any fundamental elements of the Senate, but it does open the door to an even greater number of deaths and absences due to illness. The statistics on the death rate of senators in the last 40 years show that one out of five senators died before reaching the retirement age of 75 and almost two thirds died by age 80. Consequently, the abolition of mandatory retirement may well undermine the efficiency of the Senate. Furthermore, the abolition of mandatory retirement may result in a higher average age among new appointees than at present, which undermines one long-standing motivation of senate reform, to bring more vitality into the Senate.

On the more important aspect of senatorial independence, shorter terms for senators may not have a significant impact. The evidence from the voting patterns by individual senators reveals that the traditional propensity of dissenting from caucus positions has been readily acquired by senators in their first years in the chamber. While there was a small group of very frequent dissenters among the longest serving senators, those appointed to shorter terms still evidenced a strong inclination to either abstain or to vote directly against their caucus leaders.

The prospect of senators serving eight-year terms also poses substantial problems when considered in the light of the Senate's informal seniority system. The study of the involvement in leadership positions by senators of different lengths of existing service reveals that there is indeed an informal seniority system. The high proportion of relatively new senators who have never held an official position in the Senate reflects an institutional culture that values the accumulation of experience. The Senate's important committee work, both in legislative review and policy investigations, is undoubtedly enhanced by the weight of experience. In this respect, the eight-year term limits in Bill C-19 may not immediately threaten essential aspects of the Senate, but it could well foster a division between future short-term senators and those with longer terms who will likely continue to hold most of the leadership positions.

At some point, as well, the growing body of relatively inexperienced, short-term senators will weaken the Senate's functions of legislative review and policy development, which have been largely built on the experience of many long-term senators. An amendment to Bill C-19 lengthening the term of appointment would not run afoul of Prime Minister Harper's main objection that he voiced to the Special Committee on Senate Reform: "A government can be flexible on accepting amendment to the details ... to adopt a six year term or an eight year term or a nine year term. The key point is this: We are seeking limited, fixed terms of office, not decades based on antiquated criteria of age" (Canada 2006b). However, the 15-year term that the Senate decided to insert into the former Bill S-4 may simply be too long to be politically palatable. A longer term of office than the eight years proposed, such as 12 years, would allow future senators enough time to gain valuable experience, become fully integrated into the work of the Senate, and continue the institution's cultural traditions of relative independence.

REFERENCES

Ajzenstat, J. 2003. "Bicamerlism and Canada's Founders: The Origins of the Canadian Senate," in *Protecting Canadian Democracy: The Senate You Never Knew*, ed. S. Joyal. Montreal and Kingston: McGill-Queen's University Press.

Ajzenstat, J. 2006. "Origins of the Senate," *Dialogues*, 2(Summer): 5-6.

Campbell, C. 1978. *The Canadian Senate: The Lobby from Within*. Toronto: Macmillan.

Canada. 1982. Parliament of Canada. *Report of the Special Joint Committee on a Renewed Canada*. Ottawa: Queen's Printer.

— 1984. Parliament of Canada, *Report of the Special Joint Committee on Senate Reform*. Ottawa: Queen's Printer.

— 1996. Statutes, c.1. Accessed 28 February 2008 at http://laws.justice.gc.ca/en/ShowTdm/ cs/C-36.7///en

— 2000. Statutes, c.26. Accessed 28 February 2008 at http://laws.justice.gc.ca/en/c-31.8/ text.html

— 2003. "Reforming Health Protection and Promotion in Canada: Time to Act." Senate Standing Social Affairs, Science and Technology. 19 June. Accessed online 28 February 2008 at http://www.parl.gc.ca/37/2/parlbus/commbus/Senate/com-e/soci-e/rep-e/ repfinnov03-e.htm

— 2006a. 30 *Debates of the Senate*, 6 October 6. Accessed online 28 February 2008 at http://www.parl.gc.ca/common/..%5C39%5C1%5Cparlbus%5Cchambus%5Csenate/ deb-E/035db_2006-10-05-e.htm?Language=E&Parl=39&Ses=1

— 2006b. Proceedings of the Special Senate Committee on Senate Reform. 7 September. Accessed online 28 February 2008 at http://www.parl.gc.ca/39/1/parlbus/commbus/ senate/Com-e/refo-e/02cv-e.htm?Language=E&Parl=39&Ses= 1&comm_id=599

— 2007. Statutes, c.10. *An Act to Amend the Canada Elections Act*. Accessed 28 February 2008 at http://laws.justice.gc.ca/en/showdoc/an/2007_10////en?page=1

Docherty, D. 1997. *Mr Smith Goes to Ottawa: Life in the House of Commons*, Vancouver: UBC Press, 1997.

Franks, C.E.S. 2003. "The Canadian Senate in Modern Times," in *Protecting Canadian Democracy: The Senate You Never Knew*, ed. S. Joyal. Montreal and Kingston: McGill-Queen's University Press.

Heard, A. 1991. *Canadian Constitutional Conventions: The Marriage of Law and Politics*, Toronto: Oxford University Press, pp.89-98.

Joyal, S. 2003. *Protecting Canadian Democracy: The Senate You Never Knew*. Montreal and Kingston: McGill-Queen's University Press.

Library of Parliament. nd. "Senators – 1867 to date – by name," Accessed 28 February 2008 at http://www2.parl.gc.ca/parlinfo/lists/senators.aspx?Parliament=&Name= &Party=&Province=&Gender=&Current=False&PrimeMinister=&TermEnd= &Ministry=&Picture=Fale

Nagle, J. 2003. "Database and Charts on the Composition of the Senate and House of Commons," in *Protecting Canadian Democracy: The Senate You Never Knew*, ed. S. Joyal. Montreal and Kingston: McGill-Queen's University Press.

Reference re: Authority of Parliament in Relation to the Upper House, [1980] 1 S.C.R. 54

Smith, D. 2003a. *The Canadian Senate in Bicameral Perspective*. Toronto: University of Toronto Press.

Smith, D. 2003b "The Improvement of the Senate by Nonconstitutional Means," in *Protecting Canadian Democracy: The Senate You Never Knew*, ed. S. Joyal. Montreal and Kingston: McGill-Queen's University Press.

Special Senate Committee. 2006. Unedited, verbatim transcripts of the proceedings of the Special Senate Committee on Senate Reform, 7 September.

St-Arnaud, J., M.P. Neaudet and P. Tully. 2005. "Life Expectancy," *Health Reports*, Ottawa: Statisics Canada. Vol.17, No.1, Catalogue number 82-003-XPE, 43-47.

Statistics Canada. 2003. "Life expectancy – abridged life table by sex and geography – At age 65," Accessed online 28 February 2008 at http://www.statcan.ca/english/freepub/84F0211XIE/2003000/t028_en.htm?

Thomas, P.G. 2003. "Comparing the Lawmaking Roles of the Senate and House of Commons," in *Protecting Canadian Democracy: The Senate You Never Knew*, ed. S. Joyal. Montreal and Kingston: McGill-Queen's University Press.

Weiler, P.G. 1979. "Confederation Discontents and Constitutional Reform: The Case of the Second Chamber," *University of Toronto Law Journal* 29(3): 253-283.

12

THE CONSTITUTIONALITY OF BILL C-20

Vincent Pouliot

L'auteur nous suggère d'appuyer le projet de loi C-20 de réformer le Sénat car ce projet de loi offre les moyens de concilier sur le plan légal les intérêts particuliers des provinces au sein du gouvernement dans notre fédération. Il démontre de quelle manière notre constitution fournit au Sénat la même nature représentative qu'à la Chambre des communes afin de pouvoir concilier les intérêts des provinces, alors que le projet de loi C-20 n'assure pas au sénat cette même nature représentative. Finalement, il propose certaines modifications au projet de loi afin de corriger ce problème.

Bill C-20 attempts to implement a practice (a consultation of electors) in the appointment of our senators.

This practice is either constitutional or it is unconstitutional. Either it implements the letter of the law and the legislative intent of the Constitution or it contradicts it.

If it implements the Constitution, it could rightly be said to be establishing a constitutional convention regarding the appointment of senators. If it contradicts the Constitution, it could rightly be said to be a constitutional amendment requiring approval in accordance with the provisions of our constitutional law.

Should we care about the constitutionality of Bill C-20? My answer is an unequivocal yes. Bill C-20 is meant to reform the representative and democratic character of the Senate. It is meant to affect the political structure, the constitutional balance of powers and the democratic process, that is, the constitutional framework through which the people govern themselves in Canada. In proposing to reform the Senate, the government has given Canadians an opportunity to renew Canadian federalism. We want to do it right.

THE RESPONSIBLE GOVERNMENT OF CANADA

Section 18 of the *Constitution Act, 1867* explains that the source of the powers and privileges of both the Senate and the House of Commons is the British House of Commons. On 22 May 1868, an Act of Parliament, still in force today, confirmed that both houses are entitled to the same powers and privileges as those belonging to the British House of Commons in 1867. This confirms that, contrary to the political structure of the British model of parliament providing for the legislative union of the United Kingdom, both houses of Canada's federal Parliament were meant to represent the wishes and interests of the people.

Section 22 provides that senators shall represent the provinces in Parliament. Section 23 states that, among other qualifications, a senator must reside in the province for which he or she is appointed. Section 32 provides that the governor general shall fill the vacancies that occur in the Senate by fit and qualified persons.

The 14th of the Quebec Resolutions of 1864 (on which the *Constitution Act, 1867*, is based) states that the Crown shall appoint the members of the upper house ... "so that all political parties may as nearly as possible be fairly represented." It is clear that the Fathers of Confederation intended that the provincial political parties be fairly represented in the Senate.

What is not clear is whether they meant to establish this as the principle underlying the representative character of the Senate, whether it was meant to guarantee only the representative character of the first Senate or whether it was to guarantee the representative character of the Senate until each province chose how it wished to be represented.

One must admit, however, that if all provincial political parties were proportionally represented in the Senate, then the provincial interests of the people, the people in their provincial political capacity or, put more simply, the provinces, would be truly represented in Parliament.

Because Canada is a federation of provinces, the people's political will regarding how they wish to govern themselves is divided. Under the division of powers between Parliament and the provincial legislatures that is set out in the Constitution, if this political will concerns purely local issues, the provinces are vested with the exclusive jurisdiction to govern the matter; otherwise the matter falls under federal jurisdiction. Thus, in general, the jurisdiction of the federal government over public matters is a function of them not being of a purely local nature.

Despite all this, it is thought that the Fathers of Confederation must have intended that the courts protect our local interests because, being appointed rather than elected, the senators cannot legitimately do so within the institution created for this purpose by our Constitution!

Permit me to suggest that the appointment for life of senators was meant to ensure the co-ordinate authority of the Senate by eliminating the possibility that the governor general could revoke the appointment if displeased.

The representative character of the Senate was ensured by section 30 specifically permitting a senator to resign. Within the context of the times, it was understood that if a senator was made to feel that he no longer represented the wishes and interests of the authority to whom he owed his appointment, honour would oblige him to resign. Today, the political party, when selecting their delegate, would require their choice of senator to sign an undated resignation guaranteeing he or she honours their confidence, and thus has the authority to act on their behalf and on behalf of their constituents.

Furthermore, the appointment of senators is essential to ensure a different quality of person in the Senate, one who has proven his or her ability in "sober second thought." Given the real estate or wealth qualification of some $2 million in today's terms, it is likely that our senators would also possess the quality of knowing from whence comes the "government's money."

BILL C-20

Bill C-20 enables citizens within a province to indicate, from within a "list of nominees," who they would prefer to be appointed senator. Section 16(1) charges the chief electoral officer (CEO) with confirming a prospective nominee to be included in the "list of nominees." It assumes the CEO will confirm the nominee if he or she fulfils the requirements set out in the bill. It also assumes that the prime minister of Canada will advise the governor general to appoint those persons the people prefer.

Bill C-20 does not require a nominee to reside within the province being consulted. Nowhere does it state that the nominee, if appointed senator, would represent a province in the Senate.

However, section 19(1) requires the prospective nominee to be endorsed by the political party the nominee upholds in the consultation. It does not require that this political party be provincial in nature, representing the provincial interests of the Canadian citizens living in the province being consulted. It does not permit the provinces to determine for themselves the practice by which they would select and authorize their representatives to act on their behalf in the Senate.

CONCLUSION

It would seem that the constitutionality of Bill C-20 depends on how the CEO decides to apply the law.

This is contrary to the rule of law. According to A.V. Dicey (1959, 202), the rule of law "means the absolute supremacy or predominance of regular law as opposed to the influence of arbitrary power, and excludes the existence of arbitrariness, of prerogative, or even of wide discretionary authority on the part of the government. (...) Englishmen are ruled by the law and by the law alone."

The Supreme Court of Canada explains that "[t]he principles of constitutionalism and the rule of law lie at the root of our system of government. ... At its most basic level, the rule of law ... provides a shield for individuals from arbitrary state action" ([1998] 2 SCR para. 70).

RECOMMENDATIONS

To ensure the constitutionality of Bill C-20, it should be amended
- to charge the chief electoral officer to ensure the "nominees" qualify to be senator as set out by section 23 of the *Constitution Act*;
- to change the phrase "political party" to read "provincial political party;"

- to permit the provinces to determine otherwise how they wish to be represented in the Senate.

REFERENCES

Dicey, A.V. 1959. *Introduction to the study of the Law of the Constitution, 10ᵗʰ edition*. London: Macmillan Press Ltd.

Reference re: Secession of Quebec, [1998] 2 S.C.R. 217.

13

BILL C-20'S POPULIST MODEL OF CAMPAIGN FINANCE FOR SENATE ELECTIONS: THE FIRST STEP AWAY FROM CANADA'S EGALITARIAN REGIME?

Peter Aucoin

Le projet de loi C-20 apporte de grands changements au régime de campagne de financement développé par les Canadiens dans le cadre des élections fédérales. Le régime actuel est plus juste envers la compétition car il limite la somme d'argent que les candidats et les partis politiques peuvent dépenser lors d'une campagne électorale, et il lui donne accès aux fonds publics. Ce n'est pas le cas avec le projet de loi C-20. Il permet aux candidats de dépenser autant d'argent qu'ils peuvent se le permettre, alors que le régime de Sénat proposé continue d'imposer des limites aux contributions lors des campagnes. Sous le projet de loi C-20, les candidats aux élections à la Chambre des communes peuvent également se présenter à des élections au Sénat. Si des élections avaient lieu en même temps aux deux chambres, le régime du Sénat aurait un effet négatif car il serait plus difficile de faire respecter les limites imposées à la Chambre des communes.

Canada's federal campaign finance regime has been characterized as egalitarian because its primary objective is to secure fairness in the electoral process between the contestants – candidates and political parties – and those who actively support them by engaging in activities that require the expenditure of money – so-called "third parties." The regime seeks to establish a level playing field. It does so by providing a floor of public financial support (partial reimbursement of election expenses for candidates and political parties; annual grants for political parties; tax credits for contributions to candidates and political parties; free time broadcasts for political parties) and a ceiling on contributions (to candidates and political parties) and campaign spending (by candidates, political parties, and third parties). The regime is buttressed by the requirements of disclosure on contributions and spending. And, only individual citizens may contribute money to candidates and political parties.

A contrasting model is the libertarian model in which freedom to do as one pleases with one's money constitutes the primary value. Under this model, most, if not all, of the egalitarian model's provisions disappear. This is especially the case with spending limits on candidates, political parties or anyone else. These limits infringe on an individual's right to express one's views publicly through those advertising media that impose a price for such expression or, more generally, to expend monies in campaigning in an election. The American system is a case of the libertarian model in regard to spending limits: there are none, and the Supreme Court has declared them unconstitutional (unless voluntarily accepted to gain access to public funding). Contribution limits exist in the US and have been accepted by the Court but not to promote fairness. The Court has declared them a legitimate device to diminish the risk of corruption that can emanate from undue influence on elected officials by those who otherwise could be persuaded or would want to make financially significant campaign contributions. Contributions limits, in other words, are not justified on the ground that they advance fairness in the political process. Hardcore libertarians, it should be noted, are not inclined to accept these contribution limits; at the outer edges of this position, even disclosure laws are rejected.

The Canadian regime has been relatively effective in restricting the significance of spending money in elections, and thus the impact of money in the political process generally. Campaign spending does matter, but this reality has not ruled out a high degree of competition between those candidates and political parties with some measure of public support. Participation, in short, is not financially prohibitive. By contrast, the American regime does not try to restrict the significance of spending money in elections and, as one would expect, spending is critical in American election campaigns, with a steady escalation in campaign spending, combined with a low level of competition in Congressional elections. Equally important, contribution limits in American election law have not been able to arrest the extent to which contributors regard their contributions to candidates and political parties, but especially the former, as earning them the right of influence with those they finance. The shortcomings in the American contribution limits derive primarily from the absence of *spending* limits. With candidates requiring (increasingly) large sums of money to be competitive, or to discourage serious competition before campaigns begin, the incentive is to do whatever can be achieved within the letter of the law, at a minimum, to obtain the necessary funding. The result, unintended as it may be, is a byzantine regulatory scheme with so many loopholes as to render impossible any semblance of reasonable control of financial contributions to candidates. Those who want to contribute sufficiently to be able to exert an influence on candidates are usually able to do so. Efforts to reform the campaign finance regime, of which there is a constant flow, are essentially undermined by the fact that spending limits are constitutionally off limits. To the extent that money is required by candidates to be competitive it is supplied, at least to the incumbents and those challengers who appear heading for election.

Bill C-20 proposes to change fundamentally the foundation of the Canadian regime by having no spending limits on candidates for Senate election campaigns and no direct public funding for them. By having no spending limits, Bill C-20 would create loopholes that would diminish, if not eliminate altogether, the effectiveness of the spending limits on candidates for election to the House of Commons and on their political parties if elections for the Senate and the House of Commons take place at the same time.[1] If no further changes occurred in the near future, the new Canadian regime – with different campaign finance provisions for House of Commons and Senate elections – would constitute a hybrid of the egalitarian and the libertarian models. This hybrid can be labelled a populist model.

While populism as a political ideology comes in various forms, three characteristics tend to be common. The first is an anti-elite disposition: an opposition on behalf of "ordinary" or "average" citizens against those who hold power in financial and government centres. Second, there is a dislike of political parties as the instruments of partisan politics where partisanship is perceived as a conspiracy by a cartel of political elites to restrict access to the elected offices of government, and thus to the spoils of power, by dividing the political community into competing factions that they command and control for their own benefit. These first two characteristics are clearly negative in their orientation, a negativity fuelled by the extent to which populists find themselves in opposition to those in power. The third, one that can be articulated by populists both in opposition and in power, is expressed in more positive terms. This is the preference for majoritarianism, the view that the great bulk of common folk or ordinary citizens share a homogeneous set of political values, opinions and preferences and that this popular will best finds expression when elites or other minorities, especially "special interest groups," are unable to undermine the preference of the majority by controlling or manipulating the political process to secure their minority interests and opinions. This majoritarian view assumes that there is no need to worry about fairness in political processes: the popular will is expressed by the majority of ordinary citizens. Every one is equal, equally free to have their say, and that is sufficient.

Bill C-20 is constructed in response to this populist ideology. First, its anti-elitism is expressed in contribution limits that restrict contributions to individuals and at a relatively modest amount ($1,000). Corporations and unions are thereby not allowed to contribute money at all. Elites, it is assumed, are thereby constrained. Second, political parties are also constrained. They may participate but only as one of many potential participating organizations; indeed, since a political party may participate only by registering as a "third party," they have no greater status than a single individual citizen who may likewise register as a "third party."

---

[1] If Senate elections took place at the same time as provincial/territorial elections – the second option in Bill C-20 – the federal regime would have the potential to undermine those provincial regimes where spending limits are an important element of their campaign finance regime. It could also undermine the contribution limits in provincial regimes.

Third, the absence of spending limits and public funding is predicated on the assumption that ordinary citizens, freed from domination by wealthy elites and partisan factions, are equal in all important respects, thus denying that money is a source of inequality in politics that can be offset only by restrictions on the freedom to use money.

Populism in opposition can provide a powerful critique of the economic disparities and political inequalities that exist in a political system, even if the critique invariably lacks coherence and consistency. On the other hand, when populists are elected, at least in political systems like Canada and the United States, their populism either loses its political dynamic or, whatever their protestations to the contrary, becomes mere partisanship. The former was the fate of the Progressives in the 1920s, because those elected refused to function as other than independents and thus not as a political-party formation in the legislature. The experience of the Reform Party, once it became a parliamentary party in the House of Commons and now as the Reform faction in the new Conservative Party, that from 2006 is also the governing party, provides an example of the latter. Populist partisans in power have not shown themselves to be any different than partisans of other stripes: they pursue their partisan-political interests as a political party in maintaining power. Proposing campaign finance laws that advance these interests is thus to be expected. Bill C-20 is an example. A populist campaign finance law for a populist party.

The contribution limits in Bill C-20 clearly disadvantage the Liberal opposition, given the recent fund-raising practices of the Liberals compared to the Conservatives. In this regard, what many would view as a positive measure to reduce the influence of the wealthy is also a convenient advantage to the Conservatives. That does not diminish its merits, of course. The measure extends what the Liberals under Jean Chrétien started with his amendments to limit contributions by source and amount in 2004. The Liberals, accordingly, will now simply have to adapt, as their Liberal counterparts were required to do in Quebec when low contribution limits restricted to individuals were introduced there many years ago.

The treatment of political parties as equivalent to any other political or social group is perhaps merely symbolic, a genuflection to the anti-political-party rhetoric of the populists, especially as expressed in their attack on the third-party spending limits as a measure to give preferential treatment to political parties over other social groups. For populists, the decision by the Supreme Court of Canada to uphold the constitutionality of spending limits as advancing fairness (against several decisions by Alberta courts and one British Columbia court), merely demonstrated that the SCC itself was an integral part of the elite cabal standing against the views of the majority of ordinary citizens. Populists view what the law labels "third parties" as non-partisan citizen coalitions and argue against any regulation of them in election campaigns. The fact that these groups seek the election or the defeat of particular candidates, who also almost always are the candidates of political parties, is ignored, denied, or disregarded as relevant.

Bill C-20 represents a symbolic rejection of political parties as the primary political organizations in elections in parliamentary systems, where the constitutional dynamic assumes party formations in the legislature as the basis of stable but responsive responsible governments. In this sense, the bill might be regarded as little other than an irritant to political parties. However, in parliamentary systems political parties govern and any measure that further diminishes the role of political parties in governance exacerbates an existing defect in Canadian governance. This is the increasing personalization of political parties by party leaders. This phenomenon is one factor in an increasing concentration of power in the office of the prime minister in Westminster systems. The result is the reduced effectiveness of the system of cabinet government, the collective-executive structure that is meant to constitute an important check on a prime minister's imperial ambitions to exercise power unilaterally. In practice, the capacity of the Cabinet to check the prime minister is a function of the capacity of the collective party leadership to constrain the prime minister as party leader. In Canada, it may be that this issue is largely academic because party leaders in Canada's two governing parties no longer are subject to the will of their party caucus, as is still the case in some of the governing parties in other Westminster systems where prime ministers are, on occasion, reined in by the caucus (as happened with the Conservative caucus dismissal of Margaret Thatcher in Britain and the Labour caucus dismissal of Bob Hawke in Australia in the past two decades). Nonetheless, diminishing the legitimacy of political parties as primary political institutions does not improve democracy.

Treating political parties as third parties would have the effect of lowering party spending for Senate elections and this would not necessarily be an undesired outcome from the perspective of fairness, as party spending limits that are too generous can undermine the achievement of fairness in practice. But this outcome of effective spending limits would be undermined by the absence of spending limits for candidates for election to the Senate. The absence of candidate spending limits is further compounded by the fact that political parties (and their constituency associations) are permitted to transfer unlimited goods and services to their Senate candidates without these contributions being deemed "contributions" under the law. In each respect, Bill C-20 departs from the architecture of the *Canada Elections Act*.

Bill C-20, as the chief electoral officer pointed out to the House of Commons' legislative committee on Bill C-20, allows a candidate for the House of Commons to be a candidate for the Senate, a situation that would effectively nullify the spending limit on candidates for the Commons. And, it allows a candidate for the House of Commons to register as a third party for a Senate contest and thus augment her or his spending limit. The CEO suggested that these two possibilities be shut down in order not to have "an unintended impact on the financing regime under the *Canada Elections Act*" (the CEO's assumption being that the impact of these provisions was unintended) (Mayrand 2008, 11).

The CEO also expressed concern about the possible unintended impact of two other elements of the Bill. These are the provisions for a political party (and/or its constituency associations) to contribute "goods and services" to a candidate's campaign and the absence of a spending limit on these candidates. The former would allow a political party to offload some of its campaign resources to its Senate candidates without these being deemed "contributions." The latter would allow Senate candidates to spend in support of their party's campaign their own campaign funds, including funds received as a result of their political party requesting that potential contributors make donations to the candidate's campaign, rather than directly to the party.[2] The effect would be to undermine the spending limit of those political parties willing to take advantage of this huge loophole by directing contributors to make contributions to a party's Senate candidates instead of the political party when the latter cannot use the money because it would have more than it can spend under its spending limit.

If adopted, Bill C-20 will provide those political parties with a supply of funds in excess of what they can legally spend, or the capacity to raise more funds than they can legally use, a way around their spending limit. Exploiting the loophole will require some considerable organizational and administrative capacity, of course, because the regime will be more complex than previously. But any party with a surplus of funds should have no difficulty on that front. The loopholes are, in fact, solely for the well endowed: they do not provide anything for those without the funds to spend over their limit. Moreover, the new contribution limits, designed to keep out big money, ironically also put a premium on having the organizational and administrative capacity to raise funds in the first place. Populist parties, by definition, tend to have a head start on this front by having a base of core supporters. Populist-conservative parties tend to be especially advantaged because their core will usually be financially able to make the required contributions.

The populist regime proposed in Bill C-20 would strike at the heart of the Canadian regime, as so much of the latter's architecture is predicated on effective spending limits on all contestants and participants. Regimes without spending limits find that their other provisions to limit the impact of money on elections, and then on governments, are diminished because money will find its way into the political process, one way or the other. Contributions limits may limit who may give and how much but they have not proven to have much effect on the volume of money in the political process. The government's rationale for not having spending limits is that "nominees [that is, candidates] will need to finance

---

[2] The loophole bears some resemblance to the Conservative Party's argument that its 2006 election campaign's "in and out" transfers of monies from the national party campaign to Conservative candidates for the purpose of running political party advertisements under their spending limits rather than the party's spending limit was not contrary to the *Canada Elections Act*.

province-wide campaigns" (Canada 2007). The logic here is backwards, because, other things being equal, the larger the electoral constituency the greater the need to ensure that access to money does not become an obstacle to fair elections.

The Canadian regime has demonstrated that there can be a balance in measures to promote both freedom and fairness. Indeed, with the right balance the regime can actually enhance the prospects of vigorous competition. There is no evidence that a weakening of the spending limit component of the regime, as proposed by Bill C-20, advances the cause of electoral democracy.

REFERENCES

Mayrand, M. 2008. Evidence. Legislative Committee on Bill C-20. House of Commons, 9 April.

Canada. 2007. "The Federal Government Introduces Legislation to Create a Democratic, Accountable Senate," Canada News Centre Backgrounder. Ottawa, 13 November.

14

SENATE REFORM: WHAT DOES BILL C-20 MEAN FOR WOMEN?

Louise Carbert

L'auteur s'intéresse aux conséquences de la réforme du Sénat sur les femmes. Présentement, 30 des 87 sénateurs sont des femmes, c.-à-d. 34 pourcent. Le pourcentage de femmes qui siègent au Sénat est plus élevé que dans tout autre corps législatif. Suite au projet de loi C-20, la tendance se maintiendra-t-elle? La réponse à cette question réside dans le mécanisme électoral du projet de loi. Prenant en considération quatre éléments de la proposition, premièrement, le vote préférentiel, deuxièmement, le financement des campagnes, troisièmement, la liste de candidats; et quatrièmement, l'importance de la circonscription, elle affirme que plus la liste de candidats pouvant être élu dans une circonscription est longue, toute part égale, plus une femme a de chances d'être élue.

Senate reform is in the works. Prime Minister Harper has introduced Bill C-20, the Senate Appointment Consultations Act. If this Bill passes, we could be voting for senators in the very near future. A House of Commons committee is now studying the Bill, and asking for submissions from experts and the provinces. Senate reform holds significant implications for the future of Canada, and the consequences for the federal division of powers and parliamentary procedure are being examined in great detail. The very constitutionality of Bill C-20 is in dispute.

In any case, nobody is asking another important question: what does Senate reform mean for women?

The question is worth asking because the Senate is the House where proportionally more women sit than any other legislative body – national or provincial – in the country. Women have benefited by the traditional method by which prime ministers appoint at their own discretion. As far back as the early 1990s, Prime Minister Mulroney appointed six women to the Senate. Prime Minister Chrétien came very close to achieving gender parity in Senate appointments during his time in office; 21 women and 23 men. Prime Minister Martin appointed a total of 17 senators, of whom six were women. As a result, currently, 30 of the 87 sitting senators are women – 34 percent. By comparison, 21 percent of parliamentarians in the House of Commons are female. Apparently, appointments are more effective than elections; discretion is preferable to democracy.

There is, in fact, a constitutional basis for the pattern of greater diversity of representation produced by the traditional appointments process. From the outset, a principal purpose of the upper house was to represent the religious and linguistic rights of English minorities in Quebec, and French minorities in the rest of Canada, and thus protect minority rights from the tyranny of the majority in the House of Commons. Since Confederation, the category to be protected has expanded from linguistic English and French minorities to include visible minorities, aboriginal peoples, and women. In this sense, according to Serge Joyal, the Senate has come to operate as a legislative adjunct to the *Charter of Rights and Freedoms*, in the sense that it positively contributes to the preservation of minority rights and interests in the legislative process (2005, 277). An admirable function for the Senate, but one that is rarely articulated, and defended even more rarely. Senator Claudette Tardif is an exception in her willingness to defend this function of the Senate as a reason not to proceed with elections. (In addition to her outstanding personal abilities, Senator Tardif was appointed to represent the historic French communities of Alberta.) Speaking at a panel on Senate reform, she warned:

> Let us never forget that, despite good intentions, it is difficult for a majority always to ensure that the voice of minorities is heard. The Senate must keep its role of ensuring a representation of minorities across the country, as it has done since Confederation. (2006)

The same argument was made, peripherally, on a few occasions during proceedings of the Legislative Committee on Bill-C20.

There is, therefore, the semblance of an emerging convention to make appointments that correspond to the designated equity groups. But it is a convention that rests on the opinion of one, namely the prime minister. And some prime ministers such as Jean Chrétien felt the obligation more keenly than others. Suppose that Prime Minister Harper were persuaded (or directed by the Supreme Court) to proceed with appointments without waiting for elections; would he feel obliged to appoint senators from the designated equity groups? He would probably take care to appoint official-language minorities (Acadians and FranSaskois), but would he appoint women at the same rate as Chrétien? But, supposing that Prime Minister Harper did not observe this emerging convention in appointments: who, outside the parliamentary press gallery, would notice, and who, other than disgruntled party insiders passed over for senate appointments, would care?

If so few people are prepared to make a strong, public case *against* elections in order to make the case for an appointed Senate as the chamber of women and visible minorities, it suggests a basic problem with that convention. Not even the designated equity groups being represented in the Senate are satisfied. When has a spokesperson for any equity group pointed with pride to their higher levels of representation in the Senate? Were the likes of Joyal and Tardif to launch an

advertising campaign along these lines, one can just imagine the response of conservative bloggers, ridiculing the Senate as the "House of Tokens." What sort of
legislature is this that it cannot be publicly defended?

If few people are willing to defend the convention to appoint senators on an
equity basis in order to represent women and vulnerable minorities in Parliament,
and if the penalties for ignoring that convention are light, it is a fragile convention
indeed. In a liberal democracy, there is a stronger, implicit, and default convention to select the members of any legislature on the basis of popular consultations
with the people. Democracy is, *prima facie*, more compelling than executive
discretion.

Apparently, therefore, we are caught on the horns of a dilemma – torn between
a goal to achieve the diversity in representation, and a preference for the democratic process. It is entirely possible – indeed likely – that the implementation of
elections would yield Canada even fewer women in the Senate than we have now.
If we have democratic elections for nomination to the Senate, will we end up
nominating the same sort of politicians – male politicians – we've always been
electing in the House of Commons? The devil is the details, and much of the
answer lies in the exact electoral machinery proposed in Bill-C20.

There are four operational elements contained in Bill C-20 that hold important
implications for women's representation. The first element is the preferential vote;
the second is campaign finance; the third is the panel of nominees; and the fourth
element is district magnitude. With the four elements combined, elections to the
Senate can be characterized as proportional representation (PR), but this particular combination is unique.[1]

While the Australian Senate comes close, there is simply no other electoral
system in the world like that proposed in Bill C-20. As a result of its singularity,
considerable care is required in order to disentangle the elements of PR electoral

---

[1] The closest parallel is the Australian Senate. It consists of 76 senators, twelve from
each of the six states and two from each of the territories. At twelve members, the Australian districts are of the same order of magnitude as provincial electoral districts in the
Western and Maritime Senate regions of Canada. The Australian districts are only half as
large as Ontario and Quebec districts. The results from the Australian Senate are encouraging; the proportion of women elected to the upper house has always exceeded those
elected to the lower house, in a pattern that is parallel to that of Canada. Moreover, the
proportion of women elected to Australia's upper house has ranged in the mid-to-high 30
percent range, and thus exceeded the proportion of women appointed to Canada's upper
house (Maddison and Partridge 2007, 57-61). Malta and Ireland are the only other countries to use STV in combination with multi-member districts, and their legislatures elect
few numbers of women. The experience of these small, ethnically homogenous, and traditionally Roman Catholic countries is not easily comparable to Canada or to Australia, but
does make the point that STV does not, automatically, translate into diversity of representational outcomes (Hirczy 1995).

systems that are said (in the political science literature) to promote women's election to public office, some of which are present in Bill C-20, and some of which are not. How votes are counted (by preferential ballots) and campaign finance regulations do not amount to proportional representation; the panel of nominees and district magnitude do. Furthermore, the role that political parties will play in Senate elections is a major factor in women's election, but that is not pre-determined by Bill C-20, and their role will likely vary considerably from province to province and from party to party. This paper considers each of these four key elements in turn to assess their implications for electing women. It concludes that there just might be a chance to achieve equity in Senate representation through a democratic process.

To begin with, the current bill proposes to conduct elections using a preferential voting system. Preferential voting is familiar to Canadians from the standard run-off method that is used to elect party leaders at leadership conventions and to select election candidates during nominations at the riding association level. When a run-off vote is conducted at a single time, on a single ballot, it is referred to as alternative vote (AV) for a single-member district; when it is conducted for a multi-member district, it is referred to as single-transferable vote (STV). STV sets a quota or benchmark for getting elected, selects the candidates who meet that quota on the first round of counting, re-allocates that candidates' surplus votes to second-choice candidates to see if any candidates meet the quota, and repeats the process until enough candidates meet the quota to be elected. Counting ranked choices on the ballot thus accomplishes, in one round of voting, what takes several iterations in a run-off election.[2]

The appeal of STV is its proportionality of result. The electoral outcome is nearly perfectly proportional to the choices expressed by voters on the ballot. This makes the Conservatives' proposal a version of proportional representation, but it is not like other versions of PR around the world, which use a party-list system. STV allows voters to break away from the restrictions of having to choose a party, and only one party. The connection between candidate and party is broken on the ballot, and this break is STV's defining feature. In fact, the Conservative government appears to have decided on STV for just this purpose: to structure

---

[2] The legislative summary for Bill C-20 explains how the single-transferable vote will operate (Michel Bédard, Law and Government Division, 13 December 2007). Bill C-20 proposes to use the standard Droop formula where the benchmark quota to get elected is set as (total number of votes cast / seats contested + 1) +1. On the first round, any candidate who meets the quota is immediately elected. On the second round, the winner(s)' votes are allocated to other candidates based on the voters' second-choice on the ballot. Any candidate who now meets the quota is elected. It may proceed to a third round if there are more seats to be filled. If no candidate meets the quota, the candidate with the fewest votes is eliminated and their votes are transferred to the other candidates based on the voters' second-choice on the ballot.

Senate elections as contests among individual candidates instead of opposing teams of political parties.

The ballot itself is part of the same agenda to put individual candidates ahead of political parties. The parties will not control the order of nominees on the ballot and they will not be permitted to group their candidates together on the ballot. From these conditions, it is inferred that a candidate's party affiliation will appear on the ballot, alongside his or her name.

In addition to using STV to structure people's choice at the ballot box, the government is relying on campaign finance regulation to break the connection between candidates and political parties. The government's stated goal is to preserve the traditional independent nature of the Senate as a house of legislative review. It may also want to avoid the results of Senate elections in Alberta, where voters cast ballots for the Conservative slate of candidates, and thus reproduced, in the Senate, the same pattern of regional blocs as in the House of Commons.[3] To accomplish this goal of moving parties to the periphery, Bill C-20 applies the *Canada Elections Act* to Senate consultations. Contributions to individual candidates to the Senate will be regulated in the same way as contributions to candidates to the House of Commons. Only individual persons may make contributions to Senate nominees, to a maximum of $1100 per year. Unions and corporations are not eligible to donate. Crucially, political parties are to be considered "third party" to senate consultation campaigns. As a "third-party," they could not transfer money to candidates, and they would be severely restricted in how much advertising they could do on behalf of candidates. Under the *Canada Elections Act*, a third party is limited to a total of $150,000 on election advertising, and no more than $3,000 in advertising on any one candidate.[4] Restrictions on advertising are mitigated by allowing parties and candidates to share office space and staff during campaigns. According to the government, restricting how much money parties can spend in senate campaigns will have the effect of directing citizens to vote for the individual candidate, rather than the party.

As a result, the government expects senators to be able to withstand party discipline inside and outside caucus, but we just don't know how effective these campaign finance rules will be in restricting the role of political parties. I expect

---

[3] Roger Gibbons expects a reduced role for party selection and financing of candidates to increase diversity of representation in the Senate. Judging from the Alberta experience of Senate elections, party lists herd voters into voting for the dominant regional party, and thus reproduce in the Senate the same pattern of regional bloc voting that characterizes elections to the House of Commons.

[4] Elections Canada, "Questions and answers about third party election advertising, http://www.elections.ca/content.asp?section=pol&document=index&dir=thi/que&lang=e&textonly=false#note. Also "The federal government introduces legislation to create a democratic, accountable Senate; 13 November, 2007, http://www.democraticreform.gc.ca/eng/media.asp?id=1395.

that party activity will vary considerably by region and party. A party flush with cash, like the current Conservative Party, could be expected to direct members to donate money to specific Senate races in other parts of the country where it does not expect to win seats in the House of Commons. Prairie Liberals might decide to keep their donations inside the province, focused on their own provincial Senate campaign, instead of sending their money off to the central party organization or to their own lost-cause candidates for the House of Commons. Each party will strategize where to spend its funds most effectively, and it is possible that some Senate consultations will be lavishly funded and elaborately advertised.

The first two elements of Bill C-20 – STV and restricted campaign finance – could plausibly achieve the government's stated goal of putting the individual candidate front and centre. How would women candidates fare with a diminished role for political parties? Would they be stranded or liberated? Are there women who could get elected, on their own, without (much) party support? Certainly, women who already have a high profile in the media, such as local television personalities, former lieutenant governors, university administrators, party leaders, or defeated cabinet ministers would be credible contenders. Elizabeth May, leader of the Green Party, could make a more credible run for Senate than for the House of Commons. In Nova Scotia, defeated Progressive Conservative cabinet minister Jane Purves is a credible candidate for Senate. As a Conservative in the NDP bastion of Halifax, Purves stands little chance of being elected as member either provincially or federally, but people would campaign for her, personally, without wanting to commit to joining the Conservative Party or even be seen to be supporting the Conservative Party. The same goes for Saskatchewan's Janice MacKinnon who was finance minister in Roy Romanow's New Democrat government of the early 1990s. MacKinnon no longer has a party to call home, and she could not plausibly be elected to either the House of Commons or the provincial legislature. But MacKinnon has such stature and personal appeal across party lines and beyond the party establishment to voters at large that she could walk to victory by the single-transferable vote. Similarly, in Ontario, former Deputy Prime Minister Sheila Copps would be a shoe-in for election because her profile is province-wide and her support includes both Liberals and New Democrats. The same is true of Anne MacLellan, former Liberal cabinet minister from Alberta, whose personal stature could mobilize people to campaign on a non-partisan basis. The outstanding question is: Are there sufficient numbers of high-profile women who could compete for Senate elections and come out of a preferential ballot near the top? Just how many other people, specifically how many alpha males, would they have to defeat to qualify for a seat in a rank-ordered competition? It depends on how many seats are available.

Herein lies the third relevant feature of Bill-C20. The government is proposing a system by which each province submits a list of nominees from which the prime minister selects individuals for appointment to the Senate. The text of Bill-C20 takes great care to refer to "consultations" (as opposed to elections) in order to avoid constitutional challenge. The purpose of consulting widely and democratically with the entire adult citizen population is to produce a list of nominees who may then be recommended to the governor general for appointment.[5] This list of nominees is also called a bank or panel.

The important implication for women is that the list of nominees to be voted for is longer than the list of current vacancies in the Senate. Under Bill C-20, Canadians are not voting for Senate nominees as vacancies arise; they are voting for nominees for a standing list to be used over the next few years, until the next general election. To avoid going to the polls between general elections, the prime minister requires a list with enough nominees on it to replace currently sitting senators as they retire or die. It might be that the list of nominees corresponds to the total number of Senate seats in each electoral district.[6] Seeing that the rank-ordered result of the STV ballot produces a rank-ordered list of nominees, the prime minister would presumably appoint senators in that same order.

By using STV to produce a rank-ordered list of nominees, Senate elections will have achieved proportionality. This is exactly the opposite of the "winner-takes-all" result of first-past-the-post electoral systems where a plurality of votes gets the winner elected, and all other votes are irrelevant to the composition of the legislature. Under Bill C-20, the public's voting preferences are fully and accurately translated into the composition of the Senate; this is the essence of proportionality. STV and a banked list of nominees thus amounts to proportional representation, but there are degrees of proportionality, and the degree is crucial to the number of women appointed.

The degree of proportionality depends on the size of the electoral district. District magnitude is the fourth element of Bill C-20 to hold important implications for the question of women's presence in the Senate. A solid body of political science literature establishes that the larger the size of the district, the more candidates there are to be elected, and the more candidates elected, the more likely there is to be diversity in representation. It bears repeating the obvious point that there is no mutually exclusive trade-off between women's representation and the representation of visible minorities because gender is combined with ethnicity and race in each individual, and so individual candidates – male and female – can embody more than one cleavage in their person simultaneously. The more seats

---

[5] Under cross-examination in committee, Minister Van Loan and Privy Council Officials agreed that the PM is not bound constitutionally to appoint senators from the list. Roger Gibbons envisaged a situation where the prime minister might reject certain nominees – racists, white supremacists – altogether, or a situation where the primer minister might ignore the rank-ordered results in order to preferentially recommend an Acadian nominee over another higher-ranked nominee.

[6] The ballot cannot feasibly include the names of enough candidates to produce a full list of nominees, enough to replace all senators at one fell swoop. Imagine the ballot for all of Ontario's 24 Senate seats; with even only three major parties contesting 24 seats, the ballot would contain 72 names. Perhaps the government is proposing to add only two or three extra names at a time.

being contested in an electoral district requires parties to present a longer list of candidates, and thus to go deeper down into their pool of potential candidates. As more candidacies become available, the more balanced or diverse the list becomes in terms of the type of people or the faction within the party being represented by that candidate (Matland 2002, 103).

The more seats available in a district, the less women candidates are disadvantaged. It begins at the nomination stage, inside the political party, when a woman who aspires to be the party's candidate must compete directly against all other ambitious men. In a direct, head-to-head competition, a woman candidate must defeat the most powerful male politician in the same party, and then she must go on to defeat the most powerful man in her district. Her chances are better if she can campaign alongside the most powerful man in her party, as a member on the same team, and then they can go on together to compete against teams from other parties.

Furthermore, when there are multiple seats up for election, there is an implicit obligation for political parties to design a slate that appeals to a wide variety of voters. No party wants to risk the penalty of ignoring any identifiable group in putting together a list, and the result is a mirror of a country's population in miniature. A balanced ticket is also a way to satisfy different factions inside the party, and thereby guarantee internal peace; a dream package combining United States presidential candidates Barack Obama and Hillary Clinton together could be achieved under PR, without one having to defeat the other. As a result, in electoral systems using proportional representation, the slate of candidates presented to voters becomes part of the election campaign, and part of the internal power struggles and compromises inside the party. This sort of contestation, conducted in public, thus forces the central party leadership to be accountable for gaps and absences.

By contrast, in single-member districts, there are always compelling reasons for not nominating a woman as the candidate of choice in any particular electoral district. The premium on local grassroots democracy means that the party leadership does not have to take responsibility for what the final roster of candidates looks like; the final roster is the unplanned and unpredictable result of the democratic process.[7]

But is the standard contrast between proportional multi-member elections and plurality, single-member elections to the point here? Almost all that we know about women getting elected to multi-member districts is based on elections dominated by political parties – which Bill C-20 consultations deliberately are not. In

---

[7] There are solid, countervailing strengths to the single-member, first-past-the-post electoral system that outweigh the goal of greater diversity. Local grassroots democracy at the level of the electoral district has its own value, regardless of who is elected, and the search for proportionality should not jeopardize the integrity of the electoral district and the role of the elected member in that district.

the standard model of proportional representation, each citizen has only one vote to cast, and so votes for the party. A carefully designed slate balanced by gender and race is, in fact, a product of the lack of democracy in a top-down process controlled by central party executives. By contrast, Bill C-20 is proposing a package that shifts control away from party executives and gives it back to the voters with a preferential ballot.

Hence some, but not all, the standard arguments in the literature about PR's ability to elect greater numbers of women are relevant. Under Bill C-20, the party will have the final say in determining who runs under its name in a Senate consultation, and it will produce a slate of candidates, just as in standard PR elections. Unlike PR elections, however, the party cannot depend on its party brand or its party leader to carry the vote for Senate candidates. The fate of the government in the House of Commons is not at stake, and so even loyal party supporters have the opportunity to defect (that is, to choose a Senate candidate from another party) without jeopardizing the outcome of the main race. Therein lies the discipline of putting together an appealing list of candidates to appeal to different segments of the voting public. Who the candidates are as individual people, and who they represent in their physical person and in their personal history of skills, loyalties, and affiliations, moves to the front and centre of Senate consultations.

In the end, with a reduced role for political parties, we are, in effect, pulling out the single argument of district magnitude from the PR package and relying on it to elect more women candidates. By implication, it follows that electoral districts should be as large as constitutionally possible.

In Canada, the Constitution determines district magnitude. The electoral district is the province, and the logic outlined here leads to the conclusion that getting more women nominated to the Senate means defending the province as the electoral district. The distribution of seats corresponds to the logic of four distinct regions at Confederation. Each region – Ontario, Quebec, Maritimes, and the West is guaranteed twenty-four senate seats. Could the senatorial region be the electoral district? Quebec[8] and Ontario are regions unto themselves, but could the Maritimes and the West each be an electoral district? With twenty-four seats in contention, there is ample opportunity to organize creative candidacies and plan electoral strategies accordingly. Once elected, senators could represent a province, and could be appointed as Senate vacancies arise in their province, but why couldn't election campaigns be organized and the ballots counted by region?

---

[8] Quebec is exceptional because, constitutionally, its 24 senators are appointed to represent 24 regional divisions in the province, corresponding to historic linguistic boundaries. In the rest of Canada, senators have the option to declare a self-selected division, which can be a particular street or neighbourhood. Since senators have no constituency work, there is no reason why Quebec senators appointed to a division could not purchase property in that district in order to become a resident.

If not the Senate region, the province must be the electoral district in order to maximize the crucial element of district magnitude. The more candidates there are to be elected, the lower the electoral quotient required. It becomes feasible to organize a very specialized campaign to elect a woman candidate who is Acadian, who is aboriginal, or who is indigenous African. An individual candidate may not have a province-wide profile outside a particular linguistic, ethnic, or ideological community, but a candidate can be nominated using a campaign that mobilizes intensive support among an identifiable population.

To be sure, such a campaign would take some organizational effort, but it can be done.[9] Such is the nature of democracy; it takes skill and work. The political parties and other organizations should welcome any project that gets people to work on a campaign. Senate elections that are organized around individual candidates could be the spark to re-invigorate democracy. In fact, the central party executive in Ottawa might welcome an opportunity to bypass local party strongmen at the grassroots in the regions; party elites might want to support their own favoured candidates who are more diverse than the sort of candidate than could be elected to the House of Commons through the regular nomination route.[10] For instance, Senate elections would be just the opportunity for Stephane Dion to get his aboriginal candidate of choice Joan Beatty into caucus, without having to take on David Orchard, the Métis Nation of Saskatchewan, and the Liberal Party riding executive.[11]

Personally, as an active member of Equal Voice Canada, I look forward to organizing a campaign for all three of Nova Scotia's next three Senate appointments to be women. Across Canada, there are women who are experienced parliamentarians who have enormous talent and knowledge to contribute, but whose prospects of being elected are low. Women like Anne MacLellan, Sheila Copps, Janice MacKinnon or Jane Purves are accomplished, capable individuals and the country is diminished by their absence from the centre of power and influence.

---

[9] Matland cites the 1971 example of municipal elections in Norway where campaigners mounted a campaign to have women vote only for women candidates, and strike out men's names. As a result, women became the majority of councillors in several large cities in a single election, but that strategy has its hazards, because there was, as a result of what became known as the "women's coup," a long-term backlash as men took up a habit of striking out women candidates' names (2002, 99).

[10] In Irish elections using STV, "Each candidate must build up a personal following within the electorate and within the local party, and consequently he has a power base which is not dependent upon the goodwill of the local party officers" (Gallagher 1980, 501).

[11] Stephane Dion designated former NDP cabinet minister Joan Beatty as the Liberal candidate for Desnethé–Missinippi–Churchill River in a 2008 by-election. His decision to designate Beatty without holding a nomination meeting antagonized David Orchard (and others) who had already declared his intention to seek the Liberal Party nomination. Conservative candidate Rob Clarke defeated her.

Furthermore, if our senators are to be effective parliamentarians, they should receive the legitimacy conferred by democratic elections. We all benefit from the appointment of strong, effective leadership in the Senate, and we may not get the leadership that Canada deserves without more democracy. The trick is to achieve strong effective leadership that looks like Canada in all its diversity, including that half of its population who are women.

But we need to ask: If we have democratic elections to the Senate, will we end up electing the same sort of politicians – male politicians – we've always been electing, ever since 1758? How can we get the sort of capable, effective leadership that the provinces need in the Senate? And, in particular, how can we best get more women into the Senate?

Fifteen years ago, a colleague remarked to me that it was typically and traditionally Canadian for the Canadian women's movement to celebrate Person's Day on 18 October each year. Instead of celebrating suffrage, we celebrate the date on which, in 1929, the Judicial Committee of the Privy Council decided that women were indeed, legally and constitutionally, "persons" and thereby entitled to receive a Senate appointment. In what other country, my colleague quipped, would feminists celebrate the date on which women became eligible to receive a patronage appointment? The remark still rankles.

REFERENCES

Gallagher, M. 1980. "Candidate selection in Ireland: The impact of localism and the electoral system" *British Journal of Political Science,* Vol. 10:4 (Oct.) 489-503.

Gibbons, R. 2008. Evidence. 39th Parliament, 2nd Session Legislative Committee on Bill C-20. 14 May. Accessed online at http://cmte.parl.gc.ca/cmte/CommitteePublication .aspx?SourceId=240713&Lang=1&PARLSES=392&JNT=0&COM=13493

Hirczy, W. 1995. "STV and the Representation of Women," *PS: Political Science and Politics* 28(4): 711-713.

Joyal, S. 2005. "Conclusion: The Senate as the embodiment of the federal principle," in *Protecting Canadian Democracy: The Senate You Never Knew.* Montreal and Kingston: McGill-Queen's University Press.

Maddison, S. and E. Partridge. 2007. *How Well Does Australian Democracy Serve Australian Women?* Sydney: Democratic Audit of Australia, Report No.8. Accessed online at http://arts.anu.edu.au/democraticaudit/

Matland, R. 2002. "Enhancing Women's Political Participation: Legislative Recruitment and Electoral Systems," in *Women in Parliament: Beyond numbers* Geneva: Inter-Parliamentary Union, 93-111. Accessed online at http://www.idea.int/publications/wip/ index.cfm#toc

McDougall, D. 2008. Evidence. 39th Parliament, 2nd Session Legislative Committee on Bill C-20. 2 April. Accessed online at http://cmte.parl.gc.ca/cmte/CommitteePublication .aspx?SourceId=234181&Lang=1&PARLSES=392&JNT=0&COM=13493

Tardif, C. 2006. "Parliamentary Reform: What about Minorities?" *Dialogues Senate Reform.* Calgary: Canada West Foundation. Summer, 21-22. Accessed online at http:// www.cwf.ca/V2/cnt/03b718574b6f9326872571a9004e967c.php

HOW NECESSARY IS SENATE REFORM?

15

SENATE REFORM AS A RISK TO TAKE, URGENTLY

Tom Kent

Les propositions de réforme du Sénat du gouvernement Harper comportent des risques, mais elles sont souhaitables. Le Sénat actuel n'est pas en mesure d'apporter au gouvernement fédéral le soutien dont il a besoin pour être un gouvernement fort, mais une réforme consciencieuse n'augmenterait pas plus les chances d'obtenir l'accord des provinces qu'un amendement à la Constitution afin d'abolir le Sénat. L'illégitimité électorale de la Chambre a permis aux premiers ministres des provinces de jouer un plus grand rôle dans les affaires nationales. Les premiers ministres des provinces n'ayant pas l'habitude de penser en fonction de l'ensemble du pays, les intérêts des provinces tendent à dominer dans les relations fédérales-provinciales au détriment des questions qui touchent l'ensemble du pays. Sans réforme, même si elle se limite à une loi fédérale, les provinces vont avoir de plus en plus de pouvoir et l'on tiendra de moins en compte des intérêts nationaux. Plus la situation persistera, plus elle sera difficile à changer.

The Senate reforms proposed by the Harper government are risky, not for them but for their successors a decade or two hence. Their policies could be frustrated by deadlock between the House of Commons and the "upper house." When it becomes largely elected, the Senate will still have all the legislative authority that the Constitution confers but which it has not dared to exercise, in defiance of the Commons, while unelected.

Nevertheless, the reforms deserve welcome. They should be strengthened, not weakened or abandoned. They are necessary to head off a present danger.

The national electorate is increasingly impatient with federal politics. Public participation will sink further if governmental responsibilities are increasingly confused, the federal government further weakened, because provincial premiers continue to gain a larger say in national affairs. The main countervail to that trend is an elected Senate. It is needed, quickly. Not allowing it to become, in its turn, too powerful, is the business of 2020, not today.

Federalism is more than the division of sovereignty between two orders of government. It is politically viable only if concerns distinctive to the constituent units are brought into consideration in the national business. All federations recognize this need. If they are parliamentary democracies, the chamber where the government stands or falls must be elected nationally on the principle of "rep by pop." The units of the federation are recognized in a second legislative chamber where numbers are discounted, where the smaller units have representation more than proportionate to their populations.

In almost all federations, this second chamber is elected. Canada is the exception. The *British North America Act* aped British practice by giving the trappings of an "upper house" to unelected people. Lordships could not be brought to the New World but senators appointed by the prime minister were the nearest approximation. For 140 years the Senate of Canada has survived as a copy of an anachronism. It gives superficial form to provincial representation in Ottawa. Its reality is solely to endow the prime minister with power to make prestigious patronage appointments undemanding of responsibility. For almost a century, it did no other harm. With distances long and government limited, federal politics produced its own regional leaders. As late as the 1950s, Jimmy Gardiner, for example, would have put any senator from Saskatchewan, however elected, deep into the shade.

The 1960s, however, brought a major shift in political power. Initially thanks to Lesage in Quebec, but quickly followed by Ontario, Manitoba, New Brunswick and soon by others, provincial governments cast off their parochial character. With their modernization, the paternal domination of Ottawa, which had been shaping most intergovernmental relations since 1939, faded away. Further change followed. Within Ottawa, Trudeau began the replacement of Cabinet government by prime ministerial dictatorship. Some ministers might still be strong enough to exert a regional control on patronage, but not on policy.

The vacuum in Canadian governance thus became complete. Where there should have been a Senate, significant because elected, there was effectively nothing. But politics does not long tolerate a vacuum. If created within, it is soon filled from without. Strengthened provincial premiers have been ready and willing to be the penetrators. They have no democratic mandate for the role. They are elected to run the business of their province, not for their views on national affairs. Most have little knowledge and no experience outside provincial affairs. Broader qualifications, the viewpoints of a Jean Lesage, Duff Roblin or Bill Davis, are an occasional bonus, not part of the job description.

In partisan politics, however, absence of a mandate is not an inhibition. For the past forty years, the decisive debates on national policy have often been outside federal elections and Parliament. Many policies have been shaped, deals sealed, in the exchanges, public and private, between federal and provincial leaders.

Such "executive" federalism imperils democratic accountability. It is nevertheless necessary. In contemporary society, government action commonly overlaps the distinctions of federal and provincial jurisdiction. Democracy calls not for collaboration to be limited but for its processes to be made as transparent as possible. Above all, it calls for the politics of collaboration to be made even-handed. They are not. This is the crucial, neglected reason why Senate reform is urgently important. In its absence, the national coherence of Canada will be increasingly threatened.

We have long been, by constitution and by practice, almost the most decentralized of federations. In others, the necessary intergovernmental collaboration takes place under some process of central leadership. In Canada, for the past 25 years – since, though not made inevitable by, the 1982 constitutional change – central leadership has failed. The scales of intergovernmental relations have been weighted against Ottawa.

Variations in political strengths and in personalities have produced ups and downs, but the trend has been clear. The centre is not holding. The parts increasingly determine what is done, or not done, nationally: about the economy, the environment, the society. Policies crucial for all of Canada are settled, or neglected, by dealings in which the provinces have the upper hand. That hand is inherent in the present politics of the relationship.

Ottawa needs good relations with the provinces. It scores few political points by criticizing them individually, none by attacking them collectively. In contrast, when provinces criticize Ottawa policy, or the lack of it, federal politicians are promptly put on the defensive. Whatever the issue, if it ends in agreement, provincial politicians can claim victory and appreciation from their electorates. They usually have no motive to shower gratitude on Ottawa. And if there is continuing disagreement, they have nothing to lose by further criticism of the feds. It is the Ottawa politicians, with national responsibility, who are held to have failed in their job and who may be hurt in their next election, whereas running against them is usually good for votes in provincial elections.

This asymmetry will grow greater the more thoroughly the "First Ministers" of the provinces become established as the representatives of their constituents' viewpoints on national affairs. That role has no constitutional basis, but political power is built more by practice than by right. The longer the premiers play a growing national role, the more the people elected nationally by Canadians will be diminished. Political accountability will be more than ever confused. In a world society and economy more than ever requiring firm, far-sighted policies, Canada's are threatened with more and more incoherence.

There are two possible countervails to burgeoning provincial power in national affairs, two possible competitors to the premiers. One is an elected Senate. The other is internal to the federal political parties. They do not have to be machines under central control, creating prime ministerial dictatorships when in office. The major parties could again be lively associations of like-minded people, associations from which there emerge, across the country, more men and women who command public respect, in part for the regional viewpoints they bring to national affairs.

That could be. It will not be, while one party is in shambles and a man of Mr. Harper's temperament is prime minister. Even more than under any of his predecessors, his ministers are subordinates of little account beside the premiers of their provinces.

Unelected senators are of no account at all. Some do very good work. But Hugh Segal and Michael Kirby and others do it as able individuals. They have no authority as provincial spokesmen. Their contributions are not identified with the distinctive purpose of a Senate, with the representation of provinces and regions in national affairs. They could be made equally well through commissions and task forces and non-governmental organizations.

In other words, the considerable popular sentiment in favour of abolishing the present Senate is entirely reasonable. What is strange is the identity of the political party that urges abolition. The other policies of the NDP require a strong national government. To abolish the Senate would be to jettison the one institution that could save Ottawa from further weakening before the pretensions of the premiers.

In this respect, Mr. Harper is wiser than his critics. His proposed reforms would somewhat strengthen Ottawa. But in the short run they can do only a little good, and in the long run they can create a new threat to coherent national government.

Constitutionally, the Senate of Canada has powers equal in most respects to those of the House of Commons. Hitherto that has not mattered. An unelected Senate may sometimes huff and puff, but in political reality it can never stand out against a House of Commons majority. Elected senators could. Government in Ottawa could be saved from attrition only to be enfeebled by internal deadlock.

In a parliamentary system, the second chamber of the legislature must indeed be second, not an "upper" house. The United States is different, because executive authority stems from the direct election of the president. The Senate can have power equal to, or in practice greater than, the House of Representatives, because the president is responsible to neither. In a parliamentary system, where legislative and executive authority emerge from the one electoral process, the two chambers cannot be equal. It can only be in the House of Commons, intended to mirror national opinion, that the government stands or falls. Elected senators would bring representation of Canada's regional diversities directly to bear in national politics. They could make other valuable contributions to public discussion. They could consider, criticize, improve proposed legislation. But when opinions differ, they must give way to the Commons.

Full reform therefore requires a constitutional amendment to redefine the powers of the Senate. Unfortunately, that is at present even less likely to command the necessary provincial agreement than would an amendment to abolish the Senate. Certainly no responsible government will today open the Pandora's box of constitutional change.

Mr. Harper's proposals are therefore limited to what can be done by ordinary federal legislation. Appointment to age 75 will be replaced by a fixed term. The proposed 8 years would certainly be an improvement, but it is long beside the time between general elections. A shorter term would be even better, provided senators are as entitled as MPs to run for re-election.

Within the present Constitution, the elections will be "consultative" only. Technically, they will simply advise the prime minister as to whom he should appoint to the Senate. It is therefore essential that they be federal elections under the same authority and supervision as those for the House of Commons. The past organization by Alberta of its own "election" to fill a Senate vacancy was an arrant invasion of Ottawa's jurisdiction. But provided that the election process is properly federal, there is no serious possibility that the prime minister would incur the political odium of refusing to appoint a duly elected candidate.

So far, so good. But would the public take senatorial elections seriously? How many people would bother to vote? And who would the candidates be? For a good many years, they would be seeking election to the Senate pretty much as it is. How many able people would want to go through an election for that purpose, rather than take up other forms of public service open to them?

If Mr. Harper is as serious as he seems to be, there are several ways to lessen such doubts.

The work of the Senate could be enhanced. For example, the qualifications of proposed appointees to all of the many significant posts in the prime minister's gift could be submitted to Senate committees for review and comment. Again, the Senate could be enabled and encouraged to undertake more enquiries into issues of public concern and long-term public policy. The enablement would be a legislative commitment to make adequate resources available for non-partisan enquiries initiated by the vote of, say, at least two-thirds of the Senate.

In such ways, the Senate could be made, even in the early stages of its change, more attractive to potential members. It is equally important to attract public interest. An occasional election to fill a single Senate vacancy would rouse little media or popular attention. It would be better to fix a "Senate day" – in early May, perhaps – for elections to all the seats that have become vacant during the previous twelve months.

The first one or two of such annual events could be big bangs. Present senators could be encouraged to retire before age 75. They could be offered, for a limited period, the choice of early retirement at the same pension as would be their entitlement at 75. On those terms, the Senate might quite soon be transformed from a retirement home to a largely elected, active national institution. The gain to the public interest would be well worth the cost of the pension bonuses.

Thereby, however, would come the risk inherent in reform without a constitutional amendment. Whereas senators by patronage are timid, the arrogance of elected people can sometimes know no bounds. Once they are most of the Senate, the possibility of serious conflict with the Commons cannot be ruled out. Our present Constitution could then result in deadlocks that enfeeble national policy almost as much as the present politics of provincialism.

The risk has to be weighed. Senate reform without constitutional amendment should not be lightly undertaken. In its absence, however, provincial power will continue to grow. Its politics will increasingly dilute the national interest. The longer it continues, the harder it will be to reverse this trend.

My assessment is therefore that Mr. Harper is right to take the risk of early action and would be wise to make it stronger and quicker.

Canada would never have been created, and could not have developed as it has, without optimists willing to take risks. The optimism needed now is that, once the process of electing senators has started, and particularly if it is begun with some panache, Canadians will see its value and will not allow its purpose to be thwarted. If a constitutional amendment remains long in coming, public opinion will compel politicians in the Commons and the Senate to contrive some informal arrangement that avoids deadlocks between them. The good sense of the people will make the national interest prevail.

That is not only the faith on which all democracy is built. So far it is a faith that almost always, sometimes haltingly but in the end decisively, has served Canada well.

16

SENATE REFORM AND DEMOCRATIC LEGITIMACY: BEYOND STASIS

Senator Hugh Segal

Dans cet article, l'auteur appuie la réforme du Sénat en raison du manque de légitimité démocratique du statu quo. Étant donné que les Canadiens n'ont jamais conféré la légitimité électorale à la notion d'une chambre haute élue, les efforts fournis par le Premier ministre Harper, en présentant le projet de loi C-20 sur la consultation du public dans le processus de sélection des sénateurs et le projet C-19 qui vise à raccourcir la durée des mandats des sénateurs, sont un signe positif de réforme. Bien que les institutions gouvernementales se soient toujours opposées aux réformes, il est nécessaire de consulter le public sur la question à savoir si le Sénat devrait continuer d'exister sous sa forme actuelle. Cet article affirme qu'il existe d'autres moyens démocratiques, en accord avec la constitution, pour obtenir de tels renseignements.

THE PRESENT SENATE CONUNDRUM

Democracy, as a system of government, is about many principles and operating norms. One of the most important norms, defined by the principle of public legitimacy, is how and in what way legislatures spend their time. The way that time is spent, the good that is done or the folly that may emerge from sins of omission or commission, the time used by legislators in legislatures, is the fodder of election choice and debate. This, in part, explains why, despite the many initiatives on Senate reform from many credible sources, no reform of any substance has occurred for one hundred and forty years. Senate reform strikes almost no one as urgent.

At one level, this may reflect the hard reality that whatever the Senate does or does not do is seemingly of little consequence to the way we live our lives. In consequence, the gargantuan struggle for the political, legislative and constitutional approval required for change may be perceived as simply not justified. With issues like health care, defence and foreign affairs, taxes, the rush to make our borders safe and efficient, climate change, and Iran's pursuit of the weapons of mass destruction that Israel already has, who in their right mind would argue for any time on the public agenda for Senate reform? And with Canada's self-confident, usually governing party (the Liberals) holding a commanding two-thirds majority in the Senate – one that is likely to endure given a Conservative prime minister determined not to fill vacancies with unelected individuals – the Senate itself has a structural bias against reform. Moreover, whatever Tory policy on Senate reform may actually be – at the time of writing, the introduction of eight-year term limits and statutory consultative referendums for voters in each province to identify candidates to fill Senate vacancies in their respective provinces – many Conservative senators are quite happy to see the process make no progress at all. In fact, motions I have made on televising the Senate or holding a referendum on its abolition or reform have been held up or delayed as much by Conservatives as by Liberals.

Since 1867 we have had thirty-nine federal elections and approximately 300 provincial and territorial elections. The elected legislatures that make our laws may thus surely be seen to have been legitimized on many occasions by millions of voters. And, with the referendum on the Charlottetown Accord in 1992, wherein Canadians voted against constitutional change, it is fair to conclude that there has been some measure of public involvement in a way that strengthens the legitimacy argument.

But, it is surely a reach to include the unelected Senate in that circle of reflected or *de facto* legitimacy. Except in Alberta for Stan Waters in the 1980s, or Bert Brown more recently, Canadians have never voted in any way whatever to legitimize an unelected upper chamber, one with potentially enormous legislative power.

The present government of Canada deserves credit, along with the prime minister, for attempting to address this legitimacy question through proposals in the House to consult the public on Senate vacancies before appointments are made (Bill C-20) and to shorten terms (Bill C-19). In this regard, Prime Minister Harper follows in a long and noble line of federal leaders who have attempted Senate reform.[1]

It is interesting to note that the British House of Lords, on which the Canadian Senate is modelled, is restrained in what it may do by the *Powers of Parliament Act* (1911 and 1949), which ensures that, in the event of conflict, the elected Commons shall always prevail.[2] Similarly, the powerful United States Senate can

---

[1] Since 1900 there have been 13 proposals for Senate reform. For details, see Appendix 1.

[2] The first Parliament Act, the *Parliament Act 1911,* asserted the supremacy of the House of Commons by limiting the legislation-blocking powers of the House of Lords. It was amended by the second *Parliament Act* of 1949, which further limited the power of the Lords by reducing the time that they could delay bills, from two years to one.

be stymied by the House of Representatives or simply vetoed by the president. It is surely anomalous, therefore, that the British government White Paper on upper chambers around the world, concluded that none, either elected or otherwise, was as powerful constitutionally as our unelected and unaccountable Senate (United Kingdom 2007, 23). This surely suggests that an undemocratic balance is, in terms of form if not substance, beyond equilibrium.

BENIGN DOES NOT MEAN DEMOCRATIC

To the credit of the individuals who have served in the Senate over the years, obstructionism has been the exception rather than the rule, a fact that further serves to undercut any sense of urgency around the Senate reform file.

Having campaigned honestly and sincerely on Senate reform, our present prime minister has delivered legislative proposals on term limits and protecting by statute the voters' right to be consulted about whom he recommends to the governor general for Senate appointment. Given this, he can hardly be expected to turn away; the legacy parties (Reform, Alliance and Progressive Conservative) he and Peter McKay assembled into a national, workable Conservative party and government were and are too committed to the principle here to shelve it or move on. The Liberal position – that no change can be made without formal constitutional agreement – is akin to proposing that all future tax changes require a seven-eighths majority in the House before they can pass. And, in affirming a position that underlines precisely why constitutional negotiation is unlikely to work, the Liberal governments of Quebec and Ontario have opposed any reform that does not pass their veto. While Saskatchewan, British Columbia, Alberta and Manitoba have embraced or are seriously considering a provincial electoral process, one that is provincially based like Alberta's, the difference of opinion highlights how unworkable a constitutional negotiation would be. It would not, in the end, be a negotiation about our far too powerful, profoundly unelected upper chamber. Rather, negotiation would be about everything else that provinces would demand before they would actually entertain any real consensus on the Senate. Canadians have seen this movie series before – Meech Lake in 1989–90 and Charlottetown, its genuine sequel, in 1991–92. That kind of process would be, as it has often been, a great place to send good ideas to die.

THE AMENDING FORMULA AND A REFERENDUM:
BETTER THAN CIRQUE DU SOLEIL

The present amending formula requires that, for any fundamental change in our system of government – for example, changes affecting the Crown, Parliament, regular election cycle, etc. – the concurrence of *all* provincial legislatures *and* the Parliament of Canada must be obtained (*Constitution Act, 1982*, s.41; see Appendix 3).

In the design of any referendum on the abolition or maintenance of the Senate, it would be of immense value if Ottawa and the provinces would simply agree that

- Ottawa would sign on if, nationally, a simple fifty percent plus one majority voted for abolition; and
- each premier would sign on if, within their own province, fifty percent plus one voted for abolition.

This agreement would simply be one that embraces the rather dramatic notion that the governments work for the people, even on issues of constitutional legitimacy (or perhaps especially), as opposed to the other way around.

Moreover, such a referendum would allow us to avoid another cycle of reform contortions until we had actually established whether Canadians wanted the Senate to continue in any way.

There is very little that is not intriguing about the back flips, acrobatics, artistry, creativity and physical strength and beauty of the Cirque du Soleil. On Senate reform, however, we cannot continue in perpetuity through a range of Cirque du Soleil acrobatic manoeuvres until the price of admission is paid. We need simply to know if the public wishes to have a Senate to begin with.

A WAY AHEAD

If one assumes that disengaging from the process is not an option for the Conservative government elected in 2006 and that the institutional opposition to reform of the Senate will continue on the part of the Liberal premiers of Quebec and Ontario and their Liberal colleagues who control the Senate of Canada, it is clear that we face a context of deadlock. For their part, the Conservatives have a million reasons to continue to feature Senate reform as part of their platform in the coming campaign (it continues to get strong and enthusiastic audience support in all parts of the country, in partisan and non-partisan audiences). It would seem, therefore, that barring an election shaped exclusively on Senate reform (highly unlikely) and in which the pro-reform side wins a massive majority, we are again at a stalemate – one more time since Confederation and number twenty-nine in a long list of government or party reform proposals in the last 30 years alone – not counting those put forward by the present government (Joyal 2003).

Many of those who believe we need a Senate (of whom the author is one), and even those who argue that an appointed Senate is preferable to an elected one, will argue that senators have no less legitimacy than judges who are also appointed by the duly elected government of the day. There is, however, a huge difference between the functions performed by these two classes of appointees. Judges are appointed to interpret the laws on a case by case basis. In contrast, senators get to change the law and make law and refine or reject the laws sent to it by an elected Canadian Parliament.

The illegitimacy of the status quo emerges from two realities, only one of which the government has tried to address: Canadians have no say in who sits in the Senate, and Canadians have never had a say as to whether we need a Senate.

The Senate of Canada was not always Canada's only upper house. The Maritime provinces had such chambers prior to Confederation, while those of Manitoba and Quebec were granted at that time. All but the national body have now disappeared, with that of Quebec being the most recent to do so (1968). Surely it is in the spirit of constitutional coherence and stability that we now confront the issue of the legitimacy of our last remaining bicameral institution? Fortunately, there may be a stepped and democratic way to accomplish this, a way, moreover, that does not require explicit Senate or constitutional approval (however desirable these unlikely imprimaturs may be). Such a stepped approach might embrace the following elements:

a) The NDP and Conservatives, who have both in the past few months embraced a referendum on Senate abolition,[3] could agree pursuant to the *Referendum Act, 1992* to pass legislation in the House of Commons to put the question of abolition to the Canadian voters within the next twenty-four months. If the Conservatives are re-elected in a minority, they and the NDP can proceed to that referendum. Should the Conservatives not be re-elected, a Liberal minority would have to abolish the legislation within a few months – making a stout stand against democratization in their really early days back in the saddle. But they would likely be stopped by an NDP-Tory plurality. Only a Liberal majority would stop any chance of reform.

b) In the next twenty-four months provinces considering provincial senate elections could proceed to put procedures in place to hold those elections. Elected senators would begin to take their place in the upper chamber after nomination by the prime minister. Vacancies would be filled in places like BC, Alberta, Saskatchewan and Manitoba when elections take place. Provinces where elections do not take place would see vacancies remain and increase. The collateral benefit of this, however temporary it might be, would be an increase in relative strength from the broadly under-represented Western provinces while over-represented provinces in the east would lose relative strength.

If the referendum were held, how might that process likely evolve?

Past referendum experiences in Canada indicate that however far ahead the positive proposition (in this case abolition) may be initially, the contrary side

---

[3] *"The NDP tabled a motion in Parliament for a referendum to be held by October 2009 on the abolition of the Senate. Our work builds on the motion that Senator Hugh Segal recently tabled in the Senate and years of democratic reformers in the NDP."* Jack Layton, 4 November 2007.

tends to gain ground by attrition over time. Quebec, 1980, Charlottetown, 1992, Quebec, 1995 all speak to aspects of this phenomenon. My proposal in a motion put to the Senate on 23 October 2007 called for a simple referendum on abolition. My reasoning then, which still remains salient, was and is:

> In a democracy, specifically in the key working elements of its responsible govern-ment, respect must be tied in some way to legitimacy. While questioning "legitimacy" of long established democratic institutions is usually the tactic of those seeking a more radical reform, the passage of time does not, in and of itself, confer *de facto* legitimacy, and seems a particularly undemocratic way of moving forward. The purpose of my motion regarding a referendum question put to the Canadian people is to focus squarely on the legitimacy issue. (Canada 2007; see Appendix 4)

If at least 50 percent plus one of Canadian voters nationwide vote to abolish and there is at least 50 percent plus one in each province, no premier (not even the premier of Quebec) would have any rationale to withhold the unanimity required for the constitutional amendment.

If that precise test is not met, then, as the case for non-abolition would likely include a strong series of arguments for reforms, parliamentarians and premiers would have received a strong and explicit message from Canadians on the reform agenda. The public will have been consulted *before* negotiations are begun, as opposed to after. Canadian democracy and our cherished "peace, order and good government" can, I believe, withstand that radical departure and survive very much intact.

COMPLACENCY'S SIREN CALL

The Honourable William Davis would often remind overly activist ministers and MPPs that no government ever got into trouble because of something it did not do. And for Liberals and some premiers – and perhaps Bloc Quebecois members who have little interest in validating or strengthening the federal system – doing nothing may continue to be attractive. But there are risks to the country and its institutional legitimacy if we simply keep Senate reform on a back burner:

a) Voters in Western Canada will know that the federal system is not capable of improvement, further democratization, enhanced legitimacy or responsibility. There is political cost to this – a cost we underestimate at our peril.

b) The core anti-democratic structure of the upper chamber will remain, able to emerge and create constitutional or political crisis at any time and, often, at the worst possible time.

c) The message that an institution cannot change with the times, that we are inca-pable, as a mature and stable democracy, of making adjustments and modernizing the instruments at the core of that democracy, will be ever more persuasive and endemic. How much more sense of voter alienation and elec-toral non-participation do we wish to engender? Is the Senate so perfect that it requires special protection in perpetuity from any and all change?

Serving senators who support this proposal (and admittedly, there may not be many) might be asked, "How can you serve in a Senate you feel is illegitimate?" The answer is very straightforward.

When asked by a prime minister – himself or herself duly elected under our system – to take on a task for the country, one needs to be pretty self important to say no. That being said, if one takes one's oath of service and signs it, one has a duty to serve as best one can.

But surely that obligation implies disengagement from neither the democratic imperative of legitimacy nor democratic participation in the architecture of legitimacy. The motion I proposed in the Senate (see Appendix 4) affords parliamentarians a broad opportunity to reflect on the issue and contribute their own perspectives. Should a similar motion be introduced in the House, the debate could be enjoined more broadly still. And while I would vote against abolition – for reasons that relate to both the need for a chamber that reflects regional and provincial interest and some careful reassessment of federal laws that too frequently are subject to overly hasty and careless drafting (e.g., the recent C-10) – my vote is but one vote. My opposition to abolition, however, does not in any way weaken my deeply held belief that Canadians should get to decide something on the Senate they have never been allowed to do.

One of the core premises of the development of responsible government in Canada is the process of evolution. To be relevant and engaged, all aspects of our democratic institutions must be open to reflection and possible scrutiny. The Canadian Senate, venerable, thoughtful, constructive and multi-partisan as it may be, cannot be outside the circle of public accountability.

THE INERTIAL APPEAL

Those calling for doing nothing often focus on the quality of the committee work in the Senate and the need for a constraint on a prime minister with a large majority. They also note the important role the Senate plays in cleaning up errors of substance and detail made, often in haste, in the House of Commons. And these protests are not without a measure of evidentiary substance.

One could say some of those things about the judiciary, NGOs and even hard working municipal and parish councils. But these bodies do *not* have the power to initiate legislation, stop specific spending approved by those elected precisely to approve spending in Parliament, or to do the same to laws passed by folks elected to pass laws. The Senate can, has and does engage in some or all of these activities all the time. And they do so without being elected in any way, by anyone, to do so. And, if appointed at the age of thirty (the minimum age required by the Constitution), they can serve for forty-five years under existing constitutional provisions. If a newly constructed Eastern European or African democracy had created such an assembly as a signal of their embrace of democracy, we would have been quite direct as Canadians in underlining the contemptibility of that charade.

My own experience both with the Senate and senators over three decades, and my explicit experience since being appointed in 2005 as a Conservative by Prime Minister Martin, a Liberal, leads me to agree wholeheartedly with those who extol the sense of honour, duty, diligence and public service that inspires the vast majority of those who have served or do serve in our upper chamber. Conservative ministers like Peter Van Loan, who have attacked the people in the institution, reveal more about their mean-spirited myopia and institutional inexperience than any wise government would embrace going forward. But good people working hard for causes and communities about which they care do not constitute a substitute for democratic legitimacy. And where we sanction ongoing illegitimacy and the separation of those who legislate from accountability to those for whom they legislate, we begin to gnaw at the sinews of democracy itself.

That kind of "let them eat cake" complacency and ever wilful denial of the democratic principle never occurs, especially in terms of today's intense focus on governance, coherence and accountability, without a serious price ultimately being paid.

REFERENCES

United Kingdom. 2007. The House of Lords: Reform Presented to Parliament by the Leader of the House of Commons and Lord Privy Seal by Command of Her Majesty. February. (Cm 7027) p. 23.

Joyal, S. 2003. *Protecting Canadian Democracy: The Senate You Never Knew*. Montreal and Kingston: McGill-Queen's University Press.

Canada. 2007. Parliament. Debates of the Senate. 23 October.

APPENDIX I

Attempts at Senate Reform since 1900

1. 1903 The representation of the Northwest Territories was raised from two to four seats by an Act of the Canadian Parliament.

2. 1915 The Constitution was amended so as to provide for a fourth senatorial division of 24 members, the four Western provinces being represented by six members each. The total number of senators was now 96.

3. 1949 As provided by the *Constitution Act, 1915*, Newfoundland was given six seats in the Senate upon its admission within the Federation.

4. 1965 Under a constitutional amendment, senators appointed after 2 June 1965 must retire from this House at the age of 75.

5. 1969 A White Paper published by the Government of Canada proposed the creation of a new Senate, half of its members to be appointed by the provinces and the other half being appointed by the federal government.

6. 1972 The Molgat-MacGuigan Committee recommended increasing the number of senators from Western provinces and reducing the powers of the Senate to a suspensive veto.

7. 1975 One seat was awarded to each of the two Territories, the total number of senators being raised from 102 to 104.

8. 1978 In Bill C-78, the Government of Canada proposed a reform of the Senate which was judged *ultra vires* of the federal Parliament by the Supreme Court the following year.

9. 1979 The Task Force on Canadian Unity suggested that the Senate be replaced by a council of 60 members appointed by the provinces.

10. 1980 The report of the Senate Committee on certain aspects of the Constitution reaffirmed the necessity for a nominated and substantially reformed Senate.

11. 1982 The *Constitution Act, 1982* reduced the powers of the Senate concerning certain key aspects of its organization to a suspensive veto of six months.

12. 1982 A motion by Senator Roblin proposing the election of senators by the people was discussed in the Senate.

13. 1982 Creation of a Special Joint Committee of the Senate and of the House of Commons on Reform of the Senate.
    (From *Senate Reform Proposals in Comparative Perspective*, Jack Stilborn, Political and Social Affairs Division, Research Branch, November 1992.)

14. 1984 Molgat-Cosgrove Committee

15. 1985 Macdonald Commission

16. 1992 The Beaudoin-Dobbie Proposal

17. 1992 The Charlottetown Proposal

APPENDIX 2

The House of Lords: Reform
Presented to Parliament by the Leader of the House of Commons and
Lord Privy Seal
by Command of Her Majesty
February 2007 (Cm 7027) (page 23)

> **5.10** On the face of it, one of the most powerful second chambers in the world is the wholly appointed **Canadian** Senate. When the Canadian Parliament was established, the Senate's powers were based upon those of the **pre-1911** House of Lords. Even today, Canada has no equivalent of the Parliament Acts. There are only two restrictions on the Senate's nominal powers: financial legislation must be introduced in the first chamber; and, although the Senate may amend financial legislation, it cannot increase taxation.

APPENDIX 3

Amendment by   **41.**   An amendment to the Constitution of Canada in
unanimous relation to the following matters may be made by
consent proclamation issued by the Governor General under
the Great Seal of Canada only where authorized by
resolutions of the Senate and House of Commons
and of the legislative assembly of each province:

(*a*)

the office of the Queen, the Governor General and the
Lieutenant Governor of a province;

(*b*)

the right of a province to a number of members in the
House of Commons not less than the number of
Senators by which the province is entitled to be
represented at the time this Part comes into force;

(*c*)

subject to section 43, the use of the English or the
French language;

(*d*)

the composition of the Supreme Court of Canada;
and

(*e*)

an amendment to this Part.

APPENDIX 4

23 October 2007
Notice of Motion to Urge Governor-in-Council to Prepare Referendum
on Whether the Senate Should be Abolished

Hon. Hugh Segal: Honourable senators, I give notice that, at the next sitting of the Senate, I will move:

WHEREAS the Canadian public has never been consulted on the structure of its government (Crown, Senate and House of Commons)

AND WHEREAS there has never been a clear and precise expression by the Canadian public on the legitimacy of the Upper House, since the constitutional agreement establishing its existence

AND WHEREAS a clear and concise opinion might be obtained by putting the question directly to the electors by means of a referendum

THAT the Senate urge the Governor in Council to obtain by means of a referendum, pursuant to section 3 of the *Referendum Act*, the opinion of the electors of Canada on whether the Senate should be abolished; and

THAT a message be sent to the House of Commons requesting that House to unite with the Senate for the above purpose.

17

THOUGHTS ON SENATE REFORM

Lorna R. Marsden

Si l'on réforme le Sénat, il faut que le Sénat conserve son rôle de vérificateur auprès du gouvernement en place, un organe capable de forcer le gouvernement à revoir les clauses les plus douteuses des projets de loi proposés. Jusqu'à présent, le Sénat a toujours fourni une réflexion sereine en raison de la longue durée des mandats de plusieurs sénateurs qui leur permet de jouer à merveille leur rôle de membre du Parlement, entre autres l'habileté à rédiger de bonnes lois. Pour que des élections ne nuisent pas à ce service, la durée des mandats doit être assez longue. Finalement, l'auteur nous avertit qu'un sénat élu entraînera probablement davantage de compétition entre les sénateurs et les premiers ministres provinciaux, une compétition que les Canadiens n'apprécieront pas ou ne comprendront pas.

The debate over Senate reform reminds one of the elderly wife saying to her elderly husband, after he had told an often repeated story to a visitor, "now dear, that's *always* a good one." We hear about Senate reform once again and, once again, familiar ideas abound.

Proposals for Senate reform in Canada are made by successive governments in part as a means of changing the subject because, interesting though such proposals are, reform has almost no chance of succeeding.

The reasons why Senate reform is such an extraordinarily difficult process are also familiar ground. The representation from the provinces which benefit (e.g. PEI) and the complexities of the constitutional reform process are primary among them. The discussion of what seems desirable is always interesting, however, for those who study the theory of Canadian government as well as for those in the practice of it.

As one of the latter, having spent over eight years in the Red Chamber, I have some views that have not been raised in the previous papers in this series. Foremost is the need to maintain a chamber that has checking power on the popularly elected House. A key principle for Senate reform is to maintain the countervailing, balancing powers between the two Houses of Parliament. That is, there needs to be a legitimate means to cause the government of the day to rethink and review its proposals in almost all spheres. While the courts have come to play that role in some areas, their scope is necessarily limited and often the subject of public conflict between the two institutions. This is not helpful to the orderly progress of a government's agenda and should be reserved for the most significant of disagreements. Indeed, the current Chief Justice conveys such a message repeatedly.

At present and despite the many difficulties with the structure of the Senate, the upper chamber does play that role on a regular basis. Furthermore, if it is properly composed and whether it is elected or not, that role should remain prominent in a reformed Senate for good orderly governance.

An illustration may be helpful here. When Mr. Mulroney came to power in 1984 he was anxious to demonstrate change and to get on with his program. In a previous article I have described the situation in detail (Marsden 1987). In brief, Mr. Mulroney introduced a Borrowing Bill before tabling the Main Estimates thus violating one of the most important principles of Parliament going back to the ancient disputes between king and subjects. The king was forced to explain why he needed money before imposing the taxation or borrowing to get it. In the 1984 case, the prime minister seemed to wander into this error with no idea of what he was doing and, of course, was eventually forced to back down. He did so with the help of the senators of all parties and in a way that saved his face but not until after a great deal of stormy, messy press. Subsequently and throughout my time in the Senate, there were several occasions when "back corridor" discussions allowed ministers and the government to get their legislation through without violating basic principles of democracy.

This illustrates one of the great weaknesses of the House of Commons and one of the strengths of the Senate, a strength that needs to be maintained in any reforms. What are the weaknesses? What are the strengths?

The House of Commons is unusual among lower houses in the parliamentary system for the very high rate of turnover among its members. It is a small band of members who survive three or four elections or more. Furthermore, our political parties are quite capable of electing as leaders people who may have many worthy characteristics but have very little parliamentary experience. It is the exceptional member who knows the history of Parliament, the rules governing spending powers, who has read the estimates in all their parts and who has a grasp of how parliaments really work. They can hardly be blamed for this. In Canada we teach almost nothing about civil society, the history of our parliamentary system, or the composition of governments. Most Canadians see little other than question period and election campaigns. Elections are increasingly popularity contests rather than an examination of the options with deep knowledge and consideration of the candidates' experiences.

Briefings for new members contain a great deal of essential information but it takes more than a few years to really learn about the importance of parliamentary process and why it is essential. Members do not have that time, given their incredible schedules in their ridings as well as the House. Members become ministers with almost no training. Their assistants are most often bright young things with brains, energy and no experience, and they inadvertently embarrass themselves and their ministers with proposals that are bound to fail. More recently, the PMO has gained enormous power by snatching up the experienced assistants and then demanding that all ministerial proposals go through the PMO – a slow and unfortunate development.

Senators, on the other hand, are often highly experienced parliamentarians from the House or the provincial legislatures. Prime ministers with good sense appoint senators who really have a depth of experience and knowledge about parliaments and popularity doesn't come into it – indeed the Senate and senators are quite unpopular and that is very useful. Indeed, as I argued in the article cited above, it is a good thing to have an unpopular house and one of the reasons that electing senators, desirable though that sounds, will weaken the system of checks and balances.

Senators have more time to study up on parliamentary procedures. I recall meetings of the Senate Finance Committee, on which I sat for about seven years, where senior public servants appearing to defend their estimates would be reminded by a senator that this was the third or fourth attempt to get a particular expenditure through the system and the reasons why it always failed. These senators saw the problems from a provincial and a federal point of view. They had been around the block a number of times and would often offer suggestions for reasonable modifications to help the official achieve the objectives of the minister while not running into the roadblocks that the senator could see ahead.

The role of senators as helpful brakes on the desire to implement unworkable programs and expenditures is largely non-partisan, although there are some notable exceptions. They are often very helpful to the members of the government and a great many amendments and changes are made quietly in this fashion without any great public brouhaha.

Not all senators come with experience and they can be as unknowledgeable as new members. However, they do stay longer, do not have the heavy burden of constituency work, and the great majority become sophisticated about parliamentary procedure and precedent about the crafting of good legislation and the means of implementation. Of course they also learn about blocking legislation at the same time, which can work against a government, which then advocates abolition or something worse.

But would senators gain this knowledge if elected? Election seems highly desirable but it requires three essential elements. First, the senators must not be beholden to the prime minister or the leader of their party. You may believe they are beholden under the appointments system. This is true for a few months, of course, but very shortly it dawns on all senators that once they are appointed there is little a leader can do to unseat them on a point of principle or policy disagreement, and they act accordingly if quietly. So it is essential that senate elections not be party funded, nor subject to party discipline in the way in which members of the House are. Second, senators must have a term of office sufficiently long so that they do learn parliamentary procedure and history and are therefore useful in their work and in maintaining a balance of powers. Without the ability of acting as a check or balance. there is truly no reason to have an upper chamber. Third, popularity must not trump knowledge, experience and "sober second thought" in the Senate.

Therefore I have some doubts about election and, even if election is essential, I would disagree with the proposed terms of office under the current proposal. At least ten years is needed to really learn about Parliament and legislation unless, of course, all senators are former members of a legislature or the House of Commons – which is unlikely in the extreme.

Others have raised the issue of the views of provincial governments in this matter of election to the Senate. This is an important consideration. But what if senators were elected not from provinces but from real social and economic regions that in many instances crossed provincial boundaries? What if electoral districts for senators were, for example, north-west Ontario and north-east Manitoba? Or the Rocky Mountains (BC and Alberta) or the Quebec-New Brunswick border areas or Newfoundland-Cape Breton-PEI? In short, what if the regional representation were to be a serious matter? What if the jurisdictions were not overlapping provincial boundaries which are mostly arbitrary anyway in both historical and contemporary terms?

Elected senators will want to take substantial actions. The quiet countervailing powers they now practice will be a thing of the past under an elected system. Premiers will be most frustrated by their actions. Their constituents will be confounded by their views and the views of the members of the House – double trouble in many parts of the country. Warring popularity contests in a single constituency? None of these consequences would make life easier for anyone in the governments of this country.

Far more likely than any dramatic constitutional reforms is the gradual improvement of the rules and conditions, a slow reform process that has been underway now for generations. It is not newsworthy and it does not fit with a new government's common desire to rouse the electorate with promises of "real" reform. But in many instances it does lead to success.

REFERENCES

Marsden, L.R. 1987. "What Does a Senator Actually Do? An Inside View by a Neophyte," in *Politics: Canada, Sixth Edition*, eds. P.W. Fox and G. White. Toronto: McGraw-Hill Ryerson.

APPENDIX

BILL C-19: AN ACT TO AMEND THE CONSTITUTION ACT, 1867 (SENATE TENURE)

INTRODUCED: 13 November 2007 by then Leader of the Government in the House of Commons and Minister of Democratic Reform, the Honourable Peter Van Loan.

Note: The bill died when Parliament was dissolved on 7 September 2008.

PROPOSED CHANGES: Amend clause 2 of section 29 of the *Constitution Act, 1867* – limit the tenure of senators to one eight year non-renewable term. (Currently senators, once appointed, sit until the age of seventy-five).

Note: The bill preserves the existing retirement age of seventy-five for current senators.

BILL C-20: SENATE APPOINTMENT CONSULTATIONS ACT

INTRODUCED: 13 November 2007 by then Leader of the Government in the House of Commons and Minister of Democratic Reform, the Honourable Peter Van Loan.

Note: The bill died when Parliament was dissolved on 7 September 2008.

PROPOSED CHANGES: Amend the current *Canada Elections Act* to include procedures for selecting Senate nominees. In either a federal or a provincial general election, the electorate votes for candidates as potential nominees to the Senate. Successful candidates enter a pool of potential nominees to the Senate and then are considered by the sitting prime minister as appointees for the Senate when a vacancy arises. The governor general continues to appoint senators on advice from the Prime Minister. (Currently, under section 24 of the *Constitution Act, 1867*, senators are appointed by the Governor General on advice from the sitting prime minister – the electorate has no official role in the nomination of potential appointees.)

Note: Bill C-20 does not provide for an elected Senate. The Canadian electorate vote on who they would like to see appointed to the Senate; the vote serves as a recommendation to the prime minister. The mrime minister can consider the sucessful nominees as potential appointees. The prime minister continues to advise the governor general on Senate appointments.

Bill C-20 is not a proposed amendment to the *Constitution Act, 1867*; it is an ordinary bill that requires the consent of the House of Commons, the Senate and the governor general to become valid federal law.

BILL C-20:

Sets out the procedure for electing Senate **nominees.**

- *Part 1* of the bill deals mainly with the administration of the proposed bill:

    ○ Outlines the role and responsibilities of the chief electoral officer and the consultation officers (similar to those of the chief electoral officer and the returning officers respectively under the current *Canada Elections Act*)

- *Part 2* stipulates that the consultation elections take place during a federal or provincial general election

- *Part 3* lists (1) the qualifications of nominees – they must be at least thirty years old and be endorsed by at least 100 electors who reside in the province in which they seek nomination; and (2) the rights of nominees including the right to a leave of absence from work.

- *Part 4* lists the qualifications and entitlements of the voter (identical to those stipulated in *Canada Elections Act*).

- *Part 5* sets out the rules and procedures for counting the votes in accordance with the single transferable vote system (STV). This is a system of preferential voting which takes into account the first and subsequent choices that the voters indicate on their ballots.

- *Part 6*, like the comparable section of the *Canada Elections Act,* lists the regulations vis-a-vis communications (e.g. advertising, surveys).

- *Part 7* discusses the rules of third party advertising, including spending limits, and the required information to be included in advertised messages (name of nominee, provinces, identification of third party advertiser and that the advertising has been authorized by the third party). The definition of third parties is broadened from that which is found in the *Canada Elections Act* to include an eligible party and a registered party.

- *Part 8* deals with financial contributions:

    ○ Contributions are to be made exclusively to the nominee.
    ○ Individual contributions to the nominee are limited to $1000.
    ○ Not considered contributions are professional services, shared office accommodation and lists of members or contributors provided by a registered party or a registered association of a party. This exemption does not, however, include advertising expenses.

    Note: There is no direct consultation expenses limit made explicit in bill C-20.

- *Part 9* outlines the enforcement of bill C-20.

- *Part 10* outlines transitional provisions, consequential amendments, co-ordinating amendments and coming into force clauses.

Queen's Policy Studies
Recent Publications

The Queen's Policy Studies Series is dedicated to the exploration of major public policy issues that confront governments and society in Canada and other nations.

Our books are available from good bookstores everywhere, including the Queen's University bookstore (http://www.campusbookstore.com/). McGill-Queen's University Press is the exclusive world representative and distributor of books in the series. A full catalogue and ordering information may be found on their web site (http://mqup.mcgill.ca/).

School of Policy Studies

Economic Transitions with Chinese Characteristics: Thirty Years of Reform and Opening Up, Arthur Sweetman and Jun Zhang (eds.), 2009   Paper 978-1-55339-225-5 ($39.95) Cloth ISBN 978-1-55339-226-2 ($85)

Economic Transitions with Chinese Characteristics: Social Change During Thirty Years of Reform, Arthur Sweetman and Jun Zhang (eds.), 2009   Paper 978-1-55339-234-7 ($39.95) Cloth ISBN 978-1-55339-235-4 ($85)

Politics of Purpose, 40th Anniversary Edition, Elizabeth McIninch and Arthur Milnes (eds.), 2009   Paper ISBN 978-1-55339-227-9 Cloth ISBN 978-1-55339-224-8

Who Goes? Who Stays? What Matters? Accessing and Persisting in Post-Secondary Education in Canada, Ross Finnie, Richard E. Mueller, Arthur Sweetman, and Alex Usher (eds.), 2008   Paper 978-1-55339-221-7 ($39.95) Cloth ISBN 978-1-55339-222-4 ($85)

Dear Gladys: Letters from Over There, Gladys Osmond (Gilbert Penney ed.), 2008 ISBN 978-1-55339-223-1

Bridging the Divide: Religious Dialogue and Universal Ethics, Papers for The InterAction Council, Thomas S. Axworthy (ed.), 2008 Paper ISBN 978-1-55339-219-4 Cloth ISBN 978-1-55339-220-0

Immigration and Integration in Canada in the Twenty-first Century, John Biles, Meyer Burstein, and James Frideres (eds.), 2008 Paper ISBN 978-1-55339-216-3 Cloth ISBN 978-1-55339-217-0

Robert Stanfield's Canada, Richard Clippingdale, 2008   ISBN 978-1-55339-218-7

Exploring Social Insurance: Can a Dose of Europe Cure Canadian Health Care Finance? Colleen Flood, Mark Stabile, and Carolyn Tuohy (eds.), 2008 Paper ISBN 978-1-55339-136-4 Cloth ISBN 978-1-55339-213-2

Canada in NORAD, 1957–2007: A History, Joseph T. Jockel, 2007 Paper ISBN 978-1-55339-134-0 Cloth ISBN 978-1-55339-135-7

Canadian Public-Sector Financial Management, Andrew Graham, 2007 Paper ISBN 978-1-55339-120-3 Cloth ISBN 978-1-55339-121-0

Emerging Approaches to Chronic Disease Management in Primary Health Care, John Dorland and Mary Ann McColl (eds.), 2007 Paper ISBN 978-1-55339-130-2 Cloth ISBN 978-1-55339-131-9

Fulfilling Potential, Creating Success: Perspectives on Human Capital Development, Garnett Picot, Ron Saunders and Arthur Sweetman (eds.), 2007 Paper ISBN 978-1-55339-127-2 Cloth ISBN 978-1-55339-128-9

Reinventing Canadian Defence Procurement: A View from the Inside, Alan S. Williams, 2006
Paper ISBN 0-9781693-0-1 (Published in association with Breakout Educational Network)

SARS in Context: Memory, History, Policy, Jacalyn Duffin and Arthur Sweetman (eds.), 2006
Paper ISBN 978-0-7735-3194-9 Cloth ISBN 978-0-7735-3193-2
(Published in association with McGill-Queen's University Press)

Dreamland: How Canada's Pretend Foreign Policy has Undermined Sovereignty, Roy Rempel, 2006
Paper ISBN 1-55339-118-7 Cloth ISBN 1-55339-119-5
(Published in association with Breakout Educational Network)

Canadian and Mexican Security in the New North America: Challenges and Prospects,
Jordi Díez (ed.), 2006   Paper ISBN 978-1-55339-123-4 Cloth ISBN 978-1-55339-122-7

*Global Networks and Local Linkages: The Paradox of Cluster Development in an Open
Economy*, David A. Wolfe and Matthew Lucas (eds.), 2005
Paper ISBN 1-55339-047-4 Cloth ISBN 1-55339-048-2

Choice of Force: Special Operations for Canada, David Last and Bernd Horn (eds.), 2005
Paper ISBN 1-55339-044-X Cloth ISBN 1-55339-045-8

Force of Choice: Perspectives on Special Operations, Bernd Horn, J. Paul de B. Taillon, and
David Last (eds.), 2004   Paper ISBN 1-55339-042-3 Cloth 1-55339-043-1

New Missions, Old Problems, Douglas L. Bland, David Last, Franklin Pinch, and Alan Okros
(eds.), 2004   Paper ISBN 1-55339-034-2 Cloth 1-55339-035-0

*The North American Democratic Peace: Absence of War and Security Institution-Building in
Canada-US Relations, 1867-1958*, Stéphane Roussel, 2004
Paper ISBN 0-88911-937-6 Cloth 0-88911-932-2

Implementing Primary Care Reform: Barriers and Facilitators, Ruth Wilson, S.E.D. Shortt
and John Dorland (eds.), 2004   Paper ISBN 1-55339-040-7 Cloth 1-55339-041-5

Social and Cultural Change, David Last, Franklin Pinch, Douglas L. Bland, and
Alan Okros (eds.), 2004   Paper ISBN 1-55339-032-6 Cloth 1-55339-033-4

Clusters in a Cold Climate: Innovation Dynamics in a Diverse Economy, David A. Wolfe and
Matthew Lucas (eds.), 2004   Paper ISBN 1-55339-038-5 Cloth 1-55339-039-3

Canada Without Armed Forces? Douglas L. Bland (ed.), 2004
Paper ISBN 1-55339-036-9 Cloth 1-55339-037-7

Campaigns for International Security: Canada's Defence Policy at the Turn of the Century,
Douglas L. Bland and Sean M. Maloney, 2004
Paper ISBN 0-88911-962-7 Cloth 0-88911-964-3

Understanding Innovation in Canadian Industry, Fred Gault (ed.), 2003
Paper ISBN 1-55339-030-X Cloth 1-55339-031-8

Delicate Dances: Public Policy and the Nonprofit Sector, Kathy L. Brock (ed.), 2003
Paper ISBN 0-88911-953-8 Cloth 0-88911-955-4

Beyond the National Divide: Regional Dimensions of Industrial Relations, Mark Thompson,
Joseph B. Rose and Anthony E. Smith (eds.), 2003
Paper ISBN 0-88911-963-5 Cloth 0-88911-965-1

The Nonprofit Sector in Interesting Times: Case Studies in a Changing Sector,
Kathy L. Brock and Keith G. Banting (eds.), 2003
Paper ISBN 0-88911-941-4 Cloth 0-88911-943-0

Clusters Old and New: The Transition to a Knowledge Economy in Canada's Regions,
David A. Wolfe (ed.), 2003   Paper ISBN 0-88911-959-7 Cloth 0-88911-961-9

The e-Connected World: Risks and Opportunities, Stephen Coleman (ed.), 2003
Paper ISBN 0-88911-945-7 Cloth 0-88911-947-3

Knowledge Clusters and Regional Innovation: Economic Development in Canada,
J. Adam Holbrook and David A. Wolfe (eds.), 2002
Paper ISBN 0-88911-919-8 Cloth 0-88911-917-1

Lessons of Everyday Law/Le droit du quotidien, Roderick Alexander Macdonald, 2002
Paper ISBN 0-88911-915-5 Cloth 0-88911-913-9

*Improving Connections Between Governments and Nonprofit and Voluntary Organizations:
Public Policy and the Third Sector*, Kathy L. Brock (ed.), 2002
Paper ISBN 0-88911-899-X Cloth 0-88911-907-4

Institute of Intergovernmental Relations

*Canada: The State of the Federation 2006/07: Transitions – Fiscal and Political Federalism
in an Era of Change*, vol. 20, John R. Allan, Thomas J. Courchene, and Christian Leuprecht
(eds.), 2009   Paper ISBN 978-1-55339-189-0 Cloth ISBN 978-1-55339-191-3

Comparing Federal Systems, Third Edition, Ronald L. Watts, 2008 ISBN 978-1-55339-188-3

*Canada: The State of the Federation 2005: Quebec and Canada in the New Century – New
Dynamics, New Opportunities*, vol. 19, Michael Murphy (ed.), 2007
Paper ISBN 978-1-55339-018-3 Cloth ISBN 978-1-55339-017-6

Spheres of Governance: Comparative Studies of Cities in Multilevel Governance Systems,
Harvey Lazar and Christian Leuprecht (eds.), 2007
Paper ISBN 978-1-55339-019-0 Cloth ISBN 978-1-55339-129-6

Canada: The State of the Federation 2004, vol. 18, *Municipal-Federal-Provincial Relations
in Canada*, Robert Young and Christian Leuprecht (eds.), 2006
Paper ISBN 1-55339-015-6 Cloth ISBN 1-55339-016-4

Canadian Fiscal Arrangements: What Works, What Might Work Better, Harvey Lazar (ed.), 2005
Paper ISBN 1-55339-012-1 Cloth ISBN 1-55339-013-X

Canada: The State of the Federation 2003, vol. 17, *Reconfiguring Aboriginal-State Relations*,
Michael Murphy (ed.), 2005   Paper ISBN 1-55339-010-5 Cloth 1-55339-011-3

Canada: The State of the Federation 2002, vol. 16, *Reconsidering the Institutions of
Canadian Federalism*, J. Peter Meekison, Hamish Telford, and Harvey Lazar (eds.), 2004
Paper ISBN 1-55339-009-1 Cloth ISBN 1-55339-008-3

*Federalism and Labour Market Policy: Comparing Different Governance and Employment
Strategies*, Alain Noël (ed.), 2004   Paper ISBN 1-55339-006-7 Cloth ISBN 1-55339-007-5

The Impact of Global and Regional Integration on Federal Systems: A Comparative Analysis,
Harvey Lazar, Hamish Telford, and Ronald L. Watts (eds.), 2003
Paper ISBN 1-55339-002-4 Cloth ISBN 1-55339-003-2

Canada: The State of the Federation 2001, vol. 15, *Canadian Political Culture(s) in Transition*,
Hamish Telford and Harvey Lazar (eds.), 2002
Paper ISBN 0-88911-863-9 Cloth ISBN 0-88911-851-5

Federalism, Democracy and Disability Policy in Canada, Alan Puttee (ed.), 2002
Paper ISBN 0-88911-855-8 Cloth ISBN 1-55339-001-6, ISBN 0-88911-845-0 (set)

Comparaison des régimes fédéraux, 2ᵉ éd., Ronald L. Watts, 2002   ISBN 1-55339-005-9

John Deutsch Institute for the Study of Economic Policy

The 2006 Federal Budget: Rethinking Fiscal Priorities, Charles M. Beach, Michael Smart, and Thomas A. Wilson (eds.), 2007
Paper ISBN 978-1-55339-125-8 Cloth ISBN 978-1-55339-126-6

Health Services Restructuring in Canada: New Evidence and New Directions, Charles M. Beach, Richard P. Chaykowksi, Sam Shortt, France St-Hilaire, and Arthur Sweetman (eds.), 2006 Paper ISBN 978-1-55339-076-3 Cloth ISBN 978-1-55339-075-6

A Challenge for Higher Education in Ontario, Charles M. Beach (ed.), 2005
Paper ISBN 1-55339-074-1 Cloth ISBN 1-55339-073-3

Current Directions in Financial Regulation, Frank Milne and Edwin H. Neave (eds.), Policy Forum Series no. 40, 2005 Paper ISBN 1-55339-072-5 Cloth ISBN 1-55339-071-7

Higher Education in Canada, Charles M. Beach, Robin W. Boadway, and R. Marvin McInnis (eds.), 2005 Paper ISBN 1-55339-070-9 Cloth ISBN 1-55339-069-5

Financial Services and Public Policy, Christopher Waddell (ed.), 2004
Paper ISBN 1-55339-068-7 Cloth ISBN 1-55339-067-9

The 2003 Federal Budget: Conflicting Tensions, Charles M. Beach and Thomas A. Wilson (eds.), Policy Forum Series no. 39, 2004
Paper ISBN 0-88911-958-9 Cloth ISBN 0-88911-956-2

Canadian Immigration Policy for the 21st Century, Charles M. Beach, Alan G. Green, and Jeffrey G. Reitz (eds.), 2003 Paper ISBN 0-88911-954-6 Cloth ISBN 0-88911-952-X

Framing Financial Structure in an Information Environment, Thomas J. Courchene and Edwin H. Neave (eds.), Policy Forum Series no. 38, 2003
Paper ISBN 0-88911-950-3 Cloth ISBN 0-88911-948-1

Towards Evidence-Based Policy for Canadian Education/Vers des politiques canadiennes d'éducation fondées sur la recherche, Patrice de Broucker and/et Arthur Sweetman (eds./ dirs.), 2002 Paper ISBN 0-88911-946-5 Cloth ISBN 0-88911-944-9

Money, Markets and Mobility: Celebrating the Ideas of Robert A. Mundell, Nobel Laureate in Economic Sciences, Thomas J. Courchene (ed.), 2002
Paper ISBN 0-88911-820-5 Cloth ISBN 0-88911-818-3

Our publications may be purchased at leading bookstores, including the Queen's University Bookstore
(http://www.campusbookstore.com/), or can be ordered online from: McGill-Queen's University Press, at
http://mqup.mcgill.ca/ordering.php

For more information about new and backlist titles from Queen's Policy Studies, visit the McGill-Queen's
University Press web site at:
http://mqup.mcgill.ca/

Institute of Intergovernmental Relations
Recent Publications

Available from McGill-Queen's University Press (http://mqup.mcgill.ca/ordering.php):

Canada: The State of the Federation 2006/07: Transitions – Fiscal and Political Federalism in an Era of Change, vol. 20, John R. Allan, Thomas J. Courchene, and Christian Leuprecht (eds.), 2009   Paper ISBN 978-1-55339-189-0 Cloth ISBN 978-1-55339-191-3

Comparing Federal Systems, Third Edition, Ronald L. Watts, 2008 ISBN 978-1-55339-188-3

Canada: The State of the Federation 2005: Quebec and Canada in the New Century – New Dynamics, New Opportunities, vol. 19, Michael Murphy (ed.), 2007
Paper ISBN 978-1-55339-018-3 Cloth ISBN 978-1-55339-017-6

Spheres of Governance: Comparative Studies of Cities in Multilevel Governance Systems, Harvey Lazar and Christian Leuprecht (eds.), 2007
Paper ISBN 978-1-55339-019-0 Cloth ISBN 978-1-55339-129-6

Canada: The State of the Federation 2004, vol. 18, *Municipal-Federal-Provincial Relations in Canada*, Robert Young and Christian Leuprecht (eds.), 2006
Paper ISBN 1-55339-015-6 Cloth ISBN 1-55339-016-4

Canadian Fiscal Arrangements: What Works, What Might Work Better, Harvey Lazar (ed.), 2005
Paper ISBN 1-55339-012-1 Cloth ISBN 1-55339-013-X

Canada: The State of the Federation 2003, vol. 17, *Reconfiguring Aboriginal-State Relations*, Michael Murphy (ed.), 2005   Paper ISBN 1-55339-010-5 Cloth ISBN 1-55339-011-3

Money, Politics and Health Care: Reconstructing the Federal-Provincial Partnership, Harvey Lazar and France St-Hilaire (eds.), 2004
Paper ISBN 0-88645-200-7 Cloth ISBN 0-88645-208-2

Canada: The State of the Federation 2002, vol. 16, *Reconsidering the Institutions of Canadian Federalism*, J. Peter Meekison, Hamish Telford, and Harvey Lazar (eds.), 2004
Paper ISBN 1-55339-009-1 Cloth ISBN 1-55339-008-3

Federalism and Labour Market Policy: Comparing Different Governance and Employment Strategies, Alain Noël (ed.), 2004   Paper ISBN 1-55339-006-7 Cloth ISBN 1-55339-007-5

The Impact of Global and Regional Integration on Federal Systems: A Comparative Analysis, Harvey Lazar, Hamish Telford, and Ronald L. Watts (eds.), 2003
Paper ISBN 1-55339-002-4 Cloth ISBN 1-55339-003-2

Canada: The State of the Federation 2001, vol. 15, *Canadian Political Culture(s) in Transition*, Hamish Telford and Harvey Lazar (eds.), 2002
Paper ISBN 0-88911-863-9 Cloth ISBN 0-88911-851-5

Federalism, Democracy and Disability Policy in Canada, Alan Puttee (ed.), 2002
Paper ISBN 0-88911-855-8 Cloth ISBN 1-55339-001-6, ISBN 0-88911-845-0 (set)

Comparaison des régimes fédéraux, 2ᵉ éd., Ronald L. Watts, 2002   ISBN 1-55339-005-9

Health Policy and Federalism: A Comparative Perspective on Multi-Level Governance, Keith G. Banting and Stan Corbett (eds.), 2002
Paper ISBN 0-88911-859-0 Cloth ISBN 1-55339-000-8

The following publications are available from the Institute of Intergovernmental Relations, Queen's University, Kingston, Ontario K7L 3N6
Tel: (613) 533-2080 / Fax: (613) 533-6868; E-mail: iigr@qsilver.queensu.ca

The Role of the Policy Advisor: An Insider's Look, Nadia Verrelli (ed.), 2008
ISBN 978-1-55339-193-7

Open Federalism, Interpretations Significance, collection of essays by Keith G. Banting, Roger Gibbins, Peter M. Leslie, Alain Noël, Richard Simeon, and Robert Young, 2006
ISBN 978-1-55339-187-6

First Nations and the Canadian State: In Search of Coexistence, Alan C. Cairns, 2002 Kenneth R. MacGregor Lecturer, 2005   ISBN 1-55339-014-8

The Institute's working paper series can be downloaded from our website www.iigr.ca